First World War
and Army of Occupation
War Diary
France, Belgium and Germany

3 DIVISION
Divisional Troops
Machine Gun Corps
3 Battalion
24 February 1918 - 30 September 1919

WO95/1405/1

The Naval & Military Press Ltd
www.nmarchive.com
Published in association with The National Archives

Published by

The Naval & Military Press Ltd

Unit 10 Ridgewood Industrial Park,

Uckfield, East Sussex,

TN22 5QE England

Tel: +44 (0) 1825 749494

www.naval-military-press.com

www.nmarchive.com

This diary has been reprinted in facsimile from the original. Any imperfections are inevitably reproduced and the quality may fall short of modern type and cartographic standards.

© **Crown Copyright**
Images reproduced by permission of The National Archives, London, England, 2015.

Contents

Document type	Place/Title	Date From	Date To
Heading	WO95/1405/1		
Heading	3rd Division Divl. Troops 3rd Battalion Machine Gun Corps. Feb-Dec 1918		
War Diary	Neuville-Vitasse N 19c9545	24/02/1918	27/02/1918
War Diary	Neuville Vitasse	25/02/1918	28/02/1918
Operation(al) Order(s)	3rd Div. Machine Gun Battalion Operation Order No.1	27/02/1918	27/02/1918
Operation(al) Order(s)	3rd Battalion M.G Cards Operation Order No.2	28/02/1918	28/02/1918
Operation(al) Order(s)	3rd Battalion Machine Gun Corps Operation Order No.3	28/02/1918	28/02/1918
Heading	3rd Divisional M.Gs. 3rd Battalion Machine Gun Company March 1918		
War Diary	Neuville Vitasse	01/03/1918	22/03/1918
War Diary	York Lines	23/03/1918	25/03/1918
War Diary	Railway Cutting M 21 a 6.5	26/03/1918	31/03/1918
Operation(al) Order(s)	No 1 3rd Battalion Machine Gun Corps Operation Order No 4	13/03/1918	13/03/1918
Miscellaneous	No 2 3rd Battalion Machine Gun Corps Machine Gun Instruction N.21		
Miscellaneous	3rd Battalion Machine Gun Corps. Operation Order No.5	06/03/1918	06/03/1918
Operation(al) Order(s)	No 3 3rd Battalion Machine Gun Corps Operation Order No 7	06/03/1918	06/03/1918
Miscellaneous	Machine Gun Instructions No. 6		
Operation(al) Order(s)	No 4 3rd Battalion Machine Gun Corps Operation Order No. 6	30/03/1918	30/06/1918
Heading	Operations Report by 3rd Battalion Machine Gun Company		
Miscellaneous	3rd. Battalion Machine Gun Corps		
Miscellaneous	Casualties		
Operation(al) Order(s)	No 9 3rd. Battalion M.G. Corps. Operation Orders No. 8		
Miscellaneous	Operation Orders No. 7		
Miscellaneous	D Company		
Operation(al) Order(s)	No 10 3rd. Battalion Machine Gun Corps. Operation Order No. 9	24/03/1918	24/03/1918
Operation(al) Order(s)	No 11 3rd. Battalion Machine Gun Corps. Operation Order No.10	25/03/1918	25/03/1918
Operation(al) Order(s)	No 12 3rd. Battalion Machine Gun Corps. Operation Order No.11	29/03/1918	29/03/1918
Operation(al) Order(s)	13 3rd Battalion Machine Gun Corps. Operation Order No. 11A	29/03/1918	29/03/1918
Operation(al) Order(s)	14 3rd Battalion Machine Gun Corps. Operation Order No. 12	31/03/1918	31/03/1918
Heading	3rd Division War Diary 3rd Battalion Machine Gun Corps April 1918		
War Diary	Sombrin Bruay	01/04/1918	03/04/1918
War Diary	Moeux Les Mines	04/04/1918	11/04/1918
War Diary	Gonnehem	12/04/1918	13/04/1918
War Diary	Ammezin	14/04/1918	22/04/1918
War Diary	E 14a 6.2	23/04/1918	30/04/1918

Type	Description	Date From	Date To
Operation(al) Order(s)	Appendix 1 3rd Battalion Machine Gun Corps. Operation Orders No.13	03/04/1918	03/04/1918
Miscellaneous	Report On Movements Of 3rd Battalion Machine Gun Corps From March 30th. 1913 To April 20th. 1913		
Miscellaneous	Appendix 2 3rd Battalion Machine Gun Corps		
Miscellaneous	Report Of Operations North Of Bethune		
Operation(al) Order(s)	Appendix 3 3rd Battalion Machine Gun Corps Operation No. 14	14/04/1918	14/04/1918
Miscellaneous	Battalion Orders No 35		
Miscellaneous	Appendix 4 3rd Battalion Machine Gun Corps Appendix a		
Operation(al) Order(s)	Appendix 5 3rd Battalion Machine Gun Corps. Operation Orders No.15	23/04/1918	23/04/1918
Operation(al) Order(s)	Appendix 6 3rd Battalion Machine Gun Corps. Operation Orders No.16	25/04/1918	25/04/1918
Operation(al) Order(s)	Appendix 7 3rd Battalion Machine Gun Corps. Operation Orders No.17	26/04/1918	26/04/1918
Operation(al) Order(s)	Appendix 8 3rd Battalion Machine Gun Corps. Operation Orders No.18	27/04/1918	27/04/1918
Miscellaneous	Appendix 9 Defensive Measures 3rd Battalion Machine Gun Corps Appendix 9		
Operation(al) Order(s)	Appendix 10 3rd. Battalion Machine Gun Corps. Operation Orders No.19	30/04/1918	30/04/1918
War Diary	Fouquereuil E14a. 6.2	01/05/1918	06/05/1918
War Diary	Fouquereuil	07/05/1918	09/05/1918
War Diary	E 14 C 10	09/05/1918	11/05/1918
War Diary	Fouquereuil E 14c 10	12/05/1918	31/05/1918
Miscellaneous	Appendix 1 Extracts From Divisional Routine Orders Dated 4th May 1918 Appendix 14		
Operation(al) Order(s)	Appendix 1 3rd Battalion Machine Gun Corps Operation Orders No.20 Appendix 1	02/05/1918	02/05/1918
Miscellaneous	Table Of Fire For Machine Guns		
Operation(al) Order(s)	Appendix 2 3rd Battalion Machine Gun Corps Operation Orders No.21 Appendix 2	06/05/1918	06/05/1918
War Diary	Appendix 3		
Operation(al) Order(s)	Appendix 4 3rd Battalion Machine Gun Corps Operation Orders No.7 Appendix 4	09/05/1918	09/05/1918
Operation(al) Order(s)	Appendix 5 3rd Battalion Machine Gun Corps Operation Orders No. 22.	20/05/1918	20/05/1918
Miscellaneous	Appendix 6 3rd Battalion Machine Gun Corps		
Miscellaneous	Appendix "A" Suitable Machine Gun Positions For Defence Of Various Lines		
Miscellaneous	Appendix "B" Suitable Lewis Gun Positions For Co-operation With The Machine Gun Defence Of Various Lines		
War Diary	Fouquereuil E 14c 1.0	01/06/1918	06/06/1918
War Diary	Fouquereuil	07/06/1918	30/06/1918
Miscellaneous	3rd Battalion Machine Gun Corps Appendix 1		
Operation(al) Order(s)	3rd Battalion Machine Gun Corps. Operation Orders No.23 Appendix 2	05/06/1918	05/06/1918
Operation(al) Order(s)	3rd Battalion Machine Gun Corps. Operation Orders No.24 Appendix 3	09/06/1918	09/06/1918
Operation(al) Order(s)	3rd Battalion Machine Gun Corps. Operation Orders No.25 Appendix 4	10/06/1918	10/06/1918
Miscellaneous	Blue Barrage Appendix 1		
Miscellaneous	Green Barrage Appendix 2		

Type	Description	Start	End
Miscellaneous	Locality Shooting Appendix 3		
Miscellaneous	Medical Arrangements		
Miscellaneous	3rd Battalion Machine Gun Corps.		
Miscellaneous Diagram etc	3rd Battalion Machine Gun Corps		
Miscellaneous	Report On Operations Carried Out By Left And Centre Brigade Of The 3rd. Division On Night Of 14/15th June 1918 Appendix 5		
Operation(al) Order(s)	3rd Battalion Machine Gun Corps. Operation Orders No. 20 Appendix 6	19/06/1918	19/06/1918
Operation(al) Order(s)	3rd Battalion Machine Gun Corps. Operation Orders No. 27 Appendix 7	29/06/1918	29/06/1918
War Diary	Fouquereuil	01/07/1918	31/07/1918
Miscellaneous	3rd Battalion Machine Gun Corps Appendix 1		
Miscellaneous	Order Board No. 2		
Miscellaneous	Order Board No.1 Appendix 1		
Miscellaneous	3rd Battalion Machine Gun Corps. Orders For Anti-Aircraft Positions Appendix 2		
Miscellaneous	Suitable Machine Gun Positions For Defence Of Various Lines Appendix 3		
Miscellaneous	3rd Battalion Machine Gun Corps "defence Scheme"		
Miscellaneous	War Diary (II)		
Operation(al) Order(s)	Amendment To Operation Orders No. 28	07/07/1918	07/07/1918
Miscellaneous	Amendments No. 3 To 3rd Battalion M.G.Corps "Defence Scheme"		
Operation(al) Order(s)	3rd Battalion Machine Gun Corps. Operation Orders No.26	07/07/1918	07/07/1918
Operation(al) Order(s)	3rd Battalion Machine Gun Corps. Operation Orders No.29 Appendix 3	18/07/1918	18/07/1918
Operation(al) Order(s)	Amendment To Operation Orders No.30	26/07/1918	26/07/1918
War Diary	Fouquereuil	01/08/1918	07/08/1918
War Diary	Camblain-Chatelain	08/08/1918	13/08/1918
War Diary	Ivergny	14/08/1918	19/08/1918
War Diary	Bienvillers Au Bois	20/08/1918	29/08/1918
Miscellaneous	Bienvillers	29/08/1918	31/08/1918
Operation(al) Order(s)	3rd Battalion Machine Gun Corps Operation Orders No 31 Appendix 1	04/08/1918	04/08/1918
Operation(al) Order(s)	3rd Battalion Machine Gun Corps Operation Orders No. 32 Appendix 2	06/08/1918	06/08/1918
Operation(al) Order(s)	3rd Battalion Machine Gun Corps. Addenda 1 And 2 To Operation Orders No. 31	04/08/1918	04/08/1918
Operation(al) Order(s)	3rd Battalion Machine Gun Corps. Operation Orders No.33 Appendix 3	13/08/1918	13/08/1918
Miscellaneous	Entraining Table		
Miscellaneous	Transport March Table		
Operation(al) Order(s)	3rd. Battalion Machine Gun Corps. Operation Orders No. 34 Appendix 4	19/08/1918	19/08/1918
Operation(al) Order(s)	3rd. Battalion Machine Gun Corps. Operation Orders No. 35 Appendix 5	21/08/1918	21/08/1918
Miscellaneous	3rd. Battalion Machine Gun Corps. Report On Operations Appendix 6		
Miscellaneous	Casualties		
Operation(al) Order(s)	Notes And Instructions For Forthcoming Operations No.1 Appendix 1	19/08/1918	19/08/1918
Operation(al) Order(s)	3rd Battalion Machine Gun Corps. Operation Orders No. 34 Appendix 2	19/08/1918	19/08/1918

Type	Description	Date From	Date To
Operation(al) Order(s)	3rd Battalion Machine Gun Corps. Operation Orders No. 35 Appendix 3	20/08/1918	20/08/1918
Miscellaneous	O.C. "A" Coy.		
Miscellaneous	Administrative Instructions		
Operation(al) Order(s)	3rd. Battalion Machine Gun Corps. Operation Orders No. 36	20/08/1918	20/08/1918
Operation(al) Order(s)	3rd. Battalion Machine Gun Corps. Operation Orders No. 37 Appendix 5	24/08/1918	24/08/1918
Miscellaneous	Appendix 7		
Operation(al) Order(s)	3rd Battalion Machine Gun Corps. Operation Orders No. 38 Appendix 8	26/08/1918	26/08/1918
Miscellaneous	Appendix 9		
Operation(al) Order(s)	3rd Battalion Machine Gun Corps. Operation Orders No. 39 Appendix 10	28/08/1918	28/08/1918
War Diary	Moyblain Trench A 2 D	01/09/1918	02/09/1918
War Diary	Moyblain Trench	03/09/1918	06/09/1918
War Diary	Monchy-Au-Bois	07/09/1918	11/09/1918
War Diary	Mory B 16 C.00	12/09/1918	15/09/1918
War Diary	I 25b 1.8	15/09/1918	16/09/1918
War Diary	J.26 B 0.9	17/09/1918	30/09/1918
Operation(al) Order(s)	3rd Battalion Machine Gun Corps Operation Orders No 40 Appendix 1	01/09/1918	01/09/1918
Operation(al) Order(s)	3rd Battalion Machine Gun Corps Operation Orders No 41 Appendix 2	06/09/1918	06/09/1918
Operation(al) Order(s)	3rd Battalion Machine Gun Corps Operation Orders No 42 Appendix 3	10/09/1918	10/09/1918
Operation(al) Order(s)	3rd Battalion Machine Gun Corps Operation Orders No 43 Appendix 4	14/09/1918	14/09/1918
Operation(al) Order(s)	3rd Battalion Machine Gun Corps Operation Orders No 44 Appendix 5	14/09/1918	14/09/1918
Operation(al) Order(s)	3rd Battalion Machine Gun Corps Operation Orders No 45 Appendix 6	15/09/1918	15/09/1918
Miscellaneous	3rd. Battalion Machine Gun Corps Appendix 7		
Operation(al) Order(s)	3rd. Battalion Machine Gun Corps. Operation Order No. 46 Appendix 8	26/09/1918	26/09/1918
Miscellaneous	Administrative Instructions		
Miscellaneous	Medical Arrangements Appendix II		
Miscellaneous	Signal Instructions Appendix III		
War Diary	Ribecourt L 25a 00.15	01/10/1918	09/10/1918
War Diary	Velu J 31a 1.5	10/10/1918	13/10/1918
War Diary	Flenquieres L 19a 5.7	14/10/1918	19/10/1918
War Diary	Cattenieres H 12a 6.6	20/10/1918	21/10/1918
War Diary	Quievy D 13d 55.15	22/10/1918	22/10/1918
War Diary	Solesmes E 1 C 6.8	23/10/1918	31/10/1918
Operation(al) Order(s)	3rd. Battalion Machine Gun Corps. Operation Order No.47 Appendix 1	06/10/1918	06/10/1918
Miscellaneous	3rd Battalion Machine Gun Corps. Appendix 1a		
Operation(al) Order(s)	3rd. Battalion Machine Gun Corps. Operation Order No. 47	06/10/1918	06/10/1918
Operation(al) Order(s)	3rd. Battalion Machine Gun Corps. Operation Order No.47	12/10/1918	12/10/1918
Operation(al) Order(s)	3rd. Battalion Machine Gun Corps. Operation Order No. 48.	12/10/1918	12/10/1918
Operation(al) Order(s)	3rd. Battalion Machine Gun Corps. Operation Order No.49 Appendix 3	19/10/1918	19/10/1918

Type	Description	Date From	Date To
Operation(al) Order(s)	3rd. Battalion Machine Gun Corps. Operation Order No.50 Appendix 5	27/10/1918	27/10/1918
Miscellaneous	3rd. Battalion Machine Gun Corps Appendix 5a		
Operation(al) Order(s)	3rd. Battalion Machine Gun Corps Operation Order No.51 Appendix 6	30/10/1918	30/10/1918
War Diary	Carnieres B 13d 65.40	01/11/1918	03/11/1918
War Diary	Bevillers C 22d 2.6	04/11/1918	04/11/1918
War Diary	Quievy D 13d 4.0	05/11/1918	09/11/1918
War Diary	W 15a 8.8	09/11/1918	10/11/1918
War Diary	Gommegnies M 7a 1.0	11/11/1918	11/11/1918
War Diary	Sarloton N 13d 5.5	12/11/1918	15/11/1918
War Diary	I 3ba 9.6	16/11/1918	17/11/1918
War Diary	Z 36a 9.6	17/11/1918	17/11/1918
War Diary	Sous Le Bois	18/11/1918	18/11/1918
War Diary	Q7c 0.1	19/11/1918	19/11/1918
War Diary	R 13.d.25.25 Cerfontaine	20/11/1918	20/11/1918
War Diary	R 13.d 25.25	21/11/1918	23/11/1918
War Diary	Leers Et Fosteau I26a 5.0	24/11/1918	24/11/1918
War Diary	I 26a 5.0	25/11/1918	25/11/1918
War Diary	Marbiax J5b 8.3 Sheet 52	26/11/1918	26/11/1918
War Diary	Gerpinnes	27/11/1918	27/11/1918
War Diary	Segerard	28/11/1918	28/11/1918
War Diary	Purnode	29/11/1918	29/11/1918
War Diary	Natoye	30/11/1918	30/11/1918
Operation(al) Order(s)	3rd. Battalion Machine Gun Corps. Operation Orders No.52 Appendix 1	02/11/1918	02/11/1918
Operation(al) Order(s)	3rd. Battalion Machine Gun Corps. Operation Orders No.53 Appendix 2	03/11/1918	03/11/1918
Operation(al) Order(s)	3rd. Battalion Machine Gun Corps. Operation Order No.54 Appendix 3	07/11/1918	07/11/1918
Operation(al) Order(s)	3rd. Battalion Machine Gun Corps. Operation Order No.56 Appendix 5	10/11/1918	10/11/1918
Operation(al) Order(s)	3rd. Battalion Machine Gun Corps. Operation Order No.57 Appendix 6	14/11/1918	14/11/1918
Operation(al) Order(s)	3rd. Battalion Machine Gun Corps. Operation Order No.58 Appendix 7	17/11/1918	17/11/1918
Operation(al) Order(s)	3rd. Battalion Machine Gun Corps. Operation Order No.59 Appendix 8	19/11/1918	19/11/1918
Operation(al) Order(s)	3rd. Battalion Machine Gun Corps. Operation Order No.60 Appendix 9	23/11/1918	23/11/1918
Operation(al) Order(s)	3rd. Battalion Machine Gun Corps. Operation Order No.61 App. 10	24/11/1918	24/11/1918
Operation(al) Order(s)	3rd. Battalion Machine Gun Corps. Operation Order No.62 Appendix 11		
Operation(al) Order(s)	3rd. Battalion Machine Gun Corps. Operation Order No.63 Appendix 12	27/11/1918	27/11/1918
Operation(al) Order(s)	3rd. Battalion Machine Gun Corps. Operation Order No.64 Appendix 13	28/11/1918	28/11/1918
Operation(al) Order(s)	3rd. Battalion Machine Gun Corps. Operation Order No.65 Appendix 14	30/11/1918	30/11/1918
War Diary	Natoye	01/12/1918	03/12/1918
War Diary	Mohiville	04/12/1918	04/12/1918
War Diary	Baillonville	05/12/1918	05/12/1918
War Diary	Soy	06/12/1918	06/12/1918
War Diary	Vaux-Chavanne	07/12/1918	07/12/1918
War Diary	Ottre	08/12/1918	10/12/1918

War Diary	Beho Map. Ref I.M	11/12/1918	11/12/1918
War Diary	Krombach	12/12/1918	12/12/1918
War Diary	Manderfield	13/12/1918	13/12/1918
War Diary	Hallschlag	14/12/1918	14/12/1918
War Diary	Dahlem	15/12/1918	15/12/1918
War Diary	Map. Ref. I.L Roderath	16/12/1918	16/12/1918
War Diary	Arloff	17/12/1918	17/12/1918
War Diary	Euskirchen	18/12/1918	18/12/1918
War Diary	Fussenich	19/12/1918	19/12/1918
War Diary	Duren	20/12/1918	31/12/1918
Operation(al) Order(s)	3rd Battalion Machine Gun Corps Operation Order No. 66 Appendix 1	03/12/1918	03/12/1918
Operation(al) Order(s)	3rd Battalion Machine Gun Corps Operation Order No. 67 Appendix 2	04/12/1918	04/12/1918
Operation(al) Order(s)	3rd Battalion Machine Gun Corps Operation Order No. 68 Appendix 3	05/12/1918	05/12/1918
Operation(al) Order(s)	3rd Battalion Machine Gun Corps Operation Order No. 69 Appendix 4	06/12/1918	06/12/1918
Operation(al) Order(s)	3rd Battalion Machine Gun Corps Operation Order No. 70 Appendix 5	07/12/1918	07/12/1918
Operation(al) Order(s)	3rd Battalion Machine Gun Corps Operation Order No. 71 Appendix 6	08/12/1918	08/12/1918
Operation(al) Order(s)	3rd Battalion Machine Gun Corps Operation Order No. 72 Appendix 7	10/12/1918	10/12/1918
Operation(al) Order(s)	3rd Battalion Machine Gun Corps Operation Order No. 73 Appendix 8	11/12/1918	11/12/1918
Operation(al) Order(s)	3rd Battalion Machine Gun Corps Operation Order No. 74 Appendix 9	12/12/1918	12/12/1918
Operation(al) Order(s)	3rd Battalion Machine Gun Corps Operation Order No. 75 Appendix 10	15/12/1918	15/12/1918
Operation(al) Order(s)	3rd Battalion Machine Gun Corps Operation Order No. 76 Appendix 11	14/12/1918	14/12/1918
Operation(al) Order(s)	3rd Battalion Machine Gun Corps Operation Order No. 77 Appendix 12	15/12/1918	15/12/1918
Operation(al) Order(s)	3rd Battalion Machine Gun Corps Operation Order No. 78 Appendix 13	16/12/1918	16/12/1918
Operation(al) Order(s)	3rd Battalion Machine Gun Corps Operation Order No. 79 Appendix 14	17/12/1918	17/12/1918
Operation(al) Order(s)	3rd Battalion Machine Gun Corps Operation Order No. 80 Appendix 15	18/12/1918	18/12/1918
Operation(al) Order(s)	3rd Battalion Machine Gun Corps Operation Order No. 81 Appendix 16	19/12/1918	19/12/1918
Heading	Northern Division (Late 3rd Division) 3rd Bn Machine Gun Corps Jan-Sep 1919		
War Diary	Duren	01/01/1919	12/03/1919
War Diary	Ehrenfeld	13/03/1919	06/04/1919
War Diary	Riehl	07/04/1919	30/09/1919

11/25/14
11/05 am
WO 95

3RD DIVISION
DIVL. TROOPS

3RD BATTALION
  MACHINE GUN CORPS.
Feb - Dec 1918

3RD DIVISION
DIVL. TROOPS

WAR DIARY
of 3RD BN M.G. CORPS.
INTELLIGENCE SUMMARY.

Army Form C. 2118.

Place	Date	Hour	Summary of Events and Information	Remarks and references to Appendices
NEUVILLE – VITASSE N 19.c.95.45	24.2.18	NOON	MAP 51 B S.W. The four machine gun companies of the Division were formed into a battalion, to be known hereafter as 3RD BN M.G.C. (O.B.407). They were incorporated under divisional orders (G.S.197/104). The four companies, 8th, 9th, 76th and 233rd became known respectively as Companies A, B, C, D the following H.Q. officers were appointed as such (G.S.197/104. — AG.80(a) – VI CORPS C/1357/1) C.O — LT COL W.J. CRANSTON ADJUTANT — LT R. ALLAN M.C 2ND IN COMMAND — MAJOR F.B. MACKENZIE, DSO, MC. TRANSPORT OFF: LT J.A. ROCH M.C. LT COL CRANSTON being on leave to U.K. to be appointed to command establishment and confirmed. (AG/80/7) Lt and Q.M. A.W. CRAVEN attached for duty and confirmed. To bring establishment up to strength 51 men enlisted (OB 407) authority now given by G.H.Q. (letter DAAG 26.2.18), to do no form disbanded Infantry Bns of the CB division. Lewis gun section and 'B' category men were inspected and found to be of high standard. 25 and 35" respectively of each were selected for	C.H.H. C.H.H.
	25			
	26			
	27			

Army Form C. 2118.

WAR DIARY
of 3RD BN M.G. CORPS.
INTELLIGENCE SUMMARY
(Erase heading not required.)

Instructions regarding War Diaries and Intelligence Summaries are contained in F. S. Regs., Part II. and the Staff Manual respectively. Title pages will be prepared in manuscript.

Place	Date	Hour	Summary of Events and Information	Remarks and references to Appendices
NEUVILLE VITASSE	25 26 27	2.18	duty with the M.G. Corps. "B" category men relieved for duty with B?? H.Q. 1 man, 1 ass, animals, vehicles, and eight men were also transferred from the disbanded Bn to make up the new establishment. A notable addition was one field kitchen per company.	CHA
	28.2.18		Operation orders were issued for forthcoming raid. Operation Orders were issued for relief and readjustment of divisional front.	O.O. No 1 O.O. No 2 O.O. No 3 CHA

F. B. McKenzie
Lieut.-Col. 3rd Bn M.G.C.

28.2.18.

SECRET.

3rd Div. Machine Gun Battalion Operation Order No. 1

Copy No. 10

Reference
Special Sheets
GUEMAPPE } U.T.S. 324
HENINEL } U.T.S. 252.

27.2.18

1. The following Machine Gun barrage scheme will be carried out in support of operation of the 1st Northumberland Fusiliers on the night of March 3/4 and at a zero hour to be notified later.

2. <u>Tasks.</u>

<u>101st M.G. Coy.</u>

(a) Guns 54 + 55 at U13 a 45.55 will maintain fire throughout the operation on the SUNKEN ROAD at O32 c 90.50 from Z to Z+15'.

(b) Guns 58 + 59 at T6 c 60.90 will maintain fire throughout the operation on BLOCK LANE at O32 a 50.65 from <u>Z to Z+15'.</u>

<u>9th M.G. Coy.</u>

(a) Guns 50A + 51A at N30d 15.65 will maintain fire throughout the operation on SUNKEN ROAD at O32a 75.75 from Z to Z+15'.

(b) Guns 52A + 53A at N30c 40.05 will maintain fire throughout the operation on TRENCH JUNCTION at O26d 35.90 from Z to Z+15'.

<u>76th M.G. Coy.</u>

(a) Guns ~~52A + 53A~~ 61A + 62A at ~~N30c 40.05~~ O19a 80.85 will maintain fire throughout the operation on TRENCH JUNCTION at O26c 80.70 from Z to Z+15'.

(b) Battery (Guns 56A, 57A, 58A, 59A) at N24b 70.20 will have three tasks.

(i) From Z to Z+6' to barrage a line from O26d 25.65 to O32a 95.80.

(ii) From Z+6' to Z+12' to switch & barrage a line from O26d 95.85 to O26d 70.40.

(iii) From Z+12' to Z+15' to switch & barrage a line from O32 b 45.25 to O32 d 15.90.

Operation Order No. 1 cont.

3. Rates of Fire.
Z to Z+2'   Slow fire (1 belt per 4 mins.)
Z+2' to Z+12'   Rapid fire (1 belt per min.)
Z+12' to Z+15'   Slow fire.

4. At Z+15' all guns will CEASE FIRE & lay on normal S.O.S. lines.

5. The necessary ammunition for this operation will be estimated & put in position before the operation so that establishment of S.A.A. at positions remains normal.

6. Arrangements for synchronisation of watches will be notified later.

7. ACKNOWLEDGE.

Issued at 11.55 P.M.

Copies to :-
1. 3rd Div. G.
2. 9th M.G. Coy.
3. 76th "
4. 101st "
5. 9th Inf. Bde.
6. 76th "
7. 101st "
8. C.R.A.
9. 34th T.M.G.C.
10-11. War Diary
12. File.

R. Allay
Lt & Adjt.
for O.C. 3rd Div. M.G. Battn.

SECRET.
Copy No. 14

3rd BATTALION M.G. CORPS OPERATION ORDER NO. 2.

28th February 1918.

1. The 34th Division is to take over the centre sector of the VI Corps front.

2. The following M.G. reliefs will be carried out on the night 2/3 March:-
   (a) 8th M.G. Company will be relieved in the right section by the 101st M.G. Coy. of the 34th Battalion M.G. Corps.
   (b) The 233rd M.G. Coy. will be relieved in M.G. positions 36.b. to 41b. both inclusive by the 240th M.G. Coy. of the 34th M.G. Battalion.
   (c) The 233rd M.G. Coy. will relieve the 120th M.G. Coy. of the 40th Battalion M.G. Corps in M.G. positions 48.b. to 51.b. both inclusive.
   (d) No.1 Gun numbers will remain with incoming Gun teams for 24 hours.
   (e) Reliefs will be complete by 9 p.m.
   (f) Details of the above reliefs will be arranged between Company Commanders concerned.
   (g) Completion of reliefs will be reported to Battalion H.Q. by code word (Company Commander's Name).

3. (a) L.& M. Battery Positions:-
   Will be vacated at 6 p.m. on the 2nd March by the 120th M.G. Coy. who will return to SUGAR FACTORY, NEUVILLE VITASSE and await further orders from O.C., 3rd Battalion, M.G. Corps.
   (b) At 9 a.m. they will be prepared to move to BLAIREVILLE under orders of O.C., 40th Battalion, M.G. Corps.

4. On completion of reliefs mentioned in para 2, the 8th M.G. Coy. and 1½ Sections of 233rd M.G. Coy. will be withdrawn into Divisional Reserve and will be accommodated in YORK LINES. Arrival of these Units in YORK LINES will be reported to Battalion H.Q. at once by runner. They will be prepared to move at ½ hours notice to the neighbourhood of SUGAR FACTORY, NEUVILLE VITASSE where they will occupy positions of assembly in N.25 a & b, when Company Commanders will report to Battalion H.Q. for further orders.

5. All trench stores, maps, photos, defence schemes and other documents relating to the M.G. Defence of the area will be handed over by units to relieving units.
   Receipts will be obtained and forwarded to Battalion H.Q.

6. ACKNOWLEDGE.

R. Allan
for Lieut-Colonel,
Commanding, 3rd Division M.G. Battn.

28th February 1918.
Issued at 3 P.M.
Copies to:-
1. 3rd Div. "G"
2. "A" Coy. 3rd Bn. M.G. Corps. (8th M.G. Coy)
3. "B"   do.   do.   (9th   "   )
4. "C"   do.   do.   (76th   "   )
5. "D"   do.   do.   (233rd "   )
6. 120th M.G. Coy.
7. 8th Inf. Bde.
8. 9th Inf. Bde.
9. 76th Inf. Bde.
10. O.C. 40th Bn. M.G. Corps.
11. O.C. 34th,   do.
12. Bn. Transport Officer.
13. Bn. Quartermaster.
14 & 15 War Diary.
16 & 17 File.

SECRET.

Copy No. 11

3rd BATTALION MACHINE GUN CORPS OPERATION ORDER No.3.

28th February 1918.

1. The 3rd Divisional Front will be held with 3 Brigades in the line, 9th Inf. Bde. on the Right, 8th Inf. Bde. in the Centre, and 76th Inf. Bde. on the Left.

2. M.G. Positions in the Right, Centre and Left Brigade Sections will be manned by the 9th, 8th and 76th M.G. Companies respectively, except M.Gs' 46B to 51B which will be manned by the 233rd M.G. Company.

3. Reliefs necessitated by this readjustment will be carried out as follows on the 3rd March, and will be completed by 9-0 p.m. with the exception of Guns 50A, 51A, 52A, 53A, of the 9th M.G. Company which will remain in position until completion of orders issued in Operation Order No.1.

   (a) The 8th M.G. Coy. will relieve the 9th M.G. Coy. in positions 64, 65, 66, 67, 50A, 51A, 52A, 53A, 54A, 55A,.

   (b) The 9th M.G. Coy. will relieve the 233rd M.G. Coy. in positions 42B and 43B.

   (c) 233rd M.G. Coy. will withdraw from positions 44B and 45B.

   (d) No.1. Gun Numbers will remain with incoming teams for 24 hours.

   (e) Details of above reliefs will be arranged between Company Commanders concerned.

   (f) Completion of reliefs will be reported to Battalion H.Q. by Code Word (Company Commander's Name).

4. On completion of above mentioned reliefs -

   (a) 8 guns of 9th M.G. Coy. will return to Transport Lines.

   (b) 6 guns of 8th M.G. Coy. and 10 guns of 233rd M.G. Coy. will be billetted in YORK LINES.

5. M.G. Batteries I. J. K. L. M. and positions 44B and 45B will not be manned. M.Gs' in Reserve will be prepared to man these positions on emergency as follows:-
   (a) 9th M.G. Coy. (8 guns) M.G. Batteries I and J.
   (b) 8th M.G. Coy. (8 guns) M.G. Battery K and positions 44B and 45B.
   (c) 233rd M.G. Coy. (8 guns) M.G. Batteries L and M.

6. Company Commanders and Section Officers will reconnoitre above emergency positions as early as possible and the best lines of approach to them.

7. All Trench Stores, Maps, Photos, Defence Schemes and other documents relating to the M.G. Defence of the Area will be handed over by units to relieving units.
   Receipts will be obtained and forwarded to Battalion H.Q.

8. ACKNOWLEDGE.

Issued at 3 P.M.

for R. Allen Lt. & Adjt.
Lieut-Colonel.
Commanding 3rd Division M.G. Battalion.

P.T.O.

Copie to:-

1. 3rd Div. "G"
2. "A" Coy. 3rd Bn. M.G.Corps. (8th M.G.Coy)
3. "B" Coy. "   "   "   "   (9th "   ")
4. "C" Coy. "   "   "   "   (76th "   ")
5. "D" Coy. "   "   "   "   (233rd " ")
6. 8th Inf. Bde.
7. 9th Inf. Bde.
8. 76th Inf. Bde.
9. T.O.
10. Q.M.
11. War Diary.
12. "   "
13. File.
14. "

3rd Divisional M.Gs.

3rd BATTALION

MACHINE GUN COMPANY

MARCH 1918

Appendices attached:-
Operation Orders & Instructions.
Report on Operations.

Army Form C. 2118.

WAR DIARY
INTELLIGENCE SUMMARY
(Erase heading not required.)

3RD BATT: M.G.C.

Place	Date	Hour	Summary of Events and Information	Remarks and references to Appendices
NEUVILLE VITASSE	MARCH 1st		MAP 51B S.W. 1:20,000 Artillery fire not much visibility. Snow & cross in afternoon. Conference held by Reference General attended by Major MACKENZIE D.S.O. M.C. Transport of Battalion billets together from area occupied by Infantry to M16b & 17a. Enemy aerial activity above normal. Our aerial activity above normal. Right Sector "A" Company FONTAINE 16 guns in line. Centre " "B" " CHERISY " " Left Sector "C" " activity to COJEUL RIVER 16 guns in line. Night firing on likely lines. Reserve "D" " moved down from HENIN to YORK LINES M16a. Casualties Leave to U.K. 7 O.R. Centres 3 O.R. Reinforcements 6 O.R. Evacuated 3 O.R.	VK 2
	2nd		Misty fine. Snow in afternoon. Conpt of Inquiry assembled at Batt. H.Q. to enquire into accidental shooting of soldier in 20 K.R.R. by Pte Galley, should of burst Cpl J. MOFFETT M.C. Light Actv. "A" Company Ativite in trenches by 101 Company 3rd Batt. Relief Confeld 1 a.m. moved to YORK LINES M16a.	

Army Form C. 2118.

WAR DIARY
or
INTELLIGENCE SUMMARY
(Erase heading not required.)

Place	Date	Hour	Summary of Events and Information	Remarks and references to Appendices
NEUVILLE VITASSE	March 2nd		"B" & "C" Coys engaged station targets for harassing fire at night.	
			"D" Coy in reserve.	
			Casualties —	
			Sent to U.K. 11 O.R.	Off.
			Reinforcements 4 O.R.	
			Evacuated 3 O.R.	
			Paraded 1 O.R.	
	3rd		Weather dull with snow. All machine guns registered by Corps	
			Capt W. DOWLING. R.A.M.C. attached. O.O. No 1 issued	APPENDIX No 1.
			Divisional front reduced. SOUTHERN BOUNDARY a line running T5 central through U19 c59	
			Re-distribution of Companies according to O.O. No 3 issued 28.2.18 to conform with new boundary	
			Right Sector: A" Coy four teams prior to relief evacuated with fire & reid by the	Off.
			1ST NORTHUMBERLAND FUS: firing 12,000 rounds on selected targets	
			On completion of relief two Sections march to YORK LINES M.16.d.	
			Sections now occupied 42ᴮ 43ᴮ 52ᴬ 53ᴬ 56. 57. 58. 59.	
			Centre Sector "B" Coy Relieves "B" Coy of 10 guns. Nos 60. 61. 62. 63. 54ᵃ 55ᵃ 56ᵃ 57ᵃ 58ᵃ 59ᵃ	
			Left Sector "C" Coy Remains in before. Occupies position Nos 64. 65. 66. 67 60ᴬ 61ᴬ 62ᴬ 63ᴬ 64ᴬ 65ᴬ 66ᴬ 67ᴬ 68ᴬ 69ᴬ 70ᴬ	
			Harassed with fire. The whole raid on night Sects firing 12,000 rounds.	

WAR DIARY or INTELLIGENCE SUMMARY

(Erase heading not required.)

Army Form C. 2118.

MAP 51B S.W. 1:20,000.

Place	Date	Hour	Summary of Events and Information	Remarks and references to Appendices
NEUVILLE VITASSE	March 3rd		People "D" Coy. Relief by O.O. No 3. Occupies position No 46. 47ᵃ 48. 13. 49ᵃ 50. 51ᵇ.	
			Casualties	
			Reinforcements: Sent to U.K. 10 o.R.	
			Evacuated 2 o.R. Centers 4 o.R.	
	4		Weather unsettled; visibility poor.	
			Conference of Coy Commdrs held by Major Mackenzie D.S.O. M.C. Lef Captn	A.H.
			Intakes Lemont	
			Establishment of S.A.A. made up at Latthop Batteries L.J.K.	
			Enemy Action. Enemy artillery more active.	
			Coys in line carried out harassing night firing	
			Casualties Sent to U.K. 6 o.R.	
			Reinforcements 1 o.R. Centers 3 o.R.	
			Evacuated 1 o.R.	
	5		Nearly five and well.	
			Work was proceeded with on Extrad. bathing in Captivity with M.G. Instruction No 1.	
			Left Sectors "C" Coy was relieved by "D" Coy in accordance with Bn O.O. No 4.	APPENDIX No 2. A.H.

Army Form C. 2118.

WAR DIARY
or
INTELLIGENCE SUMMARY
(Erase heading not required.)

Place	Date	Hour	Summary of Events and Information	Remarks and references to Appendices
NEUVILLE VITASSE	March 5th		MAP 51B S.W. 1:20,000	
			Relief completed 9.30 p.m. Position 43B to 51B and Tactical Command of O.C "D" Coy.	
			And occupied by team of "C" Coy. On completion of relief remainder	
			of "C" Coy. moved to YORK LINES M16d.	Off.
			1st Casualties. Leave to U.K. 6 O.R.s	
			Reinforcements 3 O.R. 3 O.R.	
			Evacuated.	
			Weather fair visibility high.	
			Lt. Col. N.J. CRANSTON returned from leave. U.K.	Off.
	6th	5.15 a.m	"A" Coy. Lewis Gun 65 fired 500 rounds on its S.O.S. line in response to enemy barrage	Off
			"C" Coy "Stood to" in centre of YORK LINES from 6.0 a.m. to 7.0 a.m. & 5.0 p.m. to 6.0 p.m.	
			in accordance with STANDING ORDERS for RESERVE O.O. No5 issued	APPENDIX 3.
			Casualties. Leave to U.K. 6 O.R. O.O. No6 issued 3/5 January 7.10	APPENDIX 4
			Reinforcements 4	
			Evacuated.	

WAR DIARY
INTELLIGENCE SUMMARY

Army Form C. 2118.

Place	Date	Hour	Summary of Events and Information	Remarks and references to Appendices
NEUVILLE VITASSE	March 1st		MAP 51 B SW. 1: 20.000.	
			C.O. visited BDE and COY H.Q. in line	
			Reconnaissance of route from transport to front line made.	
			"A" Coy 6 guns in reserve relieved 6 in line, which took up position	C.J.L.
			in "K" Battery and guns 42 & 43 B.	
			"C" Coy addressed by C.O. at YORK LINES.	
	8th		"B" Coy working on battery position I & J O.O. No 7 issued	APPENDIX 5.
			Weather fine Visibility fair.	
			C.O. inspected Reserve detail Camp	
		10 AM	Right Sector "B" Coy holds hurriedly attacked down 8 guns in reserve occupied positions I & J	S.J.L.
			Centre Sector "A" Coy Support going to ...... by 2ND SUFFOLK REGT 1000 rounds fired	
			Reserve Company training infantry recently attached.	
			Weather fine visibility good.	
	9th		Weather fine visibility good.	
			"B" Coy .... position for battery I & J Schools & constructed	
			"A" " " " " " " K " " Leave to U.K. 4 O.R.s	C.J.L.
			" " " " " " " L " " Leave to U.K. 2 O.R.s	
			"C" " " " " " " " " " Courses. 1. O.R.	

WAR DIARY
INTELLIGENCE SUMMARY

Army Form C. 2118.

(Erase heading not required.)

Place	Date	Hour	Summary of Events and Information	Remarks and references to Appendices
NEUVILLE VITASSE	July 10		MAP. 51.B. S.W. 1:20000. MACKENZIE C.O. & MAJOR Called to Confer with DIV: GEN: reference expected immediate attack by enemy.	O.R.L
	10	10.30 p.m.	"B" Coy. Heavy enemy shelling at dawn. Harassing M.G. fire copied all night. "A" & "D" Coys. Harassing fire by night on selected targets. Leave to U.K. 2 O.R.S.	
	11		Conference acced by DIV: GEN: in line, attended by C.O. ref: expected enemy attack. Much enemy aerial activity. All S.O.S. targets dropped to within 100 yards of our front line in views of expected attack. "A" "B" "D" Coys harassing fire all night. Leave to U.K. 2 O.R.S. Contues 1 O.R.	C.S.L
	12		Weather good. Division "Stood to" 5.10 a.m. — 7.10 a.m. in accordance with orders. M.G. instructions No 6 issued. Harassing artillery fire at stated intervals. LT C.D. HETTON rejoined from leave U.K. Contues 1. O.R.	APPENDIX 6. O.R.

Army Form C. 2118.

WAR DIARY
or
INTELLIGENCE SUMMARY.
(Erase heading not required.)

Place	Date	Hour	Summary of Events and Information	Remarks and references to Appendices
NEUVILLE VITASSE	March 13th		MAP 51/B SW. 1:20.000. Major MacKenzie went to Division for leave. Enemy quiet. No response to our shelling	C.S.M.
	14th		Intended attack did not materialise. Cpl in Sigs. wounded. Selected targets shelled. Leave to UK. 3 ORs	Off
			Enemy quiet & unresponsive	
	15th		COL NASMITH 15TH BN. arrived for instruction in operations in projected raid. Leave to UK. 1 OR	A.L.
	16th		New line situation normal. Leave to UK 1 OR Courses 1 OR	A.L.
			Situation Normal. Leave to UK. 2 ORs	A.L.
	17th		Situation normal. Slight enemy artillery activity. Reinforcements 3 ORs Course 1 OR	A.L.
	18th		Situation Normal. Weather rain. Leave to UK 2 ORs	A.L.

WAR DIARY
INTELLIGENCE SUMMARY

(Erase heading not required.)

Army Form C. 2118.

Place	Date	Hour	Summary of Events and Information	Remarks and references to Appendices
NEUVILLE VITASSE	March 19th		MAP 51B SW 1:20000. Weather: rain. Enemy very quiet. Gents to UK & ORs Reinforcements 2 ORs	
	20		" " 2/Lt Drury St. Weather fine.	
NEUVILLE VITASSE			Situation normal. O.C. Coys instructed of impending attack. S.O.S. lines were dropped to within 100 ft of our front line. C.O. 40th Division called to make arrangements for divisional relief. Orders were prepared O.O. No 6.	APPENDIX 7.
	21		Leave to U.K. 4 OR. Reinforcements 6 OR.	
	22		Guide key to W.K. 2/Lt Nightingale N.J. 4 Lt Darby Z.J. Leave to U.K. 4 O.R. Casualties 10 ORs	
YORK LINES	23		Reinforced 2/Lt Heyward 2 Casualties 3 OR. Casualties 1 OR	APPENDIX 9 APPENDIX 8
	24		Casualties 3 OR	APPENDIX 10
	25		Casualties 6 OR	APPENDIX 11
			CO No 10	

WAR DIARY

Army Form C. 2118.

Instructions regarding War Diaries and Intelligence Summaries are contained in F. S. Regs., Part II. and the Staff Manual respectively. Title pages will be prepared in manuscript.

(Erase heading not required.)

Place	Date	Hour	Summary of Events and Information	Remarks and references to Appendices
RAILWAY CUTTING M21 B.6.5.			MAP 51BSW 1:20,000.	
	March 26		Casualties. 2 ORs (1 killed 1 wounded)	
	" 27		Casualties. 3 ORs (wounded) Leave to UK 1 OR	
	"		Casualties: Capt. MOFFETT S. M.C. {Wounded - remaining at duty}	
			Capt. Bn. Stearne H.J.J.	
			2/Lt Rickson H.J. Killed	
			Lt Mitchell W. M.B.E. M.C.	
			" Crawshaw-Barry T.R.	
			2/Lt Thorn H.J. } Wounded	
			" Holbrook J.R.	
			" Dobson J.S.	
			" Wood J.M.	
			1Lt Adam H. } Missing	
			/6 Size L	
			" Gough A.R.	
			Other ranks 29 Killed. 68 Wounded. 60 Missing	

Army Form C. 2118.

WAR DIARY
or
INTELLIGENCE SUMMARY.
(Erase heading not required.)

Instructions regarding War Diaries and Intelligence Summaries are contained in F. S. Regs., Part II. and the Staff Manual respectively. Title pages will be prepared in manuscript.

Place	Date	Hour	Summary of Events and Information	Remarks and references to Appendices
RAILWAY CUTTING M21 a 6.5	Aug 29		Weather good. Situation quiet. O.O. 11 for relief now issued.	APPENDIX 13
	30		Bttn. was relieved by the Canadian division & marched to close billets at BRETENCOURT	AA
		Noon	Bttn. moved off to SOMBRIN	AA
	31		at SOMBRIN. Cleaning equipment, guns etc. O.O. No 12 issued. Bttn. arrived 3.30 p.m.	AA
				APPENDIX 14

W. H. ??????? LT COL.
3RD BN M.G.C.

SECRET
Copy No 9   N°1

3rd Battery Machine Gun Corps Operation Order No 4.
5.3.19

1. The following M.G. reliefs will be carried out on the night of 5/6th March.
   (a) D Coy will relieve C Coy in the left sub-sector in all positions.
   (b) C Coy will relieve D Coy in positions 46 L & 47 L and in battery positions 48 L – 51 L both inclusive.
   (c) No 1 gun numbers will remain with incoming teams for 24 hours.
   (d) Details of above reliefs will be arranged between Coy Commanders concerned.
   (e) Completion of reliefs will be reported to Battalion H.Q. by Code-word (Coy Commander's name).
   (f) Reliefs will be complete by 9 P.M.

2. On completion of above mentioned reliefs
   (a) Six (6) guns of C Coy will be in the line.
   (b) Ten (10) guns of C Coy will be in Reserve in YORK LINES and be prepared to move forward and occupy L & M Battery positions on ½ hour's notice.
   (c) Sixteen (16) guns of D Coy will be in the line.

3. Captn. DESVOEUX (O.C. D Coy) will be M.G. Group Commander. He will establish his H.Q. alongside 76th Inf. Bde H.Q. & will command the 22 guns as detailed in para 2(a) & (c) in position in 76th Inf. Bde sector.

4. All trench stores, maps showing S.O.S. lines & battle lines, range cards, order-boards, photos, defence schemes, & other documents relating to the M.G. defence of the area will be handed over by Units to relieving Units. Receipts will be obtained & forwarded to Battalion H.Q.

5. ACKNOWLEDGE.

Issued at 3 P.M.
Copies to:—
1. 3rd Div E
2. D.M.G.C.
3. C Coy (76th M.G. Coy)
4. D " (233rd ")
5. 76th Inf. Bde
6. T.O.
7. Q.M.
8. War Diary
9. — "
10. File
11. — "

R Allan
Lt & Adjt.
3rd Battn. M.G. Coy.

SECRET

3rd Battalion Machine Gun Corps

N° 2

Machine Gun Instructions N° 1.

4.5.18

O.C. Machine Gun Reserve will cause the following orders to be carried out by sections in reserve of Companies concerned.

1. 1½ Sections of "A" Coy under orders of Lt DARLEY and 2 sections of "B" Coy under orders of Lt WILLINGALE will proceed to K, I, & J battery positions at 1.30 p.m tomorrow 5th inst and at 9 a.m. each day thereafter, for the purpose of constructing & completing as early as possible the necessary Machine Gun emplacements and short trenches from the heads of the "Now" Gun Teams will work on the emplacements they will occupy on the alarm. Plan of work is attached. Sticks have been erected in the approximate positions of emplacements.

2. All work and digging must be carefully camouflaged. Camouflage must be on the spot before work is commenced and when work ceases for the day, the camouflage will be laid over same.

3. Special Instructions to "A" Coy.
The dugout for K battery has not been constructed in the proper place. The four emplacements will be constructed in old German trench 200 yards further down the hill to the right inside line Metres about N 27 a 90 70 in such a position as will command all the foreground to HENINEL & the ridge on the opposite side with no dead ground. Completion of work will be reported to this office.

4/5. (a) All ranks will proceed to above-mentioned battery positions on the 5th

(b) On the 6th inst & days thereafter two reliable & intelligent men per gun will be left behind in billets to act as guides to limbers to positions in the event of the alarm being given, while the remainder are employed in constructing emplacements as ordered.

6/ To ensure continuity of work, officers in reserve, previous to going into the line on ordinary tour of duty, will hand these orders over to officers relieving them.

R Allen Lt C Adjt
3rd Battalion M G Corps

SECRET
COPY ..2..... N°3

3rd BATTALION MACHINE GUN CORPS. O.O. No.5.

6th March, 1918.

REFERENCE MAPS.
SPECIAL SHEETS.
GUEMAPPE & HENINAL.

Scheme
1. The following M.G. Barrage will be carried out in support of Operation of the 2nd Battalion SUFFOLK Regt, on the night of 7th/8th March, & at a Zero hour to be notified later.

2. TASKS.

"D" COMPANY.

(a) Guns 60A, 61A, 62A, 63A, will maintain fire on a line between O 21 b 0.0. & O 21 c 90.10 from Z to Z plus 15'. Fire will be single gun fire & not battery fire.

(b) Guns 64A, 65A will maintain fire on a line between O 21 c 70.75 and O 21 c 60.50 from Z to Z plus 15'.

(c) Guns 70A & 71A will maintain fire on a line between O 21 c 70.50 and O 21 c 50.30 from Z to Z plus 15'.

3rd Bn.M.G.C., O.O.5. contd. (2)

(d) Guns 64, 65 will maintain fire on a line between O.21 c 70.90 and O 21 c 70.70 from Z to Z plus 15'.

"A" COMPANY.

(a) Guns 54A, 55A, 56A, 57A, will maintain fire on a line between O 26 d 90.90 & O 26 d 90.50 from Z to Z plus 15'.

3. RATES OF FIRE.

Z to Z plus 5' Rapid Fire (one belt per minute.)
Z plus 5' to Z plus 10' Slow Fire (one belt per 4 minutes)
Z plus 10' to Z plus 15' Rapid Fire.

4. At Z plus 15 minutes, all guns will "Cease Fire" & relay on normal S.O.S. lines.

5. All gun numbers given above are the new numbers.

6. The necessary ammunition for the operation will be estimated & put in position before the operation, so that establishment of S.A.A. at position remains normal.

7. Watches will be synchronised at the 76th Inf. Bde.Hd.Qrs. Time for doing same will be notified later.

8. Acknowledge.-

(3)

3rd Bn. M.G.C.   O.O. 5. continued.

Issued at 11.55 A.M.

Copy No. 1. 3rd Div. "G"
2. D.M.G.C.
3. "A" Coy.
4. "D" Coy.
5. 76th Inf. Bde.
6. War Diary.
7.   do do ✓
8. File.
9,   do

R Allan
Lieut. & Adjt.
3rd Battn. M.G. Corps.

SECRET   Copy No 4

3rd Battn Machine Gun Corps O.O. No 7
6.3.18

1. The following M.G. positions will be permanently manned from 6 p.m March 8th until further orders are issued.
   (a) Battery positions I & J by "B" Coy
   (b)   "   position "K" & positions 44B & 45B by "A" Coy
   (c)   "   positions 6 & 19 by "C" Coy.
2. Company Commanders concerned will issue the necessary orders for completion of above moves.
3. "In position" will be reported to Bn H.Q by wire & runner
4. The two guns in reserve & personnel will be at Battn H.Q.
5. Acknowledge

Issued at 11.45 AM.

Copy No 1 — DMGC
    2   A Coy
    3   B "
    4   C "
    5   D "
    6   3rd Div G
    7   War Diary
    8   Do Do
    9   File

R Alle—
Lt & Adjt.
3rd Bn. M.G. Corps.

3rd Battalion Machine Gun Corps.   SECRET
Operation Order No 7   Copy 6 No 5
                                  7.3.18

Reference MAP
WANCOURT Ed 1A

1. The following M.G. barrage scheme will be carried out in support of operation of the 15th Div on the night of 8th/9th March & at a zero hour to be notified later.

2. Tasks. D Coy.
   (a) Guns 60A, 61A, 62A & 63A will maintain harassing fire on a line between O.8.d.60.10 and O.9.c.10.10 from Z to Z+40'. Fire will be single gun fire and not battery fire.
   (b) Guns 64A & 65A will maintain harassing fire on a line between O.9.d.00.35 and O.9.d.35.55 from Z to Z+40'.
   (c) Guns 68A & 69A will maintain harassing fire on a line between O.9.c.80.25 and O.9.d.20.40 from Z to Z+40'.
   (d) Guns 70A & 71A will maintain harassing fire on a line between O.9.c.35.15 and O.9.c.90.20 from Z to Z+40'.
   (e) Guns 66 & 67 will maintain harassing fire on a line between O.9.c.20.15 and O.9.c.55.35 from Z to Z+40'.

3. Rate of Fire. 1 belt per 5 mins, throughout the practice.

4. (a) Machine Gun fire will not open before artillery fire.
   (b) All guns will cease fire at Z+40' & relay on normal S.O.S immediately.

5. The necessary ammunition for the operation will be estimated & put in position before the operation so that establishment at battery positions remains normal.

6. An officer from Batt. HQ will communicate synchronised time to O.C. D Coy at his HQ.

7. ACKNOWLEDGE.

Issued at 11 P.M.

Copies to - 1 DMGC
            2 D Coy
            3 76th Inf Bde
            4 DMGC 15th Batt
            5 3rd Div G
            6 War Diary
            7   do
            8   do

R Allan
Lt & Adjt
3rd Batt M.G.C

War Diary

S E C R E T.
COPY — N° 6

MACHINE GUN INSTRUCTIONS No. 6.

1. Extreme vigilance is now required from all M.G. detachments. All ranks will "Stand-to" from 5.10 a.m. until 7.10 a.m. on the morning of the 12th & on every succeeding morning until further orders.

2. <u>Fire Orders.</u>
   Machine Guns will put down their barrage so that the nucleus of the cone is not further than 100 yards from our front line.
   Os.C. Coys. will ascertain the exact position of all posts in the front line, so that the cones of fire will not fall on them.

3. It is clear that the enemy cannot attack without first destroying the front line wire. It is probable that he will open a bombardment to effect this at intervals of considerable length along the front during the hours of darkness preceding the attack. It is probable that he has selected certain lengths of front upon which to cut the wire as to cut the wire on the whole front must be a lengthy task. It must therefore be clearly understood that immediately the enemy opens his destructive fire the Artillery will commence their counter preparation. The "S.O.S." should not be sent up from the front line until the enemy is seen to be advancing to the assault. To bring down our "S.O.S." barrage immediately the enemy opens his destructive fire will only result in a waste of ammunition, as at the opening of his preparation the enemy will probably be some distance behind his front line, & will advance direct to the attack only after such bombardment has been put down as to ensure the destruction of the wire. <u>Immediately the enemy is seen to be advancing which may be expected shortly before or at dawn, or the enemy barrage beginning to lift forward, the S.O.S. must be sent up and immediately all Artillery and Machine Guns will respond with their S.O.S. Barrage.</u>

(No.3. cont'd)
   If the assault is made in daylight so that it can be observed from O.Ps. every post that can see the advance will put up the "S.O.S." without an instant's delay. All Commanders will arrange for an extensive issue of "S.O.S." Signals so that there may be no omission, due to casualties, in putting up the signal.

4. <u>Defensive Measures against Gas.</u>
   It is certain that the enemy will make an extensive use of Gas Shell. Nothing new is anticipated. The effect of "Mustard" shell is to cause blisters on portions of the body exposed to the effect of the Gas. Our box respirators give complete protection against internal effects. The effect of "Mustard Gas" becomes intensified in shell holes exposed to the sun. Chloride of Lime is being provided - it has a neutralising effect & should be sprinkled freely in "Mustard Gas" shell holes
   Box respirators will be worn as soon as enemy bombardment opens.
   Gloves or spare socks will be used for the protection of the hands.
   Mufflers are being issued for the protection of the neck.
   Fresh solution will be at once applied to all blankets covering Dug-out entrances.-

5. If enemy is found to be assembling in their trenches or in No Man's Land the Code word "MONCHY" will be sent.

6. In the event of enemy advancing & compelling flank divisions to withdraw, special precautions will be taken for forming a <u>defensive flank</u>

7. In the event of the Division being ordered to withdraw to Yellow Line owing to having its flanks exposed, special Machine Guns will be told off for the purpose of bluffing & holding the enemy until troops are established in new positions.-
   Special orders will be issued as to time & successive stages of withdrawal of these guns.

8. In the event of the enemy being held up on the BLUE LINE, Batteries I, J, K, & L will be prepared to move forward <u>on receipt of orders</u> to se-

Machine Gun Instructions No.6 continued.   -3-   SECRET.

(No.8 cont'd)
-lected positions for the purpose of assisting in the defence of the BLUE LINE by putting down a M.G. Barrage which will be known as: "S.O.S. Barrage BLUE". Cave Battery will also be prepared to assist in this protective barrage.-

All above mentioned Batteries will also be prepared to assist in Counter attacks which may be ordered for the recovery of any portion of the BLUE LINE & also to support as far as possible any counter attack to regain the Forward System.

On receipt of the message "BATTLE" the necessary fire orders will be issued to support a counter-attack to recover the BLUE LINE.

On receipt of the message "FORWARD" the necessary fire orders will be issued to support a counter-attack to recover the Forward System.

"Fighting Maps" must be in readiness to cope with any of above situations on the shortest of notice.-

9. Reports.
The value & importance of sending back reports must be impressed on all officers & N.C.Os. Strict attention will be given to the necessity of putting the time on all messages, also the signature & location of sender.

10. Communications.
Armoured cable has been laid forward to all Battery Positions & the fullest use should be made of same for the purpose of getting messages back quickly to Battalion Hd. Qrs.

The present system of using Brigade & Battalion wires will be maintained as long as is practicable.

Reliable & intelligent men will be told off as runners to maintain communication in the event of wires being cut.

In the case of urgent & very important messages, two runners carrying the same message should be despatched at intervals between each other.

11. Rations, Water, S.A.A. etc. Emergency Rations, Water, & additional S.A.A. will be put in position at Coy. Head Qrs.

12. Transport.
Separate orders have been issued to Transport Officer.

13. Medical Arrangements.
The Regimental Aid Posts for the Front Line System of the 3rd Division are :-

LEFT SECTOR   1. RAKE TRENCH   O. 13. b. 3.&.2
                     2. SHIKAR AV.   O. 19. d. 1.8.

CENTRE SECTOR   CUCKOO RESERVE   O. 25. c. 15.40.

RIGHT SECTOR   PUFFIN AV.   N. 36 c 4.5.

The R.A.P.s for the Battle System are -:

LEFT SECTOR   MARLIERE CAVES   N. 23 b. 7.8.

CENTRE SECTOR   THE NEST   N. 30 a 3.2.

RIGHT SECTOR.   SHAFT AV.   T.5.a.8.5.

The ADVANCED DRESSING STATIONS are :-

LEFT SECTOR   MARLIERE CAVES   N. 23 b 7.8.
                     & Eastern end of Neuville Vitasse.

Centre Sector)   A.D.S. HENIN
     &   )   and
RIGHT SECTOR.)   A.D.S. on the HENIN-CROISILLES ROAD.

CASUALTIES are to be brought to the nearest R.A.P. or A.D.S.

Machine Gun Instructions No.6 cont'd.   -5.-   SECRET.

(Medical arrangements cont'd.)

STRETCHER BEARERS of the R.A.M.C. are available at any R.A.P. or A.D.S. and also at the following places :-

SUNKEN CROSS ROADS East of HENINEL N. 29 a 8.5.

HENINEL – ST.MARTIN ROAD near end of SHAFT AV.

The LEFT SECTOR is being cleared by No.7 Field Amb. through MARLIERE CAVES.

The CENTRE SECTOR is being cleared by No.8 Field Amb. through Sunken Cross Roads East of HENINEL.

The RIGHT SECTOR is being cleared by No. 8 Field Amb. through A.D.S. on HENIN – CROISILLES ROAD.

WALKING WOUNDED from the Left Sector will make their way to A.D.S. Neuville-Vitasse.-

WALKING WOUNDED from RIGHT & CENTRE SECTORS will go to WALKING WOUNDED POST near HENIN.

DRESSINGS are being provided for each Battery Position.

STRETCHERS are being provided one to each Section.

ANTI-GAS PROTECTION. All Ranks are being provided with gloves & Cloth Head Protectors.

(Medical Arrangements continued)

A supply of Ammonia Capsules will be at each Battery Position.

CHLORIDE of LIME, if available, will be scattered in shell holes around each battery position.-

The Regimental Medical Officer Will be at ~~Batt. H.Qrs.~~ A.D.S NEUVILLE VITASSE

14.   Acknowledge .-

Issued at 7.30 P.M.

12th March 1918.

Lieut. & Adjt.

3rd Battn. M.G. Corps.

No. 1 - "A" Coy.
    2 - "B" -
    3 - "C" -
    4 - "D" -
    5 - M.O.
    6 - T.O.
    7 - Q.M.
    8 - D.M.G.C.
    9 - 3rd Div. "G".
    10 - C.M.G.O.

SECRET.   No 7

Copy..........

3rd. Battalion MACHINE GUN CORPS O.O. NO. 6.

20th. March 1918.

Reference Sheets.   GOMMECOURT 57.D.S.E. 1/34.
                         HEBUTERNE 57.D.S.E. 1/25.

1. Should the situation remain normal, the 3rd. Battn. M.G.C. will be relieved in the line by the 40th. Battn. M.G.C.

2. Reliefs will be carried out as follows:-
   (a) Night 23rd./24th. March.
      (i) A. Coy. 40th. Batt. M.G.C. will relieve D. Coy. 3rd. Batt. M.G.C. in positions 64A, 65A, 66A, 67A, 68A, 69A, 70A, 71A and positions 48B, 49B, 50B, 51B, and M Battery at present manned by personnel of C. Coy.
      (ii) D. Coy. 40th. Batt. M.G.C. will relieve B. Coy. 3rd. Batt. M.G.C. in positions 56, 57, 58, 59, 52A, 53A, 42B, 43B, and positions 60, 61, 54A, 55A, 56A, 57A, 44B, 45B, at present manned by personnel of A. Coy.

   (b) On 24th. March.
      D. Coy. 40th. Batt. M.G.C. will relieve Battery positions I, J, K, L. This relief will be complete by 5 P.M. No guides will be necessary. Company Commanders concerned will issue the necessary orders to battery detachments.

Ref. M. G.

   (c) On night 24th./25th. March.
      (i) C. Coy. 40th. Batt. M.G.C. will relieve A. Coy. 3rd. Batt. M.G.C. in positions 62, 63, 58A, 59A, and positions 64, 65, 66, 67, 60A, 61A, 62A, 63A, at present manned by personnel of D. Coy., and positions 46B, and 47B, at present manned by personnel of C. Coy.
      (ii) The two guns of C. Coy. in Batt. Reserve will move under orders of O.C. "D" Coy., in accordance with attached table.

   (d) No. 1. gun numbers will remain with in-coming teams for 24 hours.

3. Details of above reliefs will be arranged between Company Commanders concerned. All reliefs in paras. (a) and (c) will be complete by 12 midnight. Completion will be reported to Battalion H.Q. by code word (Coy. Commander's name).

4. On completion of above mentioned reliefs the 3rd. Batt. M.G.C. will move to the BEAUREGARD Area. Moves will be carried out in accordance with attached table.

5. All trench stores, maps, photos, defence schemes, and other documents relating to the M.G. defence of respective sectors will be handed over to in-coming units. Receipts will be taken. Separate receipts will be obtained for reserve rations and water, A.P. and Tracer Ammunition. Consolidated receipts will be forwarded by Companies to Battalion H.Q.

6. Special care will be taken to hand over satisfactory order boards with all necessary orders clear and legible. Special certificate
                                                                      will

(6)

O.C. NO. 6. (Contd.)

6. Will be rendered to this effect by Company Commanders.
Battle lines and S.O.S. lines will be carefully explained.
All information will be given regarding tunnelling work in progress.

7. A C K N O W L E D G E.

Signature
Lieut. & Adjt.
for O.C. 3rd. Batt. M.G.C.

Issued at 10 P.M.

1. D.M.G.C.
2. 'A' Coy. 3rd. Batt. M.G.C.
3. 'B' " " " "
4. 'C' " " " "
5. 'D' " " " "
6. T.O. " " "
7. S.M. " " "
8. M.O. " " "
9. D.M.G.C. 40th. Batt. M.G.C.
10. 3rd. Div. G.
11-12. War Diary. ✓
13-14. File.

ADDENDUM NO. 1. TO 3rd. Batt. M.G.C. O.O. No. 6. (3 PAGES.)

Para 4. After "table", add "Company Commanders will arrange with Q.M. for messes at Lumieport."

Signature
Lieut. & Adjt.
for O.C. 3rd. Batt. M.G.C.

21/3/18.

OPERATIONS REPORT

BY

3rd BATTALION

MACHINE GUN COMPANY

3rd. BATTALION MACHINE GUN CORPS.

N° 8

GROUND.
The 3rd. DIVISION held the Sector from East of GUEMAPPE to West of FONTAINE-LES-CROISILLES; its topography consisted of from the left of the lower end of the slope which ran East and West from VIS-EN-ARTOIS to TELEGRAPH HILL; from MONCHY-LE-PREUX to the long valley running North-East and South-West of the COJEUL RIVER. The remainder of the front consisted of the long ridge called the CHERISY SPUR which terminated on the right of the Division in the highest point known as HENIN HILL. Running North out of the HENIN HILL behind and nearly parallel to the CHERISY SPUR was the HENINEL SPUR. The valley between commenced at the German Line and finished at HENIN HILL in a sort of basin owing to another broad valley coming from the height North-Westerly. Behind or West of this is the valley of the COJEUL RIVER with the valleys of GUEMAPPE, WANCOURT, HENINEL and ST. MARTIN with HENIN at the foot of the slope on which was situated the YELLOW LINE. It will be seen that once the flank was turned the HENIN HILL would become untenable.

The Third System commencing on the Divisional right at HENIN ran along the WANCOURT SPUR up the HILDENBURG LINE across the Spur West of WANCOURT. The GREEN or ARMY LINE ran East of TILLOY, NEUVILLE-VITASSE, BEAURAINS and thence roughly along the RESERVE LINE of the Enemy System of the days before the battle of the SOMME.

GUNS.
The guns were sited in depth conforming with the lines of defence as laid down. There were forward positions to protect the CHERISY SPUR and heights of HENIN HILL. More guns were sited to protect the next or Divisional System which was roughly along the ridge behind the CHERISY SPUR and again on the Corps or YELLOW (3rd. System) LINE.

All guns were in pairs except three Batteries of four guns in the forward zone; each pair being under an Officer. The gun positions were all made on one type with the aid of tunnellers: A dug-out with stairs down from the nearest trench accommodated the teams and Officers, and rising from it

GUNS (Contd.)
was one or two shafts either vertical or sloping, bringing the opening away from the trench. Short camouflaged saps were constructed from these shafts and the emplacements made at the end; the whole affair giving the greatest amount of security and confidence.

The establishment of S.A.A. in forward positions, where the difficulty and danger of bringing up supplies would be felt, was doubled.

All the guns were given S.O.S. line to conform with artillery barrage gaps, and as a successful effort had been made to produce enfilade fire, the whole front was covered with a curtain fire of bullets or shrapnel. Posts were put out giving a tactical direction for battle lines.
The constant patrol of Senior Officers kept the various personnel up to concert pitch, when their interest and energy showed a natural tendency to flag as a result of eight weeks unrelieved duty in the line.
The guns in the Corps Line (3rd. System) were in batteries of four and known as lettered batteries, and were sited by Corps. Their object was to hold up the enemy should he break through the BLUE LINE (2nd. System). All the lettered batteries were connected by telephone to Battn. H.Q. and to one another by lateral wires, and these wires were in use until a fresh battle broke out on their line.
The forward guns were connected in almost every case, as far as telephones could be acquired to their Coy. H.Q.
Each gun had an establishment of 16 belt boxes, including two of tracer and two of A.P.

MEDICAL ARRANGEMENTS.
Before the action, the Reg. M.O. issued in Battalion Instructions a list of Regimental Aid Posts with their relationship to each position: stretchers and shell dressings and ammonia capsules were issued to Companies for distribution to all batteries. As an additional Anti-Gas protection chloride of lime was spread in shell holes around all positions. When the action started the Reg. M.O. took up his position in an A.D.S. where he could best deal with cases from the left half of the Division making arrangements with an A.D.S. on the right to deal with cases from that sector.

Everything that could be done to receive the impending attack was undertaken. An inspiring message was received from the G.O.C. Division stating his highest trust in the Machine Guns.
From the 12th. of March onwards, day by day, the menace of the attack was continually urged. Prisoners gave various dates which proved false, tending only to increase the alertness of the personnel. Counter preparation was vigourously undertaken by artillery assisted by Machine Gun fire on various targets. The S.O.S. lines of artillery were dropped to within 100 yards of the front line, which was held with few posts. Machine guns conformed, and firing as they were in enfilade, clearance was abundantly assured over the support line, which was the main line held by Infantry. On the night 19th./20th. prisoners were taken who stated that the attack would open on the morning of the 21st. The Officers and Men who displayed an ever-growing enthusiasm and confidence were warned of the new date.

MARCH 21st.

At 2.30 A.M. and again at 3.30 A.M. furious bombardments of our entire system took place. They lasted half an hour each and were succeeded by perfect quiet. At 5.0 A.M. with a reverberating crash the whole of the enemy's ordnance laid down an annihilating barrage both over the front trenches, and extending far to the rear, growing fiercer and of greater depth the further it proceeded to the right. He utilised gas projectors, trench mortars, guns and howitzers, and even fired heavy H.V. shells at selected towns and villages a long way in the rear. With great accuracy and without apparent previous registration, his artillery engaged especially all Brigade H.Q.'s, Divisional H.Q.'s and Batteries with gas and heavy shells. All our machine guns opened a slow rate of S.O.S. fire as ordered during the expectant period. This continued undiminished for some hours until dawn broke unusually misty, remaining so for the major part of the morning, when the attack developed on the right Brigade and was carried right down to succeeding Army fronts. Though the attack did not develope on the left and centre brigades fronts, the heavy barrage fell uninterruptedly.

Reconnaissance
Reconnaissance parties, sometimes armed with machine guns, made their way to our wire with the evident intention of engaging our Infantry and machine guns to prevent assistance being given to the right flank, and were shot down and their attempts to bring their automatic weapons into action rendered ineffective. Guns 66 and 67 had the bulk of the targets on this sector.
Almost from the beginning telephonic communication with the 8th. and 9th Infantry Brigades was severed and messages to and from Company Commanders in liaison with their Brigadiers had to be sent by runners — a service which never failed us.
On the right Brigade, the attack was carried on vigorously. The enemy gained a footing in two posts but was promptly ejected.
The guns in forward position in FIRST AVENUE and BROWN SUPPORT had many direct targets in the first assault.
About 10 A.M. another attack developed on this front and that of the Centre Brigade in which the enemy succeeded in establishing himself in the front line of the left Company. There was period of quiet suddenly broken at midday by a terrific trench mortar bombardment which continued for a long time and was succeeded by an attack on the salient on the right of the right Brigade. The enemy had formed up in "No-Man's-Land" South of the COJEUL RIVER but was caught with enfilade fire from the machine guns on the opposite slope of the COJEUL RIVER and the attempt here was abandoned. The enemy having got into the front line of the Division on our right worked along SHAFT TRENCH and then turned North into our Trench system and gradually established himself from the flank.
During all this time Guns 56, 57, 58, & 59 engaged many large targets and inflicted enormous casualties. The enemy was observed marching and massing in FONTAINE WOOD. Guns 56 and 57 thoroughly searched the locality and, with artillery help, must have inflicted very great casualties. No one debouched from here. Since the attack in the afternoon the enemy was extremely active, working up our trench system. The guns engaged him in small parties as he made advances in short bounds and wherever he showed himself for an instant. During this critical time for our right flank the guns in FIRST AVENUE 58 and 59 became isolated and unprotected. Lieut. WELLS with courageous energy and ably assisted by Sergt. Williams made a block and posted all the men he could spare from belt filling to
defend

defend the surrounding trenches. He searched for Infantry and brought them to the locality, assuming command of them, thus preventing the enemy surrounding him. He was enabled to speak to his Company Commanders over his telephone after all the incredibly heavy bombardments of the day through the undaunted courage of his signaller Pte. NODDRYDEN, who, on one occasion, seeing the hopelessness of repairing the line, because it would be cut in one place as he mended another, volunteered to carry a despatch through the barrage.

These guns fought very hard all day and at 6 P.M. the front line as occupied by us was BROWN SUPPORT, STORM AVENUE, CHIPPATE SUPPORT, SWIFT SUPPORT and our original front line.

The guns 58 and 59 were in very precarious position and liable to be suddenly rushed in a bombing attack: their location must of necessity have been known as they had fired so continuously and to such purpose.

Lieut. WELLS asked if he might withdraw to another position immediately in rear. The C.O.C. acquiesced in the request and fresh positions were taken up commanding the same ground. All supplies were replenished and six gun teams were relieved. The night passed quietly. New S.O.S. lines were worked out conforming to the line and the guns laid on them.

One gun in the YELLOW LINE WAS BLOWN UP.

Casualties for 21st. March were:
    Officers. Nil.
    O.R's. Killed 2. Wounded 6.

MARCH 22nd.
At 6 A.M. a heavy barrage was put down but no Infantry attack followed. At 11 A.M. there was a further bombardment of the System. Shortly after midday the enemy advanced again on our right Brigade and the Division on our right. On our front he was broken up into small parties and suffered severe casualties. These small units continued to press forward, and would not be denied. They became difficult as machine gun targets, flitting from cover to cover when in the open and for the most part bombing their way along the trench system. There were untold dead lying in front of the wire of BROWN SUPPORT where the wiring held unbroken. The enemy appeared to approach the wire gingerly and and linger at it as though "he was afraid of tearing his new uniform". He paid dearly during the early afternoon.

The trench fighting went on all the afternoon and as dusk started to close in, our Infantry had no more bombs and perforce had to retire from BROWN SUPPORT down both ends of which the enemy was approaching.

As soon as 2nd. Lieut. SLOPER discovered the trench was evacuated by us and grasped the position, he posted bombers 50 yards at each side of his position and withdrew his guns and teams only just in time successfully across the open to CONCRETE RESERVE where they consolidated. When a short distance away from his position 2nd. Lieut. SLOPER heard a cry for "Help". He retraced his steps and looking over the parados saw in the trench an unwounded German who fired at him. 2nd. Lieut. SLOPER shot him and returned to his men.

Owing to the Division on our right being forced back it was found necessary to form a defensive flank. The G.O.C. asked for the aid of four more guns and those of 'J' Battery were sent up to him.

The old front trench of the HINDENBURG LINE came into use and the guns about this flank were altered to cope with the new situation.

The enemy attempted to attack the Division in flank and was successfully held up on the wire in front of this line with serious casualties.

Late at night Major MacKenzie arrived at Battln. H.Q. at NEUVILLE VITASSE with orders from Division to withdraw to the YELLOW or CORPS LINE and be in position before 5 A.M. Orders were issued and despatched.

Casualties for 22nd. March were:
    Officers. Nil.
    O.R's. Killed Nil. Wounded 3.

MARCH 23rd.
These orders contained the new dispositions of all guns withdrawn and in all cases but one they were disposed in batteries of four under one or two Officers. Limbers were sent up to meet the withdrawing teams and boxes of S.A.A. were dumped at each one of the positions selected.

The night was fortunately quiet which enabled the work to proceed easily. It redounds to the Company Commander's credit and other Officers concerned that all positions stated were occupied to the best advantage with no more guidance than a map reference. Positions were constructed and guns were in by daylight. It was no inconsiderable task carried out in a most praiseworthy manner. A certain amount of equipment had to be abandoned owing to the personnel being limited but all such material was rendered useless. From later reports it appears the enemy had penetrated to within 600 yards of the place where the right Companies' limbers were loaded. Though there was much machine gun fire no casualties were sustained during the evacuation. One gun was destroyed by shell fire. The machine guns on the right are believed to be the last Infantry to have left the forward system.

It may be remarked in passing that the personnel was very depressed at the thought of retirement and the evacuation of MORCHY caused a distinct gloom. The morning passed quietly after a bombardment of the positions we had evacuated. The lettered Batteries came into action for the first time. Large bodies of the enemy were observed to be advancing over the ridge East of HENIN. 'J' and 'V' Batteries engaged them and broke them up; the advance was stopped. Shortly afterwards the enemy appeared to be advancing along the slopes of the VANCOUVER SPUR; they were caught in the withering fire of 'T' 'J' 'V' Batteries and suffered heavily. The enemy was also repulsed in an attempt to debouch from VANCOUVER. The enemy continued active patrolling all day, and many targets were thus afforded our guns, which inflicted many casualties. The enemy snipers worked their way forward and established themselves in HENIN and other commanding features, where they were very active. In this respect 'V' Battery was very unfortunate. The position they held was excellent for controlling the opposite ridge, but once that had fallen they were overlooked in their most obvious locality, more especially as they were doing a considerable amount of firing. The result was the sniping of one gunner and two guns. The Battery most gallantly remained in action until ordered to positions about 150 yards to the left. The guns were replaced at night. O.C. "B" Coy. in visiting his guns decided to withdraw 'T' Battery from HENIN which position was open to be surrounded and was annoyed by snipers, to a spot some 300 yards in rear.

Lieut. HAROLD-BARRY O.C. 'T' Battery made the move; it was a bright moonlight night and a good deal of shelling, sniping and machine gun fire. Despite everything he made a complete transference of all guns and equipment and S.A.A., but one last load, which he had to abandon as the enemy was found to be in occupation of the position.

    Casualties during day:
        Officers. Nil.
        O.R's. Killed Nil. Wounded 1.

MARCH 24th.

Our lines were heavily bombarded at dawn but no Infantry attack followed. Towards midday the enemy advanced from his positions on the lower slopes of HENIN HILL in several waves. Many batteries of machine guns got on to him and with clearly observable losses they broke up into small parties. A mass of the enemy having doubled forward in ones and twos were sheltering in dead ground about the ST. MARTIN - HENINEL ROAD. They were dislodged with difficulty by some Infantry who crawled out under our wire and the majority of them shot by one of 'J' Battery gunners, who made his way forward with one other man. They had to move over perfectly flat open ground and both men were wounded, but did not return until they had expended the last bullet they had taken out. It was a most effective piece of work. During this attempted advance 'J' Battery alone fired 30,000 rounds.

At another time O.C. "B" Battery spotted and directed his four guns on to a mass of Germans on the sunken HENIN - CROISILLES ROAD; very few moved away. This Battery also engaged and silenced an active enemy machine gun. Shortly after midday a further attempt was made by the enemy to advance from the direction of HENIN. In this attempt hardly a man escaped. It was reported later that in front of 'T' Battery there were 400 dead. At 4 P.M. some enemy field artillery was observed attempting to come into action in HENINEL. O.C. "T" Battery laid his guns in front and behind the guns. They checked and attempted to retire; they were seen to be suddenly panic stricken; at this moment they were picked up by our artillery and were totally destroyed.

The 9th. Infantry Brigade moved into the line from support. The 8th. Infantry Brigade side-stepped and joined up with the Guards Division who had withdrawn to the GREEN LINE. With the new disposition most of "B" Company's guns were with the 8th. Infantry Brigade and "A" Company's guns

guns with the 9th. Infantry Brigade. The O.C. Companies went to the
brigade where the majority of their guns were. This re-disposition made
it necessary for 'T' Battery to make another move, which was successfully
accomplished.
    Casualties during the day:
      Officers. Nil.
      O.R's. Killed 1. Wounded 2.

MARCH 25th.
   Heavy bombardment during morning; day otherwise quiet.
At 9 P.M. there was a fall of rain. Guns 56, 57, 58, and 59 were
heavily shelled at night, shells actually falling into the position.
    Casualties during the day:
      Officers. Nil.
      O.R's. Killed Nil. Wounded 6.

MARCH 26th.
   Just after daybreak the enemy was observed advancing in extended
order in two waves with the evident intention of occupying the trenches
evacuated by the Guards. They were taken in enfilade fire by several
of our machine guns Batteries and severe casualties were inflicted: the
attempt was not renewed.
    Casualties during the day:
      Officers Nil.
      O.R's. Killed 1. Wounded 1.

MARCH 27th.
   The weather was cloudy and cold. The situation was unchanged
and, except for the bombarding of the WILLOW LINE, was quiet.
Machine gun positions were selected and dug. Barrage schemes in
conjunction with the artillery defence were worked out.
    Casualties during the day:
      Officers. Nil.
      O.R's. Killed Nil. Wounded 1.

MARCH 28th.
   At 4.30 A.M. a heavy barrage fell on our lines and back areas.
On the front line it consisted chiefly of trench mortar shells, and on
the support line of heavy howitzer shells. The intensity of the barrage
and very meagre cover afforded resulted in many casualties during these
early hours as well as considerable nervous strain.
The machine guns opened a slow rate of S.O.S. fire until it should grow
light enough to see what was taking place. Soon after daybreak the
enemy advanced. The attack developed in strength towards the left.
The majority of our guns could engage him direct and did so, inflicting
casualties and causing disintegration in his waves. He was seen
advancing in large parties which divided and deployed. These parties
were often late in deploying and paid a heavy toll to machine gun
concentrations. The hostile artillery were in action on HENIN HILL
making use of direct fire.
The enemy showed as great a determination to press forward as our men
showed to pin him to the ground and so there developed a most fierce
battle. From the moment of the inception of this attack there was no
pause or cessation. The waves which had been broken worked forward in
detachments making the most skilful use of dead ground and cover; so
that after the opening of the attack very little of the enemy was seen
where the fighting was most desperate. He displayed the keenest
observation for points which checked him and unity of purpose in over-
coming them. Our line was penetrated at various points where the
barrage had fallen with more accuracy and either annihilated or
disorganised the garrison. There were many parts left who fought in a
most heroic fashion with the enemy on every side of them, until they
were all wiped out in some cases dying to a man, or as a last desperate
remedy cut their way to the rear. Our machine guns in most cases were
not in the same trench as the Infantry and their intentness in engaging
targets prevented them noticing our Infantry withdrawals. Other guns which
had an Infantry garrison in the vicinity were ordered by the Infantry
Commanders to stay and cover their retirement. Very few of these guns
were got back to consolidate in rear. Some fought to the death, some
fought rear-guard actions, some withdrew what remained to them of
equipment and fought with the Infantry. Not one withdrew until he was
                     driven

driven out with the enemy on his heels and then only far enough to come into action again. It was a day of magnificent achievement by the Officers on the spot and splendid heroism of all ranks in the fine way with which they responded to many strange things they were called upon to accomplish.

By about 4 P.M. the Division was fought back to the GREEN LINE and many incidents can be related concerning the retirement, from the opening of the battle until the surviving personnel and guns once more got into touch with their Company Commanders. 'H' Battery was on the left of the Divisional front. Two of its guns were blown up during the Infantry bombardment and all four gun Commanders became casualties. Early in the morning they were outflanked and the Infantry withdrew covered by the remaining two guns. These guns were then withdrawn to the support line where one of them was damaged. Lieut. STEWART took his remaining gun and found the remnants of another Battery which he joined.

'F' and 'J' Batteries were left in isolation owing to the forced Infantry retirement. Both Batteries, in spite of this, fought their guns with astounding coolness. Lieut. WESTROOP O.C. "F" Battery at the commencement of the advance saw the enemy appear over the ridge on his right flank not 200 yards away. His Zero Line was in the opposite direction but he switched round on to this target and inflicted most heavy casualties. The enemy worked along the Sunken Road in front of this Battery and began bombing up from the left rear. He also worked up a C.T. on the right and got a machine gun into action which destroyed the two right guns of the Battery before it was discovered and dealt with. From this precarious position the Officer decided to withdraw. He did so down a shallow C.T. with his two remaining guns and consolidated in the Support Line where shortly his two guns were destroyed by shell fire. He was pressed by the enemy but held on until two of his men were killed by a bomb and he was injured, when he joined the nearest Infantry with whom he fought, holding a block at N.26, c,50 until at 5.45 P.M. he was ordered to withdraw on account of organising the remaining M.G. personnel.

"J" Battery caused severe losses to the enemy as he entered the line in front of the Battery, evacuated by our Infantry. A report soon reached the Officer 2nd Lieut. HAYWOOD that the enemy was advancing up the old trench occupied by him. As the Officer knew the Battery to be isolated he ordered a retirement. He placed two guns at N.20 d, 50 and two at N.26, b,35 and established a bombing block at N.26, b.78. This block was held by Sergt. WEIR who killed one Officer and two O.R's at this block. From this position considerable damage was done to the enemy who failed to get through the wire on our right. The enemy had entered the YELLOW LINE on their left and started bombing inwards. As the Infantry had retired from that point the Company Commanders at the locality of the Battery formed a defensive flank; the machine guns were redistributed along it. Here the enemy was held with great loss. About 10 A.M. three men were despatched under Pte. MORGAN, who was sent on account of his trustworthiness, to obtain S.A.A. On their way back they encountered the enemy. One of their number was taken prisoner but with remarkable dexterity and courage Pte. MORGAN turned the point of a bayonet thrust at him and scampered away. He reported to his Officer with a great load of S.A.A. around his neck.

The enemy was found to be bombing up the trench in large numbers and it appeared they would be cut off, so a further retirement was ordered. One gun was kept mounted to hold the enemy. The cover back was very scant; it was necessary to crawl the whole way and the last part was across the open. The enemy had got a machine gun into action and was inflicting heavy casualties, and so accurate was his fire that it was found impossible to crawl with the guns, which therefore had to be abandoned, being first rendered useless. A number of the Infantry were unable to move forward across the open and it is thought that this accounts for the loss of the remaining team and gun who were waiting until they should have established themselves in the new position. Sergt. WEIR was with this gun.

The new position held was along the NEUVILLE-VITASSE RD, MARTIN ROAD, the machine gunners using their rifles and acting as Infantry until they were once more outflanked and retired on the GREEN LINE. "J" Battery was more fortunate in that in front of this position the wire was in good condition. This Battery was also difficult to approach unseen as it was surrounded with flat ground. They inflicted terrific casualties. When the Infantry were forced to retire, the Officer in charge Lieut. ADAM kept his guns firing and was soon afterwards wounded. The enemy was closing in on both flanks

flanks therefore the Officer who took command decided to withdraw on the Infantry. On the way this Officer was also wounded and his Sergeant was left in command. Owing to the casualties only one gun was got away; the other guns had fired until all their teams were casualties. The remaining gun joined Battery 60, 61, 62, 63. of which remained one sergeant and five men. The enemy continued to press and broke through on both flanks and commenced to advance up the valley to the left rear of these guns, and established sniping posts there. He unaccountably became panic stricken and about 200 of them attempted to retire, but were shot to a man by these guns. They fought on, engaging targets until ordered to withdraw at about 4.30 P.M. when they retired on the GREEN LINE. Two guns were despatched to assist the right flank of the ROYAL FUSILIERS. Guns 62A, 63A, were in a forward position under an N.C.O.; they did much execution before they were finally surrounded, and as it was impossible to get back, the gunners smashed their weapons. In this brave effort five of them were killed.

Magnificent work was done by Corporal WHITE of "D" Company. He advanced his guns to engage the enemy on the WANCOURT SPUR and inflicted heavy casualties. The Infantry to his front and flanks withdrew; shortly afterwards the enemy were seen in the trench 200 yards to his right. The Infantry made a further withdrawal. Cpl. WHITE elected to stay and cover them, which he did, bringing fire to bear on the hostile Infantry on his right. One of the guns was immediately put out of action by an enemy sniper. Not until the enemy had approached within bombing distance did the N.C.O. withdraw. Then, finding it impossible to dismount his gun and get away with it, he smashed it up.

At this time the four guns under Lieut. STME and 2nd./Lieut. A.P. WAUGH were engaging the enemy who had penetrated the right flank. Realising the desperate nature of the attack and the position on this flank of the Brigade, these Officers decided not to retire. The enemy dead was lying to the Battery's credit in scores. Gradually the enemy worked round them and the last seen of this brave section was a desperate resistance against great odds, fighting with gun, bayonet and revolver. There can be little doubt but that the heroic self sacrifice of this little band caused a severe check to a situation which might have ended unpleasantly for the whole Division.

Four guns under the charge of 2nd./Lieut. C.T. SMITH (M.C.) were in a support position. As soon as the Officer witnessed the penetration, he despatched a gun to assist the flank. This gun under Sergt. DUROMY was immediately engaged by snipers and the whole team and gun became casualties. The N.C.O. repaired his gun and kept it in action until ordered to withdraw. Two of the Section guns were then completely destroyed by shell fire. The Infantry withdrew through them on position 600 yards in rear; the enemy who attempted to follow was annihilated. One of these two remaining guns was sniped. The Officer then returned and got in touch with the Infantry, and disposed of his gun as the situation demanded.

42E, 43B, 52A, 53A, under 2nd. Lieut. J. KIRWIN had three guns knocked out by shell fire. The fourth gun was withdrawn to another position with the Infantry who were Officerless. He took charge and energetically made a disposition for defence in his locality. By his insistance a great quantity of rifle fire was produced, inflicting casualties. This gun was subsequently blown up.

   Casualties for the day:
    Officers. Killed 1. Wounded 9. Missing 2.
    O.R's. " 25. " 46. " 60.

Total Casualties from March 21st; to March 28th.
    Officers. Killed 1. Wounded 9. Missing 2.
    O.R's. " 29. " 66. " 60.

Total number of guns lost and destroyed: **29**

MARCH 29th.
Situation quiet.

  On MARCH 29/30th. the Division was relieved by the 2nd. CANADIAN Division.

CASUALTIES.

OFFICERS.

Killed........	2nd. Lieut.	WILSON W.J.	28/3/1918.
Wounded.......	Lieut.	MITCHELL W. McK. (M.C.)	"
	"	HAROLD-BARRY G.W.	"
	"	ADAM W.	"
	2nd. Lieut.	THOMAS W.N.	"
	"	HOLBROOK S.R.	"
	"	DOBSON T.E.	"
	"	HOOD F.E.	"
	Capt.	MOFFETT S. (M.C.)	") Remaining at
	"	DES VOEUX J.H.	") Duty.
Missing......	Lieut.	SIME T.	"
	"	WAUGH A.R.	"

3rd. BATTALION   M. G. CORPS.

OPERATION ORDERS NO. 8.

N°9

SECRET.

REFERENCE MAPS................

1. Withdrawal 3rd. Division to YELLOW LINE on night 22nd./23rd. March.

2. (a) Guns 60, 61, 62, and 63 will withdraw from present position about 1.30 a.m. or as soon as practicable after Infantry withdrawal and will occupy positions at H.26 C,8,9.
   Limbers will meet these Guns at H.23.C 2,2. (Dressing Station)

   (b) 58A, 59A, will withdraw at 2.45 A.M. or as soon as practicable after Infantry and pick up 44B, and 45B at N.23.C 2,2 where limbers meet them.

   (c) 54A, 55A, 56A, 57A, will withdraw from positions at 2.45 A.M. or as soon as practicable after withdrawal of Infantry - will withdraw to position at M.36 C 1,8.
   Limbers will meet these guns at N.23.C 2,2

   New positions in 3rd. System to be occupied not later than 5.A.m. 23rd. inst.

3. Occupation of new positions will be reported to Battln. H.Q. by runner.

(signed) F.B. MacKenzie,
                          Major
for Lt.-Col. 3rd. M.G.C.

OPERATION ORDERS NO. 7

In conjunction with Operation Orders to be issued later.
Ref:-   Withdrawal of Division to YELLOW LINE.
    Guns No.
    56 & 57   will withdraw not later than 1.15 a.m. 23rd. or as soon
               after the Infantry as Officer commanding the section may
               think advisable, and take up position S6B40.
               Limber for this party will be at advanced Ambulance car
               Station at Heninel St. Martin's Cross Road at N23,c22.

    58 & 59   will withdraw at 2 A.M. (23rd.) or as soon as practicable
               after Infantry retirement, same route and same limber as
               56 & 57 and take up position in the same place.

    52A & 53A.)   will retire at 3 A.M. or as soon as practicable
    42B,& 43B.)   after Infantry and take up position N.31,B.05.
               Limber at same place.

To O/C "B" Coy.
         The guns of J. Battery at present occupying FIELD & FOOLEY will retire on 'K' Battery position in YELLOW LINE N27,B05. Same to be notified later. (The former occupants of 'K' are now at 'J'.)

"D" COMPANY.

1. 64, 65, 66, 67, will withdraw at 1:30 A.M. or as soon as practicable after the Infantry withdrawal and will take up positions at N.15 b 1,5 Limbers for these guns will be at N.22, b, 29.

2. 64A, 65A, 66A, 67A, will withdraw at 3 A.M. or as soon as practicable after the Infantry withdrawal and will take up positions at N.21, a 9, 3. Limbers for these guns will be at N.22 b.2, 9.

3. 68A, 69A, 70A, 71A, will withdraw at 3 A.M. or as soon as practicable after Infantry withdrawal and will take up positions at N14, a, 7, 3.

4. 60A, 61A, will withdraw to CROSS ROADS at N,22, a, 8, 4.
   62A, 63A, will withdraw to N,21, b, 5, 0.
   These four guns will withdraw at 3.45 A.M. or as soon as practicable after Infantry withdrawal. No limbers will be provided for these guns.

5. 46B, 47B, 48B, 49B, 50B, 51B will withdraw to Battln. H.Q. and come under the command of O.C. "C" Coy.
   Limbers for these six guns will be at N,22, b, 2, 9.

6. New positions will be occupied by 5 A.M. on the 23rd.
7. Occupation of the new positions will be reported to Battln. H.Q. by runner.
8. A C K N O W L E D G E.

(signed) F.B. MacKenzie,
Major.
3rd. Batt. M.G.C.

23/3/18. 12.40 a.m.

SECRET.

3rd. BATTALION MACHINE GUN CORPS.

OPERATION ORDER NO. 9.

Copy No. 8

24/3/1918.

REFERENCE SHEET: 51B SW Ed 7^C

1. The 3rd. Divisional Front will be held with three Brigades in line - 8th. Infantry Brigade on the right - 9th. Infantry Brigade in the centre - and 76th. Infantry Brigade on the left.-

2. The Machine Guns will be formed in three groups:
   (a) RIGHT GROUP.
       O.C. "B" Coy. will be responsible for the tactical employment of all Machine Guns in the 8th. Infantry Brigade area, viz:
       56, 57, 58, 59, 54A, 55A, 56A, 57A, 'I' Battery, 52A, 53A, 42B, 45B.
       "B" Coy. Headquarters will be with 8th. Infantry Brigade at BOISLEUX-AU-MONT.
   (b) CENTRE GROUP.
       O.C. "A" Coy. will be responsible for the tactical employment of all machine guns in the 9th. Infantry Brigade Area, viz:
       'L' Battery, (2 guns), 'K' Battery (3 guns), 'J' Battery (4 guns), 60, 61, 62, 63, 58A, 59A, 44B, 45B.
       "A" Coy. Headquarters will be with 9th. Infantry Brigade at YORK LINES.

(2)

O.O. No. 9.

2. (Contd.)
   (c) LEFT GROUP.
       O.C. "D" Coy. will be responsible for the tactical employment of all Machine Guns in the 76th. Infantry Brigade area, viz: 60A, 61A, 62A, 63A, 64A, 65A, 66A, 67A, 68A, 69A, 70A, 71A, 64, 65, 66, 67, and 'M' Battery.
       "D" Coy. Headquarters will be with 76th. Infantry Brigade Headquarters in Square M.18.

3. O.C. "C" Coy. will be responsible for the tactical employment of the 4 gun Battery at M 18 d 7.7.
   The remaining 4 guns of "C" Coy. will remain at YORK LINES in Divisional Reserve.

4. O.C. Companies will be responsible for the tactical employment of their groups from 10 P.M. 24th. instant.

5. A C K N O W L E D G E.

Callan
Lieut. & Adjt.
3rd. Battln. M.G.Corps.

Issued at 2.30 P.M.
Copies to:-
1. D.M.G.C.   7-8 War Diary.
2. "A" Coy.   9-10. Files.
3. "B" "   11. 8th. Inf. Brigade.
4. "C" "   12. 9th. "   "
5. "D" "   13. 76th. "   "
6. 3rd. Div. "G".

3rd. BATTALION MACHINE GUN CORPS.   Copy No. 11

OPERATION ORDERS NO. 10.   SECRET.

REFERENCE MAPS. 51 b SW   25/3/1918.
51 c SE

1. In the event of the Battalion being ordered to withdraw, the under-mentioned Batteries at present holding the YELLOW LINE will remain in position with platoons detailed from Infantry Battalions and act as a covering party to the withdrawal of the Division:-
   (1) T. Battery.
   (2) Guns 52A, 53A, 42B, 43B.
   (3) J. Battery.
   (4) Guns 60, 61, 62, 63.
   (5) K. Battery and attached guns from L. Battery.
   (6) L. Battery.
   (7) Guns 62A, 63A, 60A, 61A.
   (8) Guns 64A, 65A, 66A, 67A.
   (9) M. Battery.
   These guns will withdraw at the first ZERO hour to be notified later.

2. (1) Guns 56, 57, 58, 59.   ) will remain in present position
   (2) Guns 54A, 55A, 56A, 57A.) until the 2nd. ZERO hour.
   (3) Guns 68A, 69A, 70A, 71A.)

3. On Battalions withdrawing from YELLOW LINE:-
   (1) Guns 58A, 59A, 44B, 45B, will withdraw and take up position at M.30 Central.
   (2) 64, 65, 66, 67 will withdraw on to Sunken road at N.14 a.99.

4. At First ZERO hour all guns holding the YELLOW LINE will withdraw through the troops in GREEN LINE and move back on the RED LINE to:

O.O. No. 10.   (2)

4. "C" Coy. Two Batteries East of the Railway line at M.15 Central and two Batteries at M.14dCentral.

5. At 2nd. ZERO Hour all guns detailed to hold the GREEN LINE will withdraw and take up positions as follows:
   "B" Coy. to Western edge of PICHEUX near PICHEUX MILL.
   "A" "   to the PICHEUX-WATLY Road about R.29 Central.
   "D" "   will withdraw to Battalion Headquarters at BEAMONT MILL between BEAUREVILLE and BUFFENCOURT.

6. Dispositions of Batteries with map references will be forwarded to Battalion Headquarters as soon as possible after getting into position.

7. O.C. "A" Coy. will detail L. Battery to join their own Company.
8. The above orders will be complied with on receipt of the word "MOVE"
9. A C K N O W L E D G E.

Rallan
Lieut. & Adjt.
3rd. Battln. M.G.Corps.

Issued at 2.30 A.M.
Copies to:- 1. D.M.G.C.   7. L.M.   14. 8th. Inf. Bde.
            2. "A" Coy.   8. T.O.   15. 9th. "   "
            3. "B" "   9. M.O.   16. 76th. "   "
            4. "C" "   10-11 War Diary ✓
            5. "D" "   12-13 File
            6. 3rd. Div. "Q"

3rd. BATTALION MACHINE GUN CORPS.

OPERATION ORDERS NO. 11.

<u>SECRET</u>

1. The 5th. Canadian Brigade will relieve the 8th. Brigade and half the 9th. Brigade.

2. The 4th. Canadian Brigade will relieve the 76th. Brigade and other half of 9th. Brigade.

3. Greatest care will be excercised in handing over the line.

4. Relief of every detachment will be carried out by an Officer and no detachment is to be withdrawn until regularly relieved. Except such guns as are ordered to be withdrawn unrelieved, which will withdraw on the entry of Canadian Infantry into adjacent trenches.

5. Reliefs will be as arranged between Company Commanders concerned.
Relief to be complete by 11 P.M.
Relief complete to be reported to Battln. H.Q.

6. On relief Battalion will move to close billets at RIVIERE. Guides will meet Companies on main road outside RIVIERE. Billets are being arranged.

7. Division will move on 30th. of March. Orders will be issued. All maps will be handed over.

8. A C K N O W L E D G E.

6 P.M. 29/3/18.

Capt. & Adjt.
3rd. Batt. M.G.Corps.

3rd. BATTALION MACHINE GUN CORPS.

OPERATION ORDERS NO. 11A.

SECRET.

1. The Battalion will march to the WARLUZEL Area tomorrow 30th. inst. Destination will be notified later.

2. <u>Parade Dress</u>: The Battalion will parade at 11.30 A.M., Dress - Light Marching Order, Box Respirators in the alert position. Haversacks on back, with waterproof sheets folded under flap. Steel helmets will be worn. Packs to be packed in limbers.

3. <u>Hour of Start</u>. The Battalion will move off at 12 noon.

4. <u>Order of March</u>. Battln. H.Q., "A" Coy., "B" Coy., "C" Coy., "D" Coy.

5. <u>Transport</u>. H.Q. transport will march in rear of the Battalion. Company transport behind each Coy. Field kitchens will head each Company's transport. One water cart will travel behind the field kitchen of "B" Coy. and the other behind the field kitchen of "D" Coy.

6. <u>Intervals</u>. 12 yards interval will be maintained between Companies

7. <u>March Discipline</u>. The strictest March discipline will be maintained throughout the march.

8. <u>Evacuation of Camps</u>. Coy. Commanders and Transport Officer will inspect billets and standings before moving off and render a certificate to Battln. H.Q. that these have been left in a clean and sanitary condition.

Battln. Orders.
<u>OPERATION ORDERS NO. 11A</u>.

9. <u>Billeting</u>. Arrangements regarding billeting will be notified later.

10. <u>Marching-Out-State</u>. State will be rendered to Battln. H.Q., one hour before hour of start.

11. <u>Rear Guard</u>. "D" Coy. will detail one section under an Officer to march 50 yards in the rear of the column for the purpose of collecting stragglers and assisting with transport if necessary. Stragglers will be brought along slowly and as a formed body under a Senior N.C.O. This N.C.O. before starting will be notified of destination. Officer i/c Rear guard will, on arrival at destination, render to Battln. H.Q. a return of stragglers.

12. A C K N O W L E D G E.

Company Commanders will make their own arrangements as to when Men's dinners will be served.

29/3/1918.

Lieut. & Adjt.
3rd. Batt. M.G.Corps.

3rd. BATTALION MACHINE GUN CORPS.
OPERATION ORDER NO. 12.

14

1. The Battalion will move to the BRUAY Area on 1st April.
2. The Battalion will embus at T.33.a.8.0 (Sheet 51c.) on the AVESNES-LE-COMTE----PREVENT Road, embussing to be completed by 10 a.m.
3. The Battalion will parade at 7.30 a.m. in CHURCH CRESCENT, head of Battalion on main road.
4. Order of March:---Batt. H.Q., "B" Coy., "C" Coy., "D" Coy., "A" Coy.
5. Men will carry pack and one blanket.
6. Remainder of blankets, rolled in bundles of 10, and Officers' valises will be dumped at Q.M's Stores not later than 7 a.m.
7. As Field Kitchens will not be available till late on 2nd. of April, Companies will carry sufficient dixies with them.
8. Lieut. SWANN ("B" Coy.) will act as Embussing Officer. He will proceed to the embussing point by 8.30 a.m. and make necessary arrangements for accommodation. He will obtain strength of Battalion before leaving.
9. Rations for 1st. April will be carried by men.
10. Billeting Orders will be issued later.
11. Certificate re cleanliness of billets etc. vacated will be rendered to Batt. H.Q. before the Battalion moves off.
12. Marching Out State will be handed by C.S.M's to R.S.M. on parade.
13. R.Q.M.S. and one man detailed by Q.M. will report at 10 a.m. to Supply Officer at BUNEVILLE.
14. ACKNOWLEDGE.

31/3/18.

Capt. & Adjt.
3rd. Batt. M.G.Corps.

3rd Division

WAR DIARY

3rd BATTALION

MACHINE GUN CORPS

APRIL 1918

Army Form C. 2118.

WAR DIARY
or
INTELLIGENCE SUMMARY.
(Erase heading not required.)

3rd Bn M.G. Corps

Place	Date	Hour	Summary of Events and Information	Remarks and references to Appendices
SOMBRIN. BRUAY	1st	9.0 a.m.	Bn. transport marched to LIENCOURT then they entrained 11.30 a.m. arriving at BRUAY 4.0 p.m. via the Rd. via LIGNEREUIL. Route RUE MARMOTTE. Bn. & trans. FREVENT - ST POL - DIÉVAL. Transport billeted ST POL area.	C/H/L
	2nd		Bn. cleaning up & training MAJOR MACKENZIE reconnoitering CORPS LINE Transport worked at BRUAY.	C/H/L
	3rd	2.30 p.m.	Bn. in training C.O. and COY COMMANDERS reconnoitering CORPS LINE	S/L/L APPENDIX I
		10.0 a.m.	Operation order No. 13 issued	C/H/L
NOEUX LES MINES.	4th		Bn. moved to NOEUX LES MINES. Billeted in RUE DE LA BOURSE. RUE DE SAILLY and ROUTE NATIONALE. C.O. & Coy Commanders reconnoitering CORPS LINE	
	5th		C.O. Coy Commanders, Officers & NCOs reconnoitering CORPS LINE Bn. in training. Reinforcements 2/Lt WATSON R.W. 2/Lt MANSELL D.M. 2/Lt BURKE E.J. " JONES A. 120 other ranks 6 other ranks	C/H/L
	6th		Bn. in training Lain. Platoon 2/Lt BREWER T.L. I.O.R.	S/L

A 5834. Wt. W 4973 M 687. 759,000 8/16 D.D. & L. Ltd. Forms C.2118/13.

Army Form C. 2118.

WAR DIARY
or
INTELLIGENCE SUMMARY.
(Erase heading not required.)

Instructions regarding War Diaries and Intelligence Summaries are contained in F. S. Regs., Part II. and the Staff Manual respectively. Title pages will be prepared in manuscript.

Place	Date	Hour	Summary of Events and Information	Remarks and references to Appendices
NOEUX LES MINES	April 7		BETHUNE 1: 40.000	
			Batn. Church Parade. Evacuation 2. O.R.	
	8		Rejoined 2. O.R.	
			Bn. Parade. Firing of new drafts	
			Reconnaissance of NOEUX CORPS LINE.	
			Reinforcements 2/Lt GRANT. G.J. 2/Lt EWER. A.J.	
			" DOUGLAS. J. 70 other ranks	
			Evacuation 8 other ranks	
	9		Baty.	
			Reconnaissance of NOEUX AREA	
			"A" Coy on range	
		12.0 NOON	Order to stand by and act at one hour's notice. DIV. O.O. N.230	
			Enemy action N. of LA BASSÉ. NOEUX lightly shelled	
			S.A.A. when to CORPS position.	
			Transferred to 31st Bn. 8 O.Rs. sick	
			On leave 1 other rank.	
	10		Section to like line dug in CORPS LINE but impossibility of obtaining	
			R.E. material prevented it. Buses in training	
			Evacuation 2 other ranks	

Army Form C. 2118.

WAR DIARY
or
INTELLIGENCE SUMMARY.
(Erase heading not required.)

Place	Date	Hour	Summary of Events and Information	Remarks and references to Appendices
NOEUX LES MINES	April 11	12.0 Noon	Reconnaissance of LE QUESNOY CORPS LINE. Battalion ordered to move. CAPT W. DOWLING. M.O. admitted to C.C.S. "C" Coy and "D" Coy two 2 Sections "A" Coy and "D" Coy two 2 Sections to MT BERNENCHON — HINGES Batt H.Q and "B" COY to LES HARISOIRS The detachments were changed on line of march, and "A" Coy and half of "D" Corps Nord to LONG CORNET. "C" Coy and half of "D" " — BELLERINE Batt H.Q. and "B" Coy to GONNEHEM and one "C" Coy went into position W. of LA BASSÉ CANAL around HINGES "A" Coy E. of LA BASSÉ CANAL from LES CAUDROHS to CANAL DE LA LAWE N. OF LOCON.	
GONNEHEM	April 12		Batt. H.Q and "B" Coy moved to lunch in GONNEHEM village "A", "C" & "D" Coy in line under O.C "A" Coy (right group) O.C "C" Coy (left group) four guns of "B" Coy rushed to "C" Coy MAJOR MACKENZIE to reason with disarmed	

WAR DIARY or INTELLIGENCE SUMMARY

Army Form C. 2118.

Place	Date	Hour	Summary of Events and Information	Remarks and references to Appendices
GONNEHEM		1.0 a.m.	8 R Brigade lightly attacked a force S. of LOCON. Casualties 11 O.R. Transfer to UK 1 O.R. Reinforcement 2/Lt POULTON W.G., 2/Lt MURCH A., 2/Lt ROSSER W.E., 2/Lt McNAIR. W.H. Casualties 4 O.R. & 1 injured. Enquiries in line as before. Capt. R.R. NEILSON O/C "A" Coy Carried out reconnoitring patrol from 2/Lt E.A. SHEPHERD wounded by shell. Capt DES VOEUX took Command of night post with 8 R Infantry Brigade H.Q. marching back to GONNEHEM. Lucen. 4TH DIVISION relieved 76TH BDE in line. Action round G ANNEZIN in S. edge of 13 Coy returned to base at HINGES. February. for 5000 yards.	APPENDIX 2
	April	10.0 p.m.	"B" Coy & 1 Section of 13 Coy returned to GONNEHEM. Casualties Capt R R NEILSON, Lt E A SHEPHERD. Casualties 2 O.R. 5 O.R. wounded.	
ANNEZIN	14	10.0 a.m.	Bn H.Q. & Transport march to ANNEZIN.	

Army Form C. 2118.

WAR DIARY
or
INTELLIGENCE SUMMARY.
(Erase heading not required.)

Instructions regarding War Diaries and Intelligence Summaries are contained in F.S. Regs., Part II. and the Staff Manual respectively. Title pages will be prepared in manuscript.

Place	Date	Hour	Summary of Events and Information	Remarks and references to Appendices
ANNEZIN	April 14		"C" Coy moved into line with 9th Infantry Brigade. Operation Order No.14 issued.	APPENDIX 3
		12.0 noon	"B" Coy two in relief at HINGES. Expend. BLM. H.Q. Expending fire 10,000 rounds. at ANNEZIN. Casualties 8 OR Stretcher 2 OR	
	15		Late Capt R R NEILSON died at CHOCQUES. Lt. A.S. WESTMORLAND joined vice Capt W DOWLING. C.O. visited Coys 1 conference in line. "B" Coy went into line. Expend y order fire 15,000 rounds.	
	16		C.O. visited Brigade. Conference in line. Conference issued by Major General. Warning order issued of impending re-employment of the Company fire 20,000 rounds.	

WAR DIARY
INTELLIGENCE SUMMARY

(Erase heading not required.)

Army Form C. 2118.

Place	Date	Hour	Summary of Events and Information	Remarks and references to Appendices
ANNEZIN	April 17		Conference of Coy Commanders called to discuss impending operations.	
		4.0 p.m.	Operation cancelled. Annexing fire 20,000 rounds Evacuation 2 O.R. Beyond 1 O.R.	
	18	h.	Attack on right & left flanks of division (see appendix 2) the 3rd Division was not attacked but tapped in to engage on the flank. Division front now free in S.O.S. 40,000 rounds & anti-aircraft rounds fired. Evacuation 1 O.R. Leave to U.K. 1 O.R.	

Army Form C. 2118.

WAR DIARY
or
INTELLIGENCE SUMMARY.
(Erase heading not required.)

Place	Date	Hour	Summary of Events and Information	Remarks and references to Appendices
ANNEZIN	April 19		Situation quiet. Little artillery activity. Promotion to A/Major of Company Commander & A/Capt. of 2nd in Command. C.O. visited Brigade & Companies in line & D.M.G.C. at B.H. Casualties 9 O.R.	APPENDIX CPM
	20		Lt R.N. GREGOR + 2 O.R. Heavy barrage at dawn. Otherwise situation quiet. 16th Infantry Brigade relieved its left boundary 1000 yrds from "D" and relieved two Coys of 4th Div in the line. New line OBLINGHEM ↓ VENDIN LES BETHUNE C.O. visited C.O. 1st Battalion. Casualties 2 O.R. Reinforcements 1 O.R.	CPM
	21	2.30 AM	Transport lines shelled. Gas shells were partly amongst the transport line. The first shell bursting in the afternoon to the village on Cavalry Cleared at 7pm the shrapnel shelled again. Situation in line quiet.	CPM
		7.0 pm	Casualties nil to D.24.a.3.4.	

A5834 Wt. W4973 M687 752,000 8/16 D.D. & L. Ltd Forms C.2118/13.

Army Form C. 2118.

WAR DIARY
or
INTELLIGENCE SUMMARY.
(Erase heading not required.)

Instructions regarding War Diaries and Intelligence Summaries are contained in F.S. Regs., Part II. and the Staff Manual respectively. Title pages will be prepared in manuscript.

Place	Date	Hour	Summary of Events and Information	Remarks and references to Appendices
ANNEZIN	April 21	12.0 night	Wire received ref relief of enemy 187 Regt 1st Guards Division & expected attack by 187th down Carpure & opposite Laventie. Laventie sector sent out to Arras to list of Artillery units available on Europe date. Breucher 7 pts lack. Breucher 4. 3 injured.	APPENDIX 4. a
	22	3.0 a.m.	Enemy barrage put down by our artillery & machine gun fire & much fire until dawn. Situation remained normal.	
		6.0 a.m.	H.Q. moved to E.14.a.6.2	
E.14.a.6.2	23		Situation normal. Operation order Nos received. Boy Bourne on line. Code arrangements ref by Canadian 46 Bn. C.O. visited C.O. 4 Batt. Breucher 2 O.R.	APPENDIX 5.

A834 Wt. W4973 M687 750,000 8/16 D.D. & L. Ltd. Forms C.2118/13.

Army Form C. 2118.

WAR DIARY
or
INTELLIGENCE SUMMARY
(Erase heading not required.)

Instructions regarding War Diaries and Intelligence Summaries are contained in F.S. Regs., Part II. and the Staff Manual respectively. Title pages will be prepared in manuscript.

Place	Date	Hour	Summary of Events and Information	Remarks and references to Appendices
E.14.a.6.2	24th		Misty Weather. Situation normal. Strong of took over 9 inch to that in ANNEZIN. ("C" Coy, 1 Section "D" Coy, 1 Section "B" Coy. All guns relieved on 8 dugouts new "B" Coy his 1 section) Casualties. 2. O.R.	(A)
	25th		Situation normal. Conference held by G.O.C. Division attended by C.O. On return of "A" Coy relieved by "B" Coy & Batn "D" Coy & Batn. Operation Order No. 16 issued. No 17335 Pte Ruffy J.C. awarded Military Medal. Corps C.O. No 132. Casualties 3. O.R. Evacuation 2. O.R.	(B) APPENDIX 6
	26th		On night of 25/26th Relief carried out as per O.O. No 16. Situation normal.	
		6.0 P.M.	Operation Order No 17 issued. Evacuation 1. O.R.	APPENDIX 7

Army Form C. 2118.

WAR DIARY
or
INTELLIGENCE SUMMARY.
(Erase heading not required.)

Instructions regarding War Diaries and Intelligence Summaries are contained in F. S. Regs., Part II. and the Staff Manual respectively. Title pages will be prepared in manuscript.

Place	Date	Hour	Summary of Events and Information	Remarks and references to Appendices
E14 A 6.2	Apr 27	A.M. 8.15	On night of 26/27 "C" Coy occupied nearest position as for operation order N°17. Situation normal. Bethune relieved; 12 hits on railway. C O started Dugout company in the line. 6 wounded 3 O.R.	
	28		O.O. N° 18 issued. On night of 27/28 h 1 battery of "C" Coy at W 23 d 8.1 withdrew and retired to Buists at Sharqin. Harassing fire (right group) 9,000 rounds. Artillery active on both sides. N°2 Section "C" Coy moved into position at W 13 d. 16.32. Grenadier 1. O.R. Shrapnel 1. O.R. 1. O.R. injured. Gunshot 2/Lt S R HOLBROOK + 3 O.R.	APPENDIX 3

Place	Date	Hour	Summary of Events and Information	Remarks and references to Appendices
E.14.a.6.2	Oct 29		Situation normal. Weather dull. Harassing fire (right group) 8,000 rounds. Orders re defensive measures issued. 2/Lt H.G. BARWOOD found no signal officer. Casualties. 1 O.R. Evacuation 2 O.R. Reinforced 2/Lt H.G. BARWOOD	APPENDIX 9
	30		Situation normal. Weather dull. Harassing fire 5,000 rounds. Army M.G.O. Col LINDSEY visited C.O. Casualties 1 O.R. Evacuation 4 O.R.	
		12noon	Operation Orders No 19 issued	APPENDIX 10

W.J. Bramston Lt Col
Comdg 31st Bn M.G.C

3rd. BATTALION MACHINE GUN CORPS.   APPENDIX I

OPERATION ORDERS NO. 13.

1. The Battalion will move to NOEUX-LES-MINES tomorrow 4th. instant.
2. The Battalion will parade at MARKET SQUARE at 8 A.M.
3. Order of March: Batt. H.Q., "C" Coy, "D" Coy, "A" Coy, "B" Coy.
4. Dress: Light Marching order; Haversacks on backs, ground sheets folded under flap of haversack, mess tins on haversack, steel helmets will be worn, box respirators in alert position.
5. Packs will be loaded on limbers; limbers will be packed by 7 A.M.
6. Billetting Party consisting One Officer for Batt. H.Q. and One Officer and One O.R. per Coy. will parade at Batt. H.Q. at 8 A.M. with horses or cycles.
7. Lt. St. Leger will obtain from TOWN MAJOR, NOEUX-LES-MINES Area alletted to Battalion and divide this Area amongst Companies. Certificates re cleanliness of Billets etc. will be rendered to Batt. H.Q. before moving off.
8. Parade State will be rendered on parade.
9. A rearguard consisting of One Officer and One Section detailed by "B" Coy. will march 50 yards in rear of the column for the purpose of collecting stragglers and assisting with transport, if required. Stragglers report will be rendered at conclusion of march.
10. Each transport will move in rear of its own Company. Travelling kitchens will head transport of each Company. One water cart will travel behind the kitchen of "D" Coy. and "B" Coy.
11. The strictest march discipline will be maintained throughout the march.
12. A C K N O W L E D G E.

3/4/18

Capt. & Adjt.
3rd. Batt. M.G.Corps.

SECRET.

REPORT ON MOVEMENTS
-- OF --
3rd. BATTALION MACHINE GUN CORPS.

FROM: MARCH 30TH. 1918.
TO: APRIL 20TH. 1918.

ATTACHED IS REPORT OF OPERATIONS FROM 11th. to 20th. APRIL 1918.

APPENDIX 2

3rd. BATTALION MACHINE GUN CORPS.

The period between the last date of the previous report—29th. March and the first date of that attached—the 11th. of April, was spent in a manner which precluded the rest which normal times would have warranted. For not only had the Division been through a most strenuous and nerve-racking time, but that after eight weeks of unrelieved duty in the line.

On the night 29th/30th. March the Battalion was relieved and marched to close billets in BRETENCOURT. They arrived at 5 A.M. and at Noon were on the road again, as we were out of the Divisional Area. In spite of everything they had undergone the men showed remarkable fettle throughout the long march to SOMBRIN; so much so in fact, that the G.O.C. VI Corps remarked it. One day was spent at this village and next morning the Battalion marched to LIENCOURT where they embussed for BRUAY, reaching there at 4 P.M. The same night an order was received from I Corps that there lines were to be immediately reconnoitred, and the following day a long series of protected reconnaissances was commenced starting from the LA BASSEE CANAL to NOYETTE, which lies behind SOUCHEZ. These reconnaissances were undertaken by all Officers and Non-commissioned Officers. The men, who had been heavily reinforced with new drafts were put through elementary training and when the Battalion marched to NOEUX-LES-MINES on the 4th. April, range practive was undertaken.

On the 10th. definite areas were allotted to the Division and the M.G. Battalion commenced to make emplacements and took up all the requisite S.A.A., none having been previously placed in position.

At midday on the 11th. we were ordered to move immediately as described in attached report.

W.J. Cranston
Lieut. Colonel,
Commanding 3rd. Battln. M.G.Corps.

3rd. BATTALION MACHINE GUN CORPS.

REPORT OF OPERATIONS
NORTH OF
BETHUNE.

April 11th. to April 20th. 1918.

---ooOoo---

The country in which the Battalion found itself on arriving at the battle front presented new problems to the majority of the Machine gunners, who had fought in so many battles and spent so many months in the rolling plains South of ARRAS, where good trenches could easily be dug and shelters constructed below ground level. Here it is impossible to dig deeper than 18" and much less than this in many places, the ground was so sodden. The close nature of the country however facilitated the building of breastworks behind torn hedges or broken walls, and in some places old breastworks were found and put into use.

After the open country to which the Officers had become habituated the lie of the land presented some difficulty in siting the guns. The harsh enemy treatment of the houses and compact villages of the SOMME caused the personnel to have some qualms about the use of houses in this, to them, new phase of warfare. Soon their bias was overcome, partly on account of the lack of cover in inclement weather, and partly as they realised the command possible from a house in this flat country: so guns were sited in houses where loopholed emplacements strongly covered in, could be built, for sniping purposes and special fields of fire, but were not encouraged to make defensive positions of such obvious points on account of the enemy's tactical handling of his Minnenwerfer.

At noon on the 11th. of April, the Battalion which was in billets at NOEUX-LES-MINES was ordered to proceed to HINGES (1½ Companies) and Mt. BERNENCHON (1½ Companies) the Reserve Company and Battln. H.Q. to be at LES HARISOIRS. En route the location was changed; three Companies being sent to HINGES, one Company and Battln. H.Q. to proceed to GONNEHEM. The three Companies went straight into the line; 24 guns in the environs of HINGES and 24 guns from LES GAUDRONS to the locality of LOCON.

The guns relieved in the positions occupied by the previous Division and next day were re-arranged in depth; those in front being arranged in pairs under an Officer; those behind in Batteries of four guns.

Shortly after midday on the 12th. of April the 8th. Infantry Brigade was heavily attacked and forced back to the southern outskirts of LOCON. The attack was preceded by a very trench mortar bombardment. The enemy penetrated the line on the left and pushed up machine guns and snipers. Our machine guns did great execution in the initial phase. One section of "A" Coy. under 2nd. Lieut. T.F. ARNOLD was fighting in the re-entrand formed by the infiltration; one of these guns was blown up in the preliminary bombardment. They were very intent engaging the many targets presented, doing great execution; one target among many being a party of enemy cyclists proceeding through LOCON who were shot to a man. The teams were so eagerly busy that they did not realise that they were being surrounded until two of the remaining guns were sniped, one being rendered completely useless. The Infantry then withdrew from this position and the Officer decided to withdraw with them, bringing back the good gun and slightly damaged one over the bullet swept open ground; they sustained ten casualties.

The 76th. Infantry Brigade called for the assistance of four more guns late that after-noon and they were sent up to consolidate in depth behind HINGES.

S.O.S. lines of fire were arranged in conjunction with the artillery to cover our new line.

During the morning of the 13th. Capt. R.R. NEILSON was reconnoitring forward positions when he came under machine gun fire. He took cover, but on attempting to move away was again opened on and shot through the head. Capt. DES VOEUX assumed command. 2nd. Lieut. SHEPHERD who had temporarily acted as Second in Command to his company rejoined his guns and soon after was mortally wounded by shell fire.

At 3 P.M. GONNEHEM was subjected to a bombardment H.Q. being blown up. The transport was ordered to leave the standings and move along the road – a wise precaution as it happened. The unit which moved into the vacated standings shortly afterwards suffered severe casualties – 14 killed and 23 wounded and many horses killed.

The 4th. DIVISION relieved the 76th. Infantry Brigade and the 24 guns were relieved and moved to ANNEZIN; the four extra guns were not relieved until the next night. Harrassing fire was carried out on the 8th. Brigade Front, 5000 rounds being expended.

On the 14th. April Battln. H.Q. and transport moved to ANNEZIN with Reserve Company under orders of 8th. Infantry Brigade. A prisoner taken during the day made some remarks about the deadliness of our M.G. fire. Twenty four guns moved into the line with the 9th. Infantry Brigade. The guns were re-arranged in depth in the new 9th. Brigade Sector on the 15th. and S.O.S. lines were laid out.
An organised Machine gun and artillery shoot was carried out. The houses were blown in and the fleeing occupants shot down; much damage was done. In harrassing and other fire 15,000 rounds were expended.
"B" Coy. was taken from the command of Brigade in Reserve and sent up the line to consolidate in depth.

On April 16th. the Major General called a conference.
Harrassing fire 20,000 rounds.
Nothing of special interest occurred. Aeroplanes were engaged. Prisoners gave evidence of an impending attack on this front, probably the following morning.

At dawn on the 17th. April our artillery put down a creeping barrage which was heavily replied to. Harrassing and S.O.S. fire and aeroplane fire – 20,000 rounds.

Dawn of April 18th. was ushered in with a concentrated bombardment of heavy shells and trench mortars and a prodigal use of H.V. shells on back areas. The enemy launched an attack on the right and left of our own. In an amazingly short time he threw two pontoons across the Canal at PECAUT WOOD which were promptly destroyed and every man who

who crossed either killed, wounded, drowned or taken prisoner.
Our front remained inviolate during the day but our machine guns were able to offer a good deal of assistance firing to the flanks; to some guns the enemy presented himself in enfilade and suffered accordingly owing to the scant cover in approach, so different to the ground South of ARRAS.
40,000 rounds were fired in S.O.S. harrassing, direct fire and anti-aircraft targets.

       The 19th. and 20th. of April were quiet, the situation being normal, except for a barrage on the latter morning.

Total Casualties for period April 11th. ----20th. inclusive:
- Officers.   Killed..2. (1 died of Wounds)
  - Wounded.Nil.
- O.R's.   Killed..7. (2 died of wounds)
  - Wounded.41.

W.J.Cranston.
Lieut. Colonel,
Commanding 3rd. Battln. M.G.Corps.

APPENDIX 3
SECRET.

3rd. BATTALION MACHINE GUN CORPS.
                                        April 14th. 1918.

OPERATION ORDERS NO. 14.

                                        COPY NO......1.......

REF MAPS:- Sheet 36A. S.E. 1/20000 and BETHUNE combined 1/40000.
1. (a) The 76th. Inf. Brigade will relieve the 8th. Inf. Brigade in the line between PONT TOURNANT in X.8.C. (exclusive) and PT. LEVIS at AVELETTE (inclusive) on night 14th./15th.
   (b) After relief the 8th. Inf. Brigade will move to the Area ANNEZIN - VENDIN-LES-BETHUNE and will be in Divisional Reserve.
   (c) Guns of the 3rd. Battln. M.G. Corps at present covering this front will not be relieved.
   (d) The remaining 12 guns of the 3rd. Battln. M.G. Corps ("B" Coy.) now covering the fronts of the 10th. and 11th. Infantry Brigades will be relieved tonight April 14/15th. and will move to ANNEZIN where they will come into Divisional Reserve directly under the orders of the G.O.C. 8th. Infantry Brigade together with the 4 guns now in Divisional Reserve.

2. (a) The 9th. Inf. Brigade by 6 A.M. April 15th. will be holding the left sector of the 55th. Divisional Front between X.22.a,9.2. and PONT TOURNANT in X.8.C. (inclusive). The command of the 9th. Inf. Brigade and also of the sector half by them will pass to G.O.C. 3rd. Division at this hour.
   (b) The 9th. Brigade H.Q. will be established on the LA BASSEE CANAL Bank South of and close to the 76th. Inf. Brigade H.Q.
   (c) The Company of the 1st. Battln. M.G.C. at present covering this front will be relieved by 1½ Companies of the 3rd. Battln. M.G. Corps now in Divisional Reserve on the night 14/15th. Details of relief will be arranged between D.M.G.C's of 3rd. and 55th. Divisions.
   (d) Capt. MOFFETT M.C. will be in command of the 1½ Companies referred to in para. 2.(c). His group will be composed of 4 sections "D" Coy., 1 Section "B" Coy.

OPERATION ORDERS. NO. 14. (Cont'd.)

2. (e) Completion of relief referred to in para. 2.(c) will be reported to Battln. H.Q. by Code Word (Group Commander's Name).
   (f) All maps, schemas, etc., and all information referring to the tactical defence of the Sector will be obtained from outgoing units.

3. A C K N O W L E D G E.

Issued at......4 P.M..........

Callan
Capt. & Adjt.
3rd. Battln. M.G.Corps.

Copies. to:-
1. D.M.G.C.
2. "A" Coy.
3. "B" "
4. "C" "
5. "D" "
6. 8th. Inf. Brigade.
7. 9th. Inf. Brigade.
8. 76th. Inf. Brigade.
9. R.M.C.S. 55th Bde.
10. "G" 3rd. Div.
11. War Diary.
12. " "
13. File.

APPENDIX 4

EXTRACT.

BATTALION ORDERS NO. 38.

-BY-

LIEUT. COLONEL W.J. CRANSTON.

PART II

3. GRANT OF ACTING RANK

The following Officers are granted the Acting Rank of Major whilst Commanding Companies;
Capt. MOFFETT S. (M.C.)   "C" Coy. To date from 24/2/18.
A/Capt. DES VOEUX J.H.   "D" "   "   "   "   24/2/18.
 "   THOMAS E.   "B" "   "   "   "   24/2/18.
 "   SWANN C.F.   "A" "   "   "   "   13/4/18.

The following Officers are granted the Acting Rank of Captain whilst Second in Command of Companies:-
Lieut. WETTON C.D.   "C" Coy. To date from 24/2/18.
t/Lieut. ST. LEGER C.D.   "B" "   "   "   "   28/3/18.
Lieut.   BLOWER H.E.   "C" "   "   "   "   13/4/18.

Capt. & Adjt.,
3rd. Batt. M.G. Corps.

3rd. BATTALION MACHINE GUN CORPS.   APPENDIX a
                                                 4

EXTRACT FROM DIVISIONAL ROUTINE ORDERS 21/4/1918.

REWARDS.

"The General Officer Commanding has great pleasure in announcing that the Commander of the VI Corps has awarded the Military Medal or BAR to Military Medal to the undermentioned N.C.Os and men for acts of gallantry in the Field.
All concerned should be informed if possible."

Awarded BAR to MILITARY MEDAL.

42455	Private	Robson J. (M.M.)	"B"	Company.
45929	Corpl.	Carter S. (M.M.)	"C"	"

Awarded the MILITARY MEDAL.

17546	L/Corpl.	Meadon T.	"A"	Company.
71885	Private	Lennox W.	"A"	"
17286	Sergt.	Heaney D.	"B"	"
60773	"	Jardine M.	"B"	"
60488	L/Corpl.	Whipp F.	"B"	"
17257	"	Harmer T.	"B"	"
65312	"	Sharp J.	"B"	"
37565	"	Flynn B.	"B"	"
14168	"	Greenslade T.	"B"	"
42894	Private	Morgan S.	"B"	"
33277	"	Dodridge J.	"B"	"
35904	"	Houlding T.	"B"	"
11709	"	Parker T.	"C"	"
82139	"	Parker E.	"C"	"
44418	"	Johnson R.	"C"	"
53066	"	Lougheed W.E.	"C"	"
42920	Sergt.	Dungey S.A.	"D"	"
49982	"	Long F.J.	"D"	"
128114	Private	Cowan J.	"D"	"
42040	"	Adamson D.	"D"	"
102063	"	Eakers H.	"D"	"
86005	"	Helliwell L.	"D"	"
115070	"	Berry H.	"D"	"
99922	"	Davidson W.	"D"	"

----------oo0oo----------

APPENDIX 5
SECRET.

3rd. BATTALION MACHINE GUN CORPS.

OPERATION ORDERS NO. 15.

April 23rd, 1918.

REFERENCE:- LACOUTURE Sheet 1/20,000.

1. The front of the I Corps from the LAWE CANAL (inclusive) to the present left of the 4th. DIVISION will be taken over by the XIII Corps at 12 noon 24th. April.
The XIII Corps will be composed of the 3rd., 4th., and 15th. Divisions.

2. (a) The 8th. Infantry Brigade will be relieved by the 139th. Infantry Brigade (46th. Division) on the night 24th/25th. April.
    (b) Machine guns of the 3rd. Battalion Machine Gun Corps covering the 8th. Brigade front will be relieved by machine guns of the 46th. Battalion Machine Gun Corps on the night 24th/25th. April.
    (c) Details regarding relief mentioned in para.2(b) will be arranged between Company Commanders concerned.
    (d) Nos. 1. of the guns of the 46th. Battln. M.G.C. taking over right Brigade sector will be attached to the guns of the 3rd. Battln. M.G.C. at present covering that sector on night 23rd/24th. April.

3. All secret documents, maps etc of the area will be handed over to incoming units.

4. Completion of relief will be reported to Battln. H.Q. by code word (Company Commander's Name).

5. Amount of S.A.A. handed over to incoming units will be reported to Battln. H.Q. as soon as possible after relief.

6. Destination of units after relief will be notified later.

7. The Boundary between 9th. Infantry Brigade and 139th. Infantry Brigade will be the CANAL DE LA LAWE (inclusive to 9th. Brigade) as far as LAWBRIDGE (W24,C9,1.) New Divisional Boundaries will be issued later.

8. A C K N O W L E D G E.

Callan
Capt. & Adjt.
3rd. Battln. M.G.Corps.

Issued at... 4.30 P.M.

COPY NO.... 15

Copies to:-
1. D.M.G.C.
2. "A" Coy.
3. "B" "
4. "C" "
5. "D" "
6. S.A.A.
7. P.O.
8. M.O.
9. "G" 3rd. Div.
10. 8th. Infantry Brigade
11. 9th. " "
12. 76th. " "
13. 46th. Battln. M.G.C.
14. War Diary
15. " "
16. File.

----oOo----

APPENDIX 6

3rd. BATTALION MACHINE GUN CORPS.

SECRET.

OPERATION ORDER NO. 16.

COPY NO. 15

April 25th. 1918.

REFERENCE MAP: 36A.N.E. Ed. 6. 1/20000.

1. On night 25th/26th. April the following reliefs will take place:
   (a) 4 guns "D" Coy. at present attached to "C" Coy. will relieve 4 guns of "A" Coy. (Group Commander, Major DES VOEUX). The guns to be relieved will be those occupying the most forward positions. Details of this relief will be arranged between Company Commanders concerned. On relief the 4 guns of "A" Coy. will return to AMBEZIN and occupy billets vacated by relieving Section.
   (b) 4 guns "C" Coy. will relieve 4 guns of "B" Coy. at W22.C7.7. Details of this relief will be arranged between Company Commanders concerned.
   (c) The four guns of "B" Coy. mentioned in para. 1 (b) will relieve 4 guns of 4th. Battln. M.G.Corps in LE PLOUY FARM. Guide of 4th. Battln. M.G.C. will meet this section at BRICKFIELD - W21.C6.1. at 7.P.M.

2. On night 26/27th. April "B" Coy. (less 4 guns) and 8 guns of "A" Coy. will relieve 20 guns of the 4th. Battln. M.G.Corps in the present right sector of the 4th. Division. These 20 guns with 4 guns of "B" Coy. mentioned in para 1 (c) will form left group. Major THOMAS will be in command of this group.
The 8 guns of "A" Coy. will take up the rearmost positions.
Arrangements regarding relief will be made between Company Commanders concerned, 4th. Battln. M.G.C. and Major THOMAS.

3. A return showing dispositions of guns and fields of fire (grid bearings and ranges) and copies of battery charts will be rendered to Battln. H.Q. as soon as possible. (This is only required for reliefs mentioned in paras 1 (c) and 2.) Map references of H.Q. of O.C. Group and Battery Commanders will be given in this return.

4. At each forward gun position there will be at least 16 belt boxes and ten boxes of S.A.A. per gun. At each battery of four guns there will be at least 16 belt boxes and 15 boxes of S.A.A. per gun. At each Battery position at least 10 belt boxes per gun will be reserved for direct fire.

5. A consolidated inventory of trench, mess and other stores and rations taken over will be rendered to Battln. H.Q. as soon as possible. Return of S.A.A. taken over should show class of ammunition(i.e. ordinary, tracer or A.P.)

6. Completion of relief will be notified to Battln. H.Q. by code word (in reliefs mentioned in para 1 (a) (b) and (c) by Company Commanders Name: in para 2. by Group Commander's Name)

7. A C K N O W L E D G E.

Ralla
Capt. & Adjt.
3rd. Battln. M.G.Corps.

Issued at 12 noon

Copies to:-
1. D.M.G.C.
2. "A" Coy.
3. "B" "
4. "C" "
5. "D" "
6. Q.M.
7. T.O.
8. M.O.
9. "G" 3rd. Div.
10. 8th. Inf. Brgde.
11. 9th. " "
12. 76th. " "
13. 4th. Batt. M.G.C
14. War Diary.
15. " " ✓
16. File.

3rd. BATTALION MACHINE GUN CORPS. SECRET.

AMENDMENT NO. 1. TO OPERATION ORDERS NO. 16.

REFERENCE: Para 1 (a) & (c).

These reliefs will not take place to-night but on night 26th/27th. April.

Capt. & Adjt.
3rd. Battln. M.G.Corps.

25/4/1918.

Copies to:-
All recipients of O.O. No. 16.

---o:o---

APPENDIX 7

3rd. BATTALION MACHINE GUN CORPS. SECRET.

OPERATION ORDERS NO. 17.

COPY NO. 11

April 26th. 1918.

REFERENCE: 1/20000 Sheet 36A, S.E. and
1/40000 BETHUNE Combined Sheet.

1. On night 26th/27th "C" Coy. 3rd. Battln. M.G.Corps will occupy reserve positions as follows:-
   One Battery (4 guns) at W 29, b, 9, 9.
   - ditto -   W 23, c, 2, 3.
   - ditto -   W 22, c, 6, 8.
   - ditto -   W 21, a, 9, 5.

2. These positions are at present unoccupied with the exception of position at W 22, c, 6, 8., the relief of which has been arranged by O.O. No. 16.

3. At each Battery position there will be at least 16 belt boxes and 15 boxes of S.A.A. per gun.

4. A return showing dispositions of guns, fields of fire (grid bearings and ranges) and copies of Battery charts with S.O.S. lines in cases of S.O.S. Batteries will be rendered to Battln. H.Q. as soon as possible. Map references of H.Q. of O.C. Company and Battery Commanders will be given in this return.

5. O.C. "C" Coy. will make arrangements for the taking of the time that it takes each Battery to move from present position to battery position; also time taken by limbers returning to Coy. H.Q. Times will be notified to Battln. H.Q.

6. 'In position' will be notified to Battln. H.Q. by usual code word.

7. A C K N O W L E D G E.

Ralla
Capt. & Adjt.
3rd. Battln. M.G.Corps.

Issued at 6 P.M.

Copies to:-
1. D.M.G.C.   7. T.O.
2. "A" Coy.   8. M.O.
3. "B" "   9. "G" 3rd. Div.
4. "C" "   10. War Diary. ✓
5. "D" "   11. "   "
6. Q.M.   12. File.

2nd. BATTALION/ MACHINE GUN CORPS.   S E C R E T.

ADDENDUM TO OPERATION ORDERS NO. 17.

To para. 5. add:

Order Boards will be placed at each gun position. Certificate to this effect will be rendered as soon as in position.

April 26th. 1918.   Camb. & Adjt.
                                                      2nd. Batt'ln. M.G.Corps.

To:-
    All recipients of O.O. No. 17.

APPENDIX 8

3rd. BATTALION MACHINE GUN CORPS.　　　　　　S E C R E T.

OPERATION ORDERS NO. 18.

COPY NO. 12

April 27th. 1918.

REFERENCE MAPS: 1/20000 Sheet 36A, S.E.　and
　　　　　　　　　1/40000 BETHUNE Combined Sheet.

1. On night 27th/28th. April Battery in Divisional Reserve at W 23 d,8,1. will withdraw and return to billets at ANNEZIN.

2. On night 28th/29th. April, this Battery will take up position about W 14 Central.

3. Battery in Divisional Reserve at W 23 C,3,3. will take over S.O.S. line from Battery withdrawing from W 23,d,8,1. and fire on the following line W 12 C 5,7. to W 12,d,1,6.
This change in S.O.S. line will take place at 10 P.M. night 27th/28th April.

4. Battln. H.Q. will be informed by usual code word on completion of moves in paras 1 & 2.

5. A C K N O W L E D G E.

　　　　　　　　　　　　　　　　　　　　　　Capt. & Adjt.,
　　　　　　　　　　　　　　　　　　　　　　3rd. Battln. M.G.Corps.

Issued at. 8.15 P.M.

Copies to:-
1. D.M.G.C.　　　　　8. "Q" 3rd. Div.　　15. M.O.
2. "A" Coy.　　　　　9. 8th. Inf. Bgde.　16. S.O.
3. "B" "　　　　　　10. 9th. "　"
4. "C" "　　　　　　11. 76th. "　"
5. "D" "　　　　　　12. War Diary ✓
6.　　　　　　　　　13. "　"
7. T.O.　　　　　　　14. File.

---oOo---

3rd. Division G.S.911.   APPENDIX 9   SECRET.

DEFENSIVE MEASURES.
3rd. BATTALION MACHINE GUN CORPS.

COPY NO. 12

April 29th. 1918.

REFERENCE: Sheets 36A. S.E. 1/20000.
36B. N.E.

1. It is possible that the enemy may wish to improve the flank of his Northern Battle Front. Such improvement would necessitate his occupation of the line of the LA BASSEE CANAL inclusive of HINGES and BETHUNE. It is possible that this operation might be a prelude to more extensive operations aimed at the capture of the Mine Areas.

2. To the 3rd. Division is entrusted the task of holding the line of the CANAL from LAWE RIVER inclusive E,5,A. to W.4.a.1.0.

3. It is essential that the most careful training in Anti-Gas measures and in gas discipline be carried out thoroughly throughout the Battalion. During the week commencing Monday 29th. April all troops in the Battalion (Forward and Back Areas) will wear their gas masks for one hour daily and will be worked in them in the use of their arms (Machine Guns and Rifles). All Headquarters or at least a part of all Headquarters will be made as gas proof as possible.

4. Machine Gun Battery and Section Commanders in the line will ensure that all under their command are fully acquainted with the role of their guns in the event of an attack.

5. The O.C. 3rd. Battalion Machine Gun Corps will ensure that the gap now existing between the GORDON LINE and the CANAL BANK can be swept by Machine Gun fire from the vicinity of BELZAGE FARM - BAS D'ANNEZIN.
    In addition to guns at present covering this gap, 12 guns in Reserve at W.21,a,8,5. W.22,c,8,8. W.23,c,3,3. will be employed for this purpose.

6. The Brigade in Divisional Reserve will on orders being received from Divisional H.Q. be prepared to move up two Battalions into SHROPSHIRE LINE ready to counter attack at once should the enemy gain a footing on HINGES HILL. One Battalion will be prepared to move up to the LA BASSEE CANAL to hold the CANAL in the first instance between BAS D'ANNEZIN and AVELETTE. This Battalion may be required to hold the INVERNESS and DUMBARTON LINES or to hold the ground between (a) SUFFOLK and PERTH LINES, (b) LANCASTER and INVERNESS LINES, in the event of the enemy under cover of darkness or fog endeavouring, after forcing a passage at AVELETTE to move Southward along the West Bank of the CANAL. It is intended to link up the SUFFOLK - PERTH LINE and LANCASTER - INVERNESS LINE by wire entanglements with lengths of trenches behind.
    The Battalion of the Reserve Brigade moving to the CANAL BANK will be prepared to advance along it in conjunction with a counter attack delivered on HINGES HILL from SHROPSHIRE LINE so as to take the enemy in flank as he is driven down to the CANAL from the HILL.
    O.C. Right Group, 3rd. Batt. M.G.Corps will endeavour by fire to render every assistance to this counter attack which will be supported by every available gun.
    The flanking movement will be covered by a barrage of eight Machine Guns at present in Reserve at W.23,c,3,3. and W.22,c,8,8.
    These guns should be prepared to make a forward move of 500 yards.

7. All guns on CANAL BANK will have alternate emplacements constructed to enable them to fire to flank and rear in the event of enemy succeeding in crossing CANAL.

8. ACKNOWLEDGE.

Capt. & Adjt.,
3rd. Battln. M.G.Corps.

Copies to:-
1. D.M.G.C.   6. Q.M.   11. 76th. Inf. Bde.
2. "A" Coy.   7. T.O.   12. War Diary.
3. "B" "   8. "G" 3rd. Div. 13. "   "
4. "C" "   9. 8th. Inf. Bds. 14. File.
5. "D" "   10. 9th.. "   "

APPENDIX 10

SECRET.

3rd. BATTALION MACHINE GUN CORPS.

OPERATION ORDERS NO. 19.

COPY NO. 14

April 30th. 1918.

REFERENCE: MAP 36A, S.E.

1. On night 1st/2nd. May "C" Coy. will relieve "D" Coy. in right Sector. 8 guns of "A" Coy. will remain in present positions in right Sector and will come under orders of O.C. "C" Coy. who will be O.C. Right Group.

2. On relief "D" Coy. will come into Divisional Reserve and will occupy positions at present occupied by "C" Coy.

3. Nos. 1. of both Companies will remain with incoming gun teams for 24 hours after relief.

4. Company Commanders concerned will obtain all available information regarding role of guns in positions to be taken over, work in progress etc.

5. Details of relief will be arranged direct between Company Commanders concerned.

6. Completion of relief and occupation of reserve positions will be reported to Battln. H.Q. by code words "BROWN"; and "RED" respectively.

7. O.C. "D" Coy. immediately on completion of relief by "C" Coy., will report to G.O.C. Reserve Brigade.

8. ACKNOWLEDGE.

Capt. & Adjt.,
3rd. Battln. M.G.Corps.

Issued at 12 noon
Copies to:-
1. D.M.G.C.   9. "G" 3rd. Div.
2. "A" Coy.   10. 8th. Inf. Bde.
3. "B" "   11. 9th. "   "
4. "C" "   12. 76th. "   "
5. "D" "   13. War Diary
6. Q.M.   14. "   " ✓
7. T.O.   15. File
8. C.R.A.

WAR DIARY
INTELLIGENCE SUMMARY

Army Form C. 2118.

3RD BATTN M.G.C.

VOL 4

Place	Date	Hour	Summary of Events and Information	Remarks and references to Appendices
FOUQUEREUIL E.14.a.6.2.	May 1st		MAP 36 NE 1:40,000. Situation normal. "C" Coy relieved "D" Coy as per O.O. No 19. – D Coy in divisional range.	O.O 19 APPENDIX 1.
	2nd	4.0 a.m	Operation by 2ND BATTN ROYAL SCOTS 8TH BRIGADE. Unsuccessful. 16 Guns of "C" Coy co-operated – 39,000 rounds fired. Situation normal – Harassing fire 11,000 rounds during night. O.O No 20 issued	O.O 20
		3.0 p.m	Casualties. 2. O.R.	
	3rd		Situation normal. 1,000 rounds fired at enemy aircraft during the day. Casualties 4 O.R. Reinforcements 2 O.R.	
	4th	2.30 a.m	Operation by 1st GORDONS. 76TH BRIGADE. Unsuccessful. 16 Guns of the Bn Co-operated. 43,000 rounds fired.	O.O 21
		4.55 a.m	S.O.S. signal sent up. 10,500 rounds fired on S.O.S. lines. Casualties. 7. O.R.	
		6.0 a.m	Situation normal.	

WAR DIARY
INTELLIGENCE SUMMARY

3RD BATTN. M.G.C.

Army Form C.2118.

Place	Date	Hour	Summary of Events and Information	Remarks and references to Appendices
FOUQUEREUIL E.14ᵃ 6.2	May 5	3.15am	MAP 36A N.E. 1:40,000. S.O.S. signal put up. 43,000 rounds fired on S.O.S. lines. Enemy attacked and the object of repairing the fourteen times from him. Enemy were repulsed.	
		6.0 am	Situation normal. Harassing fire 8,000 rounds during night.	
			Reinforcements :- Lt. G.H. MATTHEWS and 2/Lt. A.H. DUFFEY.	
		6.30 pm	Operation by 8th Infantry Brigade 16 Lewis & Vickers Co-operate. 45,000 rounds fired. Operation successful. Situation normal. 300 rounds fired at enemy aircraft. MAJOR MACKENZIE D.S.O. M.C. left for ENGLAND on authority A.3/801 (of 2/5/18) II Corps AB.218, 3rd DIV. 24/4/18. Hands over to Officer i/c other ranks. O.O. Inst. issued	APPENDIX 12 APPENDIX 13
		10 p.m.	Left "B" H.Q. on the way to M.G. barrage as ordered drawn up by A/B of "B" received from Gen. FISHER D.S.O. Comdg. 8th INFANTRY BRIGADE. 16,000 rounds fired.	APPENDIX 13

Army Form C. 2118.

WAR DIARY
or
INTELLIGENCE SUMMARY 3rd Batt. M.G.C.

(Erase heading not required.)

Instructions regarding War Diaries and Intelligence Summaries are contained in F. S. Regs., Part II. and the Staff Manual respectively. Title pages will be prepared in manuscript.

Place	Date	Hour	Summary of Events and Information	Remarks and references to Appendices
FOUQUEREUIL	May 7		MAP 36 NE. 1:40,000. MAJOR MOFFETT, M.C. assumed duties of 2nd in Command. 2,500 rounds fired at enemy aircraft during day. Left Sector heavily bombed at 11.0 p.m. Chinawa?? in what 12 hours in reply after firing 6,000 rounds in SOS line, also rifle C.O. of the ROYAL FUSILIERS approved the application of the second of the position in which the M.G. Barrage was put down in answer to the SOS signal on the morning of 4.5.18. "D" Coy received "A" Coy is on 00.21. Night harass fire 9,000 rounds. A/CAPT. ODJS. LEGER appointed to Command of "C" Coy vice MAJOR MOFFETT M.C. 2nd in Command. To replace 2/Lt MANSELL D.M. DCM. 9.1 O.R. Lieutenant I O.R. evacuated to Field Ambulance. 5 O.R. CAPT. W. LAWSON SMITH (Chaplain) joined Battalion. Hostile enemy toy active. 3,000 rounds fired at enemy aircraft. Report received that one hostile aeroplane was brought down in consequence of the 7th Lt M.G. Bn's machine gun fire from it. Two tanks were seen passing from the Battalion normal C.O. accompanied Capt the of "A" and B.H.Q. Lt M.G. attached to 1st in Defence of Coy Commander QM, Transport officer at B.H.Q. Lt M.G. attached to 1st 16,000 rounds nightly harrass fire.	@L @L APPENDIX 4.
		4.30 p.m.		
		6.0 p.m.		

Army Form C. 2118.

WAR DIARY
or
INTELLIGENCE SUMMARY.   3RD BATTN M.G.C.

(Erase heading not required.)

Instructions regarding War Diaries and Intelligence Summaries are contained in F.S. Regs., Part II. and the Staff Manual respectively. Title pages will be prepared in manuscript.

Place	Date	Hour	Summary of Events and Information	Remarks and references to Appendices
FOUQUEREUIL	Aug 8		MAP 36B N.E. 1:40,000	
	9		Lt. Col. J.H. DesVoeux to Lahore. Situation normal. Sent off early 2,250 rounds from a 1 Lewis Gun.	O.R.
E.14.d.10	10	12.0 noon	C.O. reconnoitred Coy. Area.	O.R.
		5 p.m.	Brit. M.G. instruction Sch. 7 wounded. Bn. HQ Batn. to E.14.d.10	
		7	Draft arrived 13 ORs. 4 in action. Training for.	
	10		C.O. returned. Coys. doing instruction normal. 15,500 rounds sent to Coys. Training for. Casualties 4 O.R. Reinforcements Draft 3 O.R. Evacuated 6 O.R.	O.R.
	11		C.O. reconnoitred Coy. line Reinforcement 2 ORs. 2,500 rounds fired at enemy aircraft. Slight damage done. 19,000 rds fired at the infantry in front of us. 1 OR reported from Sch. of Inst.	O.R.

Army Form C. 2118.

WAR DIARY
or
INTELLIGENCE SUMMARY.
(Erase heading not required.)

3RD BATT! M.G.C.

Place	Date	Hour	Summary of Events and Information	Remarks and references to Appendices
FOUQUEREUIL I/C I.O.	12/4/18		C.O. reconnoitred Corps Line. Situation normal. 1500 rounds fired at enemy aircraft. Night - 9,000 rounds fired from 3 O.R. positions.	OR
	13		C.O. reconnoitred Corps Line. Situation normal. 15,000 rounds night harassing fire. 1 Gun D Coy put out of action by enemy shell fire (Hyp Hut) Evacuated 4 O.R. Re-inforcement 5 O.R.	OR
	14		Corps M.G.O. visited C.O. Situation normal. 2,000 rounds fired at enemy aircraft. 9,500 rounds night harassing fire. Casualties 5 O.R. Evacuation 2/Lt ARNOLD J.F. 1 O.R.	OR

Army Form C. 2118.

WAR DIARY
or
INTELLIGENCE SUMMARY.
(Erase heading not required.)

3RD BATTN. M.G.C.

Place	Date	Hour	Summary of Events and Information	Remarks and references to Appendices
FOUQUEREUIL E.14.c.1.0.	May 15		MAP 36 B.N.E. 1:40.000. Situation normal. 2,500 rounds fired at enemy aircraft. 15,000 rounds night harassing fire. Casualties 3 O.R. Evacuated 3 O.R. Transferred to 4th R.W.F. 1 O.R. Reinforcements 1 O.R.	(J.W.)
	16.	10.15 a.m.	Explosion in road at E.14.c.25.40.- and scattered torpanels. Situation normal. 1,000 rounds fired at enemy aircraft. 1 Gotha plane brought down about W.14.c. 50. 60. LT. WELLS reports he inspected at 9 front at 16 he army places at dusk to think Div. Recd. by M.G. fire. 16,000 rounds night harassing fire. Evacuation 3 O.R. Reinforcements 1 O.R.	(J.W.)

Army Form C. 2118.

WAR DIARY
or
INTELLIGENCE SUMMARY. 3RD BATT. M.G.C.
(Erase heading not required.)

Place	Date	Hour	Summary of Events and Information	Remarks and references to Appendices
FOUQUEREUIL E.14.c.1.0.	Aug 17		Situation normal. 1000 round fired at enemy aircraft. 14,000 rounds night harassing fire. Vacated Lt F.W. DICKENSON 1.O.R. Evacuation 3 O.R. to duty at base 1.O.R.	O.B.
	18.		Situation normal. 500 rounds fired at enemy aircraft. 12,000 rounds night harassing fire. Reported from theatre of war 1.O.R. Evacuation 3 O.R.	O.B.
	19.		Situation normal. 2500 rounds fired at enemy aircraft. 12,000 rounds night harassing fire. Casualties 1 O.R. Cas. 3 U.K. LT. D.M. MANSELL	O.B.
	20	3.30 a.m 6.50 " 11.15 a.m	Very heavy bombardment of all gr'ph. batteries and factor area by enemy. Light shell m W.24 & 7 placed 6.95. Enemy counter from gas at Beugn & Beuville 74. Situation normal.	O.B.

WAR DIARY
or
INTELLIGENCE SUMMARY.   3RD BATT" M.G.C.

Army Form C. 2118.

(Erase heading not required.)

Place	Date	Hour	Summary of Events and Information	Remarks and references to Appendices
FOUQUEREUIL E.14.c.I.Q.	Mar 20	3:30 p.m.	MAP 36 B N.E. 1:40,000 "A" Coy relieved "B" Coy as per O.O. No 22. O.O. No 22 issued	APPENDIX 5.
			4,000 rounds S.A.A. fired at enemy aircraft Casualties 5 O.R. Wounded 3 O.R.	
	21	6 a.m.	Weather normal. 2,500 rounds fired at enemy aircraft 6,000 rounds fired. Casualties 1 OR Transferred 1 OR sent to C.C.S. 1 O.R. Wounded 5 OR	
		3:0 a.m.	Reports from the field 3 OR Wounded 5 OR A.A. distribution No 8 issued	APPENDIX 6
	22.	3:0 a.m. 6:15 a.m.	Light from enemy at LONG CORNET. 1 W.& G.B.T. 2 as M.W. & O.C.	
		6:0 a.m.	Weather normal Casualties 75. O.R.	

R. F. JOHNSON. MEDICAL OFFICER
M.O.R.C. (U.S.)

Army Form C. 2118.

WAR DIARY
or
INTELLIGENCE SUMMARY.

3RD. Bn. TH. M.G.C.

(Erase heading not required.)

MAP 36B N.E. 1:40,000

Place	Date	Hour	Summary of Events and Information	Remarks and references to Appendices
FOUQUEREUIL E.14.1.0.	Aug 23		Situation normal. 1000 rounds fired at enemy aircraft. 10,500 rounds harassing fire.	O.W.
	24		Casualties 2/Lt McNAIR & 2/Lt EVERAU & 15 O.R. Transferred to base depôt. 1 O.R. Situation normal. 8,500 rounds night harassing fire. Casualties 7 O.R. Signal for hospital. 100	O.W.
	25.		Situation normal. Slight harassing fire. 10,500 rounds. Casualties 4 O.R. Reinforcements 40 O.R.	O.W.
	26	1.40 am	LANNOY bombarded with gas shells - Blue & Yellow Cross - reaction was a period - men were apparently unharmed.	O.W.
		5.0 am	Situation normal. 6,300 rounds night harassing fire.	
		6.0 am	Evacuation 4 O.R. Casualties 2 O.R.	

Army Form C. 2118.

WAR DIARY
or
INTELLIGENCE SUMMARY.

3RD BATT'N M.G.C.

(Erase heading not required.)

Place	Date	Hour	Summary of Events and Information	Remarks and references to Appendices
FOUQUEREUIL	July 27/h		MAP 36B SE 1:40000	
E14c I.O			Normal enemy artillery & aircraft activity. 3,500 rounds fired at enemy aircraft. Night harassing fire 12,000 rounds.	O.R.
			Report from hospital 4 O.R. Evacuated 1 O.R. Casualties 1 O.R. Reinforcements 5 O.R.	O.R.
	28		Situation normal. Night harassing fire 19000 rounds. 4000 rounds fired at enemy aircraft. 8 Bursts from position A15.T.21. 9 Klms 85 Berguette Casualties 3 O.R. Evacuated 13 O.R. Dugouts 180 O.R.	O.R.
	29	3.15 p.m	Situation normal. 5,000 rounds fired at enemy aircraft 11,500 rounds night harassing fire.	O.R.
		11.30 a.m.	200 Yellow cross shells in W 16 a.	
			Evacuated 1 O.R. Reported from hospital 1 O.R. Casualties 5 O.R.	

Reinforcements: Lt. H.G. CRAIG. Lt. R.C. STREATFEILD. Lt. H.E. TIPPER. 2/Lt. I. WALKER 2/Lt. R.J. WILLIAMS. 2/Lt. W.H. WRIGHTSON. 2/Lt. J.E. WILLIAMS. 2/Lt. D.J. WILLIAMS M.M. 2/Lt. H.R. COWLISHAW.

WAR DIARY or INTELLIGENCE SUMMARY

3RD BATTⁿ N.G.C.

MAP 36 B S.E. 1:40,000

Place	Date	Hour	Summary of Events and Information	Remarks and references to Appendices
FOUQUEREUIL E.14.c.10	May 30	10 am	Relieved by 9th Brigade (RF3) Successful disengagement. 5000 rounds fired all enemy attempts	O.R.
		6.0 am	10,000 rounds night firing from Capt. Yeo Drury A (J=) Machine S.O.R	
			bunch in 5 O.R wounded. 2 O.R. reported from hospital	
	31st	6.0 am	Situation normal — Col. Lindsay D.S.O. visited O.D	O.R.
		6 am	Advance Artillery CO advised. Company Captain at BHQ. Capt. Anglin, Capt. Allan MC to left gun station	
		6.0	1,250 rounds front at enemy snipers. 10,000 rounds night firing fire	
			Casualties 10 OR Wounded 1 OR	

APPENDIX. 1A.

Extracts from divisional Routine Orders dated 4th May 1918.

The general Officer Commanding has great pleasure in announcing that the Field Marshall, Commanding in Chief, has, under authority granted by his Majesty The King awarded the undermentioned decorations for Gallantry in the field.
All concerned should be informed if possible.
Their names will appear in the "London Gazette" in due course.

Awarded Bar to the Military Cross.
T/2/Lt C.T.Smith. M.C.   "D".

Awarded the Military Cross.
Lieut C.W.Harold Barry.   "B" Coy.
T/2/Lt T.W.Wells.   "B" "
T/2/Lt L Heywood   "B" "
2/Lt B.J. Sloper.   "A" "

Awarded the Distinguished Conduct Medal.
19404   Pte (L/Cpl-a/Cpl) D.Dudley.   "B" Coy
43387   Cpl. A.P.Smith.   "C" "
65588   "   A.J.White.   "D" "
35590   Sgt. T.Kelly.   "A" "

APPENDIX 1

SECRET.

3rd. BATTALION MACHINE GUN CORPS

OPERATION ORDERS NO. 20.

COPY NO. 14

May 2nd. 1918.

1. On the night 3rd/4th May at a Zero Hour to be notified later, the 76th. Infantry Brigade in conjunction with the Brigade on the right will carry out operations, which in this sector consists of taking and occupying positions in copse W 11 a & b and establishing a line of posts along N.E. edge of copse to T. Roads in LA PANNERIE.

2. The attached Machine Gun programme will be carried out in support of the operations.

3. Requisite S.A.A. will be sent up to guns affected.

4. At Zero plus 2 hours all guns will lay on new "S.O.S."

5. A C K N O W L E D G E.

R. Allen
Capt. & Adjt.,
3rd. Battln. M.G.Corps.

Issued at 3 P.M.
Copies to:-
1. O.M.G.C. 9. "G" 3rd. Div.
2. "A" Coy. 10. 8th. Inf. Bde.
3. "B" "   11. 9th. "   "
4. "C" "   12. 76th. "   "
5. "D" "   13. War Diary
6. Q.M.   14. "   " ✓
7. T.O.   15. File
8. S.A.A.

TABLE OF FIRE FOR MACHINE GUNS

Position No.	No. of Guns	Coy and Section	Target	Nature of Target	Clearance over final position	Line of Fire	Rate of fire
10	2	A 2	N 5 c35,65 to N 5 c40,40	Organised shell holes and road.	70m	From Zero plus 15mns to Zero plus 2 hrs	1 belt per gun per 10 mins.
7	2	B 4	N 5 c45,70 to N 5 c55,65	O.A.	30m		
8	2	B 4	N 5 c45,75 to N 5 c55,70		24m	From Zero to Zero plus 30 mins.	1 belt per gun per 5 mins.
9	2	A 2	N 5 c50,90 to N 5 c55,80	PRACTICE	27m	From Zero plus 20 mins to Zero plus 2 hrs	1 belt per gun per 15 mins
11	4	A 1	N 5 c,45,75 to N 5 c,70,60	TRENCHES	45m		
Long Comet	4	C D	N 12a01 to N 12a09			From Zero plus 15mns to Zero plus 2 hrs	1 belt per gun per 10 mns.

Contour of Target regarded as 15 metres.

APPENDIX 2

Secret.

3rd. BATTALION MACHINE GUN CORPS

OPERATION ORDERS NO. 21.

COPY NO. 16.

MAY 6th. 1918.

REFERENCE MAP: 36A, S.E.

1. On night 7th/8th. May "D" Coy. will relieve "A" Coy. in positions occupied by "A" Coy. in right and left groups.

2. On relief "A" Coy. will pass into Divisional Reserve and will occupy positions at present occupied by "D" Coy.

3. Nos. 1. of both Companies will remain with incoming gun teams for 24 hours after relief and occupation of reserve positions.

4. Details of relief will be arranged direct between Company Commanders concerned.

5. Completion of relief and occupation of reserve positions will be reported to Battln. H.Q. by O.C. "D" Coy. and O.C. "A" Coy. respectively by code words---Company Commander's Name.

6. Company Commanders concerned will obtain all available information regarding role of guns in positions to be taken over, work in progress etc.

7. O.C. "A" Coy. immediately on completion of relief by "D" Coy. will report to G.O.C. Reserve Brigade.

8. A C K N O W L E D G E .

Kalla
Capt. & Adjt.,
3rd. Batt. M.G.Corps.

Issued at 4 P.M.
Copies to:-
1. D.M.G.C.
2. "A" Coy.
3. "B" "
4. "C" "
5. "D" "
6. S.O.
7. M.O.
8. Q.M.
9. T.O.
10. "G" 3rd.
11. Div.
    8th. Inf.Bde.
12. 9th. " "
13. 76th. Inf. Bde.
14. C.R.A.
15. War Diary
16. " "
17. File.

APPENDIX 3

H.Q.,
8th. Infantry Brigade,
4 - 5 - 18.

Dear Cranston,

I am writing to thank you for the excellent and very prompt way in which your Machine Gunners brought their barrage down for us this morning. Nothing could have been better, and I am told it was within 30 seconds of the S.O.S. going up.

Will you please let them know how grateful we all are,

Yours sincerely,

(signed) B. D. FISHER.

(G.O.C., 8th. Infantry Brigade.)

APPENDIX 4

SECRET.

3rd. BATTALION MACHINE GUN CORPS.

MACHINE GUN INSTRUCTIONS NO. 7.

COPY NO........

MAY 9th. 1918.

REFERENCE SHEETS: 36,b, N.E.
36,a, S.E. 1/20000.

1. According to information which is considered reliable, an attack is to be made by the enemy astride the LA BASSEE CANAL, against our positions.
   Although the actual date of the attack is not known, it is understood that this attack is to take place on the early morning of the 10th. or 11th. of May and will be preceded by a bombardment lasting three hours which is to commence at 10.30 p.m. on the night previous to the attack.

2. S.O.S. and "BATTLE LINES".
   (a) Each gun must be ready to switch on Battle Lines at a minute's notice.
   (b) S.O.S. Lines must not be altered except by sanction of G.O.C., Division.
   (c) S.O.S. must be brought down not more than 150 yards from front line.
   (d) Should the enemy commence an intense bombardment, guns will fire bursts of fire on their S.O.S. Lines, searching forward.
       Proper precautions must be taken to ensure that those guns which search forward will fire on their proper S.O.S. lines if S.O.S. goes up.
   (e) In the event of the enemy reaching the CANAL and attempting to cross, the F.O.O. at Artillery O.P., and O.C., Battalions will put up a 'shorten range' signal, which will be a rocket fired from a mortar bursting into two GREEN and one RED light.
       Up-on this signal our artillery and machine guns will put down their barrages, 100 yards North of CANAL.
       This signal applies only to the Canal Bank between W.11.d. Central and LA PANNERIE.
   (f) The enemy must not be allowed to cross the CANAL on our front.

3. PROTECTION.
   If any dead ground or covered lines of approach render guns liable to be surprised, patrols or scouts must be sent out. If necessary Infantry Commanders should be requested to furnish escorts.

4. LIAISON.
   (a) Group Commanders must be in closest touch with their Brigades, Section Officers with infantry battalion, and Company Commanders; Section Officers should make some mutual arrangement for liaison between themselves and the infantry.

   (b) In the event of aeroplanes observing signs of a hostile concentration, they will drop a RED smoke bomb opposite the front affected. This should be made known to all ranks.

5. AMMUNITION ETC.
   At each gun position, the following will be kept -
   15 boxes S.A.A.
   24 belts, inboxes, - 16 of which are to be reserved for direct fire.
   Bombs - detonated.
   Very Lights.
   S.O.S. Rockets.
   Gun Oil.
   Water.
   Chloride of Lime.

(1)

Machine Gun Instructions No. 7. (Contd.)

6. COMMUNICATIONS.
Every form of communication possible will be used.
Messages by runner must be duplicated.
Situation Reports must be sent to Battalion H.Q. as frequently as possible.

7. CASUALTY RETURNS.
Estimated number of casualties for previous 24 hours due at Battalion H.Q. not later than 4.0 p.m. daily; corrected casualties (Nominal Roll) by 5.0 p.m.

8. RESERVE GUNS.
O.C., Reserve Guns must keep in closest touch with G.O.C., Reserve Brigade.
Forward positions must be reconnoitred, constructed and ammunition put in immediately.

9. TRANSPORT.
Fighting limbers must be kept ready for any emergency.

10. ARTIFICERS.
Two artificers will be attached to each group H.Q. from 9th. instant inclusive.

11. GAS PRECAUTIONS.
All precautions must be taken against gas, both as affecting personnel and guns. It must be impressed on the Men that respirators will only be removed by orders of an Officer.
An ample supply of chloride of lime will be kept at each gun position.

12. DRESSING STATIONS.
First Aid Posts: --- LE PLOUY FARM (W,16,d,5,8.).
W,9,d,1,0.
W,23,c,9,5.
Advanced Dressing Station: --- Chateau L'ABBAYE (W,25,a) ANNEZIN.

13. ACKNOWLEDGE.

Capt. & Adjt.,
3rd. Battalion Machine Gun Corps.

Issued at............

Copies to:-
1. D.M.G.C.   7. M.O.   13. 76th. Inf. Bde.
2. "A" Coy.   8. Q.M.   14. C.R.A.
3. "B" "   9. T.O.   15. WAR DIARY
4. "C" "   10. "G" 3rd. Div. 16. "   "
5. "D" "   11. 8th. Inf. Bde. 17. FILE.
6. S.O.   12. 9th. "   "

APPENDIX 5

Secret.

3rd. BATTALION MACHINE GUN CORPS

OPERATION ORDERS NO. 22.

COPY NO. 16

May 20th. 1918.

REFERENCE MAP 36A, S.E.

1. On night 20th/21st. May "A" Coy. will relieve "B" Coy. in positions now occupied by "B" Coy. in left group.

2. On relief "B" Coy. will pass into Divisional Reserve and will occupy positions at present occupied by "A" Coy.

3. Nos. 1. of both Companies will remain with incoming gun teams for 24 hours after relief and occupation of reserve positions.

4. Details of relief will be arranged direct between Company Commanders concerned.

5. Completion of relief and occupation of reserve positions will be reported to Battln. H.Q. by O.C. "A" Coy. and O.C. "B" Coy. respectively by code words -- Company Commander's Name.

6. Company Commanders concerned will obtain all available information regarding role of guns in positions to be taken over, work in progress etc.

7. O.C. "B" Coy., immediately on completion of relief by "A" Coy. will report to G.O.C. Reserve Brigade.

8. ACKNOWLEDGE.

Capt. & Adjt.,
3rd. Batt. M.G.Corps.

Issued at 3.0 P.M.
Copies to:-
1. D.M.G.O.
2. "A" Coy.
3. "B" "
4. "C" "
5. "D" "
6. S.O.
7. M.O.
8. Q.M.
9. T.O.
10. "G"3/d.Div.
11. 8th. Inf. Bde
12. 9th. " "
13. 76th. Inf. Bde.
14. C.R.A.
15. War Diary
16. " "
17. File.

APPENDIX 6

Secret.

3rd. BATTALION MACHINE GUN CORPS.

MACHINE GUN INSTRUCTIONS. NO. 8.

COPY NO........

MAY 21st. 1918.

REAR LINE OF DEFENCE.

1. In the event of the Division being forced to withdraw in face of superior numbers from its present position, it would withdraw fighting to successive lines of defence.

   Although it is not possible to forecast the turn of events, all Commanders should be prepared for every contingency and should be thoroughly acquainted with the ground over which they may be called upon to fight.

   All lines of defence should be reconnoitred with a view to their occupation in case of necessity, so that, should the necessity arise, these successive lines of defence may be occupied without delay or confusion.

   The various lines of defence, some of which are still in process of construction, are shown on the accompanying map.

2. For the purpose of this reconnaissance it may be assumed that three Infantry Brigades of approximately equal strength are available for defence of these lines, each line being held by three Infantry Brigades in line, each Brigade being disposed with two battalions in line, with one battalion in Reserve.

3. The following is a brief description of the various lines of defence:
   (a) BETHUNE RETRENCHMENT AND LANCASTER LINE.
       Consists of a front and support line. The former consists of a series of unconnected posts.
       LANCASTER LINE forms a continuous trench line.
       As a Support Line to the above there is a continuous trench throughout, the Northern portion of this Support Line known as SHROPSHIRE LINE has a line of supporting posts in rear.
   (b) (i) CHOCQUES LINE AND CLARENCE SWITCH.
       The former consists of a front and support line of breastwork and trench - the latter runs along the West bank of the CLARENCE RIVER, the Northern portion only has been constructed, but the Bank itself is defensible.
       (ii) CHOCQUES HILL DEFENCES.
       This consists of a system of trenches on the forward and reverse slopes of CHOCQUES HILL which is an important tactical feature as it dominates the whole of the surrounding country to the North and North-East.
       These defences would be held in connection with the CHOCQUES LINE.
   (c) LILLERS - NOUCHIN LINE.
       Consists of front, support and reserve lines of trench and breastwork.
       The main tactical features in this line are the Spur in D,18 and 2,13, the village and Chateau of LABEUVRIERE, and the Spur in D,10.
   (d) RIVEILLON LINE.
       This consists of a continuous breastwork front line with breastwork support and reserve lines in places, and is designed for defence against a hostile advance from the North.
   (e) BETHUNE SWITCH.
       Consists of a front, support and reserve lines and connects our front system of trenches with the BETHUNE RETRENCHMENT.
       It is designed to protect the right flank of the left Brigade and to cover the withdrawal of the right Brigade across the LA BASSEE CANAL in case of necessity, should the enemy succeed in gaining BETHUNE as a result of an attack from the East.

Machine Gun Instructions No. 8. (contd)
3. (e) (Contd)
The front line consists of a series of posts.
The support and reserve lines have not yet been constructed, but defensible positions can be found along the railway embankment.

The front line of each of the above systems has a single, and in some places a double belt of wire.
Support and Reserve lines have no wire at present.
Much of the breastwork in the above lines still require a parados.

4. Machine Gun and Lewis Gun Positions.
Machine gun positions for the defence of each line have been selected, also certain positions for Lewis Guns which should co-operate in the Machine Gun Defence.
These positions are shown on the accompanying appendices "A" & "B"

5. Reconnaissance.
Company Commanders will arrange for the reconnaissance by all their Officers of the positions in rear of their present sectors. When this has been done, the remaining positions will be reconnoitred. Commencing 21st. instant, morning situation reports will show, until reconnaissance is complete, which positions have been reconnoitred during previous 24 hours and by whom.

6. A C K N O W L E D G E.

Issued at... 3pm

Copies to:-
1. D.M.G.C.
2. "A" Coy.
3. "B" "
4. "C" "
5. "D" Coy.
6. War Diary
7. " "
8. File

Capt. & Adjt.,
3rd. Battln. M.G.Corps.

APPENDIX "A"

SUITABLE MACHINE GUN POSITIONS FOR DEFENCE OF VARIOUS LINES.

BETHUNE RETRENCHMENT & LANCASTER LINE.			CHOCQUES LINE; CLARENCE SWITCH; and CHOCQUES LINE DEFENCES.			LILLERS - HOUCHIN LINE		
No.	Map Reference	No. of Guns	No.	Map Reference	No. of Guns	No.	Map Reference	No. of Guns

DIRECT.

18.	W,9,c,70,15.(2)		B.1	E,8,b,80,20	2	C.1	E,19,a,55,40	4
	W,9,c,20,80.(2)	4	B.2	E,2,d,50,00	2	C.2	E,19,a,25,85	4
A.6	E,3,d,45,35	2	B.3	E,2,d,35,80	2	C.3	D,18,d,35,35	4
A.7	E,3,b,60,40	2	B.4	E,2,a,20,90	4	C.4	E,13,c,40,90	4
A.9	W,27,d,05,40	4	B.4a	E,1,b,20,50	4	C.5	E,13,a,20,40	4
A.11	W,26,b,85,90	4	B.5	W,25,a,40,90	4	C.6	D,11,d,20,70	4
A.10	W,26,b,45,35	4	B.6	V,30,b,70,90	4	C.7	D,10,c,85,30	4
A.12	W,21,c,60,90	4	B.7	E,2,c,20,90	4	C.8	D,10,a,60,70	4
		24			26	C.9	D,4,c,00,00	4
						C.10	D,3,b,35,20	4
						C.11	D,3,b,05,80	4
						C.12	V,27,a,80,20	4
								48

INDIRECT.

						No. of Guns	
A.13	W,20,a,90,30(2)		B.8	E,14,c,50,80			2
	W,20,a,60,40(2)	4	B.9	E,14,a,05,65			4
A.14	W,13,d,75,20	4	B.10	E,7,b,60,15			4
A.15	W,13,c,30,90	4	B.11	E,7,b,00,90			4
B.1	E,8,d,90,95	2	B.12	E,1,d,05,90			2
B.2	E,2,d,45,55	2	B.13	E,1,a,20,20			4
B.3	E,2,d,35,80	2	B.14	V,30,a,55,00			2
B.4	E,2,a,20,90	4	C.4	E,13,c,40,90			4
B.4a	E,1,b,20,50	4	C.5	E,13,a,20,40			4
B.5	W,25,a,40,90	4					30
B.7	E,2,c,20,90	4					
		34					

REVEILLON LINE				BETHUNE SWITCH		

DIRECT

B.6	V,30,b,70,90	4		A.1	W,30,a,00,75	2
B.14	V,30,a,55,00	2		A.2	W,29,b,20,00	2
B.16	V,28,b,25,55	2		A.3	W,29,d,10,40	2
B.17	V,28,a,45,45	2		A.4	W,29,a,60,95	4
C.12	V,27,a,80,20	4		A.5	W,29,c,40,80	4
		14.		A.6	E,3,d,45,35	2
				A.7	E,3,b,30,40	2
						18.

INDIRECT.

B.15	D,5,a,05,70	2		A.8	W,28,c,15,65	4
C.6	D,11,d,20,70	4		A.9	W,27,d,05,40	4
C.8	D,10,a,60,70	4		A.10	W,26,b,45,35	4
C.9	D,4,c,00,00	4		A.11	W,26,b,85,90	4
C.10	D,3,b,35,20	4		A.12	W,21,c,60,90	4
C.11	D,3,b,05,80	4		B.1	E,8,d,90,95	2
		22		B.2	E,2,d,45,55	2
				B.3	E,2,d,35,80	2
				B.4	E,2,a,20,90	4
						30.

APPENDIX "B"

SUITABLE LEWIS GUN POSITIONS FOR CO-OPERATION WITH THE MACHINE GUN DEFENCE OF VARIOUS LINES.

BETHUNE RETRENCH- MENT AND LANCASTER LINE	CHOCQUES LINE, CLARENCE SWITCH AND CHOCQUES HILL DEFENCES	LILLERS - HOUCHIN LINE	REVEILLON LINE	BETHUNE SWITCH
E.10,a,45,60	E,9,d,95,40	E,13,c,70,50	V,30,a,90,00	E,5,a,40,65
E,4,a,05,55	E,9,d,55,55	E,13,a,15,10	V,30,d,05,35	E,5,a,15,65
W,15,b,10,90	E,9,d,15,80		V,29,b,55,00	E,4,b,10,40
W,15,b,00,80	E,9,c,00,95		V,29,b,95,30	W,29,c,10,50
W,15,d,70,90	E,8,b,60,60		D,5,a,65,50	W,28,b,70,00
	E,8,b,60,80			W,27,b,90,55
	E,2,d,60,20			
	E,2,b,25,90			
	W,25,d,20,80			
	W,25,a,90,10			
	V,30,a,90,00			
	V,30,d,70,60			
	E,14,a,40,00			
	E,14,d,90,90			
	E,15,a,00,15			
	E,15,a,80,50			

Army Form C. 2118.

3RD BATT.N M.G.C.

WAR DIARY
or
INTELLIGENCE SUMMARY.
(Erase heading not required.)

Place	Date	Hour	Summary of Events and Information	Remarks and references to Appendices
FOUQUEREUIL E.14.c.1.0	1918 June 1st	6 a.m.	MAP 36a S.E. 1:20,000 Situation normal — 5,500 rounds fired at enemy aircraft. 10,000 rounds night harassing fire.	
		4.15 p.m.	G.O.C. 3rd Divs. inspected the 1st Battn Transport. C.O. attended. The G.O.C. expressed to the Commanding Officer his great gratification on the efficiency & smartness shown by the Battn, also on the appearance of the Horses & mules in the Transport lines. Casualties 2 O.R. wounded. 3 O.R. & 2 R.A.M.C. (att.) rejoined from Hosp.tal. 2 O.R.	OR
	2nd	6.0 a.m.	Situation normal. 3,500 rounds fired at enemy aircraft. 10,000 rounds night harassing fire. Extract from "LONDON GAZETTE" dated May 20 1918. "Mentioned in Despatch. Capt (Acting Major) Wpt. Lt. Col. W.J. CRANSTON. M. Staff Regt attached M.G Corps. Extract from 'LONDON GAZETTE' dated June 2nd 1918. Awarded the D.S.O. Capt. & Brevet Major (A/Lt Col) W.J. CRANSTON. N. Staff Regt attached M.G. Corps.	OR
		12.30 a.m.	Operation by 8th K.O.R.L. — Successful. Casualties I.O.R. wounded 4. O.R. On Leave 1. O.R.	OR

Army Form C. 2118.

WAR DIARY
or
INTELLIGENCE SUMMARY.

(Erase heading not required.)

3rd Batn. M.G.C.

Instructions regarding War Diaries and Intelligence Summaries are contained in F.S. Regs., Part II. and the Staff Manual respectively. Title pages will be prepared in manuscript.

Place	Date	Hour	Summary of Events and Information	Remarks and references to Appendices
	June 3rd	6am	Situation normal - 3000 rounds fired at E.A. - 12.00 rounds to Right Harassing fire. Extract from London Gazette June 3rd 1918. Awarded the Military Cross. Lieut (acting Major) J.H. Wooders, N. Staffs Regt. Attached M.G. Corps. Casualties 1 O.R. Wounded. Horses 3 O.R. Injured for Stables 3 O.R.	O.D.
	4th	6am	Situation normal - 1500 rounds fired at E.A. - 12000 rounds Right Harassing fire. Machine Gun Instruction No 9 issued. Casualties 3 O.R. On Cadre 1 O.R.	APPENDIX 1. O.D.
		11.30pm	Some H.E. and Gas Shells (BLUECROSS) were fired on M17C. without doing any damage.	
	5th	6am	Situation normal - 1500 rounds fired at E.A. - 21,000 rounds Right Harassing fire. Operation Order No 23 issued. Casualties 2/Lt J.H. EADES + 1 O.R. Wounded 3 O.R. On Leave 1 O.R.	APPENDIX 2. O.D.
	6th		Situation normal - 1000 rds at E.A. - 8,000 rounds Right Harassing fire. Extract from London Gazette dated June 25, 1918. Awarded the Military Cross. Temp Lieut (acting Capt) E.T. Forgan C. Coy. relieved B. Coy. in Right Sector. 2 Lewis's 1st Coy came to FOUQUEREUIL & 2 Sections to Nos 1A and 2 Position. Relief complete 11.a.m. and all correct. Casualties 4 O.R.	O.D.

Army Form C. 2118.

WAR DIARY
or
INTELLIGENCE SUMMARY.   3RD BATTN M.G.C.

(Erase heading not required.)

Instructions regarding War Diaries and Intelligence Summaries are contained in F.S. Regs., Part II. and the Staff Manual respectively. Title pages will be prepared in manuscript.

Place	Date	Hour	Summary of Events and Information	Remarks and references to Appendices
FOUQUEREUIL	7.	6.0 a.m	MAP 36A. S.E. Situation normal. 25,000 rounds Night Harassing fire.	O.R
		10.15 p.m	Heavy shelling of CANAL BANK about W17 d, & W.23 b. a fire being caused. Casualties 5 O.R Wounded. 3 O.R. Transfer to R.A.F. 1 O.R.	
	8th	6.0 a.m	Situation normal. 1000 rounds fired at Enemy aircraft. 20,000 rounds night harassing fire.	O.R
		11.15 p.m	An S.O.S signal was observed in the direction of PACAUT WOOD, no action took place. Casualties 2 O.R. Wounded nil. Reinforcements 24 O.R. 2 O.R to U.K (6 mm tour of duty) 2 O.R	
	9th	6.0 a.m	Situation normal. 8000 rounds fired at E.A. 22,000 rounds night harassing fire.	APPENDIX 3. O.R
		10.0 a.m	Commanding Officer attended Divisible Conference at Divl H.Q. Operation order No 24 issued. 3 + 4 Section "C" Coy relieved 1 + 2 Sections "C" Coy at 19-20 Junction. In reply to an attacking barrage at 5.0 p.m. the enemy shelled the CANAL BANK and front line heavily. 2 O.R. Reported from Employ 3 O.R. On leave. 1 O.R.	
	10th	6.0 a.m	Situation normal. 500 rounds fired at E.A. Night harassing fire. 18,000 rounds. Increased shelling activity in the whole of the Divl Front.	O.R
		10.0 a.m	Conference of Company Commanders at BATTN H.Q. Instruction 2 O.R. Wounded 3 O.R. Reinforcements 2 O.R.	

Army Form C. 2118.

2nd Battn. M.G.C.

WAR DIARY
or
INTELLIGENCE SUMMARY.
(Erase heading not required.)

Instructions regarding War Diaries and Intelligence Summaries are contained in F.S. Regs., Part II. and the Staff Manual respectively. Title pages will be prepared in manuscript.

Place	Date	Hour	Summary of Events and Information	Remarks and references to Appendices
FOUQUEREUIL	June 11th	6 a.m.	Situation normal — 500 rounds fired at E.A. — Night harassing fire 2,000 rounds. Slight increase in shelling. Between 2-10 a.m. and 250 a.m. about 300 gas shells (Yellow Cross) were fired on roads in X13C, no casualties. Operation Order No. 5 issued. On Cortn 5. O.R.	(S) APPENDIX 4.
	12th	6 a.m.	Situation normal — Night harassing fire 5,000 rounds. Re adjustment of Groups took place during the night, the relief being carried out without any trouble and completed at 3 a.m. Two sections of "D" Company and Coy. H.Q. came into Reserve at FOUQUEREUIL. Casualties 4. O.R. Casualties 1. O.R. Returned from Hospital 6. O.R.	(S)
	13th	6 a.m.	Situation normal — 500 rounds fired at E.A. — Night harassing fire 12,000 rounds. All positions prepared for the operation and barrage lines did out. BETHUNE shelled intermittently throughout the day. Casualties 1. O.R. CAPT. H.E. BLOWER.	(S)

Army Form C. 2118.

WAR DIARY
or
INTELLIGENCE SUMMARY

3RD BATTN. M.G.C.

Place	Date	Hour	Summary of Events and Information	Remarks and references to Appendices
FOUQUEREUIL	June 14	6.0 a.m.	Situation normal.	
		11.45 p.m.	Operation by 9TH & 76TH BRIGADES with Artillery & machine gun cooperation – entirely successful. The enemy sent up numerous green, red, yellow lights on front of PACAUT WOOD & CANAL LA LAWE. Enemy barrage came down 5 mins after zero but was very weak. Rounds fired during operation 215.500. Evacuation 4. O.R.	APPENDIX 5. O.R
	15	6.0 a.m.	Situation quiet. Enemy artillery active at all points except the front. AVELETTE heavily shelled at intervals throughout the day. Nights Lowney Fire 11.500 rounds Evacuation 3. O.R.	O.R
	16	6.0 a.m.	Situation normal. 500 rounds fired at enemy aircraft. Enemy aeroplanes very active, particularly at night; a few bombs were dropped in BETHUNE. Night harassing fire 14.000 rounds Evacuation 12. O.R. Rejoined from hospital 1 O.R. Evacuation 2/LT B.F. HINGE.	O.R
	17	6.0 a.m.	Situation normal. 1200 rounds fired at enemy aircraft. Rather less hostile artillery activity; front and materials quiet during the day. Nights harassing fire 12.000 rounds Evacuation 2 O.R. Rejoined 3. O.R.	O.R

A5834 Wt. W4973 M687 750.000 8/16 D. D. & L. Ltd. Forms C.2118/13.

Army Form C. 2118.

WAR DIARY
or
INTELLIGENCE SUMMARY.
(Erase heading not required.)

3RD BATTN. M.G.C.

Instructions regarding War Diaries and Intelligence Summaries are contained in F. S. Regs., Part II. and the Staff Manual respectively. Title pages will be prepared in manuscript.

Place	Date	Hour	Summary of Events and Information	Remarks and references to Appendices
FOUQUEREUIL	July 19th	6.0 a.m.	Situation normal; 1000 rounds fired at Enemy aircraft. The CANAL BANK in vicinity of No 3 Station was shelled for 2 hours. Night harassing fire 14,000 rounds. Evacuation 1 O.R. Reported from Hospital 1 O.R. On leave CAPT. R. ALLAN. M.C.	O.P.
	19th	6.0 p.m.	Situation normal. 500 rounds fired at Enemy aircraft. Operation order No 26 issued. Night harassing fire 14,000 rounds. Evacuation 3 O.R.	APPENDIX 6
	20th	6.0 a.m.	Situation normal. Reported from Hospital 2 O.R. Enemy artillery active on back area during the day & night. "D" Coy on the Chuffy Crads billet took "A" Coy men relieved by "D" Coy in remains of FOUQUEREUIL LEFT GROUP. "A" Coy Qrs. & 2 Sections "A" Coy moved into new Qrs. Night harassing fire 11,000 rounds. Relief complete at 11.15 p.m. Evacuation 2 O.R. Reported from Hospital 1 O.R. On leave 1 O.R.	O.P.
	21st	6.0 a.m.	Situation normal. 500 rounds fired at Enemy aircraft. Slight increase in shelling the front area AVELETTE receiving particular attention this gave rounds. Night harassing fire 15,000 rounds. Guns fired 1 O.R. Reported from Hospital 2 O.R.	O.P.

A8534. Wt.W4973 M687. 750,000. 8/16 D.D. & L. Ltd. Forms C.2118/13.

Army Form C. 2118.

WAR DIARY
or
INTELLIGENCE SUMMARY.
(Erase heading not required.)

3RD BATTN. M.G.C.

Place	Date	Hour	Summary of Events and Information	Remarks and references to Appendices
FOUQUEREUIL			MAP 36 A S.E.	
	June 22nd		Situation normal. Night harassing fire 13,000 rounds. Fired at enemy aircraft 1,000 rounds. Evacuation 1 O.R. I.O.R. Rejoined from hospital. I.O.R. from leave.	O.R.P.
	23rd		Situation normal. Night harassing fire 11,000 rounds. Evacuation 7 O.R. from hospital 4 O.R.	O.R.P.
	24th		Situation normal. Night harassing fire 13,500 rounds. Evacuation 1 O.R. Joined 1 O.R.	O.R.P.
	25th		Situation normal. Evacuation 2 O.R. Night harassing fire 11,000 rounds. On leave (Paris) 2 O.R.	O.R.P.
	26th		Situation normal. Night harassing fire 13,000 rounds. Evacuation 3 O.R. From leave 1 O.R. Fired at enemy aircraft 1,000 rounds. On leave 1 O.R.	O.R.P.

CAPT. A.W. CRAVEN. 2/LT. A.R. COWKISHAW. 9 2 O.R.
LT. B.F. HINGE.

Army Form C. 2118.

WAR DIARY
or
INTELLIGENCE SUMMARY.
(Erase heading not required.)

3RD BATTN. M.G.C.

Place	Date	Hour	Summary of Events and Information	Remarks and references to Appendices
FOUQUEREUIL	Jan 30	6.0 a.m.	Situation normal. Enemy artillery active. 500 rounds fired at Enemy Aeroplane. "A" Coy relieved "C" Coy in Centre Sector as per O.O. No 27. Night harassing fire 11,000 rounds. Casualties. M.B. 21 W.6.C. 3.3 Silenced by a Concentration Operations 4 O.R. Repaired from hospital 1.O.R. LT. T.W. WELLS M.C. (Special Works) (gr) Casualties. 2. O.R.	

W.J. Cranston
LT. COL.
COMMANDING 3RD BATTN M.G.C.

SECRET.

3rd. BATTALION MACHINE GUN CORPS.

MACHINE GUN INSTRUCTIONS NO. 9.

~~SECRET~~

COPY NO....7....

JUNE 4th. 1918.

REFERENCE MAP: No. 36,A. S.E. 1/20000.

1. In the event of operations in the near future, the following is the outline of the scheme for the employment of Machine Guns.

2. ORGANIZATION.
   (a) The Divisional front will be held by three Brigades in the line; there will therefore be three Group Commanders - one at each Brigade H.Q. - The LEFT GROUP will extend from LEFT Divisional Boundary to ROAD running N.E. through W,11,a and b,.
   The CENTRE GROUP will extend from ROAD running N.E. through W,11,a and b, to W,18,a,5,7.
   The RIGHT GROUP will extend from W,18,a,5,7. to RIGHT Divisional Boundary.
   (b) Groups will be composed of the following guns:-
   LEFT GROUP.
   Positions Nos. 5, 6, 7, 13, 14, 15, 16, 19.   (18 guns)
   CENTRE GROUP.
   Positions Nos. 3, 4, 10, 11, 12, 19, 20.   (22 guns).
   RIGHT GROUP.
   Positions Nos. 1, 2, 8, 9, 17.   (16 guns).
   (c) 48 guns (Positions Nos. 1, 2, 3, 8, 9, 10, 11, 12, 13, 14, 15, 16, 17, 18, 19, 20) will be employed for barrage purposes; the distribution will be on the basis of one Machine Gun per 50 yards of front.
   (d) 8 guns (Positions Nos. 4, 5, 6, 7.) will be employed for shooting on selected localities. In addition 6 guns of 4th. Batt. M.G.C., and 6 guns of 46th. Batt. M.G.C. will shoot on selected localities.
   (e) 8 guns in Reserve and available to replace casualties.
   (f) To bring guns in range the following forward moves will take place on 'Y' night:
   No. 17. from present position to W,24,b,9,0.
   " 18.   "   "   "   to W,9,b,0,5.
   " 19.   "   "   "   to W,17,c,6,4.
   " 20.   "   "   "   to W,17,c,0,7.
   Group Commanders will reconnoitre these positions and arrange for the construction of emplacements.

3. COMMUNICATION.
   To facilitate forward liaison, Group Commanders will be connected with their Batteries by wire (as far as possible) and runners, and also by visual communication where practicable.

4. S.A.A., WATER & OIL.
   At each gun position there will be:-
   (a) 20,000 rounds of S.A.A. exclusive of belted rounds.
   (b) 2 gallons of cooling water per gun.
   (c) ½ pint of lubricating oil.

5. SAFETY PRECAUTIONS.
   (a) All Tripods used will be provided with a wooden platform, and legs must be sandbagged.
   (b) Clinometers and A.A.M's must be constantly used to enable gun numbers to maintain elevation and direction. Clinometer elevation will be checked before each belt, and in the case of the first belt after the first 50 rounds, and in soft ground more often.
   (c) Barrels for use on Zero day must be in practically new condition. They must be carefully watched for nickelling, and if wiped out after each belt will be accurate for at least 15,000 rounds.
   (d) Variation of all compasses will be checked.

6. RATES OF FIRE.
   (a) Rate of fire for Creeping and Standing Barrage, and on selected localities, will be one belt per gun per 4 minutes.
   (b) S.O.S. fire will be <u>intense</u>, and at the rate of 300 rounds per minute.

7. ACKNOWLEDGE.

Chas. H. Smith
Lieut. & Acting Adjt.,
3rd. Battln. M.G.Corps.

Issued at..........
Copies to:-
1. D.M.G.C.   6. O.C. "D" Coy.
3. O.C. "A" Coy.   7. War Diary.
4. O.C. "B" "   8. "   "
5. O.C. "C" "   9. File.
2. 2/in/Command.

Secret.

3rd. BATTALION MACHINE GUN CORPS.

OPERATION ORDERS NO. 23.

COPY NO. 16

JUNE 5th. 1918.

Reference Map, 36A, S.E.

1. On the night 6th/7th. June "B" Coy. will relieve "C" Coy. in positions now occupied by "C" Coy. in right group.

2. On relief "C" Coy. will pass into Divisional Reserve and will occupy positions at present occupied by "B" Coy.

3. Nos. 1. of both companies will remain with incoming gun teams for 24 hours after relief and occupation of reserve positions.

4. Details of relief will be arragned direct between Company Commanders concerned.

5. Completion of relief and occupation of reserve positions will be reported to Battln. H.Q. by O.C. "B" Coy. and O.C. "C" Coy. respectively by code words -- Company Commander's Name.

6. Company Commanders concerned will obtain all available information regarding role of guns in positions to be taken over, work in progress etc.

7. O. C. "C" Coy. immediately on completion of relief by "B" Coy. will report to G.O.C. Reserve Brigade.

8. ACKNOWLEDGE.

Ches V Smith
Lieut. & Acting Adjt.,
3.r.d. Battln. M.G.Corps.

Issued at 11 a.m.
Copies to:
1. D.M.G.C.   7. M.O.   13. 76th. Inf. Bde.
2. "A" Coy.   8. Q.M.   14. C.R.A.
3. "B" "   9. T.O.   15. War Diary. ✓
4. "C" "   10. "G" 3rd.Div.   16. "   "
5. "D" "   11. 8th.Inf.Bde.   17. File.
6. S.O.   12. 9th. " "

Appendix 3

SECRET.

3rd. BATTALION MACHINE GUN CORPS.

OPERATION ORDERS NO. 24.   COPY NO. 18

---oOo---   JUNE 9th. 1918.

1. Consequent on the re-adjustment of the Divisional Front, the Machine Guns will be grouped in three groups, each Group covering one Brigade Front.

2. On the night 12th/13th. June, to effect this re-adjustment, the following reliefs will take place:-

Gun
Positions.
```
   3.     4 Guns "C" Coy. will relieve 4 guns of "D" Coy.
   4.     2   "   "C"  "      "      "  2   "   "  "A"  "
  10.     4   "   "C"  "      "      "  4   "   "  "B"  "
  11.     2   "   "D"  "      "      "  2   "   "  "A"  "
  12.     2   "   "C"  "      "      "  2   "   "  "A"  "
  13.     2   "   "A"  "      "      "  2   "   "  "D"  "
  17.     4   "   "B"  "      "      "  4   "   "  "D"  "
  18.     4   "   "A"  "      "      "  4   "   "  "D"  "
  20.     4   "   "D"  "      "      "  4   "   "  "C"  "
```

3. Eight guns of "D" Coy. will be in Reserve at Battalion H.Q.

4. Details of relief will be arranged direct between Company Commanders concerned.

5. Company Commanders concerned will obtain all available information regarding role of guns in positions to be taken over, work in progress etc.

6. Completion of reliefs will be reported to Battalion H.Q. by code word (Company Commanders' Name.)

7. On completion of reliefs, the Groups will be organized as follows:-
LEFT GROUP (18 Guns) under Major C.F.SWANN.

No. of Position.	No. of Guns.	Company.
5.	2	"A"
6.	2	"A"
7.	2	"A"
13.	2	"A"
14.	2	"D"
15.	2	"A"
16.	2	"A"
18.	4	"A"

CENTRE GROUP (22 Guns) under Major C.D.ST.LEGER.

3.	4	"C"
4.	2	"C"
10.	4	"C"
11.	2	"D"
12.	2	"C"
19.	4	"C"
20.	4	"D"

RIGHT GROUP (16 Guns) under Major E. THOMAS, M.C.

1.	2	"B"
2.	2	"B"
8.	4	"B"
9.	4	"B"
17.	4	"B"

8. ACKNOWLEDGE.

R. Allan
Capt. & Adjt.,
3rd. Battln. M.G.Corps.

Issued at 8 P.M.   P.T.O.

Copies to:-
1. D.M.G.C.
2. 2/in/C
3. "A" Coy.
4. "B" "
5. "C" "
6. "D" "
7. "G" 3rd.Div.
8. 4th. Bn.M.GGC.
9. 46th. " "
10. 8th. Inf.Bde.
11. 9th. Inf. Bde.
12. 76th. " "
13. T.O.
14. Q.M.
15. M.O.
16. S.O.
17. War Diary.
18. " "
19. File
20. C.R.A.

SECRET.

3rd. BATTALION MACHINE GUN CORPS.

OPERATION ORDERS NO. 25.

COPY NO........

JUNE 10th. 1918.

REF. SHEET 36,A. S.E. 1/10,000.

1. (a) With a view to securing a greater depth in defence on the East Bank of the LA BASSEE CANAL, the 3rd. Division will advance its front on the night 14th/15th June to the line: - Q.34.d.4.2 - FORD LANE - TURBEAUTE CT at W.12.a.0.8 - thence along the West Bank of this stream to W.12.c.1.6 thence to W.18.b.5.8 where it will connect up with our present Front Line.
   (b) The 4th. Division has been ordered to conform by advancing their extreme right flank to gain touch with the left flank of the 3rd. Division about Q.34.d.40.25.
   (c) The operation will be carried out as a surprise without a preliminary bombardment.

2. The advance on the front of the 3rd. Division will be carried out by the 9th. Infantry Brigade on the Right, and the 76th. Infantry Brigade on the left.
    The 8th. Infantry Brigade will conform by advancing their extreme left to join up with the Right flank of the 9th. Infantry Brigade about W.12.c.70.10.

3. The dividing line between the 9th. and 76th. Infantry Brigades will be the road running N.E. from W.11.b.0.5 (road inclusive to 76th. Infantry Brigade).

4. The Infantry advance will be supported by the following Machine Guns:-
   (a) 48 Machine Guns will be employed for barrage purposes - the distribution being on the basis of one gun per 50 yards of front.
   (b) Eight guns will be employed for shooting on selected localities. (See Appendix 3)
   (c) Six guns 4th. Division and 6 guns 46th. Division will co-operate by fire on selected localities. (Appendix 3.)

5. TIME TABLE.
   The signal for opening fire at ZERO HOUR will be the opening of the Field Artillery barrage.
   48 Barrage Guns (See Appendices 1 & 2.)
       ZERO to ZERO plus 8 minutes.
           Fire on BLUE Barrage Line - marked on map attached.
       ZERO plus 8 minutes to 3-0 a.m.
           Fire on GREEN Barrage Line - marked on map attached.

   20 Guns shooting on localities. (See Appendix 3.)
       ZERO to 3-0 a.m.
           Fire on localities as per map attached.

   "S.O.S"
       On seeing S.O.S. the 48 Barrage guns will fire on GREEN Barrage Line (Appendix 2) and the 20 Locality shooting guns on targets as detailed in Appendix 3.
       The 6 guns of the 4th. Division and six guns of the 46th. Division will cease to operate on the 3rd. Divisional front at 3-0 a.m. 15th. June.

   Rates of Fire.
   ZERO to ZERO plus 40' -- One belt per gun per FOUR Minutes.
   ZERO plus 40' to ZERO plus 60' -- One belt per gun per EIGHT Minutes.
   ZERO plus 60' to 3-0 a.m. -- One belt per gun per TWENTY Minutes.
   "S.O.S" -- Intense and at the rate of 300 rounds per gun per minute.

O.O. No. 25.   SECRET.

6. Battery charts and gun charts will be completed and a copy will be forwarded to Battalion H.Q. by 12 noon June 12th.

7. ZERO HOUR will be notified later.

8. Group Commanders will synchronize watches with their Brigades between 5-0 p.m. and 6-0 p.m. on the 14th. June.

10. "S.O.S" LINES.
Group Commanders will draw up S.O.S. Lines to cover their respective fronts in conjunction with Artillery Group Commanders and Brigade Commanders. The new S.O.S. Lines will come into operation at 3-0 a.m. but RIGHT GROUP will be prepared to switch on to protective barrage covering fronts of CENTRE and LEFT Brigades (GREEN BARRAGE). Between ZERO and 3-0 a.m. RIGHT GROUP will be prepared to switch the fire of all guns now covering RIGHT Brigade front on to their normal S.O.S. Lines in the event of an attack developing on that front.
A map shewing new S.O.S. Lines will be forwarded to Battalion H.Q. by 12 noon June 13th.

9. ACKNOWLEDGE.

                                                                Capt. & Adjt.,
                                                                3rd. Battalion M.G.Corps.

Issued at... 9 P.M.
Copies to:-
1. D.M.G.C.   11. 8th. Inf. Bde.
2. 2/in/C.   12. 9th. "   "
3. "A" Coy.   13. 76th. "   "
4. "B" "   14. T.O.
5. "C" "   15. Q.M.
6. "D" "   16. M.O.
7. "G" 3rd.Div.   17. S.O.
8. C.R.A.   18. War Diary
9. 4th.Div.M.G.C.   19.   "   "
10. 46th. "   "   20. File.
                       21. 3rd Div G (2nd copy)
                       22. A.M.CO.
                       23. A.M.CO.

SECRET.

APPENDIX 1.

"BLUE" BARRAGE.

Position No.	No. of Guns.	Map Refs. of Gun Positions.	Grid Bearing of Barrage Line (RIGHT GUN)	Range	Duration of Fire.	Rates of Fire.
LEFT GROUP.						
13.	2	W.10.c.80.10	19°	2250ˣ		
14.	2	W.10.c.60.50	26°	2050ˣ		
15.	2	W.9.a.91.60) W.9.a.99.71)	66°	2150ˣ		
16.	2	W.3.c.65.75) W.3.c.70.70)	87°	2300ˣ		
18.	4	W.9.b.00.50	70°	2300ˣ		
CENTRE GROUP.						
3.	4	W.17.b.05.70	14°	1680ˣ	From ZERO to ZERO plus EIGHT Minutes.	One belt per gun per FOUR Minutes.
10.	4	(W.17.d.07.25 (W.23.b.05.65	17° 15°	1850ˣ 1950ˣ		
11.	2	W.16.d.95.88) W.16.d.88.92)	6°	2500ˣ		
12.	2	W.16.b.45.22) W.16.b.38.22)	7°	2650ˣ		
19.	4	W.17.c.60.40	3°	2700ˣ		
20.	4	W.17.c.05.35	15°	2700ˣ		
RIGHT GROUP.						
1.	2	X.13.c.90.50	319°	2100ˣ		
2.	2	X.13.d.45.70	338°	2100ˣ		
8.	4	W.24.b.45.15	348°	2400ˣ		
9.	4	W.24.a.15.20	358°	2500ˣ		
17.	4	W.24.d.41.95	343°	2100ˣ		

SECRET.

APPENDIX 2.

"GREEN" BARRAGE.

Position No.	No. of Guns	Map Refs. of Gun Positions.	Grid Bearing of Barrage Line (RIGHT GUN)	Range	Duration of Fire.	Rates of Fire.	Remarks.
LEFT GROUP.							
13.	2	W.10.c.80.10	38°	2500ˣ			
14.	2	W.10.c.60.50	45°	2450ˣ		From ZERO plus EIGHT Minutes to ZERO plus FORTY Minutes. One belt per gun per FOUR Minutes.	
15.	2	W.9.a.91.80) W.9.a.99.71)	53°	2500ˣ			
16.	2	W.3.c.65.75) W.3.c.70.70)	67°	2500ˣ			
18.	4	W.9.b.00.50	48°	2550ˣ			
CENTRE GROUP.							
5.	4	W.17.b.05.70	10°	2300ˣ	From ZERO plus EIGHT minutes to 3-0 a.m.	From ZERO plus 40 minutes to ZERO plus 60 Minutes. One belt per gun per EIGHT Minutes. From ZERO plus 60 Minutes to 3-0 a.m. One belt per gun per TWENTY Minutes. "S.O.S" INTENSE.	The "GREEN" Barrage will also be "S.O.S" Barrage.
10.	4	(W.17.d.07.25 (W.23.b.03.65	17° 17°	2100ˣ 2500ˣ			
11.	2	W.16.d.95.89) W.16.d.88.92)	28°	2500ˣ			
12.	2	W.16.b.45.22) W.16.b.38.22)	32°	2500ˣ			
19.	4	W.17.c.60.40	24°	2500ˣ			
20.	4	W.17.c.05.35	34°	2500ˣ			
RIGHT GROUP.							
1.	2	X.13.c.90.50	323°	1800ˣ			
2.	2	X.13.d.45.70	353°	2000ˣ			
3.	4	W.24.b.45.15	354°	2400ˣ			
9.	4	W.24.a.15.20	10°	2600ˣ			
17.	4	W.24.d.41.95	350°	2100ˣ			

SECRET.

APPENDIX 3.

LOCALITY SHOOTING.

(BROWN)

Position No.	No. of Guns.	Map Refs. of Gun Positions.	Target.	Duration of fire	Rate of Fire	Remarks.
4.	2	W.11.c.93.50) W.11.c.79.66)	Area B. W.12.d. 50.35-95.35 95.90-50.90			
5.	2	(W.10.b.65.60) (W.10.b.25.90)	Area D. W.5.d. 55.00-30.18 32.80-08.62		From ZERO to ZERO plus 40 minutes. One belt per gun per FOUR minutes.	
6.	2	(W.4.c.90.20) (W.4.c.80.25)				
7.	2	(W.3.d.05.05)		From ZERO to 3-0 a.m.	From ZERO plus 40 minutes to ZERO plus 60 minutes. One belt per gun per EIGHT minutes.	Localities will be searched on "S.O.S" Call.
4th. DIVISION.						
	2	W.3.a.00.90)	Area E. Q.35.d.15.50-70.75 70.95-15.95			
	2	W.3.d.05.90)				
	2	W.9.a.00.90)				
46th. DIVISION.					From ZERO plus 60 minutes to 3-0 a.m. One belt per gun per TWENTY minutes. "S.O.S" INTENSE.	
Pigeon (1 gun)		X.19.a.90.30	Area A. W.12.d. 05.65-15.65 15.75-05.75			
do (3 guns)		X.19.a.90.30)	Area C. W.12.b.80.30-80.50 W.6.d.30.10-W.12.b.10.90			
Thrush	2	X.20.c.10.50)				

MEDICAL ARRANGEMENTS.   O.O. No. 25.

REGIMENTAL AID POSTS are located as follows:-

    LOCON SECTION W.23.c.7.7
                                    W.23.c.7.6
                                    W.12.d.4.4
    HINGES SECTION W.9.d.4.4
                                    W.16.d.4.6
                                    W.15.a.CENTRAL.

ADVANCED DRESSING STATIONS.

    ANNEZIN E.9.b.3.7
    L'ABBAYE W.25.a.1.6

Casualties are to be brought to the nearest R.A.P. or A.D.S.

Dressings are being provided for each Battery position.

Stretchers are being provided, one for each Section.

GAS:- A supply of ammonia ampoules will be at each Battery position. Chloride of Lime will be scattered in fresh gas shell holes and then a few shovel-fulls of earth thrown over the Chloride of Lime.

Notification of arrangements for Walking Wounded and further Medical arrangements will be sent later.

Regimental Medical Officer will be at Battalion Headquarters.

10/6/1918.

3rd. BATTALION MACHINE GUN CORPS.

ADDITIONAL MEDICAL ARRANGEMENTS.

REF: O.O. 25.

WALKING WOUNDED:

From 76th. Brigade Area.
Will be directed to A.D.S. at L'ABBAYE.

From 8th. and 9th. Brigades Area.
Will be directed to A.D.S. at ANNEZIN.

There will be STRETCHER DUMPS at the following places:-

LE PLUOY FARM.
W.18.c.1.3.
W.17.c.1.8.

W.10.a.1.1.
W.4.c.8.4.
W.11.a.2.2.
W.10.b.5.7.

R.A.M.C. Bearers will be located:
In addition to R.A.P's and A.D.S's.
W.10.a.1.1.
W.17.b.1.8.
W.11.a.2.2.

-------o-------

SECRET.

3rd. BATTALION MACHINE GUN CORPS.

COMMUNICATIONS FOR IMPENDING OPERATIONS.

REPORT CENTRES WILL BE ESTABLISHED AS FOLLOWS:-

LEFT GROUP.
(W.25.a.1.6)

No. 18. Position (W.9.b.0.5).
Open Line from W.9.b.0.5 to
W15.a.5.3. From there buried
cable to W.26.b.5.1, from there
open line to Left Group H.Q.

CENTRE GROUP.
(E.4.b.3.2)

LE PLUOY FARM. (W.16.d.5.7)
Open Line from LE PLUOY FARM to
Infantry Battalion H.Q. at W.22.a.2.8
From there Infantry Open Line to
Brigade H.Q. at E.4.b.4.1, from
there open line to Centre Group H.Q.

No. 10. Position (W.23.b.08.65)
(At Infantry Battalion H.Q.)
From Infantry Battalion H.Q. at
W.23.a.9.3 to Brigade H.Q at
E.4.b.4.1 by Infantry armoured
cable line, thence to Centre Group
H.Q. by open line.

RIGHT GROUP.
(W.29.C)

LONG CORNET (W.23.b.8.1)
Open Line from LONG CORNET to
Infantry Battalion H.Q. at W.23.c.8.3
thence by Infantry armoured cable to
Brigade H.Q. at W.29.C, thence open
line to Right Group H.Q.

No. 8. Position (W.24.b.45.15)
Open line from No. 8. Position to
LONG CORNET thence open line to
Infantry Battalion H.Q. at W.23.c.8.3
thence by Infantry armoured cable
line to Infantry Brigade H.Q. at
W.29.3. thence open line to Right
Group H.Q.

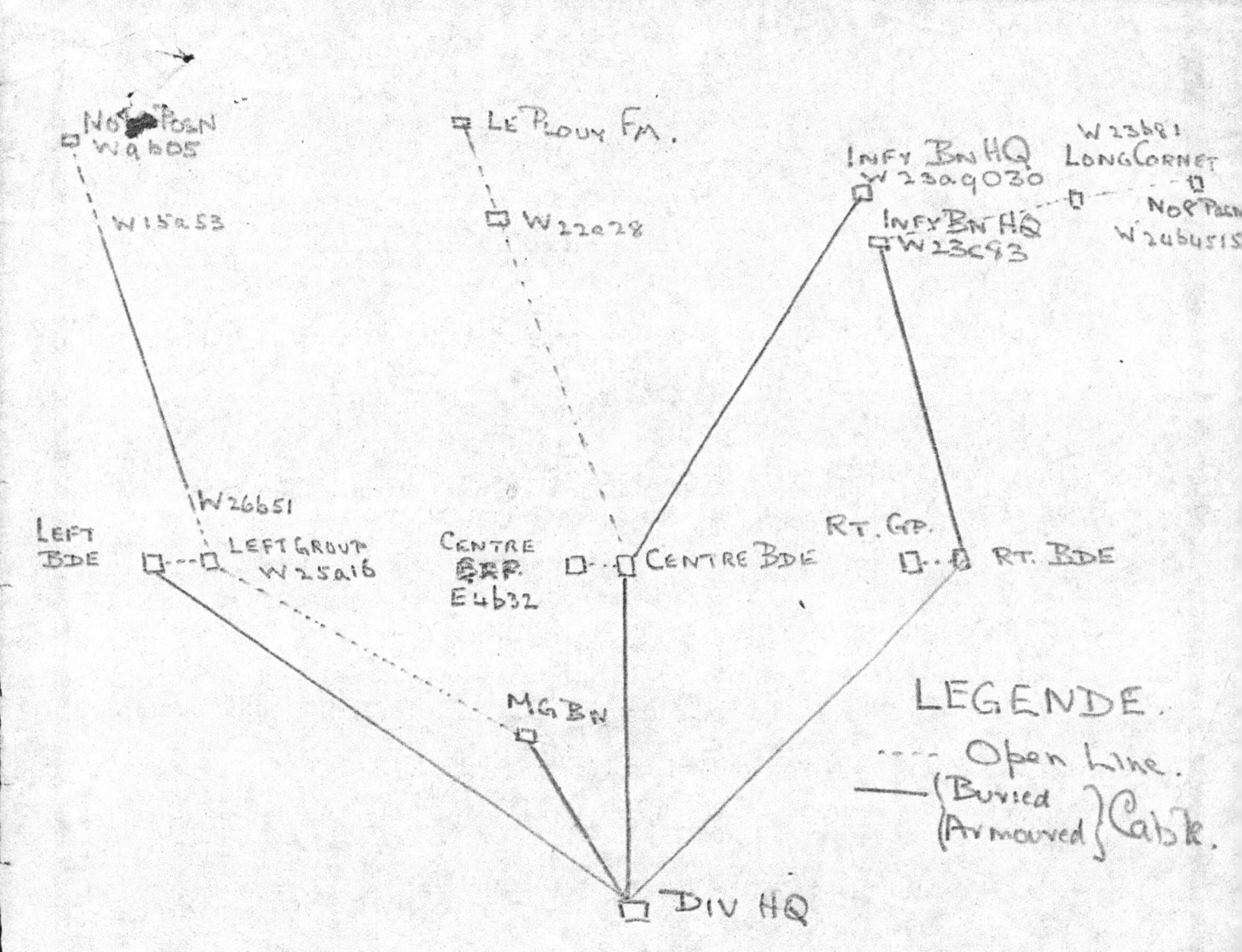

APPENDIX 5

No. 27.

Report on Operation carried out by LEFT and CENTRE
Brigades of the 3rd. DIVISION, on Night of
14/15th. June 1918.

---oOo---

11.45 p.m.   Our Artillery and Machine Gun Barrage opened promptly at 11.45 p.m. The enemy put up numerous GREEN, RED and YELLOW lights on a front between PACAUT WOOD and CANAL DELAW. Enemy barrage opened five minutes after Zero, but was very light, evidently the enemy did not at first think the operation was anything more than a raid.

1.20 a.m.   "B" Company report situation quiet, no information as to progress of operation.

2.30 a.m.   "B" Company report situation quiet, no hostile shelling. 9th. Infantry Brigade state two prisoners passed through.

7.50 a.m.   "A" Company report situation normal, nothing of interest to report.

11.50 a.m.   "B" Company report situation obscure on left Company of CENTRE Brigade.

12 noon   "A" Company report situation very quiet. Objectives on LEFT Brigade taken with but little resistance except for the extreme left which was held up for a time by Machine Gun fire, but this was soon overcome. Wounded from the 76th. Brigade state very heavy casualties were inflicted on the enemy by our barrage.

3.00 p.m.   "A" Company report situation unchanged, only slight shelling.

4.5 p.m.   "A" Company report situation unchanged, nothing further to report.

6.00 p.m.   "C" Company report enemy artillery shewed considerably more activity on forward areas. AVELETTE shelled with intermittent bursts of heavies all day. HINGETTE and System around No. 12. position shelled from 11.0 a.m. to 4.0 p.m. LE PLUOY FARM also shelled. 4.0 p.m. Heavy shelling of forward area lasting 15 minutes.

Operation was entirely successful, the Division taking 178 prisoners, the 4th. Division took 20 prisoners also.

Total Prisoners ... 198.

---oOo---

Casualties ... ... 8 O.R's Wounded.
Rounds fired during the operation ... 215,500.

APPENDIX 6

SECRET.

3rd. BATTALION MACHINE GUN CORPS.

OPERATION ORDERS NO. 2⊘.

COPY NO. 16

JUNE 19th. 1918.

REFERENCE MAP:- 38, A, S.E.

1. On the night 20th/21st. June "D" Company will relieve "A" Coy. in positions now occupied by "A" Company in LEFT GROUP.

2. On relief "A" Company will pass into Divisional Reserve and will occupy positions and billets at present occupied by "D" Company.

3. Nos. 1. of both Companies will remain with incoming gun teams for 24 hours after relief and occupation of Reserve positions.

4. Details of relief will be arranged direct between Company Commanders concerned.

5. Completion of relief and occupation of reserve positions will be reported to Battalion H.Q. by O.C. "D" Company and O.C. "A" Company respectively by code words - Company Commanders' Name.

6. Company Commanders concerned will obtain all available information regarding role of guns in positions to be taken over, work in progress etc.

7. ACKNOWLEDGE.

Lieut. & Acting Adjt.,
3rd. Battln. M.G.Corps.

Issued at 11 a.m.
Copies to:-
1. D.M.G.C.
2. O.C. "A" Coy.
3. O.C. "B" "
4. O.C. "C" "
5. O.C. "D" "
6. "G" 3rd. Div.
7. C.R.A.
8. T.O.
9. T.O.
10. 8th. Inf. Bde.
11. 9th. " "
12. 76th. " "
13. Q.M.
14. M.O.
15. S.C.
16. War Diary ✓
17. " "
18. File.

APPENDIX 7

SECRET.

3rd. BATTALION MACHINE GUN CORPS.

OPERATION ORDERS NO. 27.

COPY NO. 16

JUNE 29th. 1918.

Reference Map: 36,A. S.E.

1. On the night June 30th./July 1st. "A" Company will relieve "C" Company in positions now occupied by "C" Company in CENTRE GROUP.

2. On relief "C" Company will pass into Divisional Reserve and will occupy positions and billets at present occupied by "A" Company.

3. Nos. 1. of both Companies will remain with incoming gun teams for 24 hours after relief and occupation of Reserve positions.

4. Details of relief will be arranged direct between Company Commanders concerned.

5. Completion of relief and occupation of Reserve positions will be reported to Battalion H.Q. by O.C. "A" Company and O.C. "C" Company respectively by code word – Company Commander's Name.

6. Company Commanders concerned will obtain all available information regarding role of guns in positions to be taken over, work in progress etc. Trench Stores will be handed over and copy of same will be rendered to B.H.Q.

7. ACKNOWLEDGE.

C.N. Smith
Lieut. & A/Adjt.,
3rd. Battln. M. G. Corps.

Issued at 11 a.m.
Copies to:-
1. D.M.G.C.   10. 9th. Inf. Bde.
2. O.C. "A" Coy.   11. 76th. "   "
3. O.C. "B" "   12. Q.M.
4. O.C. "C" "   13. M.O.
5. O.C. "D" "   14. S.O.
6. "G" 3rd. Div.   15. War Diary.
7. C.R.A.   16. "   "
8. T.O.   17. File.
9. 8th. Inf. Bde.

---o---

WAR DIARY or INTELLIGENCE SUMMARY

Army Form C. 2118.

3RD BATTN M.G.C.

MAP 36a S.E.

Place	Date	Hour	Summary of Events and Information	Remarks and references to Appendices
FOUQUEREUIL	July 1st	6.0 a.m	Situation normal. Quiet day. Night harrassing fire during the day. Enemy artillery quieter. Casualties 15 O.R. Evacuated from line 1 O.R.	QR
	2nd	6.0 a.m	Situation normal. 400 rounds fired at Enemy aircraft. 500 rounds harrassing fire 6000 rounds D 27 C. enfire during the day. 7000 rounds night harrassing fire. Casualties Lt. ROCH M.C. Evacuated 3 O.R. Rejoined from hospital 2 O.R.	QR
	3rd	6.0 a.m	Situation normal. 500 rounds fired at enemy aircraft during the day. 7,500 rounds night harrassing fire Casualties 1 O.R. Rejoined from hospital 5 O.R. 2 officers and one MAJOR THOMAS M.C.	QR
	4th	6.0 a.m	Situation normal. 8,500 rounds night harrassing fire Casualties 1 O.R. Rejoined from hospital 1 O.R. From Courses LT. T.W.WELLS. M.C. From Leave CAPT. R. ALLAN. M.C. Defence Scheme (Provisional) issued. APPENDIX 1	QR

Army Form C. 2118.

WAR DIARY
or
INTELLIGENCE SUMMARY.
(Erase heading not required.)

3RD BATTN. M.G.C.

Place	Date	Hour	Summary of Events and Information	Remarks and references to Appendices
FOUQUEREUIL	July 5	6.0 a.m.	Situation normal. 8,500 rounds night harassing fire.	OR
	6	6.0 a.m.	Situation normal. Re-inforcements 21 O.R.	
		9.30 a.m.	4,500 rounds fired from No.14 section on Q.34.B.3.t. in support of 4th Division and 1800 rounds fired at enemy aircraft during the day. 8,500 rounds Night harassing fire. Evacuations 3 O.R.	OR
	7	6.0 a.m.	Situation normal. 1600 rounds fired at enemy aircraft during the day. 10,500 rounds night harassing fire. Operation order No 38 issued. Lieut. (A/Capt) C.D.WETTON is granted permission to wear the badges of the rank of A/Major whilst in command of a Company. Lt. G.H. MATTHEWS is granted permission to wear the badges of the rank of A/Capt whilst 2nd in Command of a Company. Evacuation Lt. L.L. HEYWOOD M.C. 7 O.R. Reinforcements from hospital 3 O.R.	APPENDIX 2. OR
	8	6.0 a.m.	Situation normal. 9,000 rounds night harassing fire. "C" Coy relieved "D" Coy as per O.O. No 15. Reinforcements from hospital 3 O.R.	OR

Army Form C. 2118.

WAR DIARY
or
INTELLIGENCE SUMMARY.
(Erase heading not required.)

3RD BATT^N. M.G.C.

Instructions regarding War Diaries and Intelligence Summaries are contained in F. S. Regs. Part II. and the Staff Manual respectively. Title pages will be prepared in manuscript.

Place	Date	Hour	Summary of Events and Information	Remarks and references to Appendices
FOUQUEREUIL	July 9th	6.0 a.m	Situation normal. 500 rounds fired at enemy aircraft during the day. Transport reported by Corps Commander who acknowledged this satisfaction. 3 flak lights seen about 10.0 P.M but main reported 2,000 rounds fired on S.O.S lines. 6,000 rounds night harassing fire. Presented 2/Lt W.H. WRIGHTSON. 2/Lt E.G. BURKE. 1 O.R. Returned from hospital 4 O.R. Le Roux (UK) 1 O.R. 2 officers rod. Some MAJOR F THOMAS. M.C. leave. 2 O.R.	OR
	10th	6.0 a.m	Situation normal. 12,000 rounds night harassing fire. Extract from "LONDON GAZETTE" dated 17th June 1918 Awarded the MERITORIOUS SERVICE MEDAL 6295 SGT C.D LONGFIELD. 21085 SGT B.S. COCKERTON. 17269 C.S.M J PEBDEN. 11141 CPL (A/SGT) R J EGGBEER 68327 PTE (A/L/CPL) J.W. BARNES. Rejoined from hospital 3 O.R. from leave 1 O.R. 2/Lt Captⁿ 2/Lt H.G. BEER. 2/Lt G.J. GRANT. 2/Lt R.J. WILLIAMS 1 O.R.	OR

WAR DIARY or INTELLIGENCE SUMMARY

Army Form C. 2118.

3RD BATTN. M.G.C.

Place	Date	Hour	Summary of Events and Information	Remarks and references to Appendices
FOUQUEREUIL	July 11th	6.0 a.m.	MAP 36A S.E. Situation normal. 9,000 rounds night harassing fire. From hospital 2 O.R. To reinforcements 2 O.R. Evacuation 1 O.R. From leave 1 O.R. On leave 1 O.R.	O.R.
	12th	6.0 a.m.	Situation normal. 500 rounds fired at enemy aircraft. 11,500 rounds night harassing fire. Evacuation 1 O.R. Evacuation 2 O.R. Reinforcements 9 O.R. Rejoined from Hospital 1 O.R. From leave 2/Lt. B.F. HINGE. To leave (Paris) MAJOR S. MOFFETT. M.C.	O.R.
	13th	6.0 a.m.	Situation normal. 500 rounds fired at enemy aircraft. 10,000 rounds night harassing fire. Evacuation 1 O.R. Reinforcements 2 O.R. To Corps 3 O.R. To leave (U.K.) MAJOR C.F. SWANN.	O.R.
	14th	6.0 a.m.	Situation normal. 500 rounds fired at enemy aircraft. 8,500 rounds night harassing fire. Evacuation 2 O.R. Evac. to 7 R.SCOTS 1 O.R. From leave 1 O.R. From Spare 2/Lt H.G. GEER. 2/Lt G.J. GRANT. 2/Lt R.J. WILLIAMS	O.R.

A5834 Wt. W4973 M687 732,000 8/16 D.D. & L. Ltd. Forms C.2118/13.

Army Form C. 2118.

WAR DIARY
— or —
INTELLIGENCE SUMMARY.

(Erase heading not required.)

3RD BATT N M.G.C.

Place	Date	Hour	Summary of Events and Information	Remarks and references to Appendices
FOUQUEREUIL	July 15	6.0 a.m	Situation normal. 4,000 rounds fired at enemy aircraft during the day. Hostile artillery very active. 10,500 rounds to night Barrage fire. 2 Lieut. (Rev.) 3 O.R.	O/R
	16th	6.0 a.m	(L/C KEN. CAPT. I Q'RMR. A.W. CRAVEN. to leave.) Situation normal. 2,500 rounds fired at enemy Aircraft. 13,500 rounds night harassing fire. Rejoined from hospital 9 O.R.	O/R
	17th	6.0 a.m	Situation normal. 500 rounds fired at enemy aircraft. 10,000 rounds night harassing fire. Rejoined from hospital 3 O.R. To base 1 O.R.	O/R
	18th	6.0 a.m	Situation normal. Operation Order No 29 issued Operation by Infantry on our left. 13,750 rounds fired in support 3,500 rounds fired at enemy aircraft during the day. 10,000 rounds	Appendix 3
		2.30 a.m	night harassing fire. Casualties 2 O.R. wounded 2 O.R. to base 1 O.R. Rejoined from hospital 2 O.R. Thereafter Lt R.A. COTTON. Lt L. HUTCHINSON. rejoined.	O/R

Army Form C. 2118.

WAR DIARY
or
INTELLIGENCE SUMMARY.
(Erase heading not required.)

3RD BATTN M.G.C.

Place	Date	Hour	Summary of Events and Information	Remarks and references to Appendices
			MAP 36A. S.E.	
FOUQUEREUIL	July 19	6.0 a.m	Situation normal. Enemy aircraft in active. Hostile artillery active. 24,000 rounds night harassing fire. Reports from Hospital 1 O.R. Reinforced 3 O.R. Evacuated 3 O.R.	OB
	20	6.0 a.m	Situation normal. Enemy aircraft inactive. Hostile artillery active. 19,000 rounds night harassing fire. Reports from Hospital 3 O.R.	OB
	21st	6.0 a.m	Situation normal. 500 rounds fired at enemy aircraft. 17,500 rounds night harassing fire. Fired from Coy. 1 O.R. Evacuation 1 O.R. 2 Centre 1 O.R. Brussels 1 O.R. L. Louis 1 O.R.	OB
	22nd	6.0 a.m	Situation normal. Enemy aircraft inactive. 17,000 rounds night harassing fire. Evacuation 2 O.R. Report from hospital 3 O.R. Brussels 1 O.R. Re-inforced 1 O.R.	OB

Army Form C. 2118.

WAR DIARY
or
INTELLIGENCE SUMMARY.

(Erase heading not required.)

3RD BATTALION M.G.C.

Place	Date	Hour	Summary of Events and Information	Remarks and references to Appendices
FOUQUEREUIL			MAP 36 A S.E. 1-20,000	
	July 23rd	6.0 a.m.	Situation normal. Enemy aircraft active. 14,000 rounds night harassing fire. Casualties 4. OR.	OB
	24th	6.0 a.m.	Situation normal. 15.30 rounds fired at enemy aircraft. 15,000 rounds night harassing fire. Casualties 2 OR. Severely 1 OR. Reported from hospital. 1 OR.	OB
	25th	6.0 a.m.	Situation normal. 500 rounds fired at enemy aircraft. 12,000 rounds night harassing fire. MAJOR S. MOFFETT M.C. On Leave. 2 OR. From Leave.	OB
	26th	6.0 a.m.	Situation normal. 16,000 rounds night harassing fire. Operation order No. 30 issued. Casualties 1 OR. From Hospital 2 OR. 3 OR On Leave (Pari.) 3 OR (Pari.) 3 OR To Leave (U.K.) 3 OR	APPENDIX 4. OB

Army Form C. 2118.

WAR DIARY
or
INTELLIGENCE SUMMARY.

(Erase heading not required.)

3RD BATTN. M.G.C.

Place	Date	Hour	Summary of Events and Information	Remarks and references to Appendices
FOUQUEREUIL	June 27th		MAP. 36 A. S.E. Situation normal. CHOCQUES & L'ABBAYE shelled by H.V. guns from midnight for about 3 hours. Night harassing fire 11,500 rounds	
	28th		Evacuated from hospital 2 O.R. On leave 1 O.R. Situation normal. 930 rounds fired at enemy aircraft. Enemy artillery more active than usual. Heavy shells near Gonnehem. Night harassing fire 11,000 rounds. Evacuation MAJOR DES VOEUX. 1 O.R. Gonnehem 2 O.R. Rejoined from hospital 1 O.R. From leave 1 O.R.	
	29th	6 0 a.m. 10 0 a.m.	Situation normal. Operation order No. 27 issued. 500 rounds fired at enemy aircraft. Enemy artillery active - vicinity of Gonnehem. Enemy shelling again. Night harassing fire 11,000 rounds. Shelled about midnight. Gonnehem 1 O.R. On leave 1 O.R.	APPENDIX 7.

Army Form C. 2118.

WAR DIARY
or
INTELLIGENCE SUMMARY.
(Erase heading not required.)

3RD BATT. M.G.C.

Place	Date	Hour	Summary of Events and Information	Remarks and references to Appendices
FOUQUEREUIL	July 27	6.0 a.m.	MAP 36 A S.E. Situation normal. 15,000 rounds night harassing fire. Casualties 1 O.R.	O.R.
	28	6.0 a.m.	Situation normal. 10,000 rounds night harassing fire. 500 rounds fired at enemy aircraft. On night of 28/29 2nd Coy relieved 4th Coy in accordance with Operation Order No. 30. 2nd Lt. Jas. Year (U.K.) Major C.F. SWANN. 2 O.R. Gun laplice 4 O.R. Gun Centre 1 O.R. Casualties 1 O.R.	O.R.
	29	6.0 a.m.	Situation normal. 1500 rounds fired at enemy aircraft. 15,000 rounds night harassing fire. Gun Hospital 2 O.R. To Casualties 1 O.R. 2/Lieut. (U.K.) 2 O.R.	O.R.
	30	6.0 a.m.	Situation normal. 3500 rounds fired at enemy aircraft. Col. SOMERVILLE D.S.O. started 2 weeks leave. 14,000 rounds night harassing fire. 2nd Lieut. Lee 2 O.R. Reinforcements 4 O.R. Evacuated 3 O.R.	O.R.

Army Form C. 2118.

WAR DIARY
or
INTELLIGENCE SUMMARY.

(Erase heading not required.)

3RD BATTN. M.G.C.

Place	Date	Hour	Summary of Events and Information	Remarks and references to Appendices
FOUQUEREUIL	July 31st	6.0 p.m	MAP 36A S.E. Situation normal. 2000 rounds fired at enemy aircraft. Harassing fire. 10,000 rounds night. Reinforced 1 O.R. Grenades (A.R.) 1 O.R.	OS

W. Hermaston
Lieut. Col.
Commanding 3rd Battn. M.G.C.

APPENDIX. 1.

SECRET.

3rd. BATTALION MACHINE GUN CORPS.

DEFENCE SCHEME. COPY NO. 17

(PROVISIONAL). JULY 4th, 1918.

I. **TACTICAL DESCRIPTION OF THE DEFENCE AREA AND ITS SUB-DIVISIONS.**

1. (a) The Area for the Defence of which the Division is responsible forms the CENTRE Sector of the Corps front and is subdivided into three Brigade Sections known as the LOCON (right), AVELETTE (Centre) and HINGES (Left) Sections.
   Each Section is held by one Infantry Brigade.
   (b) The front held by the Division lies to the North of the LA BASSEE CANAL and extends from the LA LAWE CANAL (inclusive) in X.8.c. to point Q.34.c.4.2, N.E. of LA PANNERIE.

2. The main tactical features on the Corps Front are the LA LAWE and LA BASSEE CANALS, the HINGES - MT. BERNENCHON RIDGE and PACAUT WOOD.
   (a) The LA LAWE CANAL provides the means of forming a strong flank in the event of the Division on our right being driven in.
   (b) The LA BASSEE CANAL forms a natural obstacle of great strength round the base of the HINGES - MT. BERNENCHON RIDGE.
   (c) The HINGES-MT. BERNENCHON RIDGE provides complete observation over the whole Corps front and denies all observation to the enemy beyond the crest of the Ridge.
      Were the enemy to capture this Ridge the position would be reversed and all the advantages which accrue to us would pass to him. Moreover, the capture of the ground about HINGES would place the enemy in a dominating position on the flank of the Corps on our right.
      It is therefore necessary, to strengthen by all possible means the defences of MT. BERNENCHON and HINGES and to ensure the rapid reinforcement of those localities. In the event of any hostile success in this Area the most vigorous and decisive action is called for.
   (d) PACAUT WOOD forms a strong bastion flanking any advance over the open ground on either edge of it, with a view to forcing the Canal crossing. Developments in gas tactics have, however, largely discounted the defensive value of a wood and the possibility of being forced to withdraw the garrison must not be lost sight of. It is therefore desirable to create the strongest possible obstacle in and behind the Wood and to make special arrangements to cover the crossing of the Canal at this point by flanking fire.

3. The whole terrain North of the LA BASSEE CANAL is flat and open except in the vicinity of the villages and outlying farms where the hedges and orchards afford cover from view during the summer months.
   This country is low-lying and intersected with ditches and would rapidly become waterlogged after heavy rain.
   It is under direct observation from the HINGES - MT. BERNENCHON RIDGE, of which HINGES HILL forms the Eastern extremity.
   The Northern slopes of HINGES HILL fall abruptly down to the CANAL.

4. The proximity of the water level to the surface both of HINGES HILL and throughout the remainder of the Area precludes the possibility of constructing deep trenches or dug-outs.

/The

(1)

The only defences possible therefore, consist of shallow trenches, as cover from fire and view can only be obtained by the building up of substantial parapets and parados and the construction of concrete shelters.

This adds considerably to the amount of work involved in the construction of a strong defensive position and is a question of time and labour.

II ORGANIZATION OF THE AREA FOR DEFENCE.

5. The defences are organized into three Zones:-
   (a) A Forward Zone.
   (b) A Battle Zone.
   (c) A Rear Zone.

(a) The "Forward Zone" (1st. System).
   This consists of a line of Section Posts with supporting Posts arranged to cover the gaps and a main continuous line of defence.

(b) The "Battle Zone" (2nd. System).
   This consists of a front and reserve line with a support line in the Centre and Left Sections and a Retrenchment, constituting the 2nd. System.
   The CANAL LINE and PERTH LINE form the front line, the SUFFOLK and INVERNESS LINES form the Reserve Line.
   GORDON LINE forms the support line in this System, in the Centre and Left Brigade Sections.
   LANCASTER LINE, SHROPSHIRE LINE and BETHUNE RETRENCHMENT form a Retrenchment for the rear defence of HINGES HILL and BETHUNE.
   Included in the "Battle Zone" is the BETHUNE SWITCH connecting the reserve line of this Zone with the BETHUNE RETRENCHMENT.

(c) The "Rear Zone" (3rd. and 4th. Systems).
   This consists of two systems of trenches with certain switch lines.
   (i) 3rd. System - The CHOCQUES LINE and CLARENCE SWITCH.
   (ii) 4th. System - The LILLERS - HOUCHIN LINE.
   These systems are so designed that if any portion of the line is penetrated it may be possible to throw back a flank to the next system without abandoning the whole line.

6. The following is a brief description of the lines of Defence in the "Rear Zone".
   (i) CHOCQUES LINE AND CLARENCE SWITCH. (3rd. System).
   The CHOCQUES LINE consists of a front and support line of breastwork and trench, and a system of trenches in rear on the forward and reverse slopes of CHOCQUES HILL, which is an important tactical feature as it dominates the whole of the surrounding country.
   The CLARENCE SWITCH runs along the Western Bank of the CLARENCE RIVER, the Northern portion only has been constructed but the River Bank itself is defensible.
   (ii) LILLERS - HOUCHIN LINE. (4th. System).
   Consists of front, support and reserve lines of trench and breastwork.
   The main tactical features in this line are the Spur in D.18. and E.13, the village and chateau of LABEUVRIERE and the Spur in D.10.
   (iii) The REVEILLON LINE forms a switch between the CHOCQUES LINE and LILLERS - HOUCHIN LINE.
   It consists of a continuous breastwork front line with breastwork support and reserve lines in places and is designed for defence against a hostile advance from the North.

7. LOCALITIES.
   In addition to the various systems of defence in the "Battle" and "Rear" Zones, it is the intention to organize a series of localities and keeps capable of all-round defence. The provision of shell-proof accommodation for the garrison is an essential factor in defences of this nature.

/Many

Many concrete Machine Gun Nests and shelters are at present under construction, and when this work is further advanced the question of grouping them to form localities will be considered.

Work has already commenced on certain localities in the "Rear" Zone, i.e. STAR KEEP (E.10.a), FOSSE NO. 1. d'ANNEZIN and L'ABBAYE.

8. The Division is responsible for the construction and maintenance of all defences forward of the CLARENCE SWITCH – CHOCQUES LINE.

The Corps is responsible for all defences in and West of the above Line.

Brigades are responsible for the construction and maintenance of all defences in the 1st, and 2nd. Systems.

III PLAN ON WHICH THE CONDUCT OF THE DEFENCE IS TO BE CARRIED OUT.

9. GENERAL PRINCIPLES.

The following are the general principles on which the defence will be conducted:-
(a) The first principle in all defensive action is the stubborn resistance of every post or trench to the last man and the last round.
(b) Every Commander will endeavour to keep a proportion of his force in hand for immediate counter attack.
(c) Every position down to Section Posts must be prepared for the contingency of having its flank turned, and steps must be taken by defilading, throwing back a flank or other means to enable the position to be fought in spite of this.
(d) All arms will be distributed for defence in depth.
(e) No withdrawals will take place without definite orders from higher command, and failing such orders, positions must be fought to the last.

DEFENCE.

10. Each Brigade will hold its front with one Battalion in the "Forward Zone" and one Battalion in the "Battle Zone" with one Battalion in Brigade Reserve in the "Rear Zone".

11. The role of the troops holding the 1st. System (Forward Zone) is to break up and disorganize a hostile attack before it reaches the "Battle Zone".

The enemy must not be permitted to approach the CANAL.

No ground will be given up and every foot of ground must be stubbornly contested.

Immediate local counter attacks by the troops holding this System will be delivered on the responsibility of the local Commander on the spot, to recapture any portion which may be temporarily lost.

12. The "Battle Zone" will be held at all costs and all the efforts of the Division will be concentrated to this end.

Brigade Commanders will utilise all the resources at their disposal including the Artillery and Machine Guns, of their respective groups to regain their ground.

13. In the event of attack and it becoming evident that the attack is confined to one flank of the Division only, or to the front of a neighbouring Division, it may, in the case of immediate and pressing urgency be necessary to send one or more of the Battalions in Brigade reserve to the threatened Area.

14. If it is decided to counter attack by troops in Brigade Reserve to retake part of the "Battle Zone" under orders of Divisional Commander, of any position of the front affected, all available machine guns will concentrate on the area affected.

15. (a) With this end in view at each machine gun position there will be a 'Fighting Map' so that the maximum fire power can be switched on to the area affected in the minimum of time. Map 'A' attached shows areas of concentration.

19. (contd)
Report Centres will be established as follows:-
Right Group.
    LONG CORNET   (W.23.b.95.20)
Centre Group.
    No. 10. Position. (W.23.b.05.80)
    LE PLUOY FARM   (W.16.b.45.80)
    LE JAUDRIE FARM (W.23.b.75.15)
Left Group.
    LE VERBANNOY   (W.9.c.8.8)
    LE PLUOY FARM   (W.16.b.45.80)
    No. 14. Position. (W.10.c.70.35)

20. ANTI-AIRCRAFT DEFENCE.
The Forward Area will be covered by several Lines of Vickers and Lewis Guns arranged in depth on the following principle:
(a) 1st. Line - 500 yards in rear of the main line of Defence of the 1st. System.
    2nd. Line - 1,000 yards in rear of the 1st. Line.
    3rd. Line - 1,000 yards in rear of the 2nd. Line.
    4th. Line - 1,000 yards in rear of the 3rd. Line.
(b) Vickers Guns in conjunction with Lewis Guns will be placed to cover the 1st. and 2nd. Lines. (See Map "C" attached).
(c) In each line, guns should be placed in pairs, at intervals of 1,000 yards.
If single guns are employed these should not be placed at a greater interval than 500 yards.
(d) In each line, the outer flank guns of the Division will not be further than 400 yards from the Divisional Boundary.
(e) At each position, a copy of the orders for Anti-Aircraft - Vickers Guns will be kept. (Appendix 2.)
(f) Belts for use by Anti-aircraft Vickers Guns will be filled as follows:-
    One round TRACER Ammunition.
    Three rounds A.P.   "
    One round TRACER   "
    Three rounds Ordinary Ammunition.

S.O.S. and 'SHORTEN RANGE' SIGNAL.

21. (a) The "S.O.S" will only be used when an actual attack is developing and will not be sent up for a bombardment only.
(b) The "S.O.S" Signal will be repeated from the Artillery O.P's.

22. A RED smoke bomb dropped by one of our aeroplanes during active operations indicates that enemy is forming up for attack opposite the front where the bomb is dropped.

23. In the event of an attack and the enemy reaching the CANAL between W.11.d. Central and LA PANNERIE a "Shorten Range" Signal which will be a rocket fired from a mortar bursting into Three lights - GREEN - RED - GREEN, will be put up from any of the following places:
    (a) Infantry Battalion H.Q. at W.22.a.2.8.
    (b) Infantry Battalion H.Q. at W.10.c.1.9.
    (c) Artillery O.P. at W.16.a.60.75.
    (d) Artillery O.P. at W.23.c.80.30.
Upon this Signal the Machine Guns covering this portion of the front will put down their barrage for the protection of the front line of the BATTLE SYSTEM as per Map "D" attached.

GENERAL.

24. All Machine Guns will be prepared to open fire on any target that may present itself or on their "S.O.S" Lines.
Should the enemy commence an intense bombardment, Machine Guns will fire bursts of fire on their "S.O.S" Lines, searching forward.

15. (b) Area "A". Should the Right Brigade front be affected, Guns Number 8, 9, 10, 11, 12, 13, 14, 17, 19, and 20. will switch their fire on Area "A" as per map attached. There will be a total of 32 guns shooting on this area.
   (c) Area "B" Should the CENTRE Brigade front be affected, Guns Number 3, 4, 8, 9, 10, 11, 12, 13, 14, 15, 17, 18 (2 guns), 19, and 20 will switch their fire on to Area "B". There will be a total of 42 guns shooting on this Area.
   (d) Area "C" Should the LEFT Brigade front be affected Guns number 3, 4, 5, 6, 7, 8, 9, 11, 12, 13, 14, 15, 16, 17, 18, 19, and 20 will switch their fire on Area "C". There will be a total of 48 guns shooting on this Area.
   (e) Should a general attack take place along the whole Divisional front, guns will shoot on their normal S.O.S. Lines as shown on Map "B" attached.
   (f) Eight guns will be in Divisional Reserve and be prepared to re-inforce any portion of the front at the shortest notice.

16. Machine Guns will be distributed in depth and will be grouped into three groups, one group for the defence by direct fire of each Brigade Area.

    Right Group ... ... 16 Guns.
    Centre Group ... ... 22 Guns.
    Left Group ... ... 18 Guns.

    The forward Guns will be in pairs; the rear guns will be arranged as far as possible in batteries of four guns.

    Machine Gun Group H.Q. will be at, or close to Infantry Brigade H.Q. Section H.Q. will be at the Battery when guns are grouped into Batteries of four guns; when guns are split up into single guns or pairs of guns, the Section H.Q. will be with the most important gun or guns.

    S.O.S. Lines and Battle Lines are shown on Map "B" attached.

    S.O.S. Lines are so arranged as to augment the artillery barrage, fill up any gaps and where possible, bring enfilade fire to bear along the Divisional Front.

    Machine Guns are therefore not/firing on S.O.S. on the front of
    necessarily
    the Brigade to which they are allotted.

    Battle Lines are so arranged so as to cover by direct fire the area of the Brigades to which they are allotted, and in conjunction with Lewis Guns to sweep by direct fire the Bridges across the CANAL.

    PROTECTION.
17. If 'dead' ground or covered lines of approach render guns liable to be surprised, patrols or scouts must be sent out. If necessary, Infantry Commanders should be required to furnish escorts.

18. At each Gun position the following stores will be maintained:-
    15 boxes S.A.A.
    16 belts in boxes (reserved for use on Battle Line).
    8 belts in S.A.A. Boxes.
    Bombs - detonated.
    Very Lights.
    ½ pint of oil.
    2 galls. of water (for use in guns).
    Chloride of Lime.
    Two picks and two shovels.
    One Ground Sheet.
    A number board showing the number of the Emplacement.
    One or more 'Order Boards' suitably constructed to protect them from the weather. (Appendix 1).
    Inventory Board.

19. COMMUNICATIONS.
    Telephones and Telegraph.
    Communication will be established from Group H.Q. forward to Report centres. The fullest use will at all times be made of existing Infantry lines.

/Report.

25. In the event of any portion of the line being broken, Machine Gun Groups concerned will come into action on their "BATTLE LINES".

They will return to their "S.O.S" Lines only if, and when, the original line has been restored.

26. OCCUPATION OF DEFENCES IN THE 'REAR ZONE'.
In the event of the Division being forced to withdraw from its present position in face of superior numbers, it would withdraw fighting, to successive lines of Defence.

All rear lines of Defence will therefore be reconnoitred by all Officers, where this has not already been done, with a view to the occupation in the case of necessity, so that, should the necessity arise, these successive lines of Defence may be occupied without delay and confusion.

These rear lines of Defence are given in para 6.

27. Machine Gun positions for the Defense of each Line have been selected. These positions are given in Appendix 3.

28. ANTI-GAS DEFENCE.
The Orders contained in Appendix iv of S.S. 534 will be strictly adhered to.

The most careful training in Anti-Gas measures and Gas discipline will be carried out by all Companies.

All troops in the Battalion will wear their gas masks for one hour at least, twice in each week, and will be worked in them in the use of the weapons with which they are armed.

All Headquarters, or at least a portion of all headquarters will be made as gas-proof as possible.

Sections in Divisional Reserve will be practised in marching in their gas-masks.

29. When an Area is shelled with 'Yellow Cross' Gas, the Gas Officer of the Company or companies concerned will at once carry out an investigation, and advise his O.C., Company, who in turn will inform Battln. H.Q., as to whether the concentration of Gas is sufficient, or is likely to become sufficient to warrant the evacuation of the Area.

30. When an Area is shelled with Gas, Section Officers in the Area affected will at once order Respirators to be adjusted, and will, when, possible, and the tactical situation permits, move their troops to a flank to windward of the shelled area.

The affected Area will NOT be re-occupied until declared free of Gas by the Gas Officer of the nearest Infantry Battalion.

If for tactical reasons it is considered essential that Posts should be left in the Area affected, these Posts must be constantly relieved.

It must be borne in mind that when the enemy bombards an Area with Gas, previous to attack, he will rarely advance over the gas-affected area but will attempt to gain ground on the flanks. The flanks of the bombarded areas must therefore be carefully watched.

31. (a) Reports of Gas-shelling will be at once forwarded by Groups to Battln. H.Q., and will give the following particulars in so far as they can be ascertained:
    (i) Nature of Gas.
    (ii) Degree of intensity in terms of the approximate number of rounds falling per minute.
    (iii) Area Affected.
    (iv) Suspected location of active hostile batteries.
(b) Reports of any gas shelling of 500 rounds and over will invariably be passed to all units within 2,000 yards radius of the area affected.
(c) Sentries will be posted round an area contaminated by "Yellow Cross" Gas, whose duties will be to warn anyone entering the area to adjust their box respirators.

/Sentries.

Sentries will not be withdrawn until the Gas Officer of the nearest Infantry Battalion has declared the Area free from Gas.

C.T. Smith
Lieut. & A/Adjt.,
3rd. Battln. M. G. Corps.

Issued at................

Copies to:-
- ✱1. D.M.G.C.
- ✱2. 2nd-in-Command.
- ✱3. O.C. "A" Coy.
- ✱4. O.C. "B" "
- ✱5. O.C. "C" "
- ✱6. O.C. "D" "
- ✱7. "G" 3rd. Div.
- ✱8. C.R.A.
- 9. 8th. Inf. Bde.
- 10. 9th. Inf. Bde.
- 11. 76th. Inf. Bde.
- 12. T.O.
- 13. Q.M.
- 14. M.O.
- 15. S.O.
- 16. War Diary ✓
- 17. " "
- 18. File.
- 19. 4? Br M G C
- 20. 46
- ✱21. C M G C

Maps to starred copies only.

POSITION NO..................

ORDER BOARD NO. 2.

IN THE EVENT OF "S.O.S"	Gun will open fire on the "S.O.S" Line at the maximum rate for 3 minutes and will then continue to fire at the rate of one belt per gun per 3 minutes for 10 minutes when fire will be directed according to the situation.

Sixteen full belts will be reserved for fire on the BATTLE ZONE.

IN THE EVENT OF HEAVY ENEMY BOMBARDMENT.	Gun will open fire on the "S.O.S" Line at the rate of one belt per gun per 5 minutes for 30 minutes. If bombardment continues gun will cease fire and the gun teams will 'Stand-to'. Fire will be re-opened according to the situation.
IN THE EVENT OF CLOUD GAS ATTACK OR SHELL GAS ATTACHMENT.	The Gun will fire on its "S.O.S" or BATTLE LINE should its fire be required. If fire is not required: (1) Belt boxes will be closed. (2) The gun covered with a waterproof sheet. (3) The recoiling portions will be worked backwards and forwards at intervals of 10 minutes. When the gas has dispersed the gun and parts will be cleaned and oiled.
IN THE EVENT OF A "BREAK-THROUGH" BY THE ENEMY.	The gun will engage any targets within range. PROVIDED ALWAYS THAT ITS FIRE IS NOT REQUIRED ON THE BATTLE LINE.

AMMUNITION AND STORES ETC., TO BE MAINTAINED
AT THE GUN EMPLACEMENT.

--------oOo--------

..........Boxes S.A.A.
16 Full Belts in boxes.
8 Full Belts in S.A.A. Boxes.
2 Gallons of Water.
½ pint of oil.
½ pint of Glycerine.
One ground sheet (for covering gun).
Chloride of Lime.
1 box bombs.
Very Lights.
2 picks and 2 shovels.
Range Card.
Position Number Board.
Order Board.
Inventory Board.
Rations.

POSITION NO.......... APPENDIX 1.

ORDER BOARD NO..1...

This Gun forms part of the framework of the Infantry Defence, and will be fought to the last man, and the last round of ammunition.

The function of the Gun is the immediate defence of:-

Gun on Right.   Gun on Left.

BATTLE LINE.

   From Gun to...

   Bearing..

   Reading on Mounting..

   Elevation..

   Direction marked by
   Stake 10 yards in front of Gun...............................

S.O.S. LINE.

   Covering...

   Bearing..

   Reading on Mounting..

   Elevation..

   Direction marked by Stake
   in front of Gun..

   Range..

The gun will cease fire on the "S.O.S" Line and prepare to fire on the BATTLE LINE, if and when it appears that the enemy has broken into our Trench System in the direction of the "S.O.S" LINE, or in the direction of the "BATTLE LINE".

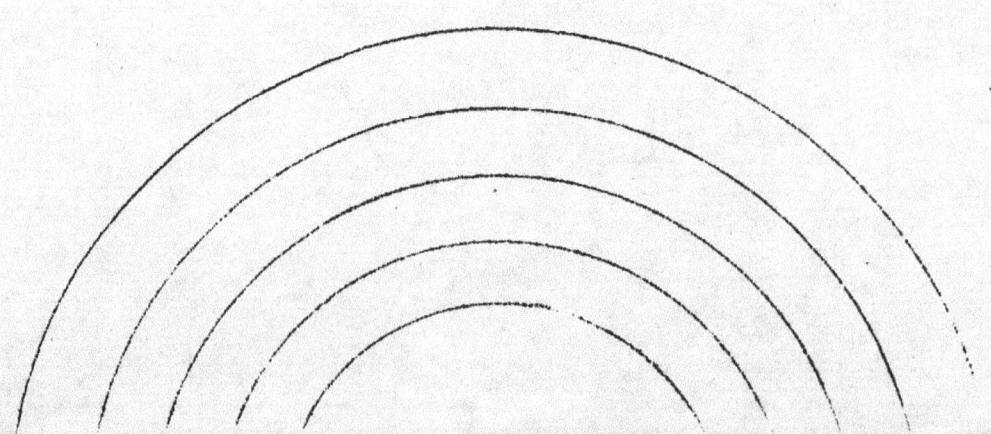

APPENDIX 2.

3rd. BATTALION MACHINE GUN CORPS.

ORDERS FOR ANTI-AIRCRAFT POSITIONS.

1. One sentry will always be on duty at the position.

2. By day fire will not be opened on hostile aircraft unless the markings or struts can be clearly seen with the naked eye.

3. By night fire will not be opened on aircraft unless they clearly demonstrate their hostility by dropping bombs, or opening machine gun fire, or their identity is clearly identified in the beam of a searchlight.

   NOTE:- As a general rule it may be taken that at night an aeroplane is within range of machine gun fire:
   (a) if the 'plane can be seen against the sky,
   (b) if the struts can be seen when in the beam of a searchlight.

4. Long bursts of fire will be used.

5. Two belts in belt boxes will be at each position.

6. Belts will be fitted as follows:-
   One round Tracer Ammunition.
   Three rounds A.P. Ammunition.
   One round Tracer Ammunition.
   Three rounds Ordinary Ammunition.

June 20th, 1918.

APPENDIX 3.

SUITABLE MACHINE GUN POSITIONS FOR DEFENCE OF VARIOUS LINES.

BETHUNE RETRENCHMENT & LANCASTER LINE.			CHOCQUES LINE, CLARENCE SWITCH and CHOCQUES LINE DEFENCE.			LILLERS – HOUCHIN LINE.		
No.	Map Reference	No. of Guns	No.	Map Reference	No. of Guns	No.	Map Reference	No. of Guns
DIRECT.			**DIRECT.**			**DIRECT.**		
18.	W.9.c.70.15 (2)		B.1	E.8.b.80.20	2	C.1	E.19.a.55.40	4
	W.9.c.20.80 (2)	4	B.2	E.2.d.50.00	2	C.2	E.19.a.25.85	4
A.6	E.3.d.45.35	2	B.3	E.2.d.35.80	2	C.3	D.18.d.35.35	4
A.7	E.3.b.60.40	2	B.4	E.2.a.20.90	4	C.4	E.13.c.40.90	4
A.9	W.27.d.05.40	4	B.4a	E.1.b.20.50	4	C.5	E.13.a.20.40	4
A.10	W.26.b.45.35	4	B.5	W.25.a.40.90	4	C.6	D.11.d.20.70	4
A.11	W.26.b.85.90	4	B.6	V.30.b.70.90	4	C.7	D.10.c.85.30	4
A.12	W.21.c.60.90	4	B.7	E.2.c.20.90	4	C.8	D.10.a.60.70	4
		24			26	C.9	D.4.c.00.00	4
						C.10	D.3.b.35.20	4
						C.11	D.3.b.05.80	4
						C.12	V.27.a.80.20	4
								48
INDIRECT (W 20 a 60.40)			**INDIRECT**					
A.13	W.20.a.90.30 (2)		B.8	E.14.c.50.80	2			
	W.9.c.20.80 (2)	4	B.9	E.14.a.05.65	4			
A.14	W.13.d.75.20	4	B.10	E.7.b.60.15	4			
A.15	W.13.c.30.90	4	B.11	E.7.b.00.90	4			
B.1	E.8.d.90.95	2	B.12	E.1.d.05.90	2			
B.2	E.2.d.45.55	2	B.13	E.1.a.20.20	4			
B.3	E.2.d.35.80	2	B.14	V.30.a.55.90	2			
B.4	E.2.a.20.90	4	C.4	E.13.c.40.90	4			
B.4a	E.1.b.20.50	4	C.5	E.13.a.20.40	4			
B.5	W.25.a.40.90	4			30.			
B.7	E.2.c.20.90	4						
		34						

REVEILLON LINE.			BETHUNE SWITCH.		
DIRECT.			**DIRECT.**		
B.6	V.30.b.70.90	4	A.1	W.30.a.00.75	2
B.14	V.30.a.55.00	2	A.2	W.29.b.20.00	2
B.16	V.28.b.25.55	2	A.3	W.29.d.10.40	2
B.17	V.28.a.45.45	2	A.4	W.29.a.60.95	4
C.12	V.27.a.80.20	4	A.5	W.29.c.40.80	4
		14.	A.6	E.3.d.45.35	2
			A.7	E.3.b.30.40	2
					18.
INDIRECT.			**INDIRECT.**		
B.15	D.5.a.05.70	2	A.8	W.28.c.15.65	4
C.6	D.11.d.20.70	4	A.9	W.27.d.05.40	4
C.8	D.10.a.60.70	4	A.10	W.26.b.45.35	4
C.9	D.4.c.00.00	4	A.11	W.26.b.85.90	4
C.10	D.3.b.35.20	4	A.12	W.21.c.60.90	4
C.11	D.3.b.05.80	4	B.1	E.8.d.90.95	2
		22.	B.2	E.2.d.45.55	2
			B.3	E.2.d.35.80	2
			B.4	E.2.a.20.90	4
					30.

DS.M/683/1.   SECRET.

3rd. Battalion Machine Gun Corps 'DEFENCE SCHEME'. (DS.M/683) dated July 4th. 1918.

Sub-paras (c) and (d) of Para. 23 will be amended to read as follows:-

(c) Artillery O.Ps' in W.16.a., W.10.a, and W.9.b. (Day only).

(d) Artillery O.Ps' at W.23.c.80.30 and W.14.b.40.70 (Night only).

July 6th. 1918.
                                                Capt. & Adjt.,
                                          3rd. Battln. M. G. Corps.

To all Recipients of Battalion 'Defence Scheme' (DS.M/683/1.)

TO:- War Diary (1) ....

DS.M/683/2.

SECRET.

3rd. Battalion Machine Gun Corps 'DEFENCE SCHEME'.
(DS.M/683) dated July 4th. 1918.

Para. 19. COMMUNICATIONS, will be amended to read as follows:
Report Centres.
Centre Group. LE JAUDRIE FARM (W.22.a.85.90)
No. 10. Position (W.23.b.05.65)

[signature]
Capt. & Adjt.,
3rd. Battln. M. G. Corps.

July 6th. 1918.

To all recipients of Battalion 'DEFENCE SCHEME' (DS.M/683).

To:- *War Diary* **SECRET** O.O./28/1.

Amendment to Operation Orders No. 28. dated July 7th. 1918.

Please read para. 1. as Follows:-

1. On the night July 9th/10th. "C" Company will relieve "B" Company in positions now occupied by "B" Company in RIGHT GROUP.
"C" and "B" Companies to ACKNOWLEDGE.

Calla

Capt. & Adjt.,
3rd. Battln. M. G. Corps.

July 7th. 1918.

SECRET.

TO:- **War Diary**

DS.M/683/3.

Amendments No. 3. to 3rd. Battalion M.G. Corps 'DEFENCE SCHEME'
(Provisional) dated July 4th. 1918. (DS.M/683).

Para. 14. is amended to read:-
If it is decided to counter attack by troops in Brigade Reserve to retake part of the 'Battle Zone' under orders of Divisional Commander, of any portion of the front affected, all available Machine Guns will be prepared to concentrate on the Area affected.

Para. 15, sub-paras. (a), (b), (c), (d), (e) and (f), are cancelled.

Para. 15. will now read as follows:-

Para. 15. (a) In drawing up their plans Brigade Commanders can only count on having at their immediate disposal the Artillery and Machine guns of their respective groups.
If time and the tactical situation permit, Artillery and machine guns covering other portions of the front will be ordered by Divisional H.Q. to co-operate.
(b) With this end in view, at each machine gun position there will be a 'Fighting Map' so that the maximum fire power can be switched on to the Area affected in the minimum of time.
(c) Eight guns will be in Divisional Reserve and be prepared to re-inforce any portion of the front at the shortest notice.

PLEASE ACKNOWLEDGE.

July 8th. 1918.

Capt. & Adjt.,
3rd. Battln. M.G.Corps.

APPENDIX 2

3rd. BATTALION MACHINE GUN CORPS.

SECRET.

OPERATION ORDERS NO. 28.

COPY NO. 15

JULY 7th. 1918.

Reference Map:— 36, A, S.E.

1. On the night July 8th/9th, "C" Company will relieve "B" Company in positions now occupied by "B" Company in RIGHT GROUP.

2. On relief "B" Company will pass into Divisional Reserve and will occupy positions and billets at present occupied by "C" Company.

3. Nos. 1. of both Companies will remain with incoming gun teams for 24 hours after relief and occupation of Reserve positions.

4. Details of relief will be arranged direct between Company Commanders concerned.

5. Completion of relief and occupation of Reserve positions will be reported to Battln. H.Q. by O.C. "C" Company and O.C. "B" Company respectively by code word — Company Commander's Name.

6. Company Commanders concerned will obtain all available information regarding role of guns in positions to be taken over, work in progress etc. Trench Stores will be handed over and copy of same rendered to Battln. H.Q.

7. ACKNOWLEDGE.

Capt. & Adjt.,
3rd. Battln. M.G. Corps.

Issued at 10.30 a.m.

Copies To:-
1. D.M.G.C.
2. O.C. "A" Coy.
3. O.C. "B" "
4. O.C. "C" "
5. O.C. "D" "
6. "G" 3rd. Div.
7. C.R.A.
8. 8th. Inf. Bde.
9. 9th. " "
10. 76th. Inf. Bde.
11. T.O.
12. Q.M.
13. M.O.
14. S.O.
15. War Diary.
16.
17. File.

APPENDIX 3

3rd. BATTALION MACHINE GUN CORPS.

OPERATION ORDERS NO. 29.

SECRET.

COPY NO...19...

JULY 18th. 1918.

Reference Map 36,A. S.E.

1. On the night July 20th/21st. "B" Company will relieve "D" Company in positions now occupied by "D" Company in LEFT GROUP.

2. On relief "D" Company will pass into Divisional Reserve and will occupy positions and billets at present occupied by "B" Company.

3. Nos. 1. of both Companies will remain with incoming gun teams for 24 hours after relief and occupation of Reserve positions.

4. Details of relief will be arranged direct between Company Commanders concerned.

5. Completion of relief and occupation of Reserve positions will be reported to Battln. H.Q. by O.C. "B" Company and O.C. "D" Company respectively by code word - Company Commander's Name.

6. Company Commanders concerned will obtain all available information regarding role of guns in positions to be taken over, work in progress etc. Trench Stores will be handed over and copy of same rendered to Battln. H.Q.

7. ACKNOWLEDGE.

Capt. & Adjt.,
3rd. Battln. M. G. Corps.

Issued at...6.15 pm

Copies to:-
1. D.M.G.C.
2. 2/in/Command.
3. O.C. "A" Coy.
4. O.C. "B" "
5. O.C. "C" "
6. O.C. "D" "
7. "G" 3rd. Div.
8. C.R.A.
9. 8th. Inf.Bde.
10. 9th. " "
11. 76th. Inf.Bde.
12. 4th. Bn.M.G.C.
13. 46th.Bn.M.G.C.
14. T.O.
15. Q.M.
16. M.O.
17. S.O.
18. War Diary.
19. " "
20. File.

Amendment to Operation Orders No. 30.   S E C R E T.

Para. 3. is CANCELLED.

                                                  [signature]
                                                  Capt. & Adjt.,
July 26th. 1918.   3rd. Battln. M.G.Corps.

To. War Diary

APPENDIX 4.

SECRET.

3rd. BATTALION MACHINE GUN CORPS.

OPERATION ORDERS NO. 30.

COPY NO. ...18...

JULY 26th. 1918.

Reference Map 56,A. S.E.

1. On the night July 28th/29th. "D" Coy. will relieve "A" Coy. in positions now occupied by "A" Coy. in CENTRE GROUP.

2. On relief "A" Coy. will pass into Divisional Reserve and will occupy positions and billets at present occupied by "D" Company.

3. Nos. 1. of both Companies will remain with incoming gun teams for 24 hours after relief and occupation of reserve positions.

4. Details of relief will be arranged direct between Company Commanders concerned.

5. Completion of relief and occupation of Reserve positions will be reported to Battln. H.Q. by O.C. "D" Company and O.C. "A" Company respectively by Company's letter, and time.

6. Company Commanders concerned will obtain all available information regarding role of guns in positions to be taken over, work in progress etc. Trench Stores will be handed over and copy of same rendered to Battln. H.Q.

7. ACKNOWLEDGE.

Capt. & Adjt.,
3rd. Battln. M.G.Corps.

Issued at 7pm

Copies to:-
1. D.M.G.C.   11. 76th. Inf. Bde.
2. 2nd/i/C.   12. 4th. Bn.M.G.C.
3. O.C. "A" Coy.   13. 46th.   do
4. O.C. "B" "   14. T.O.
5. O.C. "C" "   15. Q.M.
6. O.C. "D" "   16. M.O.
7. "G" 3rd.Div.   17. S.O.
8. C.R.A.   18. War Diary.
9. 8th. Inf.Bde.   19. "   "
10. 9th. "   "   20. File.

WAR DIARY
or
INTELLIGENCE SUMMARY 3RD BATTⁿ M.G.C.

Army Form C. 2118.

Place	Date	Hour	Summary of Events and Information	Remarks and references to Appendices
FOUQUEREUIL	Aug 1	6.0 a.m.	MAP 36A.SE Situation normal. 5000 rounds fired at enemy aircraft 13,500 rounds night harassing fire Casualties 4 O.R. injured from bombs 3 O.R. to date 1 O.R. gas shells. 1 O.R.	O.R.S
	2	6.0 a.m	Situation normal. 530 rounds fired at aircraft 13,500 rounds night harassing fire. Casualties 1 O.R.	O.R.S
	3	6.0 a.m	Situation normal. 500 rounds fired at enemy aircraft 13,000 rounds night harassing fire. At Divisional Rifle Range to fire Lewis gun course Ex Lt Watts Lt Humber, Lt Oscar, Lt L.D. Burton, 1st A/C Knox A/Cpl, 3rd Lt Leasdale B4 Lt Carr, Lt O.B Sadler, L/Cpl Brice 'C' 2nd Pte Balaam A. Consionson M.O. S. Beaton 3rd Pte Smith A Cpl Officers from Army 3rd at LA ROCH M.C. Casualties 2 O.R. to Base 1 O.R. From Brigade 2 O.R. to U.K. pn Commsn 1 O.R.	O.R.S

WAR DIARY or INTELLIGENCE SUMMARY

3RD BATTN. M.G.C.

Army Form C. 2118.

Place	Date	Hour	Summary of Events and Information	Remarks and references to Appendices
FOUQUEREUIL	Aug 4th	3.0 a.m	MAP. 36A. S.E. FOUQUEREUIL Shelled by 4.2" Gun 3 shots fell near Church	
		6.0 a.m	Situation normal 1000 rounds fired at enemy aircraft during the day	APPENDIX 1
			C.O. visited by Lt Col. COX M.C. O/c Battn M.G.C. re Mg supplies to relief Operation Order No 31 issued	
		8.45 p.m	Smoke bomb dropped by enemy aircraft at about	
		W.4.b.85.85	12,000 rounds Mg's harassing fire	
			Strength 2 O.R. to reinforce 12 O.R. 2/Lt S.R. HOLBROOK 2/Lt W.L. SIMS & 3 O.R. from hospital 3 O.R.	
	5th	6.0 a.m	Situation normal 500 rounds fired at enemy aircraft during day	
			3,000 rounds of night harassing fire by centre group Reg.ts & left group relieved by 19 "B" Battn M.G.C. "A" "B" & "C" Coys in FOUQUEREUIL	
			Strength 2 O.R. on leave 3 O.R. Transferred to RE 1 O.R. from hosp. 1 O.R.	
	6th	6.0 a.m	Situation normal	
		1.30 p.m	Lunatic bomb dropped No 32 aeroplane Operation Order No 32 arranged H.Q. 19th Battn M.G.C.	APPENDIX 2
		4.30 p.m	Centre group ("D" Coy + Section of "A") relieved from hospital 2/Lt R.J. WILLIAMS 1 O.R.	
		11.0		

Army Form C. 2118

WAR DIARY
or
INTELLIGENCE SUMMARY.
(Erase heading not required.)

3RD BATTN M.G.C.

Place	Date	Hour	Summary of Events and Information	Remarks and references to Appendices
FOUQUEREUIL	Aug 7th		MAP 36A. SE	
		6.15 a.m.	"D" Coy for BEUGIN plus 1 Rnk. Section of "A" 1.20 O.R. of	JB
			"B" "D" "C" Coy for CAMBLAIN - CHATELAIN.	
		7.30 a.m.	"D" Coy reported arrived at BEUGIN.	
		10.0 a.m.	Battn. less "D" Coy, 1 R.B. section of "A" 1.20 O.R. of CAMBLAIN - CHATELAIN.	
			"A" "B" "C" Coy commenced the march for CAMBLAIN - CHATELAIN.	
		11.30 a.m.	"D" Coy transport in charge of 2/Lt STOCKDALE reported arrived at BEUGIN.	
		12.45 p.m.	Battn arrived & billeted at CAMBLAIN - CHATELAIN. Evacuation 2. O.R. Reported from hospital 2. O.R.	
CAMBLAIN-CHATELAIN.	8h		Baths. Taking gun kit & limbers to Extension 8. O.R. from hospital 1. O.R. from leave (Paris) 3. O.R. (UK) 1. O.R.	JB
	9h		Reconnaissance by all Officers of OURTON for intended Tactical Scheme Extension 1. O.R. Reinforcement 2/Lt R. BALKWELL from hospital 1. O.R. from leave 5. O.R. Evacuation 1. O.R. 4. O.R. to leave (UK) 4 O.R. (Paris) 2. O.R.	JB

Army Form C. 2118.

WAR DIARY
or
INTELLIGENCE SUMMARY.

(Erase heading not required.)

3RD BATT^N M.G.C.

Place	Date	Hour	Summary of Events and Information	Remarks and references to Appendices
CAMBLAIN-CHATELAIN	Aug 10.		Corps on range for rifle & revolver practice. To date (UK) 1.O.R. Transferred to Scot Rifles 1.O.R.	
	11.	10.45 a.m.	Battalion church parade. Evacuation 5.O.R. To date (UK) 2.O.R. From bombers ½ Lt S.R. HOLBROOK 2/Lt W.L. SAMS 3.O.R.	
	12.	5.0 p.m.	Corps training shooting - revolver drill. Warning Order received from Division to prepare for move. From Leave 1.O.R. To Leave 3.O.R.	
	13.	6.30 a.m.	Operation order 33 issued	APPENDIX 3
		9.0 a.m.	"B" Coy from CAMBLAIN-CHATELAIN & "D" Coy from BEUGIN marched to BRYAS & entrained for WARLINCOURT under command of MAJOR MOFFETT M.C.	
		2.30 p.m.	D.H.Q. "A" & "C" Coys marched to PERNES & entrained for WARLINCOURT.	
		9.0	D.H.Q. "A" & "C" Coys billeted at BOUQUE-MAISON. Evacuation 5.O.R. To Cadre U.K. 1.O.R. From Leave 1.O.R. From Leave 2.O.R. To Leave 1.O.R.	

Army Form C. 2118.

WAR DIARY
or
INTELLIGENCE SUMMARY.

(Erase heading not required.)

3RD BATTⁿ M.G.C.

Place	Date	Hour	Summary of Events and Information	Remarks and references to Appendices
IVERGNY	Aug 14	1.30 a.m.	All Companies in billets at IVERGNY. Transport arrived by road from PERNES & ANVIN.	O.R
		2.5 a.m.	Transport arrived march from ANVIN	
		8.0 p.m.	Transport 2 late 1 O.R. Evacuated 2 O.R	
	15 "	5.30 a.m.	Transport arrived at IVERGNY. 2 Rank 2 O.R. Evacuated 2 O.R	O.R
	16 "		Companies reorganised for tactical scheme. 2 late 3 O.R.	O.R
	17 "		All Companies on tactical scheme. Evacuated 8 O.R. from Centre 1 O.R. 2 Ranks 3 O.R. from Ranks CAPT A.W. CRAVEN + 1 O.R	O.R
	18 "	11.45 a.m.	Battalion Church Parade.	O.R
		9.0 p.m.	C.O. attended Conference at Divisional Head Quarters.	
		11.30 "	Conference at Battⁿ H.Q. of Coy Commanders + Transport Officer. Evacuated 1 O.R. 2 late 1 O.R	

Army Form C. 2118.

WAR DIARY
or
INTELLIGENCE SUMMARY

3RD BATT^N M.G.C.

(Erase heading not required.)

Place	Date	Hour	Summary of Events and Information	Remarks and references to Appendices
IVERGNY	Aug 19	2.0 a.m.	Awam Operation order No 259 received.	APPENDIX 4
		11.30 a.m.	All officers & N.C.O's attended lecture by G.S.O. 2nd Tank Corps at SUS ST. LEGER	O.R.
		12.0 noon	Operation Order No 34 issued	
		9.30 p.m.	Battalion commenced the march from IVERGNY. Evacuation 7 O.R. Jo hole 2. O.R.	
MAP ERVILLERS EDITION 1A LOCAL 1:20000				
BIEHVILLERS AU BOIS	20	4.30 a.m.	"A" Coy billeted at MONCHY AU BOIS	
			"B" " " HANNESCAMPS	
			"C" " " BERLES AU BOIS	
			"D" " " BIEHVILLERS	
			C.O. & BATT. H.Q.	
		11.0 a.m.	C.O. visited 2nd Bn M.G.C. & obtained information & a guide for purpose of acting forward B.H.Q. & locality for "D" Coy in Ivancourt.	
		2.30 p.m.	Operation Order No 35 issued	APPENDIX 5
		8.30 "	B.H.Q. (less details) from staff and "D" Coy marched to F 8 d 6.6. Ivancourt to S.W. corner of ADINFER WOOD. Jo tiale 3 O.R	O.R.

Army Form C. 2118.

WAR DIARY
or
INTELLIGENCE SUMMARY.
(Erase heading not required.)

3RD BATT'N M.G.C.

Place	Date	Hour	Summary of Events and Information	Remarks and references to Appendices
BIENVILLERS AU BOIS	Aug 21st	4.55 a.m	MAP. ERVILLERS 1A LOCAL 1:20,000 Battalion in action. 2 A.M. steps noted to MONCHY AU BOIS W.30 C.3.0. Junction of roads RANSART & ADINFER. Operation Order No. 36 issued. Casualties ¹/Lt H LOCKERBIE (Killed) and 25 O.R. Evacuation 3 O.R. From hospital 3 O.R. To duty 1 O.R.	
	22nd		Battalion in action. Casualties 6 O.R. Reinforcements 10 O.R. From hospital 1 O.R. From duty 1 O.R. To duty 4 O.R.	APPENDIX 6.
	23		Battalion in action. Casualties Lt A. JONES (Wounded) 9.25 O.R. Evacuated 3 O.R. On leave 1 O.R. From leave 2 O.R.	
	24.		Battalion in action in Cam out of action in the evening to rest & re-organise at DOUCHEY AVENUE F.3. B&D. From hospital 2 O.R. Evacuation 1 O.R. To leave 2 O.R. To leave 1 O.R. Operation Order No. 37 issued.	

Army Form C. 2118.

WAR DIARY
or
INTELLIGENCE SUMMARY.

(Erase heading not required.)

3RD BATT'N M.G.C.

Instructions regarding War Diaries and Intelligence Summaries are contained in F. S. Regs., Part II. and the Staff Manual respectively. Title pages will be prepared in manuscript.

Place	Date	Hour	MAP. ERVILLERS EDITION 1A LOCAL 1:20000 Summary of Events and Information	Remarks and references to Appendices
BIENVILLERS AU BOIS	Aug 25		Battalion resting & re-organizing. Letter of appreciation received from Comdr. of VI Corps. from Empire 1 OR. Reinforcement 1 OR. Casualties 6 OR. Evacuation 2 OR. To W.K. for Commission 2 OR. To Leave MAJ. G.D. ST LEDGER. 9 2 OR.	APPENDIX 7
	26.	2.30 p.m.	Operation order No. 38 issued. "D" Coy with No. 16 Infy Brigade acted in accordance with O.O. 38 "A" "B" "C" Coys resting & re-organizing. Casualties 1 OR. Evacuation 2 OR. To sick for Commission 1 OR.	APPENDIX 8
	27.		"A" "C" Coys resting & re-organizing. "B" Coy with 9th Brigade noted & for A.R. 911. "D" Coy on Gunfire 2 OR. Evacuation 4 OR. From Emp. 3 OR. To Leave Lt. T. A. WORRALL	APPENDIX 9
	28.	4.15 p.m.	"A" "C" Coys resting & re-organizing. Operation order No. 39 issued. Advance from MOYOLPIN TRENCH. Evacuation 1 OR. issued to be employed by L/S CLEGG, S.C. 15th Brigade. Went into line in relief of 1st Guard Brigade.	APPENDIX 10

Army Form C. 2118.

WAR DIARY
or
INTELLIGENCE SUMMARY.
(Erase heading not required.)

3RD BATTALION M.G.C.

Instructions regarding War Diaries and Intelligence Summaries are contained in F. S. Regs., Part II. and the Staff Manual respectively. Title pages will be prepared in manuscript.

Place	Date	Hour	Summary of Events and Information	Remarks and references to Appendices
BIENVILLERS	Aug 29		"B" Coy moved to BEAUVOIR. Brigade area. "A" Coy attached 8 Brigade and remained with it. B"33 Q Sm Baptiste 1 OR to the information Bm OR Brandon 3 OR to Lieut F.T. SMITH MC Capt 3rd FIELD (OK)	CA
	30		16th Brigade attached & captured ECOUST. "D" Coy Co operating ECOUST Evacuated owing to franks being exposed. 2 OR	CA
	11.0 am		"B" Coy moved to line in support of attack by 9th Brigade "D" Coy remained in line	CA
	Sept 1st			
	31st 2.45am & 5.15		"D" Coy fired Barrage from R.E. 5.15 am 9th Brigade attacked ECOUST. "B" Coy advanced by bounds with line Section Guns each supported by Platoon and captured position on a line from G.2.d 85 C.14.b 19 C.14.c 5.3. Casualties 7hr B.J.SLOPER MC ♦ 2/Lt. WILLIAMS R.J. Killed 2/Lt. M STOEHER LT. R.A. COTTON 7/LT. WRIGHTSON Wounded. und. 22 OR.	CA

W.Hammerton. - Lt. Col.
COMDG. 3RD BATT'N M.G.C.

APPENDIX 1

SECRET

3rd BATTALION MACHINE GUN CORPS

Operations Orders No 31.   Copy No.........

August 4th 1918.

Ref. Lens Sheet   )
      Hazebrouck Sheet) 1:100.000.

1. The 3rd Division is to be relieved in the line by the 19th Division.

2. The following reliefs will take place.

   (a) Night 5/6th August
   The Right and Left Groups 3rd Battn M.G.Corps will be relieved by the 19th Battn M.G.Corps. For the purposes of relief No 19 position will come under right group.
   Nos 1 of Machine Gun detachments of ~~Centre~~ RIGHT & LEFT Groups 3rd Battn M.G.Corps will remain in the line with the relieving Machine Gun detachments of 19th Batallion M.G.Corps for 24 hours.

   (b) Night 6/7th August
   Centre Group 3rd Battn M.G.Corps will be releived by the 19th Battn M.G.Corps
   Nos 1 of Machine Gun detachments of Centre Group 3rd Battn M.G.Corps will remain in the line with the releiving Machine Gun detachments of 19th Battn M.G.Corps for 24 hours.

   (c) Details of above releifs will be arranged direct between GROUP Commanders concerned.
   Completion of releifs will be reported to Battalion H.Q. by 'RIGHT', 'LEFT' and 'CENTRE' by the respective groups.

3. The following will be handed over to releiving unit:-
   All Order boards, 'T' bases, S.O.S. and Battle Line sticks;
   Iron rations and tins of water in Nos 14, 20 and 9 positions; reserve ammunition at Centre and Left Groups H.Q.with instructions appertaining thereto. All maps, documents, photos, schemes etc relating to the Area.
   All information relating to the defence of the sector, concrete emplacements, work in progress etc, will be communicated to releiving unit

4. On releif, Groups will be Billeted in FOUQUEREUIL.
   O's C RIGHT and LEFT Groups will each detail an officer to take over billets in FOUQUEREUIL on 5th inst.
   Orders regarding CENTRE Group will be issued later, also orders relating to further moves and billeting parties.

5. Acknowledge.

                                          Capt & Adjt
                                          3rd Battn M.G.Corps.

Issued at ....

SECRET.

Amendment No 1. to 3rd Battn. M.G.Corps Operation Order No 31.

Para. 2. (b) is cancelled and the following substituted.

2.   (b) Night 6/7th August

        CENTRE GROUP, 3rd Battn M.G.Corps will be relieved by the 19th Battn M.G.Corps.
        Nos 1 of relieving detachments of 19th Battn M.G. Corps will join the Machine Gun detachments of The Centre Group 3rd Battn M.G.Corps on the night of the 5/6th August.

                                        Capt & Adjt
                              3rd Battalion M.G.Corps.

August 5th 1918.

To..................................

APPENDIX 2.

SECRET

3rd. BATTALION MACHINE GUN CORPS

OPERATION ORDERS NO. 32

COPY NO ....

AUGUST 6th. 1918.

Reference Sheet 36.B. 1;40.000

1. On 7th inst. the Battn will move to the new Area. Battn H.Q., "A" "B" & "C" Coys will be billeted at CAMBLAIN-CHATELAIN and "D" Coy at DIEVAL.

2. BUS ARRANGEMENTS
   Nine Lorries have been alotted to the Battn for the transport of 1½ Companies.
   Embussing point will be on FOUQUEREUIL - CHOQUES Road D 13 d central head of column facing north, tail at E.13.d.55.
   These lorries will be allotted as follows:-
   ~~One sub-section under Lieut Duffey and 20 men each from "A" "B" & "C" Coys~~
   The leading six to "D" Coy proceeding to DIEVAL; the other three for the half Compy proceeding to CAMBLAIN-CHATELAIN.
   This half Compy will be composed as follows:-
   One sub-section under "/Lt Duffey and 20 men each from "A" "B" and "C" Companies.
   Embussing will commence at 5.30.a.m.
   Breakfast for those travelling by bus 510.a.m.
   Convoy will move off at 6.0.a.m.

   The two men ("A" Coy 1), (C Coy 1.) who are proceeding to the First A Army Rest Camp will report to O.C. "D" Coy at 5.30.a.m. and will travel by bus. O.C. "D" Coy will be responsible that these men are dropped at CALONNE RICOURT, where they will entrain at 9. 0.a.m.

3. MARCH ARRANGEMENTS.
   Battn H.Q., "A" Coy, "B" Coy. & "C" Coy will march to new area.
   Time of start 10.a.m. Starting point, bend in road E.19.c.o.7.
   Order of march; Battn.H.Q. "A" Coy "B" Coy "C" Coy.
   Route will be:- FOUQUEREUIL - GOSNAY- North side of Railway d.30. b.1.9. Junction of roads J.2.c.7.1.- CALONNE RICOUART- CAMBLAIN-CHATELAIN. Transport will join up, behind Companies at J.2.c.7.1.
   Each Coy will be followed by its own transport.
   Battn H.Q.Transport will be attached to "A" Coy.
   Field Kitchen and water cart will be at the head of each Company's transport.

4. Packs will be carried and helmets worn.

5. Strictest attention will be paid to march discipline.

6. There will be a halt of ten minutes à 10 minutes to each clock hour,

7. Troops and Transport will not be halted in villages. When halted care will be taken that junctions in roads are not blocked.

8. All men falling out on line of march must have written Authority. These authority slips should be prepared before moving off.

3rd Battln. M. G. Corps Operation Orders No. 32. (Contd).

9. O.C. "C" Coy. will detail one Section under an Officer to act as Battalion rearguard for the purpose of collecting stragglers and assisting Transport. They will march in rear of "C" Coy's Transport.

10. Mounted Officers will not ride between Sections, but at head and tail of Companies. Dismounted Officers will march with their Sections. Company, Second in Command will ride in rear of each Company.

11. Marching out state and certificates re cleanliness of billets will be rendered to Battalion H.Q. half hour before moving off. Certificates by billets owners, two hours before moving off.

12. On arrival in new billets, fire orders will be read out and posted up and all fire precautions taken.
Men will walk about villages clean and properly dressed.
No one will leave billeting area unless in possession of a pass.
Companies will detail a police patrol for duty on their billets and in the villages where they are billeted.
O.C. Companies will forward to Battln. H.Q. Stragglers Return and certificate as to arrival in billets.
List of billets will be rendered to Battln. H.Q. as soon as possible.

13. ACKNOWLEDGE,

Callan
Capt. α Adjt.,
3rd. Battln. M.G. Corps.

Issued....1.30. p.m...

Copies to:-
1. Commanding Officer.
2. 2/in/C.
3. O.C. "A" Coy.
4. O.C. "B" "
5. O.C. "C" "
6. O.C. "D" "
7. 3rd. Div. "G"
8. C.R.A.
9. 8th. Inf. Bde.
10. 9th. " "
11. 76th. " "
12. T.O.
13. Q.M.
14. S.O.
15. M.O.
16. War Diary
17. " "
18. File.
19. File.

SECRET.

AUGUST 5th. 1918.

3rd. BATTALION MACHINE GUN CORPS.

ADDENDA 1 and 2 to OPERATION ORDERS NO. 31, dated AUGUST 4th. 1918.

1. **TABLE OF MOVES.**

Serial No.	Date.	Group or Coy.	From	To	Instructions.
1.	August 5/6th.	RIGHT and LEFT Groups.	Right and Left Sectors.	FOUQUEREUIL.	By Route March.
2.	August 6/7th.	CENTRE Group.	CENTRE Sector.	FOUQUEREUIL.	-do-
3.	August 7th.	Battln. H.Q. "A" Coy. "B" " "C" "	FOUQUEREUIL -do- -do- -do-	CAMBLAIN CHATELAIN. -do- -do- -do-	By Route March. -do- -do- -do-
4.	August 7th.	"D" Coy.	-do-	BOURS	By bus from FOUQUEREUIL.

The following distances will be maintained by Companies on the march:-
Between Companies ... ... 100 yards.
Between Rear Section of a Coy. and its Transport ... 100 yards.
Between every six vehicles ... ... 50 yards.

Particular attention will be paid to March Discipline.

2. **BILLETING PARTY.**

A billeting party consisting of one Officer from Battalion H.Q. and One Officer per Company will leave FOUQUEREUIL by horse at 10 a.m. TUESDAY 6th. and proceed to new Billeting Area to obtain billets. Transport Officer will detail the necessary number of grooms to accompany party. One Officer of the CAMBLAIN-CHATELAIN billeting party will be delegated to obtain all billets from TOWN MAJOR and allot them to the different Companies. Billeting party will remain in the new area.

TO:- ......War.Diary........

Capt. & Adjt.,
3rd. Battln. M. G. Corps.

APPENDIX 3

3rd. BATTALION MACHINE GUN CORPS.   **SECRET.**

OPERATION ORDERS NO. 33.

COPY NO. 17

Ref. Map 1/100000 Lens 11.   AUGUST 13th. 1918.

1. The Battalion, with certain transport will entrain on 13th. August in accordance with attached table.

2. For purposes of move, the Battalion will be included in Infantry Brigade Groups as follows:-
   8th. Infantry Brigade Group - 2 Coys. ("B" and "D").
   9th. Infantry Brigade Group - Battln. H.Q. and 2 Coys. ("A" & "C")
   Major S. MOFFETT, M.C. will be in command of "B" and "D" Coys.

3. ALL Transport will move by road, with the exception of 1 water-cart, 1 Cooker, and 1 G.S. limbered wagon per Company in accordance with March Table of Transport attached.

4. Destination of 8th. Infantry Brigade Group will be SAULTY - LARBRET Area; of 9th. Infantry Brigade Group LE SOUICH Area.

5. **Entraining Officers.**
   An Entraining Officer of each Infantry Brigade will be at the Entraining Station half an hour before the arrival of the first Unit of the Group.
   A complete MARCHING OUT STATE in duplicate showing the number of men, horses, limbered G.S. Wagons, and 2-wheeled wagons and cycles will be made out by each Company. A combined State in duplicate, of "B" and "D" Companies will be handed to the Entraining Officer by Major MOFFETT, and of Battln. H.Q., "A" and "C" Coys. by a Battln. H.Q. representative.
   Limbered G.S. Wagons will be entered on the State as two 2-wheeled vehicles.

6. **Loading and Unloading Parties.**
   BRYAS. There will be a Company from 8th. Infantry Brigade.
   PERNES. There will be a Company from 9th. Infantry Brigade.
   These Companies are responsible for loading and unloading trains.

7. Probable length of journey 2½ hours.

8. **ARRIVAL AT ENTRAINING STATION.**
   Dismounted personnel will arrive at the Entraining Stations 1 hour, and Transport 3 hours, before the time of departure.

9. **Water Carts.**
   Water Carts will be full on entrainment.

10. **Completion of Entrainment.**
    The entrainment of all Units must be completed half an hour before the time of departure of the train, when it will be moved from the loading siding.

11. **Breast Ropes and Lashings.**
    Breast Ropes for Horse trucks must be provided by the Units themselves; ropes for lashing vehicles on the flat trucks will be provided by the Railway.

12. **Piquets.**
    Piquets will be provided at all stops for each end of the train to prevent troops leaving.

(1)

O.O. 53. (contd.)

13. **Closing of Doors.**
   All doors of covered trucks and carriages on the right hand side of the train on the main line will be kept closed.

14. **Brake Vans.**
   No personnel or Stores will be allowed in the Brake Van at each end of the Trains, or on the roofs of the trucks. No covered truck should be used for baggage as it restricts the space available for personnel.

15. **Supplies.**
   In addition to the Iron Rations, Units will carry the unconsumed portion of the current day's rations on the man. Rations for the day following will be delivered to Companies before leaving billets.

16. **Railhead.**
   Railhead will be changed from CALONNE RICOUART to FREVENT on 14/8/18.

17. **Lorries.**
   Two lorries will report at Q.M. Stores at 10.0 a.m. 13th. Aug., Destination of these lorries is MONDICOURT where loads will be dumped and lorries released immediately. The loading parties will remain in charge of dumps until further instructions from Battalion.

18. **Billeting Parties.**
   One Officer and one Other Rank per Coy., will travel by these lorries for the purpose of billeting.

19. **ACKNOWLEDGE.**

                                                Capt. & Adjt.,
                                           3rd. Battln. M.G.Corps.

Issued at................
Copies to:-
1. D.M.G.C.
2. 2/in/C.
3. O.C. "A" Coy.
4. O.C. "B" "
5. O.C. "C" "
6. O.C. "D" "
7. 3rd. Div. "G".
8. C.R.A.
9. M.O.
10. Q.M.
11. T.O.
12. S.O.
13. 8th. Infantry Brigade.
14. 9th. " "
15. 76th. " "
16. War Diary.
17. " "
18. File.
19. R.S.M.

ENTRAINING TABLE.

Coys.	Entraining Station.	Train No.	Hour and Date of Departure.	Detraining Station. Personnel	Transport.
"B") "D")	BRYAS	1(Personnel) 5(Transport.)	13/8/18 15.23 hours 13/8/18. 20.23 hours.	WARLINCOURT.	MONDICOURT.
tt.H.Q.) "A") "C")	PERNES	2(Transport) 4(Personnel.)	13/8/18 15.32 hours. 13/8/18 17.44 hours.	WARLINCOURT.	MONDICOURT.

TRANSPORT MARCH TABLE.

For Night..13th./14th. August, 1918. (To accompany 3rd. Batt. M.G.C. O.O.No.33.).

1. All Transport of the Battalion will proceed under orders of 9th. Infantry Brigade Group.

2. These Transport Groups will be commanded on the march by the Officer commanding their prospective Train Companies who will send on Billeting parties furnished with the number of Officers, O.Rs and animals to the Area Commandant, ANVIN.

Unit.	Route.	Destination.	Instructions.
All Transport of 9th. Infantry Brigade Group and M.G. Battln. not proceeding by rail.	PERNES - SAINS LEZ PERNES - HEUCHIN.	ANVIN - HAVRANS Area.	To pass PERNES at 1.30 a.m. Orders for march on night 14/15th. August will be received from Area Commandant, ANVIN.

APPENDIX 4

SECRET.

3rd. BATTALION MACHINE GUN CORPS.

OPERATION ORDERS NO. 34.

COPY NO. 19

AUGUST 19th. 1918.

Reference Maps: 51.C.) 1/40,000.
57.D.)

1. The Battalion will move to the Area MONCHY-AU-BOIS -- BERLES-AU-BOIS -- BIENVILLERS-AU-BOIS -- HANNESCAMPS on night 19th./20th. August.

2. Companies will march in accordance with March Table, over leaf.

3. Distances between Units will be reduced to 50 yards.

4. No Units will march off from billets before 8.30 p.m.

5. Strictest attention will be paid to March Discipline.

6. There will be a halt of 10 minutes at 10 minutes to each clock hour.

7. When halted care will be taken that junctions of roads are not blocked. Troops and transport will not be halted in villages.

8. All men falling out on line of march must have written authority. These authority slips should be prepared before moving off.

9. Each Company provide its own rearguard. In addition O.C. "D" Coy. will detail one section under an Officer, to act as Battalion Rearguard as far as POMMIER, for the purpose of collecting stragglers and assisting transport. They will march in rear of "C" Company's Transport.

10. Marching out State will be rendered to R.S.M. 1 hour before moving off. Certificates re cleanliness of billets will be rendered to B.H.Q. half an hour before moving off.

11. All ranks will take on the march fighting kit only. A dump will be formed at the Q.M. Stores IVERGNY. All packs, Q.M. Stores and Officers' valises will be stored here as soon as possible. Caps will not be taken on the march. Greatcoats will be taken and carried on limbers.

12. On arrival in new billets, Companies will render certificate re arrival, both to their own Brigade and to Battalion H.Q.

13. Battln. H.Q. will close at IVERGNY at 8 p.m. 19th. August and open at BIENVILLERS on arrival.

14. A C K N O W L E D G E.

Allan
Capt. & Adjt.,
3rd. Battln. M.G.Corps.

Issued at... 12 noon
Copies to:-
1. Commanding Officer.   8. C.R.A.   15. T.O.
2. 2/in/command.   9. 8th. Inf.Bde.   16. S.O.
3. O.C. "A" Coy.   10. 9th. " "   17. R.S.M.
4. O.C. "B" "   11. 76th. " "   18. War Diary.
5. O.C. "C" "   12. Area Cmndt.LE SOUICH. 19. " "
6. O.C. "D" "   13. M.O.   20. File. "
7. "G" 3rd. Div.   14. Q.M.

SECRET.

3rd. BRIGADE MACHINE GUN CORPS.

OPERATION ORDER NO. 34.

Copy No.............
Ref. Map. SHEET 57C.

1. The BATTALION will move to-night 19/20th. August from present area to position in support of 9th. Infantry Brigade Group from U.3.B.8.2. which point the latter will clear by 11.25 p.m.

2. Guides will meet Coys. at present area.

3. Baggage will be reduced to a minimum.

4. No dumps will be formed.

5. Rations for to-morrow, 20th., will be carried on the limbers.

6. Dress:- Fighting Order, with one day's rations & full water bottle.

7. MARCH TABLE OF 3rd. BATTALION MACHINE GUN CORPS, TO ACCOMPANY OPERATION ORDER NO. 34.

Starting Point.	Time.	Route.	Order of March	Destination.	Instructions.
Cross Roads, U.22.a.4.7.	9.30 p.m.	SUS-ST-LEGER, WARLUZEL, COUTURELLE, GOUBRETETZ, Cross Roads ½ mile E. of 2 of GOUBRETETZ, HUMBERCAMP (vic Northorn Road) to POMMIER.	"B" Coy. "A" " B.H.Q. "D" Coy. "C" "	HANNESCAMPS MONCHY-AU-BOIS BIENVILLERS -do- BERLES-AU-BOIS	To keep to Southorn Road. Through SUS-ST-LEGER.

8. ACKNOWLEDGE.

W. BARNETT BARKER Lt.Col.,
O.C. 3rd............

Issued at 7.30 p.m.
Copy No.
1. Divisional Signals.
2. B/MGC 9th.
3. O.C. "A" Coy.
4. O.C. "B" "
5. O.C. "C" "
6. O.C. "D" "
7. O.C. 3rd. Bn.
A/R.

10. "H.Q."
11. "A"
12. "B"
13. "C"
14. "D"
15. War Diary.
16. H.Q.
17. File.
18. "
19. "
20. "

APPENDIX 5

SECRET.

3rd. BATTALION MACHINE GUN CORPS.

OPERATION ORDERS NO. 35.

COPY NO. 20

Ref. Maps:- AVELETTE - Ed. 2.c. 1/20,000 AUGUST 21st. 1918.
ERVILLERS Special Sheet Ed. 1.a. 1/20,000.

1. The Third Army has been ordered to press the enemy back energetically in the direction of BAPAUME without delay and to make every effort to prevent the enemy from destroying Road and Rail communications.

2. (a) On 'Z' day which will be notified later the IV and VI Corps have been ordered to capture BUCQUOY - ABLAINZEVILLE and the ABLAINZEVILLE - MOYENNEVILLE Spur.
   This attack will be carried out as a surprise.
   (b) The objective of this preliminary operation is shown in BLUE on map already issued. This operation will be carried out by the 2nd. Division and Guard Division.
   The 37th. Division (IV Corps) will attack on the right of the 2nd. Division.
   (c) The 99th. Infantry Brigade (2nd. Division) will carry out the attack on the right and the 2nd. Guard Brigade (Guard Division) will carry out the attack on the left of the VI Corps.

3. Provided the preliminary operation is successful:-
   (a) The IV and VI Corps have been ordered to exploit the success by pushing through Infantry and Tanks to the line IRLES - BIHUCOURT - GOMIECOURT, then Northwards along the line of the ACHIET-LE-GRAND - ARRAS Railway.
   (b) The 1st. Cavalry Division has been ordered to be prepared to take advantage of every opportunity which may present itself of passing through the exploiting troops and continuing the success in the general direction of BAPAUME.

4. (a) The operation mentioned in para. 3. will be carried out by the 3rd. Division on the right and the Guard Division on the left of the VI Corps.
   The 63rd. Division (IV Corps) will be attacking on the right of the 3rd. Division.
   (b) The 2nd. Guard Brigade (Guard Division) will be on the immediate left of the 3rd. Division.
   The 188th. Infantry Brigade (63rd. Division) will be on the immediate right of the 3rd. Division.
   (c) The 3rd. Division will attack with the 9th. Infantry Brigade on the right, and 8th. Infantry Brigade on the left.
   The 76th. Infantry Brigade will be in Reserve.

5. Boundaries are as shown on map already issued.

6. On the night Y/Z, the 8th. and 9th. Infantry Brigades will be assembled in trenches ready to follow the tanks which will pass through them, and so timed that the leading Infantry cross the BLUE Line on map, i.e. the objective of the leading Divisions - Guards and 2nd. - at ZERO plus 90 minutes, and will move direct on the RED Line i.e. RAILWAY objective.
   The 76th. Infantry Brigade will advance in the centre and at about 1,000 yards distance from the rearmost troops of the leading Brigades.

(1)

6. (Contd).
The supporting Battalions of the leading Brigades will be echeloned on their outer flanks.
Thus the dispositions of the Infantry of the Division in the advance to the RAILWAY objective will be:-

   1 Battalion.   1 Battalion.   1 Battalion.   1 Battalion.
       8th. Infantry Brigade.   9th. Infantry Brigade.

   1 Battalion.   1 Battalion.
             1 Battalion.   1 Battalion.
              76th. Infantry Brigade.

               1 Battalion.

7. The RAILWAY Objective will be captured and patrols at once pushed forward to secure the crossings over the Railway.
These crossings will be prepared for the passage of Tanks and Cavalry.

8. As soon as the RAILWAY objective and the exits to the East have been thoroughly secured, 24 Whippet Tanks will pass through and prepare the way for the Cavalry.
The 2nd. Cavalry Brigade will be ordered to pass through and to move on the RED dotted line.

9. After the capture of the RAILWAY objective and pending the passing through of the Cavalry the G.Os.C. 8th. and 9th. Infantry Brigades will organize their Brigades so that the RAILWAY objective is held by the four Battalions who have led the attack.
The two leading Battalions of the 76th. Infantry Brigade will come up in the centre.
The right battalion coming under the orders of the G.O.C. 9th. Infantry Brigade and the left battalion of the G.O.C. 8th. Infantry Brigade.
After the Cavalry Brigade have passed through, these two battalions together with the supporting battalions of the 8th. and 9th. Infantry Brigades on the outer flanks will advance in support of the Cavalry, will gain the RED dotted line and will consolidate on that line pushing out patrols in support of the Cavalry.
The third Battalion of the 76th. Infantry Brigade will remain in Reserve in about the sunken road from COURCELLES - ACHIET-LE-GRAND, A.21.d. - A.28.a. and will be prepared at once on the initiative of the Commander on the spot to reinforce the advancing Battalions in order to deal with GOMMECOURT if serious opposition is not met with there.

10. The action of the Artillery will be:-
(a) Enfilade fire from the North of Heavy Artillery on the Railway objective.
(b) A concentration of Heavy Artillery on COURCELLES.
(c) The searching of all sunken roads in enfilade by Heavy Artillery.
(d) A barrage of Field Artillery which will move back in jumps in front of the Tanks, using Smoke, H.E. and Shrapnel.
Special arrangements will be made to deal with all sunken roads and trenches and with COURCELLES Village.

11. When the RED dotted line has been gained the Divisional front will be held by three Brigades 9th. - 76th. - 8th.

12. One Machine Gun Company will be attached to each Infantry Brigade as follows:-
   "A" Coy. 3rd. Bn. M.G.Corps. ... 8th. Infantry Brigade.
   "B" " -do- ... 9th. " "
   "C" " -do- ... 76th. " "
   "D" " -do- ... In Divisional Reserve.

13.   The 15th. Battalion (2nd. Tank Brigade) (less two Sections - total 20 Tanks - will co-operate in the attack.
    Four Tanks of the First Gun Carrier Company are allotted to the Division for the carriage of supplies &c. Two of these tanks are allotted to the G.O.s.C. 8th. and 9th. Infantry Brigades respectively who will arrange load tables with the Officer in command.
    Company Commanders will arrange with the Brigade to which they are attached for supply tanks to take forward Machine Gun ammunition, supplies etc.

14.   The following signals between Tanks and Infantry will be employed:
  (a) Tanks to Infantry.
        RED and YELLOW Flag -- Broken down - go on.
        GREEN and WHITE Flag .. Come on.
        RED, WHITE and BLUE -- British Tank coming back to rally.
                Flag.
  (b) Infantry to Tanks.
        Helmet on rifle pointed in direction required - Tank wanted.

15. (a) The "S.O.S" Signal on the VI Corps front during the operations will be GREEN - GREEN - GREEN.
    (b) The "S.O.S" Signal on the IV Corps on our right will be RED - GREEN - RED.

16.   The 12th. Squadron R.A.F. will arrange to drop S.A.A. for troops holding forward positions.

17.   In addition to the iron ration, rations for (2) day will be carried on the man.
    Two full waterbottles per man will be carried if available.

18.   Battalion H.Q. and the H.Q. of the Company in Reserve will be at Advanced Division H.Q. The H.Q.s of Companies attached to Brigades will be at the H.Q. of the Brigade to which they are attached.
    Moving of H.Q.s of Companies during operations should be notified to Battln. H.Q. at the earliest possible moment.

19. (a) Machine Guns must be handled boldly throughout the operation and the fullest use made of the offensive powers of the weapon.
    (b) Limbers and pack animals will be exploited to the fullest extent.
    (c) When the situation permits the D.C.L.I. (2nd. Division) will make 3 tracks forward. Posts will be put up as soon as possible, directing persons to crossings over trenches. These tracks will be called 'X' 'Y' and 'Z' from right to left.

20. GAS.   All precautions will be taken against gas.

21. REPORTS.   Frequent reports will be sent to Battalion H.Q. The importance of negative information and the timing, dating and signing of all messages is impressed on all ranks.

22. CASUALTIES. Wires.
        Period to be covered - past 24 hours.
        Nature of and time - Estimated - to reach Battln. H.Q. not later than 4.0 p.m. daily.
        Accurate - To reach Battln. H.Q. not later than 5.30 p.m. daily. DATES to be given.
        NIL returns required.

23. MEDICAL ARRANGEMENTS.
    For the period of the assembly the existing Medical Arrangements of the 2nd. Division will be conformed to.
    A.D. Station at RANSART Brewery X.7.d.9.9.
    b: MONCHY-AU-BOIS. W.29.d.8.3.

23. (cont).
R.A.Ps. X.29.c.5.2.
F.4.c.7.6.
F.15.c.2.1.
and
F.16.b.9.9.
F.16.d.7.7.
F.16.c.8.5.

Walking Wounded Collecting Station will be at BERLES-AU-BOIS.
Stretchers have been supplied at rate of one per Section.
Extra Shell dressings are being obtained.
On the attack being launched, Field Ambulances Bearer Divisions keep in close touch with the Advancing R.A.Ps. Motor and horsed Ambulances will be used as far as the ground permits.
Battln. Medical Officer will be at Advanced Battln. H.Q.

24. COMMUNICATIONS.
All available means of communication will be taken advantage of. The importance of visual signalling in this type of warfare should not be lost sight of.

25. All information re existing dumps and proposed arrangement after first stage of the operation will be obtained from the Division holding the line. Care must be taken that the ammunition supply is maintained.

26. Companies attached to Brigades will arrange with Brigade for synchronization of watches.
"D" Company will synchronize at Battln. H.Q. at 7.30 p.m. on 'Y' Day.

27. ZERO hour will be notified later.

28. ACKNOWLEDGE.

Capt. & Adjt.,
3rd. Battln. M. G. Corps.

Issued at ....
Copies to:-
1. Commanding Officer.
2. 2nd/in/C.
3. O.C. "A" Coy.
4. O.C. "B" "
5. O.C. "C" "
6. O.C. "D" "
7. 3rd.Div."G"
8. C.R.A.
9. 8th. Inf.Bde.
10. 9th. " "
11. 76th. " "
12. 2nd.Bn.M.G.C.
13. 37th.Bn.M.G.C.
14. 63rd.Bn.M.G.C.
15. M.O.
16. Q.M.
17. T.O.
18. S.O.
19. I.O.
20. War Diary.
21. " "
22. File.
23.

Amendment to Operation Orders No. 35. d/- 20/8/1918.

For Reference Map - Read AILETTE., instead of AVALETTE.

R. Allan
Capt. & Adjt.,
2nd. Battln. M.G.Corps.

20/8/1918.

To was Dray

Amendment to Operation Orders No. 35. d/- 20/8/1918.

For Reference Map - Read AILETTE., instead of AVALETTE.

R. Allan
Capt. & Adjt.,
2nd. Battln. M.G.Corps.

20/8/1918.

Amendment No. 2. to Operation Orders No. 35, d/- 20/8/1918.   S E C R E T.

Para. 18. Cancel 1st. sentence of para and read:-
   Advanced Battln. H.Q. and H.Q. of Company in Reserve will be at Junction of Trenches F.8.d.60.55.

Addendum No. 1. to Operation Orders No. 35 d/- 20/8/1918.

   All first line Transport will move to S.W. Edge of ADINFER WOOD on Y/Z night.

                                          [signature]
                                          Capt. & Adjt.,
August 20th, 1918.   3rd. Battln. M.G.Corps.

TO..........War Diary..........

APPENDIX 6

SECRET.

3rd. BATTALION MACHINE GUN CORPS.

REPORT ON OPERATIONS.
21st. -- 24th. August 1918.

Reference Maps - LENS, 11, 1/100,000.
ERVILLERS, 1/20,000.

1. On 18th. August 1918, the Battalion was in billets at IVERGNY. At 9.0 p.m. the Commanding Officer was summoned to a Conference at Divisional H.Q., and on his return he held a Conference at Battalion H.Q. at 11.30 p.m. He explained the general scheme of the operations and allotted companies as follows:-
   "A" Coy. to 8th. Infantry Brigade.
   "B" " to 9th. Infantry Brigade.
   "C" " to 76th. Infantry Brigade.
   "D" " to remain in Divisional Reserve.

2. The role of Machine Guns in open warfare was most carefully explained and the necessity for using Transport - both Limber and Pack - to the fullest extent, and thereby saving unnecessary fatigue to men in carrying forward guns for long distances, and enable the guns to be more rapidly brought into action, was impressed on all.

3. On the morning of the 19th., Instructions were issued to all Companies as a general guide to forthcoming operations. (See Appendix 1.)

4. On the night 19th/20th. the Battalion moved from IVERGNY to Area of concentration; the Companies allotted to Brigades proceeding to their Brigade Areas en route. (Appendix 2.)
   On the morning of the 20th. the disposition of the Battalion was as follows:-
   Battln. H.Q. and "D" Coy.   ERVILLERS.
   "A" Company   MONCHY-AU-BOIS.
   "B" "   HANNESCAMPS.
   "C" "   BERLES-AU-BOIS.

5. On the morning of the 20th. a reconnaissance was made of the Area allotted for the 'forming up' for attack.
   Operation Orders No. 35. (Appendix 3) was issued at 2.30 p.m. giving a general idea of the scheme of attack and definitely allotting Companies to Brigades.
   Map "A" attached show the objectives mentioned in these Operation Orders.

6. "A", "B", "C" Companies proceeded to the line under the arrangements of the Brigades to which they were attached. Battln. H.Q. and "D" Coy. proceeded to F.8.d.60.55, where the Headquarters of the Battalion were established at 3.30 p.m.
   The complete Battalion Transport was moved to the South-West corner of ADINFER WOOD (F.1.a.10.50) so as to be close at hand ready to meet the requirements of an anticipated situation.

7. At 2.0 a.m. 21st. August, the Battalion was in assembly positions as follows:-
   "A" Company - (LAUREL LANE F.3.a. - X.27.a.
                 (AYETTE TRENCH.
                 (PURPLE Front Line - F.3.a.
   "B" Company - From F.20.b.9.6. To F.9.c.1.0.
   "C" Company - Trenches S.E. of MONCHY-AU-BOIS.
   Battalion H.Q. and "D" Company - F.8.d.60.55.

/The

The H.Q.s. of "A", "B" and "C" Companies were at the Brigade H.Q. to which they were attached at,
"A" Coy. - 8th. Infantry Brigade - F.5.a.5.9.
"B" " - 9th. Infantry Brigade - F.15.d.5.5.
"C" " - 76th. Infantry Brigade - F.8.d.9.8.

AUGUST 21st. 1918.

ZERO Hour (4.55 a.m.) was accompanied by a mist of unusual density which made it a matter of the utmost difficulty to keep in touch.

The distance from the assembly positions to the BLUE Line where the Division came into action was anything over 5,000 yards and the RAILWAY objective another 3,000 yards on the right.

To facilitate action over this very large Area of naturally unexplored ground, it was decided that Machine Gun Sections should follow the Infantry Battalions and keep in touch with them. Each Section was given its especial task and whilst ordered to keep in touch, was warned not to become mixed up in any melee in the early stages of the battle, but to reserve themselves for their definite task.

Promptly at ZERO Hour the Artillery barrage opened and the Infantry, with Machine Guns in rear, advanced in artillery formation behind the 2nd. Division, who were to carry out the first stage of the operation. (See Appendix 3, para. 2).

The 2nd. Division reached the BLUE Line according to Time Table when our Infantry deployed and advanced to the BLUE Line which was where we passed through the 2nd. Division and carried on with the attack.

"A" COMPANY had one Section with each of the leading Infantry Battalions, the remaining two Sections were kept under the control of the Brigade Commander and advanced about 1200 yards in rear of the leading Battalions.

The leading Sections of this Company advanced by bounds and took the greatest advantage of cover throughout. The left Section deployed in AERODROME TRENCH (A.8.a & c) and advanced to the SUNKEN ROAD in A.9.a.20.40, keeping on the flank of the Brigade ready to form a defensive flank if necessary. Then, having ascertained their correct position, they advanced to TRENCH at A.9.d.20.90. Touch was established with the Guards on the left and positions taken up in this trench.

The right Section on nearing COURCELLES came under very heavy artillery and Machine Gun fire, yet they took up positions in COFFEE REDOUBT at A.15.a & b, which were retained throughout the remainder of the operations.

The two Sections in the hands of G.O.C. Brigade advanced and were ordered to take up Battery positions at A.16.a.50.90 and A.15.c.30.30.

"B" COMPANY had one Section with each Infantry battalion and one Section in Brigade Reserve. The Sections attached to Infantry Battalions advanced behind the Battalions, whilst the reserve Section remained at Brigade H.Q.

The enemy artillery fire was very considerable during the advance. Very few targets were actually engaged by Machine Guns during the advance owing to the dense fog.

One Section came up against a party of the enemy with rifles, in a shell hole at about 10 yards range. The party opened fire on the Section who immediately laid down and took cover; a couple of men were detailed to work round each flank and take the party in the rear, the four enemy occupying the shell-hole were thus killed. The Section suffered no casualties. It is assumed that this pocket of the enemy was passed unseen in the fog by our Infantry.

On reaching the crest from A.27.a.5.4. to A.21.d.7.7. heavy Machine gun and rifle fire, and considerable artillery fire was met with which for a time held up the advance. The machine guns were pushed forward on to the crest, but owing to the dense fog, it was impossible to ascertain the location of the enemy. Ultimately the RAILWAY was captured, except on the extreme right where a strong machine gun nest existed - the fire was so deadly, it was impossible to approach it.

The three machine gun Sections took up positions on the high ground overlooking the Railway where they were able to defend the

/Brigade

Brigade front by direct fire, and the Reserve Section was moved forward in close support. The guns were placed as follows:-
    2 guns - A.22.c.2.2.
    2 guns - A.27.b.8.8.
    2 guns - A.27.b.3.7.
    2 guns - A.21.d.6.5.
    2 guns - A.27.b.1.8.
    2 guns - A.27.a.6.5.
    4 guns - A.20.a.4.3.

Coy. H.Q. along with Brigade H.Q. then moved forward to RIDGE WORK at A.14.c.8.8.

"C" COMPANY was attached to Infantry Battalions as follows:- One Section with each of the leading battalions. Two Sections under the command of the 2nd - in - Command of the Company with the Reserve Battalion. The 76th. Brigade to which "C" Coy. was attached was in Divisional Reserve and moved forward as the attack progressed ready to render assistance at any point on the Divisional front if required. With this point in view, the O.C., Coy. made the fullest use of his Transport so as to give greater mobility. The two leading Sections moved off with their 'fighting' limbers which they unloaded at AYETTE. The Sections were disappointed that they did not proceed further with their limbers as the advance led to COURCELLES, but the lack of opportunity to reconnoitre thoroughly routes beforehand and the impossibility of going far from the limbers, owing to the easiness with which it would have been possible to lose them altogether, suggested to the Officers the slower but surer plan of following on the heels of the infantry along the tracks they used.

The two Sections attached to the Reserve battalion decided owing to the fog and lack of time for reconnaissance, to use pack animals from the start; this proved most successful. If they had used limbers, the time taken to transfer from limbers to pack would no doubt have caused loss of touch with the infantry. The mule drivers and their animals worked splendidly, nothing better could have been wished for; no animals were lost.

The advance progressed steadily. The left forward Section was advancing to to take up positions on the RAILWAY Line. On topping the crest North of COURCELLES the mist cleared and the enemy put down a heavy barrage. The Section Officer (2nd. Lt. H. LOCKERBIE) and the Section Sergeant were killed and two O.Rs. wounded. No. 59206 Sergeant H. ROWE immediately assumed command of the Section, retired behind the crest, reorganized and despatched a runner to Coy. H.Q. reporting the situation. His coolness and ability gained for him great admiration.

He again attempted to move forward, but being under direct observation found it impossible; he thereupon waited till dusk and advanced and consolidated with the Battalion to which he was attached. The runner No. 72049 Private C. HAYHOW despatched to Coy. H.Q. by Sergeant H. ROWE arrived after a considerable time and much misdirection in a most exhausted condition. He gave a correct and most detailed account of the day's happenings and the Company of the battalion with which he had left his Section. The tremendous difficulties he experienced in finding his way hindered him from making his way back, but his keen observation enabled the location of his Section to be fairly established. The determination and thoroughness he displayed cannot be too strongly emphasised.

Sergeant ROWE cannot be too highly commended for the most excellent way he rallied his men and assumed command in a difficult situation. Later, when he was withdrawn, he volunteered to return and fetch the bodies of his Section Officer and Section Sergeant.

The Right forward Section advanced without incident. On one occasion touch with the infantry was lost but with great skill on the part of the Section Officer, liaison was again established.

The two Sections with the Reserve Battalion were handled in a praiseworthy manner by Captain MATTHEWS, Second in Command of the Company. The use made of pack animals has already been commented on. The very closest liaison was maintained throughout the operation.

When they got to their final destination about F.20. c & d there were one or two dug-outs. No. 56867 Private G. LEGGETT was assuring himself all was correct when he heard voices, and shouted down the stairs; he got no reply so fired a shot when a German appeared; he

/was

was followed by 30 or 40 more including an Officer. He marshalled them and handed them over to the Infantry for escort.

In praise of Captain G. H. MATTHEWS who so ably commanded the half Company, his Company Commander states:-
"He handled them with the greatest skill and it is due to his
"liaison that their progress was rendered so satisfactory.
"It was a most difficult operation under the prevailing conditions
"and Company H.Q. was never out of touch with him."

The remainder of the day was spent in consolidation; the forward guns engaged parties of the enemy moving over the open ground, East of the Railway. The rear guns carried out harassing fire on known enemy localities.

At 8.0 p.m. orders were received from Division H.Q. that "D" Coy. was placed at the disposal of G.O.C., 76th. Infantry Brigade.

It was to be employed to relieve guns of "D" Coy. 2nd. Battln. M.G.Corps holding the BLUE Line.

At 10 p.m. the following message was received from Division H.Q.:
"G.O.C. congratulates all ranks on excellent work carried
"out under trying and difficult conditions."

AUGUST 22nd. 1918.
At 4.30 a.m. under cover of a heavy bombardment the enemy counter-attacked our new positions at the RAILWAY; he was forced back with heavy casualties.

At 8.0 a.m. the enemy was observed on the crest in A.11.c. Machine gun fire was concentrated on the target at about 1200 yards range and heavy casualties inflicted.

At 11.0 a.m. "D" Company moved forward in relief of "D" Coy. 2nd. Battln. M.G.Corps. Limbers were used and taken up to the gun positions. Positions occupied were as follows:-

2 guns - A.8.a.84.74.
2 guns A.9.Central.
2 guns - A.14.a.15.50.
2 guns - A.14.Central.
2 guns - A.13.d.20.30.
2 guns - A.19.b.60.40.
4 guns - in reserve at F.17.c.15.80.

"D" Coy. H.Q. were moved to 76th. Brigade H.Q.

Throughout the day, the transport - both limber and pack - were very busy establishing forward ammunition dumps and replenishing the supply at the gun positions.

At 1 p.m. a Conference was held at Divisional H.Q. and the capture of GOMIECOURT ordered.

The 76th. Brigade with "C" and "D" Companies attached, were to capture GOMIECOURT and the 8th. Brigade with "A" Coy. attached on the left, and 9th. Brigade with "B" Coy. attached on the right, were to advance on the flanks. The Second-in-Command of the Battalion proceeded to 76th. Brigade H.Q. and attended a Conference at 3.0 p.m. and arranged a Machine Gun barrage for the capture of GOMIECOURT.

At 7.30 p.m. Operation Orders No. 36 (Appendix 4) was issued.

AUGUST 23rd. 1918.
ZERO hour was at 4.0 a.m.
From ZERO - 30' to ZERO harassing fire was carried out on tracks and known enemy localities to cover the noise of the approach of Tanks.

"A" COMPANY fired a barrage from ZERO to ZERO plus 30' on road running from CROSS ROADS in A.18.c to JUNCTION OF TRENCH and ROAD in A.18.a.

"B" COMPANY fired a barrage on G.4.a. where the enemy was still holding on and on known enemy machine gun nests. 12 guns in all were employed.

"C" and "D" COMPANIES worked together, O.C. "D" Coy. acting as Group Commander. 24 guns were employed on barrage fire (16 guns of "D" Coy. and 8 guns of "C" Coy.) (See Appendix 4 and Map "A" attached). All guns of "D" Coy. were collected from their defensive positions on the BLUE Line and placed in barrage positions in A.27.b.

Section Officers were sent out to reconnoitre positions. In carrying out this reconnaissance Lieut. JONES and 2nd./Lt. SAMS ran into a German fighting patrol and had a most lively experience.

At 9 p.m. the Sections moved to their barrage positions using their limbers. Great difficulty was experienced in getting the

/Limbers

limbers forward as the ground was very badly cut up by shell fire; there was a great number of dead horses on the tracks at which the animals took fright.

During this move Lieut. JONES was mortally wounded.

The two Sections of "C" Company took up their barrage positions in DOROTHY TRENCH (A.21.d.). Although these Sections were tired out with the exhaustive advance of the previous days, all ranks were most remarkably cheerful and behaved magnificently.

Four guns of "C" Company were ordered to proceed early after ZERO to protect the right flank of the attack, as the enemy still held the RAILWAY in G.4.a. The Section Officer reported as follows:-

"At 10 p.m. on the night 22nd/23rd. I received orders to take my Section forward to assist in the capture of GOMIECOURT. My instructions were to find out what troops were going to guard the right flank, cross the Railway with them and get my guns in such positions as would enable me to protect the right flank. Limbers were taken as far as SUNKEN ROAD in A.20.b. from where kit was carried to A.27.b.50.80. This entailed two journeys. At the latter place I found that "A" and "D" Companies, 1st GORDON HIGH-LANDERS were going to protect the flank.

'At ZERO 4.0 a.m. 23rd. the Section moved forward immediately in rear of the above mentioned Companies and established positions at A.28.b.20.70. In the meantime the GORDON HIGHLANDERS pushed towards the SUNKEN ROAD in A.28.b. and faced right. Hostile machine guns were in great evidence in SUNKEN ROAD and DIP in A.28.d. and RAILWAY EMBANKMENT and one was firing from CUTTING at A.28.b.00.20.

'On the crest about A.28.c.85.20 was an enemy field gun and a Trench Mortar. We engaged them with good results, but not before the field gun put one of our guns out of action.

'Two GORDON HIGHLANDERS conducting about 100 prisoners were killed, the enemy having turned on the escort. Our guns were immediately turned on the prisoners and did great execution.

'After about three hours fighting, a party of about fifty of the enemy issued from a dug-out in the SUNKEN ROAD within 20 yards of our Infantry. About a score of GORDON HIGHLANDERS were taken prisoners by these and two men of my Section as eventually transpired. We could not fire on the enemy in this case, our own men being between them and us. This party went along the RAILWAY to ACHIET-LE-GRAND. When the attack at 11 a.m. began, the enemy emerged from the Railway towards ACHIET-LE-GRAND, offering fine targets from 400 to 1000 yards range. This opportunity was not wasted. Two enemy horsemen who were making for the Railway were shot down by us. In the evening I walked round the vicinity of the SUNKEN ROAD and RAILWAY EMBANKMENT and found eleven enemy machine guns. 'The dug-outs near the Railway were found full of enemy wounded, evidently due to our fire."

The great determination shown by this Officer to hold on to his position in spite of the loss of a gun and casualties, where he was able to engage the enemy in the RAILWAY EMBANKMENT with enfilade fire ~~from the re arear~~ and fire from the rear, undoubtedly was instrumental in the successful capture of GOMIECOURT. He must have saved many casualties to the Infantry by keeping this vulnerable enemy strong point constantly under a concentrated machine gun fire.

At 11 a.m. the 2nd. Division passed through us to continue the attack; in the early stages of their attack the three remaining guns fired enfilade fire across the front of the 2nd. Division and again must have saved the Division many casualties by preventing the enemy from using his machine guns.

It is thought interesting to relate the experiences of two of our Machine Gunners who were captured. The following is their own account:-

On

"On leaving the 'jumping off' position we went forward with the Section, our team leading. Just before reaching the Railway Cutting, we saw the two men who carrying the gun fall over they were killed and their gun destroyed. We got across the Railway and a Sergeant of the GORDON HIGHLANDERS asked if we had got our gun; we replied 'No' so he told us to go along with them. Not seeing any of the Section near, we did this. When we reached the SUNKEN ROAD we started to dig in; machine gun fire was so intense from the rear that this was given up and we again commenced digging on the road facing the Railway. Machine guns now opened fire from the Sunken Road on our left, so we left the Road and took up positions behind two banks of earth about twenty yards away, between the Sunken Road and Railway. These breastworks ran parallel with the Railway and about 10 yards apart. Two Lewis guns were mounted here and we took one of them over after the team had been knocked out. We fought in this position for three hours, all the time being subject to machine gun fire from the Railway and Sunken Road. A field gun on the crest also caused us casualties.

About 7 a.m. a party of the enemy emerged from a dug-out on the Sunken Road about 20 yards away and rushed our position. I shot one Officer through the head with my revolver, then we were taken prisoners, with about 12 GORDON HIGHLANDERS, two of whom were wounded. We were taken along the Railway and put in a small sandpit with three of the enemy to guard us. We tried to take our wounded with us, but a 'Hun' Officer refused to let us get them all. This Officer started beating one of the GORDONS with a stick and told him to hurry up. He said he was going to shoot the two machine gunners because they had inflicted heavy casualties on German troops. At that moment a German Colonel appeared who was exceedingly nice to us and ordered us to take our wounded with us under escort to ACHIET-LE-GRAND. He said we and the GORDONS were brave fellows. He then went away and was not seen any more. Just then our barrage opened at 11 a.m., we were hurried to ACHIET-LE-GRAND and the 'Huns' took refuge in a dug-out and left us at the top of the stairs. We saw our fellows advancing and waved for them to come on, and they took prisoners all the 'Boche' in the dug-out, about 3 Officers and 50 men. On going back to our own lines we told the K.R.Rs, 37th. Division about the Officer who had beaten the GORDON with the stick; the K.R.Rs. then bayonetted the Officer."

At 5 p.m. on 23rd. orders were received for the Division to concentrate by Brigades and be in readiness for a further advance. "A" Coy. concentrated at A.16.b. and "B" Coy. at G.4.a.3.4. "C" Coy. at A.21.d. and "D" Coy. in SUNKEN ROAD (A.20.b.). All transport was sent to Companies and in every respect they were complete and ready again for independent movement. The men had hot meals and rested. The night passed quietly.

AUGUST 24th. 1918.
On the morning of the 24th. orders were received that the Division was to be withdrawn into VI Corps Reserve. Operation Order No. 37. (Appendix 5) was issued at 11.45 a.m. All Companies rendezvoused at DOROTHY AVENUE Area, and once again were under the direct control of the Battalion. Improvised shelters were made of ground sheets and all ranks got down to a well earned rest.

The spirit of the men throughout the operations was perfectly magnificent under the most trying conditions, and suffering with the fatigue of the first day's sudden strain their efforts were wonderful.

The skill displayed by all Officers must not be belittled. The advance was a test of the severest nature combining as it did totally new and unreconnoitred country with a most appalling mist. To many it is the first time opportunity has arisen for the bold use of transport, and the way Section Officers handled their Sections, Guns and Transport generally, calls for most praiseworthy remarks.

1. **COMMUNICATIONS.**

   Report Centres were established and Companies and Transport were in telephone communication with Battalion H.Q. throughout the operations. The fullest use was made of visual signalling which worked well, the ground being most suitable. A relay runner service was established, the bravery of the runners generally is beyond reproach.

   The various means of communication worked well and the rapid transmission of orders thus enabling movement of guns to meet any required situation, gained the highest praise from the Infantry Commanders, when on all occasions the Machine Guns proved invaluable in an offensive operation.

2. **TRANSPORT.**

   The Transport was handled with boldness and skill.

   Before ZERO it was picquetted well forward ready for any emergency. Limbers were used freely, taking ammunition to forward dumps as the attack progressed. The 'off' animals at all times wore pack saddlery and were used to take ammunition forward from the dumps to the gun positions and for the forward movement of guns during the attack.

   Sections were at no times found waiting for ammunition, rations or water.

3. **GENERAL.**

   Experience gained in previous operations together with notes received of the experience of others were carefully reviewed before the operations. It was decided that the guns should be employed in pairs and in fours, which proved as in previous operations a great advantage, the guns being more easily controllable and increased the steadiness of the gun teams.

   The greatest advantage of direct fire was taken throughout, and on several occasions the effect of the destructive fire of the guns inflicting severe casualties on the enemy was observed, the enemy being fired on at various ranges as he rapidly retired.

   At all times the guns advanced in echelon, so as to keep the enemy constantly under fire. The guns worked forward on the flanks of Brigades during the attack, ready to form a defensive flank in the event of units on either side being unable to get forward.

   At no time were guns actually placed in villages. They were placed on the flanks making use of the tactical features and by means of direct fire carefully arranged locked all entrances and approaches.

   Guns in rear, in batteries of four, were used for bringing down a barrage on an S.O.S. Line in conjunction with the artillery and for harassing enemy roads and tracks at night.

August 27th. 1918.

Lieut. Colonel,
Commanding 3rd. Battln. M.G. Corps.

/CASUALTIES.

CASUALTIES.

<u>Officers.</u>
    Killed ----------- 2nd/Lieut. H. LOCKERBIE 21/8/18.
    Died of Wounds ------ Lieut. A. JONES, 23/8/18.
    Wounded ---------- Nil.
    Missing ----------- Nil.

<u>Other Ranks.</u>
    Killed ------------ 6.
    Died of Wounds ------- --
    Wounded ----------- 50.
    Missing ------------ 3.

<u>Transport.</u>
    Killed - Light Draught ---- 3.
    Wounded - Light Draught --- 3.
    Limber - destroyed ------- 1.

APPENDIX....1.

NOTES AND INSTRUCTIONS FOR FORTHCOMING OPERATIONS.
NO. 1.

I. All Officers will make a careful study of their Maps and note any features that may be of use as Gun positions for the covering of their respective Infantry Groups.

II. It is suggested that each advance be done by bounds preceded by a Reconnoitring Party, usually consisting of Section Officer, Nos. 1 etc.

III. It is also suggested that a Scheme be prepared for every available gun in the Brigade Groups to cover the Railway (crossing the Divisional Front) and all its crossings and approaches.

IV. The final bound should be made with a view of bringing guns into a position for consolidation in depth and also to bring fire to bear on Fleeting Targets.

V. The utmost possible use will be made of Limbers and Pack Saddlery, not only for bringing guns into action, but also Pack Horses or Mules to act as Ammunition, Water and Ration Carriers.

If Packs are resorted to, the Limber Driver must receive clear instructions as to where he is to proceed, or if he is to remain where he is until he receives further instructions.

VI. Company Commanders will note very carefully any lesson learnt re use of Limbers or Packs for immediate report after operation.

VII. All information that is possible should be collected from the Division at present holding the line.

    Information required,
        Re Dumps (Ammunition).
        " Water.
        " Lines of approach.
        " Gun Positions etc. etc.

                                        Capt. & Adjt.,
                                        3rd. Battln. M.G.Corps.

August 19th. 1918.

TO:-
    O.C. "A" Coy.
    O.C. "B" "
    O.C. "C" "
    O.C. "D" "

APPENDIX....2.

SECRET.

3rd. BATTALION MACHINE GUN CORPS.

COPY NO..........

OPERATION ORDERS NO. 34.

AUGUST 19th. 1918.

Reference Maps - 51.C.)
57.D.) 1/40,000.

1. The Battalion will move to the Area HOUCHY-AU-BOIS -- BERLES-AU-BOIS --- BIENVILLERS-AU-BOIS -- HANDESCAMPS on night 19th/20th.

2. Companies will march in accordance with March Table overleaf.

3. Distances between units will be reduced to 30 yards.

4. No Units will march off from billets before 8.30 p.m.

5. Strictest attention will be paid to March Discipline.

6. There will be a halt of 10 minutes at 10 minutes to each clock hour.

7. When halted, care will be taken that junction of roads are not blocked. Troops and Transport will not be halted in villages.

8. All men falling out on line of march must have written authority. These authority slips should be prepared before moving off.

9. Each Company provide its own rearguard. In addition O.C. "D" Coy. will detail one Section under an Officer, to act as Battalion Rearguard as far as POMMIER, for the purpose of collecting stragglers and assisting Transport. They will march in rear of "C" Coy's Transport.

10. Marching Out State will be rendered to Adjutant 1 hour before moving off. Certificates re cleanliness of billets will be rendered to B.H.Q. half an hour before moving off.

11. All packs will take on the march fighting kit only. A dump will be formed at the Q.M. Stores IVERGNY. All packs, Q.M. Stores and Officers' valises will be stored here as soon as possible. Caps will not be taken on the march. Greatcoats will be taken and carried on limbers.

12. On arrival in new billets, Companies will render certificate re arrival both to their own Brigade and to Battalion H.Q.

13. Battalion H.Q. will close at IVERGNY at 8.0 p.m. 19th. August and open at BIENVILLERS on arrival.

14. ACKNOWLEDGE.

R. Allen
Capt. & Adjt.,
3rd. Battln. M. G. Corps.

Issued at 12 noon.
Copies to:-
1. Commanding Officer.
2. 2nd/in/Command.
3. O.C. "A" Coy.
4. O.C. "B" "
5. O.C. "C" "
6. O.C. "D" "
7. "G" 3rd. Divn.
8. C.R.A.
9. 8th. Inf. Bde.
10. 9th. " "
11. 76th. " "
12. Area Comdt. LE SOUICH.
13. M.O.
14. Q.M.
15. T.O.
16. S.O.
17. R.S.M.
18. War Diary.
19. "   "
20. File.

SECRET.

LARGE TABLE OF 3rd. BATTALION MACHINE GUN CORPS TO ACCOMPANY OPERATION ORDERS NO. 34.

Starting Point.	Time.	Route	Order of March	Destination.	Instructions.
Cross Roads; N.22.d.4.7.	9.30 p.m.	SUS ST. LEGER, WAILLIZEL, COUTURELLE, COMBRIETZ, Cross Roads ¼ mile East of GOMBRIETZ, HUMBERCAMT,—(via Northern Road) to POMMIER.	"B" Coy. "A" Coy. B.H.Q. "D" Coy. "C" Coy.	HAMESCAMP, FLIGHY-AU-BOIS, BIENVILLERS, -do- BERLES-AU-BOIS.	To keep to Southern Road through SUS-ST-LEGER.

APPENDIX...3.

SECRET.

3rd. BATTALION MACHINE GUN CORPS.

OPERATION ORDERS NO. 35.

COPY NO..........

AUGUST 20th. 1918.

Ref. Maps:- ERVILLERS Special Sheet Ed. 1.a. 1/20,000.
AYETTE Ed. 2.c. 1/20,000.

1. The Third Army has been ordered to press the enemy back energetically in the direction of BAPAUME without delay and to make every effort to prevent the enemy from destroying Road and Rail communications.

2. (a) On 'Z' day which will be notified later the IV and VI Corps have been ordered to capture DUCQUOY - ABLAINZEVILLE and the ABLAINZEVILLE - MOYENNEVILLE Spur.
   This attack will be carried out as a surprise.
   (b) The objective of this preliminary operation is shewn in BLUE on map already issued. This operation will be carried out by the 2nd. Division and Guards Division.
   The 37th. Division (IV Corps) will attack on the right of the 2nd. Division.
   (c) The 99th. Infantry Brigade (2nd. Division) will carry out the attack on the right and the 2nd. Guard Brigade (Guard Division) will carry out the attack on the left of the VI Corps.

3. Provided the preliminary operation is successful:-
   (a) The IV and VI Corps have been ordered to exploit the success by pushing through Infantry and Tanks to the line IRLES - BIHUCOURT - GOMIECOURT, then Northwards along the line of the ACHIET-LE-GRAND - ARRAS Railway.
   (b) The 1st. Cavalry Division has been ordered to be prepared to take advantage of every opportunity which may present itself of passing through the exploiting troops and continuing the success in the general direction of BAPAUME.

4. (a) The operation mentioned in para. 3. will be carried out by the 3rd. Division on the right and the Guard Division on the left of the VI Corps.
   The 63rd. Division (IV Corps) will be attacking on the right of the 3rd. Division.
   (b) The 2nd. Guard Brigade (Guard Division) will be on the immediate left of the 3rd. Division.
   The 188th. Infantry Brigade (63rd. Division) will be on the immediate right of the 3rd. Division.
   (c) The 3rd. Division will attack with the 9th. Infantry Brigade on the right, and 8th. Infantry Brigade on the left.
   The 76th. Infantry Brigade will be in Reserve.

5. Boundaries are as shewn on map already issued.

6. On the night Y/Z, the 8th. and 9th. Infantry Brigades will be assembled in trenches ready to follow the Tanks which will pass through them, and so timed that the leading Infantry cross the BLUE Line on map, i.e. the objective of the leading Divisions - Guards and 2nd. - at ZERO plus 90 minutes, and will move direct on the RED Line i.e. RAILWAY objective.
   The 76th. Infantry Brigade will advance in the centre and at about 1,000 yards distance from the rearmost troops of the leading Brigades.

6. Contd.
The supporting Battalions of the leading Brigades will be echeloned on their outer flanks.
Thus the disposition of the infantry of the Division in the advance to the Railway objective will be:-

<u>1 Battalion</u>   <u>1 Battalion</u>   <u>1 Battalion</u>   <u>1 Battalion.</u>
8th. Infantry Brigade.   9th. Infantry Brigade.

<u>1 Battalion.</u>   <u>1 Battalion.</u>
              <u>1 Battalion. 1 Battalion.</u>
                 76th. Infantry Brigade.

<u>1 Battalion.</u>

7. The RAILWAY objective will be captured and patrols at once pushed forward to secure the crossings over the Railway.
These crossings will be prepared for the passage of Tanks and Cavalry.

8. As soon as the RAILWAY objective and the exits to the East have been thoroughly secured, 24 Whippet Tanks will pass through and prepare the way for the Cavalry.
The 2nd. Cavalry Brigade will be ordered to pass through and to move on the RED dotted line.

9. After the capture of the RAILWAY objective and pending the passing through of the Cavalry the G.O.s.C. 8th. and 9th. Infantry Brigades will organize their Brigades so that the RAILWAY objective is held by the four Battalions who have led the attack.
The two leading Battalions of the 76th. Infantry Brigade will come up in the centre.
The right Battalion coming under the orders of the G.O.C. 9th. Infantry Brigade and the left Battalion, of the G.O.C. 8th. Infantry Brigade.
After the Cavalry Brigade have passed through these two Battalions together with the supporting Battalions of the 8th. and 9th. Infantry Brigades on the outer flanks will advance in support of the Cavalry, will gain the RED dotted line and will consolidate on that line pushing out patrols in support of the Cavalry.
The 3rd. Battalion of the 76th. Infantry Brigade will remain in Reserve in about the sunken road from COURCELLES - ACHIET-LE-GRAND; A.21.d. - A.28.a. and will be prepared at once on the initiative of the Commander on the spot to reinforce the advancing Battalions in order to deal with GOMIECOURT if serious opposition is met with there.

10. The action of the artillery will be:-
(a) Enfilade fire from the North of Heavy Artillery on the RAILWAY objective.
(b) A concentration of Heavy Artillery on COURCELLES.
(c) The searching of all sunken roads in enfilade by Heavy Artillery.
(d) A barrage of Field Artillery which will move back in jumps in front of the Tanks, using Smoke, H.E. and Shrapnel.
Special arrangements will be made to deal with all sunken roads and trenches and with COURCELLES Village.

11. When the RED dotted line has been gained the Divisional Front will be held by three Brigades 9th. - 76th. - 8th.

12. One Machine Gun Company will be attached to each Infantry Brigade as follows:-
"A" Coy. 3rd. Bn.M.G.Corps.   ... 8th. Infantry Brigade.
"B" "   "   "   -do-   ... 9th.   "   "
"C" "   "   "   -do-   ... 76th.   "   "
"D" "   "   "   -do-   ... In Divisional Reserve.

13. The 15th. Battalion (2nd. Tank Brigade) less two Sections - total 20 Tanks - will co-operate in the attack.

Four Tanks of the First Gun Carrier Company are allotted to the Division for the carriage of supplies &c. Two of these Tanks are allotted to the G.Os.C. 8th. and 9th. Infantry Brigades respectively who will arrange load tables with the Officer in Command.

Company Commanders will arrange with the Brigade to which they are attached, for supply tanks to take forward Machine Gun ammunition, supplies etc.

14. The following Signals between Tanks and Infantry will be employed:-
   (a) <u>Tanks to Infantry.</u>
       RED and YELLOW Flag   ---   Broken down - go on.
       GREEN and WHITE Flag   ---   Come on.
       RED, WHITE & BLUE Flag ---   British Tank coming back to rally.

   (b) <u>Infantry to Tanks.</u>
       Helmet on rifle pointed in direction required - Tank wanted.

15. (a) The "S.O.S" Signal on the VI Corps front during the operations will be GREEN - GREEN - GREEN.
    (b) The "S.O.S" Signal on the IV Corps front on our right will be RED - GREEN - RED.

16. The 12th. Squadron R.A.F. will arrange to drop S.A.A. for troops holding forward positions.

17. In addition to the iron ration, rations for 'Z' day will be carried on the man.
    Two full waterbottles per man will be carried if available.

18. Battalion H.Q. and the H.Q. of the Company in Reserve will be at Advanced Division H.Q. The H.Q.s of Companies attached to Brigades will be at the H.Q. of the Brigade to which they are attached.
    Moving of H.Q.s of Companies during operations should be notified to Battln. H.Q. at the earliest possible moment.

19. (a) Machine Guns must be handled boldly throughout the operation and the fullest use made of the offensive powers of the weapon.
    (b) Limbers and pack animals will be exploited to the fullest extent.
    (c) When the situation permits the D.C.L.I. (2nd. Division) will make 3 tracks forward. Posts will be put up as soon as possible, directing persons to crossings over trenches. These tracks will be called 'X' 'Y' and 'Z' from right to left.

20. <u>GAS.</u> All precautions will be taken against Gas.

21. <u>REPORTS.</u> Frequent reports will be sent to Battalion H.Q.
    The importance of negative information and the timing, dating and signing of all messages is impressed on all ranks.

22. <u>CASUALTIES.</u> Wires.
        Period to be covered - past 24 hours.
        Nature of and time   - Estimated - to reach Battln. H.Q. not later than 4.0 p.m.
                               Accurate - To reach Battln. H.Q. not later than 5.30 p.m. daily. DATES to be given.
        NIL Returns required.

23. <u>MEDICAL ARRANGEMENTS.</u>
    For the period of assembly the existing Medical arrangements of the 2nd. Division will be conformed to.
    A.D. Station a} BASSART Brewery - X.7.d.9.9.
                 b} MONCHY-AU-BOIS - W.29.d.8.3.

23. (Contd) R.A.Ps. X.29.c.5.2.
F.4.c.7.6.
F.15.c.2.1.
and
F.16.b.9.9.
F.16.d.7.7.
F.16.c.8.5.

Walking Wounded Collecting Station will be at BERLES-AU-BOIS.
Stretchers have been supplied at rate of one per Section.
Extra shell dressings are being obtained.
On the attack being launched, Field Ambulances Bearer Divisions keep in close touch with the Advancing R.A.Ps. Motor and horsed Ambulances will be used as far as the ground permits.
Battln. Medical Officer will be at Advanced Battalion H.Q.

24. COMMUNICATIONS.
All available means of communication will be taken advantage of. The importance of visual signalling in this type of warfare should not be lost sight of.

25. All information re existing dumps and proposed arrangements after first stage of the operation will be obtained from the Division holding the line. Care must be taken that the ammunition supply is maintained.

26. Companies attached to Brigades will arrange with Brigade for synchronization of watches.
"D" Coy. will synchronize at Battln. H.Q. at 7.30 p.m. on 'Y' ~~night~~ day.

27. ZERO Hour will be notified later.

28. ACKNOWLEDGE.

Issued at...2.30 p.m....
Copies to:-
1. Commanding Officer.   9. 8th. Inf. Bde.   17. T.O.
2. 2nd./in/Command.   10. 9th. "   "   18. S.O.
3. O.C. "A" Coy.   11. 76th. "   "   19. I.O.
4. O.C. "B" "   12. 2nd.Bn.M.G.C.   20. War Diary.
5. O.C. "C" "   13. 37th.Bn.M.G.C.   21. "   "
6. O.C. "D" "   14. 63rd.Bn.M.G.C.   22. File.
7. 3rd.Div."G"   15. M.O.
8. C.R.A.   16. Q.M.

Capt. & Adjt.,
3rd. Battln. M. G. Corps.

Amendment to Operation Orders No. 35. d/- 20/8/1918.

Para. 13. Cancel 1st. sentence of para. and read -
"Advanced Battln. H.Q. and H.Q. of Company in Reserve will be at junction of Trenches F.8.d.60.55.

Addendum No. 1. to Operation Orders No. 35. d/- 20/8/1918.

All First line Transport will move to S.W. Edge of ADINFER WOOD on Y/Z night.

August 20th. 1918.

Capt. & Adjt.,
3rd. Battln. M. G. Corps.

SECRET.

TO:-
O.C. "A" Coy.
O.C. "B" "
O.C. "C" "
O.C. "D" "
"G" 3rd. Division.
Transport Officers.

As soon as rations have been delivered tonight, which will be as early as possible, all Gun limbers, with mobile reserve, cookers and water carts (filled) will rendez-vous tonight at the South Western Edge of ADINFER WOOD (F.1.d. -(57.d.).

Forage and rations for Transport will be brought, as it is unlikely that the Transport will go back to its present area.

It will be prepared to move forward in support of operations if required. Company Commanders will make arrangements for communicating with Transport at ADINFER WOOD.

Transport Officers will ascertain nearest watering places for horses.

Water carts will be refilled as soon as emptied at nearest available place, possibly MONCHY-AU-BOIS.

Capt. & Adjt.,
3rd. Battln. M.G. Corps.

August 20th. 1918.

TO:-
O.C. "A" Coy.
O.C. "B" "
O.C. "C" "
O.C. "D" "

3rd. Div. No.W.35/6.

SECRET.

ADMINISTRATIVE INSTRUCTIONS -- 3rd. DIVISION.

1. AMMUNITION SUPPLY (S.A.A., Grenades etc.).
   S.A.A. and Grenades can be drawn from the following 2nd. Division dumps as required by Units:-

   Main S.A.A. Dump on POMMIER - LA CAUCHIE Road at W.25.a.1.7.

   Brigade Dumps.
Right.	Centre.	Left.
E.4.a.8.3.	W.30.c.7.2.	W.23.b.1.1.
	E.6.b.0.3.	

   Method of Supply.
   From ZERO plus 90 minutes a Divisional Ammunition Dump will be formed at X.26.a.3.3. from which Units will be able to draw.

August 20th. 1918.

Capt. & Adjt.
3rd. Bn. M.G.Corps.

APPENDIX......4.

SECRET.

3rd. BATTALION MACHINE GUN CORPS.

OPERATION ORDERS No. 36.

COPY NO..........

AUGUST 24th. 1918.

Reference ERVILLERS 1/20,000.

1. The Division has been ordered to capture and hold GOMIECOURT tonight.

2. The capture of GOMIECOURT is entrusted to the 76th. Infantry Brigade. Simultaneously with this operation the 8th. Infantry Brigade will advance their line to the general line of the RED dotted line on maps already issued.

3. The 76th. Infantry Brigade will form a defensive flank watching to the South and South-East about the grid line A.28 and 29 Central.

4. The 9th. Infantry Brigade will arrange to straighten out the situation along the Railway on the Southern portion of their front.

5. Eight Mark IV Tanks will co-operate in operation by 76th. Brigade.

6. Machine Guns will co-operate in the attack and Companies will be attached as follows:-
   - 8th. Infantry Brigade - "A" Coy. - 16 guns.
   - 9th.   "   "   - "B" "   - 16 guns.
   - 76th.   "   "   - "C" "   - 8 guns (and 8 in reserve)
   -                          "D" "   - 16 guns.

7. The operation will be supported as far as possible by direct overhead fire.

8. The 24 Guns of "C" and "D" Company will fire on barrage as under:-
   (a) From ZERO to ZERO plus 20' on a line from A.29.a.55.00 to A.23.c. 80.75.
   (b) From ZERO plus 24' to ZERO plus 56' enfilade flanks of village.
       12 guns from A.29.b.00.25 to A.30.a.00.20.
       12 guns from A.23.d.40.65 to A.24.c.40.75.
       These guns will lift in accordance with Artillery Barrage Time Table.
   (c) From ZERO plus 60' to ZERO plus 90' on a line from A.30.c.00.40 to A.24.c.60.75.
       This Barrage Line will be "S.O.S" Line.
   (d) At ZERO plus 90' all guns will cease fire and be prepared to fire on "S.O.S" Lines when required.
   (e) Rates of fire:- Barrage ... One belt per gun per 10 minutes.
       "S.O.S" ... 300 rounds per minute per gun.

9. "A" and "B" Companies will operate as arranged verbally by D.M.G.C. with G.Os.C. of their respective Brigades at Divisional Conference this afternoon.

10. Companies will ensure that sufficient ammunition is dumped at gun positions for operation and in the event of an "S.O.S" after the operation.

11. Watches will be synchronized by Company Commanders at their respective Brigade H.Q.

12. ZERO Hour will be notified to Company Commanders by the G.Os.C. of their respective Brigades.

13. Guns will be re-organized and consolidated in depth as soon as possible after the close of the operations.

14. All reports will be forwarded to Battalion H.Q. through the Report Centre at F.11.b.6.4.

15. Battalion H.Q. will be at F.5.d.60.55.

16. Medical arrangements will be as in 3rd. Battln. M.G.Corps, Operation Orders No. 35. of 20th. August 1918.

17. A C K N O W L E D G E.

                                          Capt. & Adjt.,
Issued at.....7.30 p.m.   3rd. Battln. M.G.Corps.
Copies to:-
Commanding Officer.
2nd/in/Command.
O.C. "A" Coy.
O.C. "B" Coy.
O.C. "C" "
O.C. "D" "
"G" 3rd. Division.
C.R.A.
8th. Inf. Bde.
9th. " "
76th. " "
War Diary.
etc.

APPENDIX...5.

SECRET.

3rd. BATTALION MACHINE GUN CORPS.

OPERATION ORDERS NO. 37.

COPY NO............

AUGUST 24th. 1918.

Reference Map -- ERVILLERS 1/20,000.

1. The 3rd. Division (less Artillery) will be withdrawn to VI Corps Reserve Area tonight 24th/25th. August.
No move to take place before 8.0 p.m. tonight.

2. 3rd. Battln. M.G.Corps will move to the area DOUCHY AVENUE F.3.b & d.

3. Each Company will send a representative to meet the 2nd. in Command at FORKED ROADS at F.3.d.95.15 at 4.0 p.m. today when Area will be allocated.

4. Lieut. ROCH will arrange re Transport Lines for the Battalion.

5. The Quartermaster will arrange direct with Transport Officer for movement of stores, site for which will be in area mentioned in para 2.

6. Rations will be delivered to Companies in the new area.

7. Rear H.Q. will move to new Area.

8. Location of new Battln. H.Q. will be notified later.

9. ACKNOWLEDGE.

Capt. & Adjt.,
3rd. Battln. M.G.Corps.

Issued at....11.45 a.m.....

Copies to:-
1. Commanding Officer.
2. 2nd-in-Command.
3. O.C. "A" Coy.
4. O.C. "B" "
5. O.C. "C" "
6. O.C. "D" "
7. "G" 3rd. Division.
8. T.O.
9. Q.M.
10. Rear Bn. H.Q.
11. War Diary.
12. " "
13. File.

AMENDMENT NO. 1. to OPERATION ORDERS NO. 37.   August 24th. 1918.

Reference paras. 4, 5, 7, and 8.
Transport Lines will remain at S.W. Corner of ADINFER WOOD.
Q.M. Stores will remain in MONCHY-AU-BOIS at Junction of MONCHY-RANSART and MONCHY - ADINFER Roads.
Rear Battln. H.Q. will remain at BIENVILLERS.
Advanced Battln. H.Q. will remain at F.3.d.50.55.

Capt. & Adjt.,
3rd. Battln. M. G. Corps.

Issued at....1.20 p.m.....

TO:- All recipients of Operation Orders No. 37.

APPENDIX 7.

The Corps Commander wishes to say to all ranks of the Division how proud he is of their gallant conduct in the VI Corps.

The capture of COURCELLES, GOMIECOURT and the very strong position on the Railway line were very fine pieces of work, and broke the resistance of the Germans on a front which they had been ordered to hold at all costs.

The enemy hoped by holding strongly the Railway to prevent tanks from crossing, but before the determined advance of the old fighting Division, they were driven back with heavy losses.

August 25th. 1918.

(signed) J.N.LUMLEY, Major,
for Lieut. Colonel,
General Staff, 3rd. Division.

APPENDIX 8

SECRET.

3rd. BATTALION MACHINE GUN CORPS.

OPERATION ORDERS NO. 38.

COPY NO..........

AUGUST 26th. 1918.

Reference AYETTE - 1/20,000.

1. The 76th. Infantry Brigade will move today into the Area between the ACHIET-LE-GRAND -- ARRAS Railway and the BAPAUME -- ARRAS Road within the Guards Divisional Boundary, where it will become the support Brigade of the Guards Division, relieving the 3rd. Guards Brigade.
    Battalions will move forward by platoons with at least 200 yards distance.
    On arrival in the Area, it will come under the command of the G.O.C. Guards Division.

2. "D" Company, 3rd. Battln. M. G. Corps is allotted to the 76th. Infantry Brigade.

3. Completion of move and location of new Headquarters will be reported to Battln. H.Q.

4. ACKNOWLEDGE.

　　　　　　　　　　　　　　　　　　　　　　　　Capt. & Adjt,,
　　　　　　　　　　　　　　　　　　　　　3rd. Battln. M.G.Corps.

Issued at....2.30 p.m.
Copies to:-
Commanding Officer　　　"G" 3rd. Div.
Second in Command.　　　Rear Bn. H.Q.
O.C. "A" Coy.　　　　　　T.O.
O.C. "B" "　　　　　　　Q.M.
O.C. "C" "　　　　　　　War Diary.
O.C. "D" "　　　　　　　 "   "
　　　　　　　　　　　　　File.

APPENDIX 9

SECRET.

August 27th. 1918.

TO:-
    O.C. "A" Coy.
        "B" "
        "C" "
        "D" "
    Rear Bn. H.Q.
    T.O.
    Q.M.
    War Diary.
    " "
    File.
xxxxxxxxxxxxxxxxxx

A.R. 311.

1. The 9th. Infantry Brigade will move today from their present Area, Squares S.20, S.26, S.27, S.21,c, & d. S.28,

2. "B" Coy., 3rd. Battln. M.G.Corps will be attached to the 9th. Infantry Brigade. O.C. Company will obtain further instructions re move from G.O.C., 9th. Infantry Brigade.

3. Battalions will move by platoons at 200 yards distance.

4. Completion of move and new location of Coy. H.Q. of "B" Coy. will be reported to Battln. H.Q.

5. ACKNOWLEDGE.

Issued at 8.30 p.m.

Capt. & Adjt.,
3rd. Battln. M.G.Corps.

APPENDIX. 10.

SECRET.

3rd. BATTALION MACHINE GUN CORPS.

OPERATION ORDERS NO. 39.

COPY NO..........

AUGUST 28th. 1918.

Reference ERVILLERS - 1/20,000.

1. Advanced Battln. H.Q. "A" Coy. and "C" Coy. will move this afternoon to MOYBLAIN TRENCH in A.2.d. and A.3.a & c.

2. "A" Coy. will occupy that part of MOYBLAIN TRENCH in A.3.a & c. "C" Coy. that part in A.2.d. Advanced Battln. H.Q. will also be in A.2.d.

3. The T.O. will select Transport Lines in A.2.c.4.7. (approx.).

4. The Q.M. Stores will move to Transport Lines this evening.

5. The MOVE will take place at 5.30 p.m.

6. Location of Coy. H.Q. will be reported to Battln. H.Q.

7. "C" Coy. will be prepared to attach a half-Company to "D" Coy. to relieve Guards Brigade.

8. ACKNOWLEDGE.

Capt. & Adjt.,
3rd. Battln. M.G.Corps.

Issued at 4.15 p.m.
Copies to:-
Commanding Officer.   "G" 3rd. Div.
2nd/in/Command.   Rear Bn. H.Q.
O.C. "A" Coy.   T.O.
O.C. "B" "   Q.M.
O.C. "C" "   War Diary.
O.C. "D" "   "   "
                        File.

Army Form C. 2118.

WAR DIARY
or
INTELLIGENCE SUMMARY.
(Erase heading not required.)

3RD BATT^N M.G.C.

Place	Date	Hour	Summary of Events and Information	Remarks and references to Appendices
MOYALAIN A TRENCH A 2 D	Sept 1st		MAP. ERVILLERS. EDITION 1.	
			On night of 31 Aug/1 Sept 9th Brigade + 10th Coy took left sector. 76th Brigade + "D" Coy took right sector. Operation order No 40 issued	APPENDIX I
			On morning of 1st Sept Brigade + "A" Coy moved to support Brigade area. Coy Hqts 26.Q. moved from BERVILLERS to MOYBAIN TRENCH in A 2 d. Evacuated 2/Lt R. BALKWILL + 3 O.R. A 2 d 6.	
	2nd 5.30 a.m.		9th Brigade + "A" Coy advance through the 9th + 16th Brigade under cover of a M.G. Barrage from "B" + "D" Coy, attacked the enemy organisation at LAGNICOURT. Between our left + right Coy. objective — Officers pushed forward — 2/Lt. H.H. SHEPPARD from Cache 27 O.G. + Capt H.M.E BENSON AT T. WELLS M.C. + 4 OR. to 3rd Army Last Cpt. 3 O.R.s	
	Night 2/3		Coys under orders, moved forward thro Lagnicourt to take up a line from MOYBAIN TRENCH A 2 d. A 1 3 a + c for no opposition met.	

Army Form C. 2118.

WAR DIARY
or
INTELLIGENCE SUMMARY.
(Erase heading not required.)

3RD BATT. M.G.C.

Summary of Events and Information — Edition LOCAL

Place	Date	Hour	Summary of Events and Information	Remarks and references to Appendices
MOYRLAIN TRENCH	3/3	3 PM	Battalion resting & re-organizing. Reinforcements 30 O.R's & Lt SCHOFIELD.A. 2/LT LLEWELLYN J.E.B. 2/LT FORSTER A.O. 2/LT ROBINSON M.E. to the Batt. and sent to 3 O.B. From Hospital 2 O.R. To Leave 2 O.R. From Leave 2 O.R.	C.A.
	4		Battalion resting & re-organizing. Corp. Tracey. Expedition 1 O.R. To Leave 2 O.R.	C.A.
	5		Battalion resting & re-organizing & Corp. Tracey. —	C.A.
			Reinforcements Lt G. PETCHES 2/LT KNOWLES.T. & 53 O.R. From Hospital 1 O.R. Evacuation 1 O.R. From Leave 2 O.R. To Leave 2 O.R.	
	6th	10.0 PM	Operation order No 41 issued. Battalion moved from MOYBLAIN TRENCH to village of MONCHY-AU-BOIS arriving in billets at 4.30 AM.	APPENDIX 2 C.A.
MONCHY-AU-BOIS	7th		2 Lieuts. 2 OR's Battalion resting & re-organizing. Corp. Instnr. training. Expedition 1 O.R. From Hospital 4 O.R. To Leave 2 O.R. From Leave 3 O.R.	C.A.

Army Form C. 2118.

WAR DIARY
or
INTELLIGENCE SUMMARY.
(Erase heading not required.)

3RD BATTN M.G.C.

Place	Date	Hour	Summary of Events and Information	Remarks and references to Appendices
MONCHY-AU-BOIS	Sept. 8		Battn. resting & re-organizing. Re-inforcements Lt RYDER S.R.S., Lt SMITH A.G.G.G., from leave (France) Lt C.T. SMITH M.C. from leave (UK) 2 O.R. to Leave. Capt H.H.E. HENSON Transfer to 3rd Cavalry Divn 1 O.R. from Hospital 2 O.R.	CM
	9		Battn. resting. Capt Fishwick training from leave. Cpl 1 O.R. to leave. Capt'BLOWER + 1 O.R.	CM
	10		Battn. tactical training.	CM
		6.30 p.m	Operation order No 1 2 issued. from leave 1 O.R. Gun team 3 O.R. Gradation 1 O.R. 2Lt STOCKDALE + 1 O.R. to leave.	Appendix 2 CM
	11	1.30 p.m	Battn. in accordance with O.O. 42. marched to MORY & came in billets 4.30 p.m. Battn. billeted in B15, B16, B21, B22. BHQ B.16 C.00. 2 Leave 2 O.R.	CM

WAR DIARY
INTELLIGENCE SUMMARY

Army Form C. 2118.

3RD BATT^N M.G.C.

MAP. BUCQUOY 1:40,000

Place	Date	Hour	Summary of Events and Information	Remarks and references to Appendices
MORY B.16.C.00	Septr 12		Battⁿ on tactical training	R.A.
			To base "ETAPLES" 1 O.R.	
			To Infinements to GRANTHAM 2 O.R.	
			Re inforcements 27 O.R. from base 1 O.R.	
	13th		To base 2/Lt LITTLER J. & 1 O.R. Lt A.J DEATON Reinforced	R.A.
			Battⁿ on tactical training	
			To base 3 O.R. from base Lt T.A.WORRALL branch 1 O.R. base; 1 O.R.	
	14th		Battⁿ on tactical training	APPENDIX A
		11.0 a.m	Operation order No 43 issued	
		2.0 p.m	"A" & "B" Coy with 9th Infantry Brigade moved to BEUGNY	
			acting in duties to at From	
		11.55 p.m	Operation order No 44 issued	APPENDIX 5
I.25.d.1.8.	15th		From to R.A.F. 7/Lt KNOWLES J. & n.k base hrs of duty Lt T.A WORRALL	
			From base Capt. S.FIELD & 5 O.R. to base 1 O.R.	
	15th	10.0 a.m	Operation order No 45 issued "D" Coy with 8th Infantry Brigade	APPENDIX 6
			acting in accordance with O.O. 1459 to BEAUMETZ - MORCHIES area	
I.25.b.1.8.			Battⁿ H.Q. moved to FREMICOURT I.25.b.1.8.	R.A.

Army Form C. 2

WAR DIARY
or
INTELLIGENCE SUMMARY.
(Erase heading not required.)

3RD BATTALION M.G.C.

Place	Date	Hour	Summary of Events and Information	Remarks and references to Appendices
	Sept 1916		MAP 57C S.E.	
	Sept 15th		"A" & "B" Coys moved with 9th Brigade into right Brigade Sector. Evac. 5 OR. Casualties 6 OR. To Leave 2 OR.	CA
L.25.b.1.8.	16		Battalion HQ moved to VÉLU area. map reference J26.B.0.9. and "C" Coy to BEAUMETZ. "D" Coy moved into left Sector with 8 Brigade. Casualties 1 OR. From Leave 2 OR. To Leave 2 OR.	CA
J.26.B.0.9.	17.	6.0.a.m.	Situation normal. Enemy artillery active. Wounded 4 OR. Casualties 2 OR. To Leave 2 OR. From Leave MAJOR C.D. ST LEGER.	CA
	Sept 18th		2000 rounds fired on retreams.	
	18	3.45 p.m.	Enemy attacked front after intense artillery barrage. 75,000 rounds on S.O.S. line, & rapid fire; attack unsuccessful. Wounded 8 OR. Casualties 2/Lt G. PETCHES (Wnds) & 1 OR. To Leave 2 OR.	CA
	19		Situation normal. Enemy artillery inactive. Wounded 3 OR. From Hospital 1 OR. Casualties 1 OR. Lieut. F.W. WATSON (W'ds) From 3rd Army and Corps. 3 OR. From Leave 3 OR. 2nd Lieut L/C T. SMITH M.C. & 1 OR.	CA

Army Form C. 2118.

WAR DIARY
or
INTELLIGENCE SUMMARY.
(Erase heading not required.)

3RD BATTALION M.G.C.

Place	Date	Hour	Summary of Events and Information	Remarks and references to Appendices
MAP 57C S.E.	Sept 19		The undermentioned O.R's are awarded the MILITARY MEDAL (D.R.O. 259 19/9/18)	C.O.
			20604 Sgt M. O'DWYER.	
			53296 Pte T. JONES.	
			46570 " A. SALMOND	
			20230 SGT J RALPHS (Bar to Military Medal)	
	20		Situation normal. Enemy artillery inactive.	C.O.
			Evacuation 10 O.R. Reinforcements 2/Lt T.A.C. CHAMPION, 2/Lt C.J. DERRY.	
			To duty 2 O.R.	
	21st		Situation normal. 12,600 rounds fired on Jerries again, morning	C.O.
			hostile patrols.	
			Evacuation 2 O.R. Reinforcement 11 O.R. from Leave 5 O.R.	
			To leave 1 O.R.	
	22nd		Situation normal. Enemy artillery active.	C.O.
			Evacuation 3 O.R. from Lafitte 2 O.R. from Leave 3 O.R.	
			To Leave Lt W.L. SAMS. Le Contre 4 O.R.	

WAR DIARY
or
INTELLIGENCE SUMMARY.

(Erase heading not required.)

3RD BATTN M.G.C.

Army Form C. 2118.

Instructions regarding War Diaries and Intelligence Summaries are contained in F. S. Regs., Part II. and the Staff Manual respectively. Title pages will be prepared in manuscript.

Place	Date	Hour	Summary of Events and Information	Remarks and references to Appendices
J.26.b.0.9.	Sept 20th		MAP 51c S.E.	
			Situation normal. Enemy artillery active	CG
			From hospital 1 O.R. Brouelles & O.R. from limits 1 O.R.	
			To leave 2/Lt S.R. HOLBROOK, 3 O.Rs	
	21st		Situation normal. Hostile artillery & aircraft active	CG
			Preliminary instructions to 1 issued	APPENDIX 1
			Wounded 3 O.R. From hospital 1 O.R. Brouelles 1 O.R.	
			From leave 2 O.R. To leave 3 O.R.	
			To VI Corps reception camp re commission 1 O.R.	
			Situation normal. Hostile artillery & aircraft active	CG
	25th		Wounded 3 O.R. Brouelles 4 O.R. SCHOFIELD A. 2/Lt H.H. SHEPPARD & 1 O.R.	
			From leave CAPT H.H.E. HENSON. CAPT H.E. BLOWER. To leave 2 O.R.	APPENDIX 1
	26th	10.0 pm	Operation order No 46 issued	
			Situation normal. Enemy artillery & aircraft active throughout day and fired at night.	CG
			From hospital 6 O.R. Brouelles 1 O.R. Reinforcements 51 O.R.	
			From leave 2/Lt W. STOCKDALE & 2 O.R. To leave 1 O.R.	

WAR DIARY
or
INTELLIGENCE SUMMARY.

3RD BATTN M.G.C.

Army Form C. 2118.

Place	Date	Hour	Summary of Events and Information	Remarks and references to Appendices
J.26.b.o.g.	Sept 26/9		Formed Head quarters moved to J.26.b.8.3.	CA
	Sept 27/9	5.20 a.m.	Attack commenced by division as reported in appendix	APPENDIX 9
			Casualties 2 O.R. 6 November 2/Lt I WALKER 2/Lt J F WILLIAMS + 13 O.R.	CA
			From Lewis 1 O.R. To Lewis 2 O.R. from Corps 1 O.R.	
	28th		Division not known to Corps wards Battn in trenches	CA
S.W. of HAVRINCOURT			Casualties 1 O.R. From Lewis 1 O.R. To Lewis 3 O.R.	
			To Corps 3 O.R.	
	29th		2/Lt Halin wading Lt J LITTER + 2 O.R.	CA
			From Lewis Lt A DRURY + 1 O.R.	
			To Lewis Lt A DRURY + 1 O.R.	
	30/1/00		Division relieved 62nd Division "D" Coy attached to	CA
			8 Brigade, "C" Coy attached to 76th Brigade "A" + "D" Coy	
			in Division wards in trench South of RIBECOURT.	

Army Form C. 2118.

WAR DIARY
or
INTELLIGENCE SUMMARY.
(Erase heading not required.)

3RD BATTN M.G.C.

Place	Date	Hour	Summary of Events and Information	Remarks and references to Appendices
J26 b 09	Sept 30	early	Battn H.Q. moved to RIBECOURT.	E.g.
			2 Secs Lt J.A. ROCH M.G. & 2 O.R.	

W.H. Kirkpatrick
Lieut. Col.
Commanding 3RD BATTN M.G.C.

APPENDIX 1

SECRET

3rd BATTALION MACHINE GUN CORPS.

OPERATION ORDERS NO 40

COPY NO. . . . .

September 1st 1918.

Ref. Maps 57c.N.W. 1/20,000
57c.N.E. "

1. The Vlth Corps is to advance tomorrow in conjunction with the XVllth Corps on its left.

2. The attack on the 3rd Division front will be carried out by the 8th Infantry Brigade which will pass through the 9th and 76th Brigades at Zero hour.

3. One Battalion each of the 9th and 76th Brigades will come under the orders of the G.O.C. 8th Infantry Brigade and will move forward in support to the 8th Infantry Brigade.

4. The attack will be made under a creeping barrage and will be supported by tanks.

5. 10 Mark 1V tanks and 8 Whippet tanks are placed at the disposal of the G.O.C. 8th Infantry Brigade. The mark 1V tanks will operate against all trenches between the line of objective and departure. The Whippet Tanks will operate in the NOREUIL VALLEY and round the South and East of LAGNICOURT.

6. Machine Guns will Co-operate as under:-
(a) 16 Guns of B Company will barrage (1) MACAULEY AVENUE and BOLTON ALLEY from SUNKEN ROAD in C 16b 3.1.to C.12c.5.7. from Zero to Zero plus 8. (2) LAGNICOURT TRENCH and SUNKEN ROAD from C.17c.o.9. to C.17.d.3.0. from Zero plus 8 to Zero plus 18 (3) DUNELM AVENUE from C.28.a.9.6. to C 17.d.3.0. from Zero plus 18 to Zero plus 30.
(b) "C" Coy will assemble east of L'HOMME MORT (B.17.b.) and as soon as the high ground in C.21.central has been captured will advance as swiftly as possible making full use of limbers. Unlimbering will take place in the valley West of the ridge. Scouts will be sent out and the guns placed in such position on the ridge so as to command LAGNICOURT and its approaches. From this commanding position every effort should be made to bring surprise on the enemy.
(c) "A" Coy will send one Section forward in support of the attacking Battalions and one Section will remain in reserve. Every advantage will be taken of fleeting targets and whenever possible the Infantry will be supported by direct fire.
(d) "D" Coy will barrage with 16 guns as under:-
Zero to Zero plus 8 - barrage SUNKEN ROAD in C.15.d. and VRAUCOURT TRENCH. Zero plus 8 to Zero plus 18 enfilade ROAD (C 22a.& d.) Zero plus 18 to Zero plus 30 enfilade VRAU WOOD SWITCH in C.22.d.

7. Ammunition dumps will be established at L'HOMME MORT (B.17.a.) and at C.2d.8.4.

8. S.A.A. Limbers will be used and an ammunition dump will be established with each Section.

9½. A report centre will be established at FORKED ROADS at B.13.b.2.2. to where all reports will be sent. The report centre will be established at 5.30.a.m. 2nd September. Frequent situation reports will be sent and the fullest use made of Visual signalling.

9. (Cont'd)
Visual stations will be established as follows:-
- MORY COPSE ... B.16.a.
- ERVILLERS ... B.13.b.
- MOYENVILLE CHURCH.

The Battalion Signal Officer will arrange these Stations.

10. Company Commanders will synchronize watches at their respective Brigade Headquarters.

11. Zero hour will be notifued by Brigades.

12. Acknowledge.

[signature]

Capt & Adj't.,
3rd Battalion M.G. Corps.

Issued at 10.p.m.

Copies to:-
1. Commanding Officer.
2. 2nd in Command
3. O.C. "A" Coy
4. O.C. "B" "
5. O.C. "C" "
6. O.C. "D" "
7. "G" 3rd Division
8. C.R.A.
9. 8th Infantry Brigade.
10. 9th Infantry Brigade
11. 76th Infantry Brigade.
12. T.O.
13. Q.M.
14. S.O.
15. War Diary
16. "
17. File

SECRET.

3rd. BATTALION MACHINE GUN CORPS.

Appendix 2

OPERATION ORDERS NO. 41.   COPY NO... 13.

SEPTEMBER 6th. 1918.

Reference BUCQUOY Combined Sheet.
ERVILLERS 1/20,000.

1. The Division (less Artillery) will move into the VI Corps Reserve Area today September 6th. 1918.
   The Area at present occupied will be cleared by 6-0 p.m.

2. 3rd. Battalion M.G.Corps will move to MONCHY-AU-BOIS.
   Company Billeting parties will report to Lieut. STREATFIELD at that village at 10.30 a.m. today, when billeting Area will be allocated.

3. Packs will be carried on limbers, helmets worn.

4. The order of march will be Battln. H.Q., "B" Coy., "C" Coy., "D" Coy., "A" Coy.   Starting point will be junction of Roads F.5.d.3.2.   Time of Starting 2.30 p.m.
   Route for personnel - AYETTE - DOUCHY - S.W. Corner of ADINFER WOOD.   Route for Transport - AYETTE - DOUCHY - ADINFER.

5. Strictest attention will be paid to march discipline, usual intervals will be kept.

6. Trenches and vicinity will be left clean and sanitary.

7. A C K N O W L E D G E.

Capt. & Adjt.,
3rd. Battln. M.G.Corps.

Issued at....11 a.m....
Copies to:-
1. C.O.
2. 2/in/C.
3. O.C. "A" Coy.
4. O.C. "B" "
5. O.C. "C" "
6. O.C. "D" "
7. "G" 3rd. Div.
8. M.O.
9. T.O.
10. Q.M.
11. R.S.M.
12. War Diary.
13. "   "
14. File.

SECRET.

3rd. BATTALION MACHINE GUN CORPS.

OPERATION ORDERS NO. 42.

COPY NO....1......

SEPTEMBER 10th. 1918.

REF. BUCQUOY, Combined Sheet
1/40,000.

1. The Battalion will move tomorrow 11th. instant to MORY Area, Squares B.15, B.16, B.21, B.22,.

2. Starting Point - E.6.a.6.0.
   Time of Starting - 1 p.m.
   Order of March - Battln. H.Q., "B" Coy., "D" Coy., "C" Coy., "A" Coy.
   Route - DOUCHY-LES-AYETTE -- AYETTE -- COURCELLES -- LE - COMTE
   -- ERVILLERS -- MORY.

3. Dress - Fighting Order. Packs will be carried on limbers.

4. Billeting party consisting of One Officer and two cyclists per Company will leave Battalion H.Q. at 9 a.m. 11th. instant under the 2nd-in-Command, who will allocate the billeting Area.

5. Marching out State will be rendered to Orderly Room by 12 noon.

6. The regulation intervals between Companies and transport will be observed.

7. There will be a 10 minutes halt at 10 minutes to every clock hour.

8. "A" Coy. will provide a rearguard, consisting of one Section under an Officer. This rear-guard will march in rear of the Battalion for the purpose of helping the Transport and collecting stragglers.

9. No one will be allowed to fall out on the line of march without written permission.

10. Arrival and Straggler Report will be rendered to Battln. H.Q. immediately on arrival.

11. Strictest march discipline will be maintained on the march.

12. ACKNOWLEDGE.

Capt. & Adjt.,
3rd. Battln. M.G.Corps.

Issued at 6.30 p.m.
Copies to:-
1. Commanding Officer.
2. 2nd/in/Command.
3. O.C. "A" Coy.
4. O.C. "B" "
5. O.C. "C" "
6. O.C. "D" "
7. "G" 3rd. Divn.
8. C.R.A.
9. 8th. Inf.Bde.
10. 9th. "   "
11. 76th. "   "
12. M.O.
13. Q.M.
14. T.O.
15. I.O.
16. S.O.
17. War Diary.
18. "   "
19. File.

Appendix A

SECRET.

3rd. BATTALION MACHINE GUN CORPS.

OPERATION ORDERS NO...43.

COPY NO.........

SEPTEMBER 14th, 1918.

Reference Sheets - BUCQUOY 1/40,000.
57.C. N.E. 1/20,000.

1. 9th. Infantry Brigade (with 7th. Field Ambulance) will move today, September 14th. to the BEUGNY Area (I.21, I.22 and BEUGNY).

2. "A" and "B" Companies, 3rd. Battln. M.G.Corps will be attached to the 9th. Infantry Brigade.

3. Order of March - "A" Coy., "B" Coy.
   Starting Point - Cross Roads B.23.a.0.7.
   Time of Start - 2 p.m.
   Route   - VRAUCOURT - BEUGNY.

4. Distances as laid down will be maintained on the march.

5. "A" and "B" Companies will each detail an Officer to report to Staff Captain, 9th. Infantry Brigade at Cross Roads I.22.a.4.8. at 2 p.m. today to obtain billeting Area.

6. Billets in the MORY Area will be left in a clean and sanitary condition.

7. Completion of move and location of H.Q. will be reported as soon as possible after arrival in new Area to Brigade H.Q. and Battalion H.Q.

8. A C K N O W L E D G E.

Capt. & Adjt.,
3rd. Battln. M. G. Corps.

Issued at...11 a.m.....
Copies to:-
1. Commanding Officer.   10. 76th. Infantry Brigade.
2. 2/in/Command.   11. M.O.
3. O.C. "A" Coy.   12. T.O.
4. O.C. "B" "   13. Q.M.
5. O.C. "C" "   14. S.O.
6. O.C. "D" "   15. War Diary.
7. "G" 3rd. Div.   16. "   "
8. 8th. Infantry Brigade   17. File.
9. 9th.   "   "

Appendix 5

SECRET.

3rd. BATTALION MACHINE GUN CORPS.

OPERATION ORDERS No. 44.

COPY NO........

SEPTEMBER 14th. 1918.

Reference Map - 57.C. 1/40,000.

1. 8th. Infantry Brigade and "D" Company, 3rd. Battalion Machine Gun Corps will move tomorrow September 15th. into BEAUMETZ - MORCHIES Area in relief of 5th. Infantry Brigade and on arrival will come under the orders of G.O.C., 2nd. Division as reserve Brigade.

2. "D" Company will start at 10 a.m. and march via VAULX VRAUCOURT MORCHIES.

3. An Officer will be detailed to meet the Staff Captain, 8th. Infantry Brigade at J.13.a.8.2. to receive details of new area. "D" Company will take over the H.Q. of the M.G.Company. of the 2nd. Battalion Machine Gun Corps at J.8.d.3.9.

4. The 76th. Infantry Brigade will move into the FREMICOURT Area tomorrow September 15th.. The Area available is FREMICOURT inclusive, I.25., I.26., I.27., I.20.c & d.

5. 76th. Infantry Brigade will allot accommodation to Battalion H.Q. and "C" Company 3rd. Battalion Machine Gun Corps.

6. Staff Captain, 76th. Infantry Brigade will meet billeting representatives at 10 a.m. 15th. instant at Cross Roads FREMICOURT I.19.c.6.1.

7. Battalion H.Q. and "C" Company will move to new Area at 2 p.m. 15th. instant and will march via BEUGNATRE.

8. A C K N O W L E D G E.

Capt. & Adjt.,
3rd. Battalion Machine Gun Corps.

Issued at.....11.55 p.m.
Copies to:-
1. Commanding Officer
2. 2nd/in/Command.
3. O.C. "A" Coy.
4. O.C. "B" "
5. O.C. "C" "
6. O.C. "D" "
7. "G" 3rd.Divn.
8. 8th. Inf.Bde.
9. 9th. Inf.Bde.
10. 76th. " "
11. M.O.
12. T.O.
13. Q.M.
14. S.O.
15. R.S.M.
16. War Diary
17. "   "
18. File.

Appendix 6

SECRET.

3rd. BATTALION MACHINE GUN CORPS.

OPERATION ORDERS NO. 45.

COPY NO.

SEPTEMBER 15th. 1918.

Reference Map - 57.^{C} N.E. 1/20,000.

1. (a) The VI Corps front is to be held with two Divisions in the line.
   (b) The 3rd. Division is to take over the 62nd. Division Front and the Southern portion of the 2nd. Division Front.
   (c) The Guards Division is taking over the Northern portion of the 2nd. Division Front North of KEY TRENCH (exclusive) on the night 15/16th. September.
   (d) The 3rd. Division will take over the remainder of the 2nd. Division Front South of KEY TRENCH (inclusive) on the night 16/17th. September.

2. Night 15/16th. September.
   (a) 9th. Infantry Brigade will relieve the 185th. Infantry Brigade and a portion of the 186th. Infantry Brigade of the 62nd. Division between TRIANGLE WOOD (exclusive) and CLARGES AVENUE (inclusive). Brigade Headquarters - J.36.b.9.3.
   (b) "A" and "B" Companies, 3rd. Battalion Machine Gun Corps will relieve three Companies, 62nd. Battalion Machine Gun Corps covering 62nd. Division Front.
   Major THOMAS, M.C., "B" Company will be in command of this Group.
   (c) Details of reliefs of Machine Guns will be arranged direct between D.M.G.Cs. concerned.

3. Night 16/17th. September.
   (a) The 8th. Infantry Brigade will relieve a portion of the 6th. Infantry Brigade (2nd. Division) between CLARGES AVENUE (exclusive) and KEY TRENCH (inclusive).
   Brigade Headquarters - J.23.d.5.0.
   (b) "D" Company, 3rd. Battalion Machine Gun Corps will relieve the Machine Guns, 2nd. Battalion Machine Gun Corps covering the front Between CLARGES AVENUE and KEY TRENCH (inclusive).
   (c) Details of reliefs of Machine Guns will be arranged direct between D.M.G.Cs concerned.

4. 76th. Infantry Brigade and "C" Company 3rd. Battalion Machine Gun Corps will be in Divisional Reserve.

5. Machine Guns will be disposed in depth and will have S.O.S. lines allotted to them to cover the vulnerable portions of the front.
   These will be arranged by D.M.G.C. in consultation with G.O's.C. 8th. and 9th. Infantry Brigades.

6. Machine Gun Group H.Q. will be established at or near the Infantry Brigade H.Q. of the front which they are covering.

7. Completion of reliefs will be reported to Battalion H.Q. by letter of Company and time.

8. Battalion H.Q. will close at MORY at 2 p.m. on 15th. instant and will open at FREMICOURT on arrival. Location of Advanced Battln. H.Q. will be notified later.

9. Companies are warned against low-flying aeroplanes which have recently been active over this front and adequate A.A. precautions must be taken.

10. A C K N O W L E D G E.

                                                                                   Capt. & Adjt.,

Issued at....10 a.m...   3rd. Battln. M. G. Corps.
Copies to:-
1. Commanding Officer.   19. 2nd. Bn. M.G.C.
2. 2/in/Command.   20. 62nd. " "
3. O.C. "A" Coy.
4. O.C. "B" "
5. O.C. "C" "
6. O.C. "D" "
7. "G" 3rd.Div.
8. C.R.A.
9. 8th. Inf. Bde.
10. 9th. " "
11. 76th. " "
12. M.O.
13. T.O.
14. Q.M.
15. S.O.
16. War Diary.
17. " "
18. File.

SECRET.

3rd. BATTALION MACHINE GUN CORPS.

PRELIMINARY INSTRUCTIONS.

NO....1.

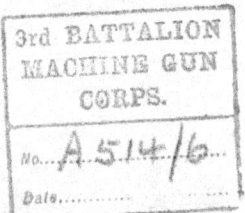

During forthcoming operations the following will be the roles of Companies:-

1. "A" Company will be in Divisional Reserve.

2. During the first stage of the operations it will be employed in protecting the right flank of the Division by firing enfilade fire on to TRIANGLE (front and support) TRENCH in K.35.b. and on UNSEEN (front and support) TRENCH in K.36.a., b. and d., and K.31.c. as far as the Sunken Road.

3. O.C. "A" Company will establish forward dumps and be prepared to move his Company forward and assist the 9th. Infantry Brigade in the capture of RIBECOURT.
    For this operation "A" Company will be under the orders of 9th. Brigade M.G.Group Commander.

4. "B" Company will be attached to 9th. Infantry Brigade and will cover the Brigade during their advance on RIBECOURT.

5. "C" Company will be attached to 76th. Infantry Brigade, one Section with each Battalion and one Section in PUTNEY SUPPORT. The latter will enfilade Sunken Road in K.22.b & c., K.16.d. and WHITEHALL. This Section will then move in rear of 76th. Infantry Brigade and take up position in RAVINE AVENUE about K.24.d.30.40 with the view of covering 76th. Brigade front.

6. "D" Company will be attached to 8th. Infantry Brigade. Eight guns will make their first bound to WHITEHALL to put a protective barrage in front of 8th. Brigade's objective. The remaining eight guns will move to SNAKE TRENCH with the Brigade and will assist in the consolidation of this line.

7. It is hoped to have the assistance of 16 guns of the 62nd. Battalion M.G.Corps for the purpose of assisting in the advance of the 8th. Brigade.

8. S.A.A. Dumps have been formed at:-
RAILWAY TRENCH	--- K.27.a.	---	450 boxes.
PUTNEY TRENCH	--- K.21.d.	---	55 boxes.
LONDON SUPPORT	--- K.21a & c.	---	112 boxes.
JERMYN STREET	--- K.21.a.	---	56 boxes.
SLOANE STREET	--- K.20.d.	---	56 boxes.
K.27.c.			200 boxes.
STAR TRENCH	--- K.34.b.	---	40 boxes.
K.28.Central	---		64 boxes.

Capt. & Adjt.,
3rd. Battalion M.G.Corps.

September 24th, 1918.
Issued at.....6.30 p.m....
Copies to:-
1. Commanding Officer.
2. 2/in/C.
3. O.C. "A" Coy.
4. O.C. "B" "
5. O.C. "C" "
6. O.C. "D" Coy.
7. "G" 3rd.Div.
8. 8th. Inf.Bde.
9. 9th. " "
10. 76th. " "
11. War Diary.
12. " "
13. File.

Appendix 8

SECRET.

3rd. BATTALION MACHINE GUN CORPS.

OPERATION ORDER NO. 46.

COPY NO. 17

SEPTEMBER 26th. 1918.

Reference Sheets 57.C. N.E.
57.C. S.E. 1/20,000.

1. (a) In conjunction with operations being undertaken by the First Army, the Third Army will attack on a date to be notified later, with the objective of driving the enemy over the CANAL DE ST. QUENTIN and DE L'ESCAUT.
(b) The IV Corps is attacking on the right and the XVII Corps on the left of the VI Corps.

2. (a) The VI Corps has been ordered to capture the FLESQUIERES Ridge clearing up the HINDENBURG SUPPORT LINE on that Ridge and the trenches on the East side of the CANAL DU NORD up to its Northern Boundary.
(b) The IV Corps is to capture BEAUCAMP RIDGE and HIGHLAND RIDGE clearing the HINDENBURG FRONT SYSTEM as far East as the COUILLET VALLEY and is to protect the Right flank of the VI Corps.

3. (a) The attack on the 1st. and 2nd. objectives on the VI Corps front will be carried out by the Third Division on the right and Guards Division on the left.
(b) On the front of the Guards Division the 2nd. Guards Brigade will attack the first objective, the 1st. Guards Brigade will attack the 2nd. objective passing through the 2nd. Guards Brigade on the 1st. objective.
(c) The 42nd. Division (IV Corps) will be attacking on the right of the 3rd. Division, with the 127th. Infantry Brigade leading.

4. The attack on the final objective (BLUE) will be carried out by the 62nd. and 2nd. Divisions which will pass through the 3rd. and Guards Divisions respectively on the 2nd. objective.

5. The objectives of the VI Corps and the Divisional boundaries are shown on Map already issued to Companies.

6. (a) The attack on the 1st. objective (RED) on the 3rd. Division front will be carried out by the 9th. Infantry Brigade on the right and 8th. Infantry Brigade on the left.
(b) The attack on the 2nd. objective (BROWN) will be carried out by the 9th. Infantry Brigade on the right and 76th. Infantry Brigade on the left which will pass through the 8th. Infantry Brigade on the 1st. objective.

7. (a) The dividing line between Brigades is shown on the Map.
(b) The Railway will be inclusive to the 9th. Infantry Brigade as far as the 1st. objective and inclusive to the 76th. Infantry Brigade East of the 1st. objective.

8. The advance by the 3rd. Division will be supported by six Brigades Field Artillery and one Brigade Heavy Artillery.

9. Machine Gun Companies are allotted as follows:-
"D" Coy. to 8th. Infantry Brigade.
"B" " to 9th. Infantry Brigade.
"C" " to 76th. Infantry Brigade.
"A" " In Divisional Reserve.

10. During the first stage of the operations "A" Company will be used to enfilade TRIANGLE TRENCH and UNSEEN TRENCH.
It will subsequently be available to assist in covering the advance of the 9th. Infantry Brigade through RIBECOURT.

11. For Targets etc. see ~~Appendix~~. MAP. Div & Coys only.

12. All guns will be warned to keep a sharp look-out to their front in case any Friendly Troops pass immediately in front of their guns, and to cease fire if there is any likelihood of their being hit.

13. As soon as the 62nd. Division has passed through, the 3rd. Division will be re-organized in depth as follows:-
8th. and 76th. Infantry Brigades - between FLESQUIERES and the CANAL DU NORD.
9th. Infantry Brigade - West of the CANAL DU NORD.

14. (a) In order to indicate that the 1st. and 2nd. objectives have been gained the 'success signal' will be fired (3 white lights).
This signal will only be made on the order of a Company Commander.
(b) The leading troops will light RED flares when called for by a contact aeroplane sounding its Klaxon horn or dropping white VERY lights.
Flares will be called for at the following hours:-
ZERO plus 90' (1½ hours).
ZERO plus 210' (3½ hours).
(c) A counter-attack machine will be in the air from ZERO onwards.
The signal to denote the assembly of the enemy to counter-attack is the dropping of a RED smoke bomb over the place where the enemy is seen assembling.

15. (a) All means of communication will be employed, i.e. - Telephone, Visual, Wireless, Power Buzzer - Amplifier, Runners, Pigeons.
(b) All ranks will be made acquainted with the Signals to be used between Tanks and Infantry.

16. (a) One Supply Tank is allotted to each Infantry Brigade.
(b) 12th. Squadron R.A.F. will arrange to drop ammunition to the forward troops if required.

17. Troops are to be warned against using dug-outs before they have been examined and found safe.

18. It must be impressed on all concerned that the success of the operation depends on the maintenance of secrecy. No wireless stations additional to those already in the line are to operate before ZERO hour.
No Code Calls in addition to those of the Units already in the line are to be used beyond Divisional Headquarters before ZERO hour.

19. "Z" day and ZERO hour will be notified later.

20. Watches will be synchronised at Brigade H.Q. between 4-0 p.m. and 5-0 p.m. on "Y" day.

21. Advanced Battalion H.Q. will open at J.36.b.9.3. at 6-0 p.m. on "Y" day.
    Rear Battalion H.Q. will remain at J.20.d.1.0.
    TRANSPORT & QM STORES. I.36. Central.
22. A C K N O W L E D G E.

                                            Callan
                                            Capt. & Adjt.,
Issued at....1 p.m....   3rd. Battln. M. G. Corps.

Copies to:-
1. Commanding Officer.
2. 2/in/Command.
3. O.C. "A" Coy.
4. O.C. "B" "
5. O.C. "C" "
6. O.C. "D" "
7. "G" 3rd.Div.
8. C.R.A.
9. 8th. Inf. Bde.
10. 9th. "   "
11. 76th. "   "
12. M.O.
13. T.O.
14. Q.M.
15. S.O.
16. War Diary.
17. "   "
18. File.

ADMINISTRATIVE INSTRUCTIONS.

The following arrangements are being made with regard to Water, Ammunition and Supplies:-

WATER.
Storage Tanks will be installed at,
K.15.a.Central   and   K.27.c.Central.
The filling of the Tanks will probably not commence till the evening of "Z" Day.
Water Carts can then be filled from these two points.
A Water point at J.15.b.4.3. (DOIGNIES) is nearing completion. There will be troughs at this point and it will also be available for the filling of water lorries and Water Carts.
Water Point at P.4.a.9.9. (SLAG HEAP) is available for filling Water Lorries. There are Water Troughs both sides of the CANAL at J.36.Central which can be taken into use on "Z" Day.
At K.31.a.0.3. there is a Water Point at bottom of CANAL (approached by the Ramp) for small lorries to fill up from.
Water at FLESQUIERES and RIBECOURT should be plentiful and will be exploited immediately we occupy these places.

AMMUNITION.
Corps Light Ammunition Dump will be formed at SLAG HEAP at P.4.a.
The S.A.A. Section of the 3rd. D.A.C. will move to a site in the vicinity of HAVRINCOURT WOOD by noon on "Z" Day.

SUPPLIES.
On 26th. instant, two days' rations for consumption 27th. and 28th. instant will be issued.

TRANSPORT.
Extra G.S. Baggage Wagons from an Aux. H.T. Coy. for the carriage of surplus stores will be issued on the 25th. inst. as follows:-
    2 per Infantry Brigade.
    1 for Machine Gun Corps.
These will be retained during operations.
It must be impressed on all concerned that there is no further spare transport, and units must be prepared to move 'light'.
Anything that has to be left behind must be collected together and placed under a Guard.

APPENDIX.....II.

MEDICAL ARRANGEMENTS.

Wounded should be brought to the nearest R.A.P. or Field Ambulance Dressing Station.

All ranks should know the location of the nearest AID.Posts.

Arrangements for the Left Sector:-

All 3 R.A.Ps. of 8th. Infantry Brigade will be in LONDON TRENCH.
Wounded will be cleared from there by the 8th. Field Ambulance across the CANAL by JERMYN STREET to the Advanced Dressing Station at K.13.d.7.5.
Walking Wounded Posts will be at:-
 K.13.d.9.5.,   J.29.b.4.9.,   J.28.b.9.0.

Arrangements for right Sector:-

R.A.Ps. will be at:-
        (1) K.27.a.7.2.
        (2) K.33.a.4.8.
        (3) K.32.b.5.1.
Walking Wounded Posts:-
    J.35.d.3.6.
    Q.7.b.6.4.
Ambulance Car Post:
    K.32.b.2.2.
Ambulance Bearer Post:
    K.32.b.5.5.
Wounded will be cleared by 142nd. Field Ambulance through HAVRINCOURT WOOD to RUYAULCOURT.

The following are Posts of Guards Division which may be nearer some Sections:
    Leading Post - K.8.Central.
Advanced Dressing Station - K.7.c.2.5.

APPENDIX...III.

SIGNAL INSTRUCTIONS.

1. Battln. H.Q. at old 9th. Infantry Brigade H.Q. will be in direct communication with ~~this~~ DN H.Q. in J.24.a. by buried cable line.

2. Battln. H.Q. at old 9th. Brigade H.Q. will be in communication with Rear H.Q. at J.~~26.b.2.8.~~ 20.d.1.0. by buried cable line.

3. Battalion H.Q. will be in communication with Transport and Q.M. Stores by buried cable as far as J.2.c.6.6. from there by open field cable.

4. Battalion H.Q. will be in communication with "D" Coy. H.Q. by means of buried cable as far as J.24.d.8.5., thence by field cable.

5. All Companies will lay lines to Infantry Brigade H.Q.

6. A Report Centre will be formed at K.26.b.4.1. approx. This Centre will be in telephonic communication with Battln. H.Q. and efforts will also be made to obtain telephone communication to Coy. H.Q. from there, Visual communication to Companies will also be attempted from this position.

7. It is suggested that Companies should place "S.O.S" and barrage batteries in telephonic communication with Coy. H.Q.

8. Divisional Central Visual Station for 3rd. and 62nd. Divisions is being established at K.19.c.5.5.
All messages sent out by troops in and about FLESQUIERES will be picked up here if conditions are favourable.

Army Form C. 2118.

WAR DIARY
or
INTELLIGENCE SUMMARY.
(Erase heading not required.)

3RD BATTN. M.G.C.

Place	Date	Hour	Summary of Events and Information	Remarks and references to Appendices
RIBECOURT	1918 Oct 1		MAP 57C. S.E.	
L 25 a		00.15	76th Brigade attacked supported by "C" Coy with 9th Brigade on	
			Report with "D" Coy. "A" & "B" Coy in reserve trenches south of	
			RIBECOURT.	
			Casualties 20 OR. From Hospital 2 OR. Evacuations 12 OR.	
			To Lusks 3 OR. From Lusks 2 OR.	
	2nd		Previous orders received for 9th Brigade to hold front area	
			Whilst 76th Brigade moved up in response for defence of RUMILLY & "D"	
			Coy Co-operating.	
			Casualties 4 OR. From Hospital 2 OR Evacuation 1 OR	
			To Lusks 2 OR. From Lusks 8 OR	
	3rd		Much harassing fire carried out during night 9 organised	
			shoots fired on known enemy strong points	
			The following awards made to Officers, 1 O.R. of the Battn.	
			MILITARY CROSS. CAPT W.J. DOWLING	
			T/Lt (A/Capt) C.H. MATTHEWS D.C.M. 2103 PTE J. HASSALL	
			T/2/Lt W.L. SAMS 2ND BAR to M.M. 85992 L/CPL D. WATERS D.M.	
			" S.R. HOLBROOK. SIG COY ATT'D M.G.C.	

Army Form C.2118.

WAR DIARY
or
INTELLIGENCE SUMMARY.
(Erase heading not required.)

3RD BATTN. M.G.C.

Instructions regarding War Diaries and Intelligence Summaries are contained in F. S. Regs., Part II. and the Staff Manual respectively. Title pages will be prepared in manuscript.

Place	Date	Hour	Summary of Events and Information	Remarks and references to Appendices
RIDGECOURT L.25.a.00.15	MAP 57C			
	Oct 3rd		Casualties 2 O.R. To leave 1 O.R. From leave LT C.T. SMITH M.C. & 1 O.R.	CC
			Re inforced 2/LT H.G. WALLACE LT R. SUMMERS LT D. MORRIS LT P. DANGERFIELD	
	Oct 4th		2/LT S.G. MEDLOCK 2/LT M. McGILL and 16 O.R.	CC
			Enemy heavily barraged front line & supports	
			Casualties 3 O.R. Evacuation 4 O.R. To leave 2 O.R. From leave 3 O.R.	
			Reinforcement LT G.S. BALL LT A.H. SHAW	CC
	Oct 5		Situation normal C.O. attended Conference at DIV. H.Q.	
			To leave 2 O.R. From leave 4 O.R.	CC
			The following awards were made to Officers & other ranks of the Battalion.	
			MILITARY CROSS 2/LT A. DRURY 2/LT M.S. TURNER R. 2/LT M.S. TURNER R. SGT PENNINGTON A.S.	CC
			D.C.M. 60773 SGT. M. JARDINE M.M. 61124	APPENDIX 1
			Situation normal Enemy artillery active	
	6th	21.30 hr	Operation Order No 47 issued.	
			From hospital MAJOR C.D. WETTON Casualties 2 O.R.	
			To leave LT H.G. GEER CAPT LAWSON-SMITH C.F. LT H.G. BARWOOD & 2 O.R.	CC
	7th		Casualties 2 O.R. From hospital 1 O.R.	
			Situation normal	
			Evacuation 1 O.R. To leave 2 O.R. From leave 2 O.R. To officers cadet corps 1 O.R.	CC

Army Form C.2118.

WAR DIARY
or
INTELLIGENCE SUMMARY.
(Erase heading not required.)

3RD BATTN. M.G.C.

Instructions regarding War Diaries and Intelligence Summaries are contained in F. S. Regs., Part II. and the Staff Manual respectively. Title pages will be prepared in manuscript.

Place	Date	Hour	Summary of Events and Information	Remarks and references to Appendices
RIBECOURT L25a 00.15	Sept 1/18	MAP 57 C	"A" & "B" Coy. moved from RIBECOURT to assembly position in front	
			at MASNIERES. "C" & "D" Coy to barrage positions at "C" Coy G 22 &	
			"D" Coy G 22 c. Advanced B.H.Q. to Catacomb, MASNIERES.	APPENDIX 1/A.
	Oct 8		Battalion in action. Report on operation.	
		5.30 p.m	"C" & "D" Coy withdrew to RIBECOURT.	
			Casualties Lt H.A. SHAW (killed) Lt G.S. BALL & 2/Lt ROBINSON H.E (wounded)	
			" 48 OR from hospital 1 OR evacuation 1 OR	
			Reinforcements 21 OR To duty MAJ THOMAS & 2 OR from leave 2 OR	
	9th		B.H.Q. "C" & "D" Coy marched to YELU WOOD.	
			"A" & "B" Coy withdrew to RIBECOURT.	
			Reinforcements 25 OR To duty 2 OR	
			from leave LT W.L. SAMS. LT S.R. HOLBROOK & 1 OR	
VELU J31a 1.5.	10th		"A" & "B" Coy arrived in billets at YELU WOOD at 16.30 hr.	
			Reinforcements 40 OR	
			Evacuation 1 OR	
			To duty MAJ S. MOFFETT MC & 3 OR from leave 1 OR	

WAR DIARY
or
INTELLIGENCE SUMMARY. 3RD BATT^N M.G.C.

(Erase heading not required.)

Army Form C. 2118.

Place	Date	Hour	Summary of Events and Information	Remarks and references to Appendices
VELU J.31.a.1.5.	Oct 11		Battalion training	
			Evacuation 2/Lt LLEWELLYN J.C.B. To base 2/Lt BURKE + 3 O.R. from base 4 O.R.	
	12		Battalion training	
			Operation order No 48 issued	APPENDIX 2
			From hospital 10 O.R. Evacuation 7 O.R. To base 2/Lt DOUGLAS J. 7 O.R.	
			From base Lt T.W.WELLS M.C. + 6 O.R. To base at GRAHTHAM 2 O.R.	
			Reinforcement 2/Lt KIRK J.H. 2/Lt MOULE L. Lt MYHILL H.T. + 60 O.Rs	
	13		Battalion in accordance with O.O. No 48 moved to FLESQUIERES at L.19.a.5.7.	
FLESQUIERES L.19.a.5.7.	14		Evacuation 2/Lt A.H. DUFFY + 18 O.R. To base 3 O.R. From base 2 O.R.	
			Battalion training.	
			Evacuation 5 O.R. To base 3 O.R.	
	15		Battalion training	
			From hospital 10 O.R. Evacuation 7 O.R. To base 3 O.R. from base Lt A. DRURY and 3 O.R.	

Army Form C. 2118.

WAR DIARY
or
INTELLIGENCE SUMMARY.
(Erase heading not required.)

3RD BATTN M.G.C.

Place	Date	Hour	Summary of Events and Information	Remarks and references to Appendices
FLESQUIERES Oct 16 L19 A 57			MAP 57C	
	Oct 16		Battalion training	
			To 6 months tour of duty to U.K. Lt T WELLS M.C. & Lt A DRURY M.C.	
			To leave 4 O.R. To M.G School G.H.Q. Lt R.C. STREATFIELD	
	17		Battalion training	
			Reinforcements 2/Lt F HOPE 2/Lt R TALKWILL To leave 2 O.R. from leave 2 O.R.	
	18		Battalion training	
			Warning order (S.D. 474) received for "C" Coy to move with 76th Brigade	
			To leave CAPT DOWLING M.C. & 4 O.R. From leave Lt ROCH M.C.	
	19	09.30 hr	C.O. attended conference at DIV H.Q.	
			"C" Coy moved to CATTENIERES under orders of 76th Brigade	
		16.00 hr	Warning order No 49 issued	
			Insertions 9 O.R. To leave 2 O.R. from leave 3 O.R.	
CATTENIERES H12 a 6.6.	20		Battn HQ. A'd Coy moved to CATTENIERES arriving in billets at 17.15 hrs. BHQ at 12a 6.6. "B" Coy moved to BEVILLERS & "C" Coy to QUIEVY	
			Insertions 3 O.R. To leave Lt T DANGERFIELD & 3 O.R.	

WAR DIARY
INTELLIGENCE SUMMARY

3RD BATTⁿ M.G.C.

Army Form C-2118

MAP 57B

Place	Date	Hour	Summary of Events and Information	Remarks and references to Appendices
COTTENIERES H12a 6.6	Oct 21	11.00 hrs	Commanding Officer attended conference at DIV. H.Q.	H.B.
		14.45	Officers of "A" Coy attended conference at Battⁿ H.Q.	
			"D" Coy moved to QUIEVY Evacuation 2 OR. Jo kindc MAJ. C.D. WETTON, 9, 2 OR from kindc 2 OR	
QUIEVY D13a 55.15	22ⁿᵈ		B.H.Q. & "A" Coy moved to QUIEVY arriving at 11.00 hrs Advanced B.H.Q. & "A" Coy moved to SOLESMES. "B" Coy moved to QUIEVY arriving at 19.30 hrs Operation orders No 49 issued Reinforced 2 OR. Jo kindc 4 OR. Battalion in action. Report on operations	H.B. APPENDIX 3 APPENDIX 4
SOLESMES E10 6.8	23	07.15 hrs	"B" Coy moved to SOLESMES Rear H.Q. moved to SOLESMES "D" moved to VERTAIN Evacuation 18 OR. From hospital 3 OR. Reinforced 12 OR. Jo kindc 3 OR. From kindc CAPT LAWSON-SMITH C.F from - LT. H.G. BARWOOD, 2/LT H.C. GEER & 5 OR	H.B.

WAR DIARY
INTELLIGENCE SUMMARY

3RD BATTN M.G.C.

Army Form C-2118

Place	Date	Hour	Summary of Events and Information	Remarks and references to Appendices
SOLESMES E.I.C.6.8.	Oct 24		MAP 57B	
			Battalion in action. Zero hour 04.00 hr.	
			Addresses B.H.Q, "B" + "D" Coy moved to ESCARMAIN W5 & 5.5	Rd
			Casualties 1 OR 2/Lt G J GRANT + 5 OR	APPENDIX A
	25		from hostile 1 OR	
			Battalion in action	Rd
			Casualties 1 OR Evacuation 3 OR	
	26th		2/Lt A MURCH + 3 OR from hostile + artillery action	
			To hostile enemy aircraft + artillery action	Rd
			"C" Coy moved to ESCARMAIN	
			Evacuation 1 OR Evacuation 1 OR	
			To hostile 2/Lt W.E. ROSSER 1 + 2 OR	
27 to	15.30		Operation order No 50 issued.	APPENDIX B
			A" + "D" Coys moved to RUESHES	
			Evacuation 4 OR Evacuation 3 OR To hostile 2 OR	Rd
			from hostile 4 OR	

Army Form C.2118.

WAR DIARY
or
INTELLIGENCE SUMMARY.
(Erase heading not required.)

3RD BATT'N M.G.C.

Instructions regarding War Diaries and Intelligence Summaries are contained in F. S. Regs., Part II. and the Staff Manual respectively. Title pages will be prepared in manuscript.

Place	Date	Hour	Summary of Events and Information	Remarks and references to Appendices
SOLESMES E I C 6.8.	Oct 28		Situation normal. Enemy artillery active. Casualties 1 O.R. to hosp. 5 O.R. from leave 1 O.R.	R.O.
	29		Situation normal. Enemy artillery active. "C" Coy moved to St PYTHON. Operation order No A 49 issued. Casualties 5 O.R. evacuated. 2 O.R. from leave. MAJOR S. MOFFETT M.C. To hosp. 1 O.R. Reinforcements 2/Lt T. CUNLIFFE 2/Lt H.G. TAWN.	R.O. APPENDIX 5 A
	30		Battalion re-assembled at St PYTHON, being relieved in the Line by 2nd Batt'n M.G.C. Operation orders No 51 issued. Casualties 1 O.R. evacuated 2 O.R. to Leave 2 O.R.	R.O. APPENDIX 6
	31	21.00	Battalion marched to CARRIERES arriving in bivouac at	
		16.00 hrs.	B.H.Q at B. 19. d. 65. 40. Casualties 2 O.R. from leave 12 O.R. from hosp.	R.O.

W. Thornton
LT. COL
COMMANDING 3RD BATT'N M.G.C.

APPENDIX I.

SECRET.

3rd. BATTALION MACHINE GUN CORPS.

OPERATION ORDER NO. 47.

COPY NO. 18

OCTOBER 6th. 1918.

Reference Sheet 57.B. N.W. 1/20,000.

1. The Third Army is to continue its advance towards the general line LE CATEAU --- SOLESMES.

2. The objectives allotted to the VI Corps are WAMBAIX and IGNIEL DIT LES FRISETTES.

3. (a) The attack of the VI Corps will be carried out by the 3rd. Division on the right and the 2nd. Division on the left.

   (b) The Guards Division will be prepared to pass through the 3rd. Division under orders of the Corps according as the situation develops, and will in any case take over from, or pass through the 3rd. Division on the night "Z"/"Z" plus 1 night.

   (c) The New Zealand Division will be attacking on the right of the 3rd. Division.

4. The boundaries between 3rd. Division and flank Divisions, and the objectives are shewn on the Map already issued to Companies.

5. (a) The advance on the 3rd. Division front will be carried out by the 9th. Infantry Brigade which will pass through the 8th. Infantry Brigade at ZERO Hour.

   (b) The line of departure of the 9th. Infantry Brigade will extend from the East and West grid line between Squares G.23. and G.29. to L'EPINE (inclusive).
   9th. Infantry Brigade H.Q. - G.20.d.7.2.

   (c) The 99th. Infantry Brigade (2nd. Division) will pass through the 8th. Infantry Brigade.

6. One Battalion 76th. Infantry Brigade and "A" and "B" Companies, 3rd. Battalion Machine Gun Corps will come under the orders of the G.O.C., 9th. Infantry Brigade.

7. 76th. Infantry Brigade (less one Battalion) and "C" Coy. 3rd. Battln. Machine Gun Corps will be in Divisional Reserve and will be prepared:-

   (a) Either to support the 9th. Infantry Brigade in their attack on the 2nd. objective for which purpose they will come under the orders of the G.O.C., 9th. Infantry Brigade, or -

   (b) On receipt of orders from Divisional H.Q., to pass through the 9th. Infantry Brigade on the 2nd. objective and capture the 3rd. objective under the orders of the G.O.C., 76th. Infantry Brigade.

(1)

8. "C" Company, 3rd. Battln. Machine Gun Corps, after completion of task allotted them by D.M.G.C. will be prepared to join 76th. Infantry Brigade, as the Brigade moves forward.

9. On night Y/Z 9th. Infantry Brigade and "A" and "B" Companies will move forward under orders of the G.O.C., 9th. Infantry Brigade and will be clear of their present area by 19.00 hours.
    No move to take place before 17.30 hours.

10. The following tasks are allotted:-

(a) "D" Company. 16 guns in Trench in G.22.c. (not East of a line running North and South through G.22.c.4.5) will fire a creeping barrage starting on road in G.24.b & d. Each lift will be 200 yards and will be in accordance with Map issued.

Time of Fire.
   Road G.24.b & d.   ZERO to ZERO plus 10'.
   1st. Lift.   ZERO plus 10' to ZERO plus 18'.
   2nd. Lift.   ZERO plus 18' to ZERO plus 26'.

Rate of Fire: One belt per gun per five minutes.

"D" Company will remain in their barrage positions until further orders are received from D.M.G.C.

(b) "C" Company. 16 guns will occupy positions in Trench in G.22.b. (not East of a line running North and South through G.22.b.4.5). and will barrage 1st. objective from ZERO plus 30' to ZERO plus 65'.
Rate of fire -- One belt per gun per five minutes.

(c) "B" Company. 16 guns will follow 9th. Infantry Brigade and, where possible, will support the advance by covering fire. They will support the consolidation of the 2nd. objective, the following positions being occupied:-
    4 guns at H.13.d.40.60.
    4 guns at H.14.a.20.00.
    4 guns at H.20.c.30.65.
    4 guns at H.20.b.20.00.

If the 3rd. objective is attacked by either/the 9th. or 76th. Infantry Brigade the following positions of consolidation will be occupied when objective is taken:-
    4 guns at H.14.b.50.40.
    4 guns at H.15.a.50.60.
    4 guns at H.15.c.90.60.
    4 guns at H.21.b.85.90.

(d) "A" Company. 16 guns will follow 9th. Infantry Brigade as closely as possible and will take up following positions:-
    8 guns at H.13.c.30.15.
    8 guns at H.19.a.60.15.

They will support by covering fire from ZERO plus 150' to ZERO plus 182' the attack on the 2nd. objective and cover consolidation. They will then cover the advance on the 3rd. objective and will cease fire on Infantry approaching within 300 yards of WAMBAIX.

When the 3rd. objective has been taken, the following positions will be occupied:-
    8 guns at H.14.a.20.00.
    8 guns at H.21.a.25.40.

(e) "S.O.S" Lines will be arranged with G.O.C., Forward Brigade by Group Commanders of "A" and "B" Companies.

11.	There will be a pause of 30 minutes on the 1st. objective.

Troops advancing to the 2nd. objective will pass the 1st. objective at ZERO plus 130'.

12.	Six Mark IV Tanks will co-operate in the attack and will follow in rear of the 9th. Infantry Brigade.

Four Tanks will operate against SERANVILLERS and two tanks on the high ground West of the Village.

13. (a)	In order to indicate that the 1st. and 2nd. objectives have been gained, the "success signal" will be fired (3 white lights).

(b)	The leading troops will light RED Flares when called for by contact aeroplane sounding its Klaxon Horn or dropping white Very lights.

(c)	A counter-attack machine will be in the air from ZERO onwards. The signal to denote the assembly of the enemy to counter-attack is the dropping of a RED smoke bomb over the place where the enemy is seen assembling.

14. (a)	All means of communication will be employed, i.e. telephone, Visual, Wireless, Runners, Pigeons.

(b)	All Ranks will be made acquainted with the signals to be used between Tanks and Infantry.

15.	The closest liaison will be kept between Companies and Brigades and between Sections and Battalions.

16.	Attention is again called to the necessity of frequent reports.

17.	The boldest use of Transport, limbers and pack, will be made during the operations.

18.	Advanced Battalion H.Q. will open at G.20.d.7.2. at 18,00 hours on 'Y' day.

19.	"Z" day and ZERO Hour will be notified later.

20.	Orders as regards synchronization of watches will be issued later.

21.	ACKNOWLEDGE.

Capt. & Adjt.,
3rd. Battln. M. G. Corps.

Issued at 2130 hrs.
Copies to:-
1. Commanding Officer.
2. 2nd/in/Command.
3. O.C. "A" Coy.
4. O.C. "B" "
5. O.C. "C" "
6. O.C. "D" "
7. "G" 3rd. Div.
8. C.R.A.
9. 8th. Inf. Bde.
10. 9th. "   "
11. 76th. Inf. Bde.
12. T.O.
13. Q.M.
14. S.O.
15. 2nd. Bn. M.G.C.
16. New Zealand Bn. M.G.C.
17. War Diary.
18.   "   "
19. File.

Tracings to:-	Company Commanders.
3rd. Div. "G".
8th., 9th., 76th., Infantry Brigades.

APPENDIX 1a

SECRET.

3rd. BATTALION MACHINE GUN CORPS.

REPORT ON OPERATIONS.

FROM - 29th. September 1918.

TO - 9th. October 1918.

Reference Sheets - 57.C. N.E.
57.C. N.W.

-x-

1. On the 28th. and 29th. September, the Battalion was resting and reorganizing in the Trench System at K.32. Battalion H.Q. were at J.36.b.9.3.

2. At 5-0 p.m. on the 30th. orders were received that the Division would move forward and be prepared to pass through the 62nd. Division in the line, and in conjunction with the 2nd. Division continue the advance on the morning of the 1st. October.

3. The necessary orders were issued to Companies. Battln. H.Q. and "A" Coy. moved to Trench System in K.24.a. on the South side of FLESQUIERES, "B" Coy. moved to TRIANGLE WOOD at K.29.c.3.0. "C" Coy. was attached to the 76th. Infantry Brigade and moved to Sunken Road at L.31.b.8.8. "D" Coy. was attached to 8th. Infantry Brigade and moved to Trench System in L.20.c.

4. At 6-0 a.m. on the 1st. Battalion H.Q. and "A" and "B" Companies moved to Area L.25.c. & d. Battln. H.Q. were established at L.25.a.00.15.

5. "C" Company moved to the line during the night with 76th. Infantry Brigade. Company H.Q. were established near Brigade H.Q. at L.22.a.9.4.
At 6 a.m. the 76th. Brigade passed through the 62nd. Division and advanced to the attack. One Battalion supported by two Companies of the 1st. GORDONS was to advance North-East from RUMILLY Support through RUMILLY to line of Sunken Road G.17. and 23 Central, the other Battalion supported by two Companies 1st. GORDONS was to conform on the right by advancing East of MASNIERES.
The right of the attack progressed favourably, the left however was seriously checked by Machine Gun fire from Railway in G.9.c. Such troops of ours as were in RUMILLY were withdrawn and the village was heavily bombarded.

"C" Company used its transport as far as MON PLAISIR FARM - G.27.d. from which place they took up positions along the original line. The roads were heavily shelled but no casualties were sustained by the transport.
"C" Company occupied positions as follows:-
4 guns at G.28.a.Central.
4 guns at G.28.b.0.7.
4 guns at G.21.c.4.8.
4 guns at L.24.a.Central.
Meanwhile 8th. Infantry Brigade reinforced the 76th. Infantry Brigade in the jumping off trenches.

6. "D" Company attached to 8th. Infantry Brigade allotted one Section to each of the leading Infantry Battalions and two Sections to the Reserve Infantry Battalion.

The Company Commander proceeded to the line and reconnoitred positions for his two Sections with the Reserve Infantry Battalion with a view to doing barrage fire. These two Sections followed on and occupied the selected positions on the reverse slope in G.22.c.

An Officer was sent to 8th. Brigade H.Q. as Machine Gun Liaison Officer and Company H.Q. were established at the H.Q. of an Infantry Battalion at G.27.b.3.6.

7. At 18.30 the 8th. Infantry Brigade which had assembled during the afternoon attacked to establish the objective of the morning whilst the 76th. Brigade mopped up RUMILLY under a barrage.

(a) One Section of "C" Company followed the barrage through RUMILLY and established themselves at G.9.d.6.1. where they were able to protect the Northern approaches and Eastern front of the Village.

Four guns were placed at G.21.b.4.1. which protected RUMILLY from the South.

Four guns at G.22.c.5.7. all of which positions gave good Battle Line protection to the Sector.

Four guns were in depth at G.20.a.0.8.

(b) "D" Company disposed of its guns as follows:-
8 guns at G.22.c.   laid on indirect targets from which counter attacks might develop.
Four guns at G.22.c.75.00.
Four guns at G.26.b.50.70.

There was scattered but heavy enemy shelling during the night including a lot of gas.

8. On the 2nd. October Division issued orders that the 8th. Infantry Brigade would hold the forward area whilst the 76th. Infantry Brigade would be responsible for the defence of RUMILLY.

By midnight on the 2nd./3rd. October the guns were redisposed according to the wishes of Brigades, as follows:-

"C" Company.
4 guns at G.15.b.8.9.
2 guns at G.15.b.7.3.)
2 guns at G.15.d.7.9.) Along the Eastern edge of
2 guns at G.21.b.2.8.)   RUMILLY.
2 guns at G.21.b.2.2.)
4 guns at G.14.c.5.9.

"D" Company.
4 guns at G.27.b.99.30.
4 guns at G.21.d.25.82.
4 guns at G.21.b.20.15.
4 guns at G.21.a.00.25.

9. "S.O.S" Lines were arranged in conjunction with the Artillery and in accordance with the wishes of the G.O.C., 8th. Infantry Brigade.

10. During the night of the 3rd/4th. October "C" Company moved their guns to the following positions -
4 guns at G.15.b.8.9.
2 guns at G.21.b.2.2.
2 guns at G.21.c.3.9.
4 guns at G.20.a.3.5.
4 guns at G.14.c.48 & 87.

11. Much harassing fire was carried out during the hours of darkness and organised shoots were fired on known enemy strong points.

12. At 9.50 a.m. on October 5th, the Commanding Officer attended a Conference at Divisional Headquarters.

13. At 6.20 p.m. on the 5th, Operation Orders were received from Division ordering operations for the 8th.

14. (a) The Third Army was to continue its advance towards the general line LE CATEAU – SOLESMES.
(b) The objective allotted to the VI Corps was WAMBAIX and IGNIEL DIT LES FRISETTES.
(c) The attack of the VI Corps was to be carried out by the 3rd. Division on the right and the 2nd. Division on the left.

15. At 9-30 p.m. Operation Order No. 47. (Appendix 1) was issued. Officers of "A" and "B" Companies made a reconnaissance of Sector.

16. At 6-0 p.m. on the 7th. Battalion H.Q. moved to G.20.d.7.2. MASNIERES. During the night 7th/8th. October "A" and "B" Companies moved from RIBECOURT to assembly positions in front of MASNIERES, whilst "C" and "D" Companies moved from their last positions to barrage positions at,

"C" Coy.   G.22.b.
"D" Coy.   G.22.d.

The forward movement and assembly was a matter of great difficulty, owing to darkness, and in itself quite a creditable feat. More than one journey was required by the Section already in line to move up their material and supplies of S.A.A.

17. At ZERO Hour 04.30 everything was in readiness.
Arrangements had been made to protect our troops advancing in front of our machine guns firing barrage, and all guns were able to fire their full programme; it is believed with great success.
On completion of their barrage "C" and "D" Companies came under the command of 76th. Infantry Brigade and the D.M.G.O. respectively.

18. "A" and "B" Companies were attached to the 9th. Infantry Brigade to advance with the Infantry putting down barrages as shown in Operation Order No. 47 and to consolidate the positions won.

19. At ZERO Hour "A" Company which was assembled in G.23.a. & b. advanced with its limbers. The rapidity and heaviness of the enemy barrage prevented the limbers being further exploited. Dumps were formed and the limbers sent away.

At this stage it is regretted that Lieut. W. H. SHAW was killed. The Sections followed closely to the Infantry sustaining severe casualties; they continued however and took up positions directed,

8 guns at H.13.c.30.15.
8 guns at H.12.a.60.15.

From these positions the barrage on the BLUE LINE was opened as in Operation Order No. 47.

At about 10.30 the enemy counter attack developed, tanks being employed. The Officer in charge of battery at H.13.c.30.15 directed the fire of his eight guns on the Tanks at 600 yards range causing them to retire. The fire of this massed battery was then directed on to the ground North of SERANVILLERS where the enemy was observed to be debouching, inflicting casualties for 15 minutes at only 1200 yards range.

20. "B" Company moved off with limbers at ZERO Hour; they advanced a certain distance with them but had to abandon transport on having three horses killed. The casualties suffered in this preliminary advance were very heavy. Two Sections were moving forward when they discovered the Tanks; these they promptly engaged but it was an unequal struggle in which they suffered severely.

/The

(3)

The positions occupied at noon were,
H.20.c.4.8.
H.20.b.3.0.
H.13.d.0.8.
H.13.c.8.5.

21. Owing to the obscurity in the situation caused by the enemy counter-attack it was decided to continue the attack at 12.35.
The D.M.G.C. consulted with the Brigadier General 9th. Infantry Brigade and issued orders for a barrage to be produced to aid this movement.

22. "A" and "B" Companies undertook this task. 2nd. Lieut. MEDLOCK of "B" Company who was going up to replace a casualty took the orders for the shoot with him. He was unable to find his own guns but found ten guns of 2nd. Division at G.18.d.8.5. and they responded and put down the required barrage.

23. After this operation the situation was still obscure. The D.M.G.C. again arranged for a machine gun barrage to assist the advance to take place at 18.00.

24. The operation this time succeeded and the whole of the 2nd. objective was consolidated.

25. In all 146,000 rounds were fired by the four Companies in support of operations.

26. "A" and "B" Companies withdrew from their positions after the Guards had passed through them.
"C" and "D" Companies withdrew the evening of "Z" Day.
All Companies marched to VELU spending one night at RIBECOURT en route.

27. The highest praise is due to Officers for the accurate way in which the various barrage shoots were conducted. Requiring as it did careful reconnaissance and precautions to protect our own troops advancing in the open in front of the guns.
No complaints were received.

28. Too much cannot be said of the magnificent spirit of N.C.Os. and men, who, tired out by the many movements imposed upon them, undertook each new task without a grumble and never stopped short of doing their work thoroughly.

29. A special word must be said for the Transport drivers and N.C.Os. who had a very arduous time, especially when they helped to move their Sections forward through the heavy shelling. They were dauntless.

30. CASUALTIES.
Officers - Killed ... Lieut. W. H. SHAW 8/10/18.
Wounded ... Lieut. G. S. BALL, "
2nd/Lieut. H.E.ROBINSON, "

O.Rs. - Killed ... 12.
Wounded... 42. (1 wounded Gas).
Wounded at Duty 4.

W J Cranston
Lieut. Colonel
Commanding 2nd. Battln. M.G.Corps.

SECRET.

3rd. BATTALION MACHINE GUN CORPS.

OPERATION ORDER NO. 47.

COPY NO........

OCTOBER 6th. 1918.

Reference Sheet 57.B. N.W. 1/20,000.
---:X:---

1. The Third Army is to continue its advance towards the general line LE CATEAU --- SOLESMES.

2. The objectives allotted to the VI Corps are WAMBAIX and IGNIEL DIT LES FRISETTES.

3. (a) The attack of the VI Corps will be carried out by the 3rd. Division on the right and the 2nd. Division on the left.

(b) The Guards Division will be prepared to pass through the 3rd. Division under orders of the Corps according as the situation develops, and will in any case take over from, or pass through the 3rd. Division on the night "Z"/"Z" plus 1 night.

(c) The New Zealand Division will be attacking on the right of the 3rd. Division.

4. The boundaries between 3rd. Division and flank Divisions, and the objectives are shewn on the Map already issued to Companies.

5. (a) The advance on the 3rd. Division front will be carried out by the 9th. Infantry Brigade which will pass through the 8th. Infantry Brigade at ZERO Hour.

(b) The line of departure of the 9th. Infantry Brigade will extend from the East and West grid line between Squares G.23. and G.29. to L'EPINE (inclusive).
9th. Infantry Brigade H.Q. - G.20.d.7.2.

(c) The 99th. Infantry Brigade (2nd. Division) will pass through the 8th. Infantry Brigade.

6. One Battalion 76th. Infantry Brigade and "A" and "B" Companies, 3rd. Battalion Machine Gun Corps will come under the orders of the G.O.C., 9th. Infantry Brigade.

7. 76th. Infantry Brigade (less one Battalion) and "C" Coy. 3rd. Battln. Machine Gun Corps will be in Divisional Reserve and will be prepared:-

(a) Either to support the 9th. Infantry Brigade in their attack on the 2nd. objective for which purpose they will come under the orders of the G.O.C., 9th. Infantry Brigade, or -

(b) On receipt of orders from Divisional H.Q., to pass through the 9th. Infantry Brigade on the 2nd. objective and capture the 3rd. objective under the orders of the G.O.C., 76th. Infantry Brigade.

8. "C" Company, 3rd. Battln. Machine Gun Corps, after completion of task allotted them by D.M.G.C. will be prepared to join 76th. Infantry Brigade, as the Brigade moves forward.

9. On night Y/Z 9th. Infantry Brigade and "A" and "B" Companies will move forward under orders of the G.O.C., 9th. Infantry Brigade and will be clear of their present area by 19.00 hours.
No move to take place before 17.30 hours.

10. The following tasks are allotted:-

(a) "D" Company. 16 guns in Trench in G.22.c. (not East of a line running North and South through G.22.c.4.5) will fire a creeping barrage starting on road in G.24.b & d. Each lift will be 200 yards and will be in accordance with Map issued.

Time of Fire.
Road G.24.b & d.   ZERO to ZERO plus 10'.
1st. Lift.   ZERO plus 10' to ZERO plus 18'.
2nd. Lift.   ZERO plus 18' to ZERO plus 26'.

Rate of Fire: One belt per gun per five minutes.

"D" Company will remain in their barrage positions until further orders are received from D.M.G.C.

(b) "C" Company. 16 guns will occupy positions in Trench in G.22.b. (not East of a line running North and South through G.22.b.4.5) and will barrage 1st. objective from ZERO plus 30' to ZERO plus 65'.
Rate of fire -- One belt per gun per five minutes.

(c) "B" Company. 16 guns will follow 9th. Infantry Brigade and, where possible, will support the advance by covering fire. They will support the consolidation of the 2nd. objective, the following positions being occupied:-
4 guns at H.13.d.40.60.
4 guns at H.14.a.20.00.
4 guns at H.20.c.30.65.
4 guns at H.20.b.20.00.

If the 3rd. objective is attacked by either/the 9th. or 76th. Infantry Brigade the following positions of consolidation will be occupied when objective is taken:-
4 guns at H.14.b.50.40.
4 guns at H.15.a.50.60.
4 guns at H.15.c.90.60.
4 guns at H.21.b.85.90.

(d) "A" Company. 16 guns will follow 9th. Infantry Brigade as closely as possible and will take up following positions:-
8 guns at H.13.c.30.15.
8 guns at H.19.a.60.15.

They will support by covering fire from ZERO plus 150' to ZERO plus 182' the attack on the 2nd. objective and cover consolidation. They will then cover the advance on the 3rd. objective and will cease fire on Infantry approaching within 300 yards of WAMBAIX.

When the 3rd. objective has been taken, the following positions will be occupied:-
8 guns at H.14.a.20.00.
8 guns at H.21.a.25.40.

(e) "S.O.S" Lines will be arranged with G.O.C., Forward Brigade by Group Commanders of "A" and "B" Companies.

11. There will be a pause of 30 minutes on the 1st. objective.

Troops advancing to the 2nd. objective will pass the 1st. objective at ZERO plus 130'.

12. Six Mark IV Tanks will co-operate in the attack and will follow in rear of the 9th. Infantry Brigade.

Four Tanks will operate against SERANVILLERS and two tanks on the high ground West of the Village.

13. (a) In order to indicate that the 1st. and 2nd. objectives have been gained, the "success signal" will be fired (3 white lights).

(b) The leading troops will light RED Flares when called for by contact aeroplane sounding its Klaxon Horn or dropping white Very lights.

(c) A counter-attack machine will be in the air from ZERO onwards. The signal to denote the assembly of the enemy to counter-attack is the dropping of a RED smoke bomb over the place where the enemy is seen assembling.

14. (a) All means of communication will be employed, i.e. telephone, Visual, Wireless, Runners, Pigeons.

(b) All Ranks will be made acquainted with the signals to be used between Tanks and Infantry.

15. The closest liaison will be kept between Companies and Brigades and between Sections and Battalions.

16. Attention is again called to the necessity of frequent reports.

17. The boldest use of Transport, limbers and pack, will be made during the operations.

18. Advanced Battalion H.Q. will open at G.22.d.7.2. at 18,00 hours on 'Y' day.

19. "Z" day and ZERO Hour will be notified later.

20. Orders as regards synchronization of watches will be issued later.

21. ACKNOWLEDGE.

Ralla
Capt. & Adjt.,
3rd. Battln. M. G. Corps.

Issued at..............
Copies to:-
1. Commanding Officer.
2. 2nd/in/Command.
3. O.C. "A" Coy.
4. O.C. "B" "
5. O.C. "C" "
6. O.C. "D" "
7. "G" 3rd. Div.
8. C.R.A.
9. 8th. Inf. Bde.
10. 9th. " "
11. 76th. Inf. Bde.
12. T.O.
13. Q.M.
14. S.O.
15. 2nd. Bn. M.G.C.
16. New Zealand Bn. M.G.C.
17. War Diary.
18. " "
19. File.

Tracings to:-   Company Commanders.
3rd. Div. "G".
8th., 9th., 76th., Infantry Brigades.

SECRET.

ADDENDUM TO OPERATION ORDER NO. 47, dated OCTOBER 6th, 1918.

3rd. BATTALION MACHINE GUN CORPS.

1. 'Z' Day will be October 8th.

2. Watches will be synchronized at Brigade Headquarters between 16,00 hours and 17,00 hours on 7th. October.

3. Reference Para.13.(b) A Contact aeroplane will call for flares at ZERO plus 1 hour 55 minutes and ZERO plus 3 hours, 20 minutes.

4. When the Guards Division has passed through and taken over responsibility for the front the Division will be withdrawn to the HAVRINCOURT - HERMIES Area and become Right Reserve Division.

5. ACKNOWLEDGE.

OCTOBER 7th, 1918.

Capt. & Adjt.,
3rd. Battln. M. G. Corps.

Issued at:..........

Copies to:-
1. Commanding Officer.
2. Second in Command.
3. O.C. "A" Coy.
4. O.C. "B" "
5. O.C. "C" "
6. O.C. "D" "
7. Q.M.
8. T.O.
9. S.O.
10. War Diary.
11. "   "
12. File.

SECRET.

No. 1

ADDENDUM TO OPERATION ORDER NO. 47. dated OCTOBER 6th. 1918.

3rd. BATTALION MACHINE GUN CORPS.

1. "Z" Day will be October 8th.

2. Watches will be synchronized at Brigade Headquarters between 16,00 hours and 17,00 hours on 7th. October.

3. Reference Para.13.(b)   A Contact aeroplane will call for flares at ZERO plus 1 hour 55 minutes and ZERO plus 3 hours, 20 minutes.

4. When the Guards Division has passed through and taken over responsibility for the front the Division will be withdrawn to the HAVRINCOURT - HERMIES Area and become Right Reserve Division.

5. ACKNOWLEDGE.

Capt. & Adjt.,
3rd. Battln. M. G. Corps.

OCTOBER 7th. 1918.

Issued at: 0930 hrs.

Copies to:-
1. Commanding Officer.
2. Second in Command.
3. O.C. "A" Coy.
4. O.C. "B" "
5. O.C. "C" "
6. O.C. "D" "
7. Q.M.
8. T.O.
9. S.O.
10. War Diary.
11. "   "
12. File.

APPENDIX 2.

SECRET.

3rd. BATTALION MACHINE GUN CORPS.

OPERATION ORDER NO. 48.

———x———

COPY NO. 16

OCTOBER 12th. 1918.

Reference Sheet - 57.C N.E.

1. The Battalion will move tomorrow 13th. instant to the FLESQUIERES Area.

2. Order of March, and Time of Starting.
   B.H.Q. and "C" Company ... 11.30 hours.
   "D" Company ... ... 11.45 hours.
   "A" Company ... ... 12.00 hours.
   "B" Company ... ... 12.15 hours.

   Dress - Fighting Order with Caps. Helmets will be slung over shoulder. Officers Valises and Packs will be carried on limbers.

3. Companies will halt near the Crucifix on the South side of HERMIES for dinner.
   The dinner of Battln. H.Q. will be cooked on "C" Company's cooker.
   Transport will be halted off the roads during dinner.

4. Companies will resume the march in the original order and at 15 minutes intervals. The leading Company moving off at 15.00 hours.

5. Route will be via CANAL RAMP at K.31.a.0.3.

6. A billeting party of one Officer and necessary cyclists per Company will leave VELU Chateau gates at 11.00 hours.
   Lieut. SAMS, M.C. will accompany this party and allocate billeting Area, which consists of Squares K.18, K.24. and L.19.

7. Strictest attention will be paid to March Discipline. 200 yards interval will be maintained between a Company and its Transport.

8. Huts and vicinity thereof will be left in a clean and sanitary condition.

9. Battln. H.Q. will reopen at L.19.a.5.7. (Old 3rd. Divn. H.Q.) on arrival.

10. Marching out state will be rendered to Battln. H.Q. by 10.00 hours 13th. instant. Arrival Reports are due within one hour of arrival.

11. ACKNOWLEDGE.

Capt. & Adjt.
Issued at...21.50 hours... 3rd. Battln. M.G. Corps.
Copies to:-
1. Commanding Officer. 7. G 3rd. Div.   13. 8th. Inf. Bde.
2. 2nd in Command.   8. T.O.   14. 9th. "   "
3. O.C. "A" Coy.   9. Q.M.   15. 76th. "   "
4. O.C. "B" "   10. M.O.   16. War Diary.
5. O.C. "C" "   11. S.O.   17. "   "
6. O.C. "D" "   12. T.O.   18. Town Major. VELU.

APPENDIX 3

SECRET.

3rd. BATTALION MACHINE GUN CORPS.

WARNING ORDER NO. 49.

COPY NO. 16

OCTOBER, 19th. 1918.

Reference Maps - Sheets 57.C.)
                           51.A.)   1/40,000.
                           57.B.)

1. The Division (less Artillery) is to be prepared to move as under, at two hours' notice after 07.00 hours October 20th.

   (a) 76th. Infantry Brigade Group from CATTENIERES to QUIEVY.

   (b) 9th. Infantry Brigade from present Area to BEVILLERS.

   (c) 8th. Infantry Brigade from present Area to CATTENIERES.

Times at which these moves will take place and routes are to be notified later.

2. Reference above moves, Companies of the Machine Gun Battalion will be allotted as follows,

    "C" Company to 76th. Infantry Brigade.
    "B" Company to 9th. Infantry Brigade.
    "D" Company to 8th. Infantry Brigade.

The above Companies will move under the orders of their respective G.Os.C.

3. Orders for move of Battalion H.Q. & "A" Company will be issued later.

4. ACKNOWLEDGE.

                                                     Capt. & Adjt.,
Issued at 1600   3rd. Battln. M.G.Corps.

Copies to -
1. Commanding Officer.   11. "G" 3rd. Div.
2. 2/in/Command.   12. 8th. Inf. Bde.
3. O.C. "A" Coy.   13. 9th. " "
4. O.C. "B" "   14. 76th. " "
5. O.C. "C" "   15. War Diary.
6. O.C. "D" "   16. " "
7. Q.M.   17. File.
8. T.O.
9. S.O.
10. I.O.

APPENDIX 5

SECRET.

3rd. BATTALION MACHINE GUN CORPS.

OPERATION ORDER NO. 50.

COPY NO........

OCTOBER 27th. 1918.

Reference Sheet, 51,A. S.E.

The following re-arrangement of the Divisional front will take place commencing tonight.

99th. Infantry Brigade of the 2nd. Division will be withdrawn into Corps reserve.

The Corps front will then be held by the 3rd. Division alone with two Brigades in the line and one in reserve.

8th. Infantry Brigade will be on the right and 76th. Infantry Brigade on the left.

Boundaries between 8th. and 76th. Infantry Brigades will be BOSQUET - DES - QUATORZE -- Cross Roads R.14.c.4.4. -- Road junction R.14.b.2.1. (all inclusive to 8th. Infantry Brigade) HALT R.9.b.1.6. (inclusive to 76th. Infantry Brigade).

1½ Companies M. G. Battalion will be attached to 8th. and 76th. Infantry Brigades respectively under a Group Commander at each Brigade H.Q.
"A" Company and 8 guns of "D" Company (4 guns at R.16.c.1.5. and 4 guns at R.15.c.5.5.) will constitute the 8th. Brigade Machine Gun Group under Major SWANN, Group Commander.
"C" Company and 8 guns of "D" Company (2 guns at R.14.b.95.95, 2 guns at R.14.b.90.75, 2 guns at R.2.d.3.2. and 2 guns at R.3.b.6.5) will constitute the 76th. Brigade Machine Gun Group under Major ST. LEGER, Group Commander.

The 16 guns of "C" Company will relieve the guns of the 2nd. Division at R.13.d.4.5. (4 guns) R.19a.2.8. (4 guns), R.7.c.1.1. (2 guns) and Q.12.c.0.5. (2 guns).

The position of the 4 guns of the 2nd. Battalion at Q.23.a.7.6. will not be relieved but positions about R.13.a.6.4. will be occupied instead.

"B" Company will be in Divisional reserve but will remain in their present battle positions.

"S.O.S" lines will remain as at present in force.

Relief of guns of 2nd. Battalion by "C" Company will be arranged between Company Commanders concerned.

Relief will be complete by 10.00 hours October 28th.

Reliefs will be carried out so that there will be no movement in positions exposed to direct ground observation by the enemy during the hours of daylight.
Relief of troops not exposed to direct observation should be carried out in daylight so as to avoid gas shelling which takes place at night.

/O.C.

O.C., 76th. Infantry Brigade Machine Gun Group will forward to Battln. H.Q. as soon as possible the grid bearings of the battle lines of the guns of his group.

The 8 guns of "D" Company will come under the command of O.C., 76th. Infantry Brigade Machine Gun Group at 10.00 hours 28th. October.

A C K N O W L E D G E.

                                                Capt. & Adjt.,
                                          3rd. Battln. M.G.Corps.

Issued at.....15.30 hours.
Copies to:-
1. Commanding Officer.
2. O.C. 8th. Brigade Machine Gun Group.
3. O.C.   "C" Coy.
4. O.C.   "B" "
5. "G" 3rd. Divn.
6. 8th. Inf. Bde.
7. 9th. "   "
8. 76th. "   "
9. War Diary.
10.   "   "
11. File.

APPENDIX 5A

SECRET.

3rd. BATTALION MACHINE GUN CORPS.

A.49.

OCTOBER 29th. 1918.

Reference Sheet 51,A. S.E.

On the 29th. October 2nd. Division (less Artillery) will relieve 3rd. Division (less Artillery).

Companies of Machine Gun Battalion will be relieved by Companies of 2nd. Battalion as follows:

All guns of the 76th. Infantry Brigade Machine Gun Group (less 2 guns at Q.13.d.3.1., 2 guns at Q.24.b.95.45. and 4 guns of "D" Company in R.14.b.) will be relieved on evening of 29th. October.

The two guns at Q.18.d.3.1. and 2 guns at Q.24.b.95.45. will be relieved on morning of 30th. October.

For purposes of relief the 4 guns of "D" Company in R.14.b. will come under the 8th. Infantry Brigade Machine Gun Group.

The following guns of the 8th. Infantry Brigade Machine Gun Group will be relieved on the morning of the 30th. October:
4 guns of "D" Coy. in R.14.b., 4 guns of "D" Coy. in R.15.c., 8 guns of "A" Coy. in R.21.b.
The 4 guns of "D" Coy. in R.16.c. and the 8 guns of "A" Coy. in R.21.a. will withdraw at an hour to be notified later.
The 16 guns of "B" Coy. (8 guns in R.19.d. and 8 guns in R.26.b.) will be relieved by 12 guns of the 2nd. Battalion on the morning of the 30th.

Completion of relief will be reported to Forward Battalion H.Q. in ESCARMAIN.

On completion of relief Companies will concentrate about cottage in W.10.a. and move to billets at ST. PYTHON.

Captain MATTHEWS "C" Coy. with one Officer from each Company will proceed today to Town Major ST. PYTHON to obtain billets for the Battalion.

In the event of another move on 30th. or 31st. October the same billeting party will be prepared to go ahead and obtain billets.

ACKNOWLEDGE.

Callen
Capt. & Aj.,
3rd. Battln. M.G.Corps.

Issued at 11.00 hours.
Copies to:- Commanding Officer.
O.C. "A" Coy.
O.C. "B" "
O.C. "C" "
O.C. "D" "
"G" 3rd. Div,
8th. Inf. Bde.
9th. " "
76th. " "
War Diary

APPENDIX 6

COPY NO..........

SECRET.

3rd. BATTALION MACHINE GUN CORPS

OPERATION ORDER NO...51. OCTOBER 30th. 1918.

Reference Sheets 51.A. S.E. 1/20,000.
57.B.

1. The 3rd. Division is being withdrawn into Corps Reserve.

   76th. Infantry Brigade Group including the 3rd. Battalion Machine Gun Corps will move into CARNIERES Area tomorrow.

2. The Battalion will march in rear of the 8th. K.O.R.L.

3. Companies will parade outside their billets prepared to move off at 11.30 hours.
   Orders as to actual moving off will be issued tomorrow.
   Transport at SOLESMES will join their Companies by 11.30 hours.

4. Order of March - Battalion H.Q. and "C" Coy.
                    "B" Company.
                    "A" Company.
                    "D" Company.
   Dress - Fighting Order. Steel helmets will be worn.
   Route - Railway Crossing D.5.d.3.8. - Road Junction D.10.d.4.1. - QUIEVY - BEVILLERS - BOUSSIERES.

5. 1st. Line transport of each Company will march in rear of its Company.
   Cookers, Mess Cart and Maltese Cart will march in rear of the Battalion.
   Baggage and supply wagons, and water carts will march under O.C., No. 2. Coy. 3rd. Divn. Train. They will rendezvous at Road Junction D.5.d.9.5. at 11.45 hours reporting to O.C., No. 2. Coy. Train on arrival.

6. The distances to be maintained on the march will be as follows -
   Between Battalions and their Transport ... 100 yards.
   Between Battalions ... ... 300 yards.
   i.e. Battalion H.Q. and "C" Company will keep a distance of 300 yards behind the 8th. K.O.R.L. and a distance of 100 yards will be maintained between "D" Company's transport and the Cookers, Mess Cart and Maltese Cart (as in para. 5).

7. The strictest march discipline must be observed.

8. A Billeting party of 1 Officer per Company (with requisite guides) under the Second in Command will leave Battalion H.Q. at 07.30 hours and will meet the Staff Captain, 76th. Infantry Brigade at Town Major's Office, CARNIERES at 09.00 hours.

9.) Guides from Billeting parties will be at BOUSSIERES Church to meet their Companies at 14.15 hours.
   Billeting Officers will ensure that one guide per Company is detailed to meet the Water Carts moving under No. 2. Coy. Train.

10. All billets now occupied must be left scrupulously clean.

11. Machine Gun Companies to ACKNOWLEDGE.

Ralla

Capt. & Adjt.,
3rd. Battln. M.G.Corps.

Issued at..............

Copies to:-
1. Commanding Officer.
2. Second in Command.
3. O.C. "A" Coy.
4. O.C. "B" "
5. O.C. "C" "
6. O.C. "D" "
7. 3rd. Div. "G"
8. 76th. Inf. Bde.
9. Battln. T.O.
10. T.M. ST.PYTHON.
11. Q.M.
12. I.O.
13. R.S.M.
14. War Diary.
15. " "
16. File.

WAR DIARY
or
INTELLIGENCE SUMMARY.
(Erase heading not required.)

Army Form C. 2118.

3RD BATTN. M.G.C.

Place	Date	Hour	Summary of Events and Information	Remarks and references to Appendices
CARMIERES B13d 6.40.	Mrch 1st		MAP 57 B.	
			Battalion cleaning up & re-organizing.	
			To duty 1 O.R. From Courts 1 O.R.	
	2nd		Battalion training.	
		14.00 hrs	Operation order No 52 issued.	APPENDIX I.
			Re-inforcement 57 O.R. from lends 3 O.R.	
			To lends 2/Lt. W.G. POULTON & 4 O.R.	
	3rd 11.00		Battalion Church Parade.	
	16.00		Brigade Officers attended conference at Division H.Q.	
	18.00		Battalion moved to BEVILLERS arriving in busses at 18.45 hrs.	
			B.H.Q. at C 22 d 2.6.	
			Evacuations 8 O.R. To Base depot 1 O.R.	
			To duty 4 O.R. From lends Capt. DOWLING & 7 O.R.	
BEVILLERS C 22 d 2.6	4th		B.H.Q. "A" & "B" Coys moved to QUIEVY arriving in busses at 10.15 hrs.	
			B.H.Q. at D 13d 4.0. "C" Coy moved to ESCARMAIN "D" Coy to SOLESMES.	
			To lends 3 O.R.	

Army Form C. 2118.

WAR DIARY
or
INTELLIGENCE SUMMARY.
(Erase heading not required.)

3RD BATTN M.G.C.

Instructions regarding War Diaries and Intelligence Summaries are contained in F.S. Regs., Part II. and the Staff Manual respectively. Title pages will be prepared in manuscript.

Place	Date	Hour	Summary of Events and Information	Remarks and references to Appendices
QUIEVY D.13.d.4.0	1918 Nov 5		Coy training. Evacuation 5 O.R. To leave 2 O.R. From leave Lt P. DANGERFIELD M.C. & 3 O.R.	
	Nov 6		Coy training. Evacuation 2 O.R. To leave 2/Lt D.J. WILLIAMS MM & 2 O.R. From leave MAJ. C.D. WETTON & 3 O.R.	
	7	22.00	Operation Order No 54 issued. Evacuation 6 O.R. To leave 2 O.R. From leave MAJ. E. THOMAS M.C. & 1 O.R.	APPENDIX 3/III
	8	09.00	B"HQ "A" & "B" Coy moved to YERTAIN arriving in billets at 13 hr. B.H.Q at W.15.a B.8. (Map 57B) "C" Coy moved to GOMMEGNIES. Evacuation 1 O.R. To leave 4 O.R.	
MAP 57A	9		Coy training. Operation order N°55 issued. From hospital 1 O.R. Evacuation Lt A.J. DEATON & 17 O.R. Re-inforcement 2/Lt T. VOSE. From leave 2 O.R. To leave CAPT. G.A. MATTHEWS M.C. & 2 O.R.	APPENDIX 4/III
W 15a.8.8.				

WAR DIARY
or
INTELLIGENCE SUMMARY.
(Erase heading not required.)

Army Form C. 2118.

3RD BATTN. M.G.C.

Place	Date	Hour	Summary of Events and Information	Remarks and references to Appendices
W 15 a. 8.8	Nov 10		MAP. 51a.	
			B.H.Q. "A" & "B" Coy marched to GOMMEGNIES arriving in billets at 15.00 hr. B.H.Q. M7a.1.0. (App 51)	
			"D" Coy moved to VERTAIN arriving at 11.00 hr	
		18.00 hr	Operation Order No 56 issued	APPENDIX 51
			To Canteen 2 O.R. To Baths MAJ. E. THOMAS M.C.	
GOMMEGNIES M. 7a 1.0	11		MAP. 51.	
			B.H.Q moved to SARLOTON N.13 d 5.5	
			Evacuation 1 O.R. To Leave LT. H.E.TIPPER. 2 O.R.	
			From leave LT. A MURCH + 2 O.R.	
SARLOTON N. 13 d 5.5	12	11.00	Company Officers attended Conference at Division	
			To Leave 2 O.R. From leave LT G.J.GRANT & 2 O.R	
			To Canteen 1 O.R.	
		13	"D" Coy marched to SARLOTON arriving in billets at 13.00 hr	
			Evacuation 4 O.R. To leave LT. A.G.CRAIG & 2 O.R.	
			From leave 2/LT W.E. ROSSER & 3 O.R.	

Army Form C. 2118.

WAR DIARY
or
INTELLIGENCE SUMMARY.
(Erase heading not required.)

3RD BATTN M.G.C.

Instructions regarding War Diaries and Intelligence Summaries are contained in F. S. Regs., Part II. and the Staff Manual respectively. Title pages will be prepared in manuscript.

Place	Date	Hour	Summary of Events and Information	Remarks and references to Appendices
SABLOTON M13.d.5.5	Nov 14		MAP 51	
			Battalion cleaning up & training	APPENDIX 6(1)
		22.00	Operation Order No 57 issued	(1)
			From Infants 1.O.R. Evacuations 6 O.R. To leave 2 O.R.	(1)
			From leave 6 O.R. Reinforcements 24 O.R.	(1)
	15		B.H.Q. "A" "B" & "D" Coys marched to LA LONGUEVILLE arriving at	(1)
			Which 13.15. Ln. B.H.Q. at 136.a.9.6.	
136.a.9.6	16		Evacuations 9. O.R. To leave. 2. O.R. From leave 10 R	(1)
			Battalion training. To leave 1. O.R.	(1)
	17		O.O. No 58 issued 18 others Evacuations 2 O.R. To leave 5 O.R.	APPENDIX (1)
236.a.9.6.			From leave 3. O.R.	(1)
Sous LE BOIS	18		Battalion moved to Sous LE Bois arriving @ 16 the Battn. H.Q. Q.7.C.0'.	(1)
			Sheet 51. Evacuations (2.O.R.) to leave 3. O.R. from leave 2.O.R.	(1)
Q.7.C.0.1	19		O.O. No 59 issued. Battle Training. To leave 2 O.R. Evacuation 40.O.R.	APPENDIX 8
R.13.D.12.15	20		Battn. moved to CERFONTAINE arriving in billets @ 10-45 hrs	(1)
CERFONTAINE			Battn. H.Q. (17 Rue a) R.13.D.25-25. Sheet 51. To leave 2.O.R.	(1)

WAR DIARY
or
INTELLIGENCE SUMMARY.

3RD Battn M.Q.C.

Army Form C. 2118.

Place	Date	Hour	Summary of Events and Information	Remarks and references to Appendices
R.13.D.25.25 GERZONTAINE	NOV 20		MAP 51. Continued. Evacuations 2 O.R. From Leave 3.O.R.	
R.13.D.25.25	21		Battn training. Evacuations (9 O.R.) To leave 2 O.R. From Leave 3. O.R.	
R.13.D.25.25	22		Battn training. TO LEAVE 8. O.R. From Leave 2 O.R. 2nd D.J.Williams	
R.13.D.25.25	23		Battn training. Operation order N°2 issued @ 15.30 hrs 24 Evacuations (To leave 2 O.R. Capt Field) From Leave 2 O.R.	APPENDIX 9
LIGERS ET. FOSTEAU	24	12.50 hrs	Battn marched to LIGERS ET FOSTEAU arriving in billets @ 13.30 hrs Battn H.Q. @ TACPESSE Ref I.26.a 5.0. Sheet 52. Operation Order N° 6 issued @ 17.45 hrs TO LEAVE 5. O.R. FROM LEAVE 4. O.R.	APPENDIX 10

Army Form C. 2118.

WAR DIARY
or
INTELLIGENCE SUMMARY.

3rd Battn. M.G. Corps

(Erase heading not required.)

Instructions regarding War Diaries and Intelligence Summaries are contained in F. S. Regs., Part II. and the Staff Manual respectively. Title pages will be prepared in manuscript.

Place	Date	Hour	Summary of Events and Information	Remarks and references to Appendices
			MAP 51	
I 26 c 5.0.	Nov 25		Battn. marched to MARBIAX arriving @ 14-15 hrs Battn. H.Q. Chateau J.52.C.3. Sheet 52. Operation Order No 62 issued @ 21-35 hrs	APPENDIX 11
MARBIAX	Nov 26		To leave 2.O.R. from leave 2.O.R. Evacuations 4.O.R.	Nil
J.52.B.3. Sheet 52.			Battn. marched to GERPINNES arriving @ 14.00 hrs Battn. H.Q. CHATEAU GERPINNES. Evacuation (1 O.R.) to leave 2.O.R. from leave 5.O.R. & Lt. T. SMITH M.C. To leave 2.O.R.	Nil / Nil
GERPINNES	27		Battn. training. Operation Order No 63 issued @ 22 hrs. To leave 2.O.R.	APPENDIX 12
ST GERARD	28		Battn. marched to ST GERARD arriving in billets @ 12·45 hrs Battn. H.Q. Chateau. Operation Order No 64 issued. To leave 2.O.R. from leave 3.O.R. AT 29 hrs	Nil / APPENDIX 13
PURNODE	29		Battn. marched to Purnode arriving in billets @ 13-20 hrs Battn H.Q. in AWAGNE. To leave 2.O.R.	Nil / Nil
NATOYE	30		Operation Order issued @ 02.00 hrs Battn. marched to NATOYE arriving in billets @ 14hrs B.H.Q. FRANCESSE. Chateau. To leave 2.O.R.	APPENDIX 14 / Nil

W. Horgan Lieut. Colonel
Comdg. 3rd Bn. M.G. Corps

APPENDIX 1

SECRET.

3rd. BATTALION MACHINE GUN CORPS.

OPERATION ORDERS NO. 52.

COPY NO. 16

NOVEMBER 2nd, 1918.

Reference Map - 57.B. 1/40,000.

1. The Battalion will march to the BEVILLERS Area via BOUSSIERES on November 3rd.

   Starting Point - Cross Roads in BOUSSIERES C.21.a.5.4.

   Battalion H.Q.) pass starting Point at 18.01 hours.
   "B" Company)
   "A" Company   -do-   18.10 hours.
   "D" Company   -do-   18.19 hours.
   "C" Company   -do-   18.28 hours.

2. Distances to be maintained -
   100 yards between Company and its Transport.
   300 yards between Companies.

3. Each Company will be followed by its own Transport including cooker and water cart.
   B.H.Q. Transport will travel in rear of "B" Company.

4. Dress - Marching Order.
   Officers' valises and Company blankets will be carried on limbers.

5. Each Company will provide a rearguard for the purpose of issuing straggler slips.
   "C" Company will provide a Battln. rearguard of one Section under an Officer.

6. A billeting party of one Officer and necessary guides per Company will proceed to BEVILLERS under the Second in Command on 3rd. November, leaving Battln. H.Q. at an hour to be notified later.

7. Billets at present occupied will be left in a clean and sanitary condition.

8. Machine Gun Companies to Acknowledge.

Capt. & Adjt.,
3rd. Battln. M.G.Corps.

Issued at 1400
Copies to :-
1. Commanding Officer.   9. Town Major CARNIERES.
2. 2/in/Command.   10. T.O.
3. O.C. "A" Coy.   11. Q.M.
4. O.C. "B" "   12. I.O.
5. O.C. "C" "   13. S.O.
6. O.C. "D" "   14. R.S.M.
7. "G" 3rd. Div.   15. War Diary.
8. 76th. Inf. Bde.   16.   "   "
                           17. File.

ADDENDA 2

SECRET.

3rd. BATTALION MACHINE GUN CORPS.

OPERATION ORDER NO. 53. COPY NO. 16

NOVEMBER 3rd, 1918.

Reference Maps - 57.B.
51.A.

1. The following moves will take place tomorrow 4th. November:-

    (a) "C" Company attached to 76th. Infantry Brigade will move to ESCARMAIN under orders of G.O.C., 76th. Infantry Brigade.

    (b) "D" Company, attached to 8th. Infantry Brigade will move to SOLESMES under orders of G.O.C., 8th. Infantry Brigade.

    (c) Battln. H.Q., "A" and "B" Companies will move to QUIEVY.

2. Reference para. 1. (c).
    Dress - Fighting Order.
    Starting Point - C.29.a.8.9. (57.B).
    Order of March - "B" Company to pass Starting point 09.00 hrs.
    Battln. H.Q.) "   "   "   09.10 hrs.
    "A" Company)

3. "A" Company will provide a Battalion Rearguard of one Section under an Officer.

4. Companies will be accompanied by their Transport.

5. Strictest march discipline will be observed.

6. A billeting party of one Officer and necessary guides from "A" and "B" Companies under the Second in Command will leave Battln. H.Q. at 08.00 hours.

7. Billets at present occupied will be left in a clean and sanitary condition.

8. A kit dump has been formed in BEVILLERS (C.23.c.0.4, Sheet 57.B) at which all packs, blankets, valises and surplus kit will be stored. Each Company will detail one man to remain with the kits.

9. Greatcoats will be carried on limbers carried in bundles of teams.

10. M.G. Units to ACKNOWLEDGE.

Capt. & Adjt.,
3rd. Battln. M. G. Corps.

Issued at... 22.00 hours.
Copies to:-
1. Commanding Officer.
2. Second in Command.
3. O.C. "A" Coy.
4. O.C. "B" "
5. O.C. "C" "
6. O.C. "D" "
7. "G" 3rd. Div.
8. 9th. Inf. Bde.
9. M.O.
10. Q.M.
11. T.O.
12. I.O.
13. S.O.
14. R.S.M.
15. War Diary.
16. " "
17. File.
18. Town Major, BEVILLERS.

APPENDIX 3

SECRET.

3rd. BATTALION MACHINE GUN CORPS

OPERATION ORDER NO. 54.

COPY NO...15...

NOVEMBER 7th. 1918.

Reference Sheets – 57.B. 1/40,000.
                       51.A. 1/40,000.

1. The following moves will take place tomorrow.

    (a) 76th. Infantry Brigade with "C" Company attached to FRASNOY.
    (b) 9th. Infantry Brigade to ROMERIES.
    (c) Machine Gun Battln. H.Q., "A" and "B" Companies to ROMERIES.

2. Reference para. 1. (c).
    Battln. H.Q., "A" and "B" Companies will move in rear of 9th. Infantry Brigade Group.

    Route – AUTERTRE FARM – SOLESMES STATION.

    Parade – 09.00 hours in front of billets.

    Order of march – "B" Company, Battln. H.Q., "A" Company.

3. Each Company will be followed by its own Transport.

4. Strictest march discipline will be maintained.

5. "A" Company will provide a rearguard of one Section under an Officer.

6. Billets at present occupied will be left in a clean and sanitary condition.

7. A billeting party of one Officer and necessary guides per Company under the Second in Command will leave B.H.Q. at 08.00 hours.

8. Machine Gun Units to ACKNOWLEDGE.

                                                     Capt. & Adjt.,
                                         3rd. Battln. M. G. Corps.

Issued at...22.00 hours.
Copies to:-
1. Commanding Officer.   9. T.O.
2. Second in Command.   10. Q.M.
3. O.C. "A" Coy.   11. I.O.
4. O.C. "B" "   12. S.O.
5. O.C. "C" "   13. R.S.M.
6. O.C. "D" "   14. War Diary.
7. "G" 3rd. Divn.   15. " "
8. Town Major QUIEVY. 16. File.

Appendix 5.

3rd. BATTALION MACHINE GUN CORPS.   SECRET.

OPERATION ORDER NO. 56.

COPY NO. 14

NOVEMBER 10th. 1918.

Sheet 51, 1/40,000.

1. The following moves will take place tomorrow.

   (a) 76th. Infantry Brigade Group (with "C" Coy. attached) to ASSEVENT.

   (b) 9th. Infantry Brigade Group (with "B" Coy. attached) to LA LONGUEVILLE.

   (c) 8th. Infantry Brigade Group (with "D" Coy. attached) to FRASNOY.

   (d) Battln. H.Q. and "A" Coy. to LA LONGUEVILLE.

2. Referenced para. 1. (d).
Route - AMFROIPRET - BERMERIES - BAVAI.
Starting Point - Road Junction H.32.d.7.0.
Time of passing Starting Point - 11.30 hours.
Parade (Ready to move off at 11.00 hours) - Battln. H.Q. in BRUCKEN STR.
"A" Coy. in RUE DE LA GARE.

3. Strictest march discipline will be maintained.

4. Personnel will be moved off the road at each halt.

5. "A" Company will provide a rearguard.

6. Billets at present occupied will be left in a clean and sanitary condition.

7. Billeting party under Second in Command will leave Battln. H.Q. at an hour to be notified later.

8. Machine Gun Units to ACKNOWLEDGE.

Capt. & Adjt.,
3rd. Battln. M.G.Corps.

Issued at...18.00 hours.
Copies to:-
1. Commanding Officer.   9. T.O.
2. Second in Command.   10. Q.M.
3. O.C. "A" Coy.   11. Lt. Smith.
4. O.C. "B" "   12. S.O.
5. O.C. "C" "   13. R.S.M.
6. O.C. "D" "   14. War Diary.
7. "G" 3rd. Divn.   15. " "
8. Town Major GOMEGNIES   16. File.

APPENDIX 6

SECRET.
COPY NO. 16

3rd. BATTALION MACHINE GUN CORPS

OPERATION ORDER NO. 57.   NOVEMBER 14th. 1918.

Reference Sheet 51 1/40,000.

1. Battln. H.Q., "A" "B" and "D" Companies will move tomorrow 15th. instant to LA LONGUEVILLE.

2. Order of march - Battln. H.Q.
   "A" Coy.
   "B" "
   "D" "

   Companies will not be followed by their Transport.
   All Transport will march in rear of "D" Coy. in the same order as the Companies.
   Starting Point - Junction of Roads M.7.a.5.5.
   Time of passing Starting Point - = 10.00 hours.
   Route - AMFROIPRET - BERMERIES - TO BAVAI

3. Dress:- Marching Order as detailed in Administrative Instructions Nos. 1 and 2. Packs, containing articles enumerated in Administrative Instructions will be carried.
   Greatcoats rolled by gun teams and Officers' valises will be carried in limbers.

4. At each halt, poles will be dropped and personnel moved off the road. On resumption of march files will be changed over.

5. "D" Coy. will provide a Battalion Rear-guard.

6. Billets at present occupied will be left in a clean and sanitary condition. Certificates to this effect will be rendered.

7. Billeting party will start from School, GOMMEGNIES at 09.00 hours. Transport Officers will accompany billeting party for purpose of obtaining stables.
   Lieut. BARWOOD will allot billets to Companies.

8. Machine Gun Units to ACKNOWLEDGE.

                                        Capt. & Adjt.,
                                        3rd. Battln. M. G. Corps.

Issued at.....22.28 hours.
Issued to:-
1. Commanding Officer   9. M.O.
2. 2/in/Command.   10. Q.M.
3. O.C. "A" Coy.   11. T.O.
4. O.C. "B" "   12. I.O.
5. O.C. "C" "   13. S.O.
6. O.C. "D" "   14. R.S.M.
7. "G" 3rd. Divn.   15. War Diary.
8. Town Major GOMMEGNIES.   16. " "
                            17. File.

APPENDIX. 7

SECRET.
****

3rd. BATTALION MACHINE GUN CORPS

OPERATION ORDER NO. 58.

COPY NO. 12

NOVEMBER 17th. 1918.

Reference Map - VALENCIENNES,
1/100,000.

---***---

1. The Battalion will move tomorrow November 18th to SOUS - LE - BOIS.

2. Route - Main MAUBERGE Road - Road Junction 200 yards South of "Z" in DOUZIES.

   Starting Point - Cross Roads 600 yards South of "L" in LONGUEVILLE.

   Time to pass Starting Point - 14.18 hours.

   Order of march - Battln. H.Q., "B" "C" "D" and "A" Coys.

   Time and place of parade will be notified later.

   Dress - As per Administrative Instructions Nos 1 & 2.

3. Companies will not be followed by their Transport. Transport will march in the same order as their Companies, with 9th Brigade 1st line Transport.
   2nd line Transport will move with No. 4 Coy., A.S.C.
   Battln. T.O. will make all arrangements re transport joining column.

4. Distances - 10 yards between Companies.
   50 yards between Battalions.

5. Blankets and Officers' Valises will be dumped at Q.M. Stores under arrangements made by Q.M.

6. Greatcoats will be packed neatly on limbers.
   Limbers should be packed as flatly as possible.

7. Billets at present occupied will be left in a clean and sanitary condition.

8. Billeting party under Lieut. MORRIS will leave Battln. H.Q. at 09.00 hours, 18th inst.

9. Machine Gun Units to ACKNOWLEDGE.

Capt & Adjt.,
3rd. Battln. M. G. Corps.

Issued at....18.00 hours.
Copies to -
1. Commanding Officer   7. M.D.   Town Major LA LONGUEVILLE
2. 2/in/Command: 8. Q.M.
3. O.C. "A" Coy.   9. Battln T.O.
4. O.C. "B" "   10. I.O.
5. O.C. "C" "   11. R.S.M.
6. O.C. "D" "   12. War Diary
                        13. "   "
                        14. File.

APPENDIX 8

3rd. BATTALION MACHINE GUN CORPS.   S E C R E T.

OPERATION ORDER NO. 59.
                                                               COPY NO...14...

                                                               NOVEMBER 19th 1918.

Reference Maps - VALENCIENNES) 1/100,000.
                 NAMUR   )

1. The Battalion will move tomorrow November 20th to CERFONTAINE.

2. Route - MAUBERGE - Railway Bridge 1200 yards South of 'M' in MAUBERGE.
    Starting Point - Cross Roads 600 yards North-East of last 'S' in
    SOUS - LE - BOIS.
    Time to pass Starting Point - 09.06 hours.
    Order of march - Battln. H.Q., Divisional Band - "C" Coy., "D" Coy.,
    "A" Coy., "B" Coy.
    The Battalion will parade in Rue de Foigny, head of column at
    Southern end, ready to move off at 08.15 hours.
    Dress - As per Administrative Instructions Nos 1 & 2 except that
    Box Respirators will be worn on top of pack.

3. The Battalion will be followed by the cookers and mess cart.
    The 1st line transport will follow on behind the Battalion, in
    same order as Companies, until the Battalion joins the Brigade
    when 1st line transport less cookers and mess cart will join
    Brigade transport.
    2nd line transport will travel with No. 4 Company Train.

4. Distances will be as already laid down.

5. Blankets and Officers' Valises will be dumped at Q.M. Stores
    under arrangements made by Q.M.

6. Billets at present occupied will be left in a clean and
    sanitary condition.

7. Billeting party under Lieut. MORRIS will leave Battln. H.Q.
    tomorrow at 07.00 hours. Lieut. MORRIS will meet Staff
    Captain, 9th Infantry Brigade at 08.00 hours at Cross Roads
    500 yards South of 'O' in CERFONTAINE.

8. Machine Gun Units to ACKNOWLEDGE.

                                            Capt. & Adjt.,
Issued at.....21.DF hours.   3rd Battln. M. G. Corps.
Copies to:-
1. Commanding Officer   9. M.O.
2. Second in Command.   10. Battln T.O.
3. O.C. "A" Coy.   11. Q.M.
4. O.C. "B" "   12. Lt. Smith.
5. O.C. "C" "   13. R.S.M.
6. O.C. "D" "   14. War Diary.
7. "G" 3rd Divn.   15. "   "
8. 9th Inf. Bde.   16. File
                             17. Town Major SOUS LE BOIS.

appendix 9

SECRET.
****

3rd BATTALION MACHINE GUN CORPS

OPERATION ORDER NO 60.

COPY NO ..... 13 ...

NOVEMBER 23rd. 1918.

Reference Map - NAMUR 1/100,000.
***

1. The Battalion will march to LEERS - ET - FOSTEAU tomorrow 24th November.

2. Starting Point - Road Junction 900 yards South-East of "T" in COLLERET.
   Time of Passing Starting Point - 09.21 hours.
   Route - Cross Roads 50 yards North of "E" in COUSOLRE - BOUSIGNIES
   - Road Junction 100 yards North of "B" in BOUSIGNIES -
   Road Junction 200 yards North of "S" in MONTIGNIES -
   Road Junction 500 yards South-West of "M" in MALAISE.
   Order of March - Battln. H.Q., "D" Coy., "A" Coy., "B" Coy., "C" Coy.

   The Battalion will parade at 08.00 hours on Main Road COUSOLRE - CERFONTAINE, head of column at junction of Roads 500 yards South of "I" in CERFONTAINE.

   Dress and Distances as already laid down.

3. Cookers will follow immediately behind the Battalion.
   1st line transport will march with 9th Brigade 1st line transport.
   2nd line transport will march under orders of O.C., No. 4, Coy. A.S.C.

4. Billeting party under Lieut. MORRIS will leave Battln. H.Q. at an hour to be notified later.

5. Blankets, Officers' Valises will be dumped at Q.M. Stores under arrangements to be made by Q.M.

6. Billets at present occupied will be left in a clean and sanitary condition.

7. Machine Gun Units to ACKNOWLEDGE.

Capt. & Adjt.,
3rd Battln. M. G. Corps.

Issued at .....15.30 hours...
Copies to:-
1. Commanding Officer.   7. 9th Inf. Bde.   13. War Diary.
2. 2/in/Command.   8. Battln. T.C.   14. "   "
3. O.C. "A" Coy.   9. M.O.   15. File.
4. O.C. "B" "   10. Q.M.
5. O.C. "C" "   11. Lt. Smith.
6. O.C. "D" "   12. R.S.M.

SECRET.
****

3rd BATTALION MACHINE GUN CORPS.

app. 10

OPERATION ORDER NO. 61.

COPY NO. 13.....

NOVEMBER 24th 1918.

Reference Map - NAMUR 1/100,000.

1. The Battalion will march to MARBAIX tomorrow 25th November.

2. Route - THUIN - GOZEE.
   Starting Point - Cross Roads 200 yards South of "L" in LOCK.
   Time to pass Starting Point - 10.48 hours.

3. The Battalion will parade on main road LEERS - LOBBES at 09.45 hours; head of column at Road Junction 100 yards South-East of second "N" in INN.
   Order of March - Battln. H.Q., Divisional Band, "A" Coy., "B" Coy., "C" Coy., "D" Coy.

4. Dress, Distances and Orders re Transport as already laid down.

5. Billets at present occupied will be left in a clean and sanitary condition.

6. Billeting Party under Lieut. MORRIS will leave Cross Roads in LEERS at 07.30 hours.

7. Blankets and Officers' Valises will be dumped at Q.M. Stores under arrangements to be made by Q.M.

8. "D" Coy. will detail a rearguard consisting of a Section under an Officer. This Officer will render a rearguard report to Battalion Orderly Room on arrival at destination.

9. Machine Gun Units to ACKNOWLEDGE.

Issued at 17.45 hours.

Capt. & Adjt.,
3rd Battln. M. G. Corps.

Copies to -
1. Commanding Officer.
2. Second in Command.
3. O.C. "A" Coy.
4. O.C. "B" "
5. O.C. "C" "
6. O.C. "D" "
7. M.O.
8. Q.M.
9. T.O.
10. Lt. Smith.
11. Lt. Morris.
12. R.S.M.
13. War Diary ✓
14. War Diary.
15. File.

SECRET.
****

3rd BATTALION MACHINE GUN CORPS

OPERATION ORDER NO. 62.

13
appendix 11

Reference Map NAMUR 1/100,000.

1. The Battalion will march to the VILLERS - POTERIE area tomorrow 26th November.

2. Route - THY - LE - CHATEAU - SOMZEE - TARCIENNE - GERPINNES
   Starting Point - Road Junction 100 yards South of "T" in
   in BERZEE STA .
   Time to pass Starting Point - 10.18 hours.

3. The Battalion will parade on MARBAIX - HAM Road at 08.15 hours head of column on Cross Roads 300 yards North West of "H" in HAM. Order of march - Battln H.Q., "B", "C", "D", "A" Coys.

4. Dress, Distances, and Orders re transport as already laid down.

5. Billets at present occupied to be left in a clean and sanitary condition.

6. Billeting party under Lieut. MORRIS will leave Church, MARBAIX at a time to be notified later.

7. Blankets and Officers' Valises will be dumped at Q.M. Stores under arrangements to be made by Q.M.

8. "A" Coy. will detail a rearguard consisting of a Section under an Officer to march behind the cookers. This Officer will render rearguard Report to Battalion Orderly Room on arrival at destination.

9. Machine Gun Units to ACKNOWLEDGE.

Callan
Capt. & Adjt.,
3rd Battln. M. G. Corps.

Issued at.....21.30 hours.
Copies to -
1. Commanding Officer.
2. Second in Command.
3. O.C. "A" Coy.
4. O.C. "B" "
5. O.C. "C" "
6. O.C. "D" "
7. T.O.
8. M.O.
9. Q.M.
10. Lt. Smith.
11. Lt. Morris.
12. War Diary.
13. War Diary.
14. File.

S E C R E T.
****

3rd BATTALION MACHINE GUN CORPS,

APPENDIX 12

OPERATION ORDER NO. 63.

COPY NO. ....

NOVEMBER 27th 1918.

Reference Map - NAMUR, 1/100,000.
***

1. The Battalion will march to ST. GERARD BIOUL Area tomorrow 28th November.

2. The Battalion (less Transport) will parade on the GERPINNES - ACOZ Road at 07.45 hours (unless otherwise ordered), head of column on Road Junction 100 yards South-West of "C" in CHau.
Order of March - Battln. H.Q., "C", "D", "A", "B" Coys.
"A" Coy. with transport will join the column at FIGOTTERIE at 08.30 hours.
The Transport of Battln. H.Q.,"C" & "D", Coys. and 2nd line will be formed up on the GERPINNES - VILLERS POTERIE Road, head of column 500 yards North-East of first Railway crossing.

3. Dress, Distances and orders re Transport as already laid down.

4. Billets at present occupied will be left in a clean and sanitary condition.

5. Billeting party under Lieut. MORRIS, will leave Q.M. Stores at hour to be notified later.

6. Blankets and Officers' Valises will be dumped at Q.M. Stores under arrangements to be made by Q.M.

7. "D" Company will detail a rearguard consisting of a Section under an Officer to march behind the cookers. This Officer will render rearguard Report to Battalion Orderly Room on arrival at destination.

8. ACKNOWLEDGE.

Capt. & Adjt.,
3rd Battln. M. G. Corps.

Issued at ...22.00 hours.
Copies to:-
1 Commanding Officer   7. T.O.   13 Lt. MORRIS.
2 Second in Command.   8. M.O.
3 O.C. "A" Coy.   9. Q.M.
4 O.C. "B" "   10. War.Diary.
5 O.C. "C" "   11. "   "
6 O.C. "D" "   12. File.

SECRET.

3rd BATTALION MACHINE GUN CORPS.   APPENDIX 13

OPERATION ORDER NO. 64.

COPY NO. ....

NOVEMBER 28th 1918.

Reference Map – NAMUR – 1/100,000.

1. The Battalion will march to the EVREHAILLES Area tomorrow, 29th November.

2. Route – Cross Roads 200 yards East of "N" in BOUILLON – West Bank of MEUSE to Bridge West of YVOIR STA. – YVOIR – EVREHAILLES.
Starting Point – Road Junction 800 yards South of "H" in BOUCHAT.
Time to pass Starting Point – 09.31 hours.

3. The Battalion will parade in street in front of Battalion Orderly Room at 07.35 hours.
Order of march – Battln. H.Q., "D" Coy., Divisional Band, "B" Coy., "A" Coy. "C" Coy.

4. Dress and distances as already laid down.
Cookers and H.Q. Limber of each Coy. will march with Battalion. Remainder of Transport will march via Cross Roads 600 yards South-East of "X" in GRAUX passing through BIOUL at about 10.50 hours.

5. A divisional Staff Officer will be on the hill North of YVOIR with orders to dump excess baggage on overloaded wagons.

6. Billets at present occupied will be left in a clean and sanitary condition.

7. Billeting party under Lieut. MORRIS will leave Orderly Room at an hour to be notified later.

8. Blankets and Officers' Valises will be dumped at Q.M. Stores at 06.45 hours.

9. "A" Coy. will detail a rearguard consisting of a Section under an Officer to march behind the cookers. This Officer will render rearguard report to Battalion Orderly Room on arrival at destination.

10. ACKNOWLEDGE.

Capt. & Adjt.,
3rd Battln. M. G. Corps.

Appendix 14

SECRET.

3rd BATTALION MACHINE GUN CORPS

OPERATION ORDER NO. 65.

COPY NO.........

NOVEMBER 30th 1918.

Reference Maps - NAMUR & MARCHE - 1/100,000.

1. The Battalion will march to NATOYE today, 30th instant.

2. The Battalion will parade on the PURNODE - DORINNE Road at 0745 hours head of column 1200 yards East of Cross Roads at Q.M. Stores. Order of march - B.H.Q., "B", "A", "C", "D" Coyys.

3. Dress and distances as already laid down.

4. Transport will follow Battalion

5. One man only will march behind each vehicle.

6. Billets at present occupied will be left in a clean and sanitary condition.

7. Billeting party under Lieut. MORRIS will leave Q.M. Stores at 0700 hours. The billets of the 20th K.R.R.C. at NATOYE will be taken over. Billeting party should arrive at new billets by 08.00 hours.

8. Blankets and Officers' Valises will be dumped at Q.M. Stores at 06.30 hours.

9. "D" Coy. will detail a rearguard consisting of a Section under an Officer to march behind the cookers. This Officer will render rearguard report to Battalion Orderly Room on arrival at destination.

10. ACKNOWLEDGE.

Capt & Adjt.,
3rd Battln. M. G. Corps.

Issued at....02.00 hours.
Copies to
Commanding Officer   M.O.
Second in Command.   T.O.
O.C. "A" Coy.   Q.M.
O.C. "B" "   Lt. Morris.
O.C. "C" "   R.S.M.
O.C. "D" "   War Diary.
    "   "
    File.

Army Form C. 2118.

WAR DIARY
or
INTELLIGENCE SUMMARY.

3RD BATTLN M.G.C.

(Erase heading not required.)

Place	Date	Hour	Summary of Events and Information	Remarks and references to Appendices
			MAP. MARGHE. 9	
NATOYE	DEC. 1		Battn. training, Evacuations 2.O.R., To leave 1.O.R.	RA
"	2		Battn. training. Reinforcements 1.O.R. To leave 2.O.R.(1 officer transferred to U.K. 2nd. R. BALKWILL.	RA
"	3		Battn. training Operation order No.66 issued @ 22.00 hrs. Evacuations 5.O.R. Reinforcements MAJOR J.R. BELLERBY, M.C. To leave 2.O.R. From leave LT. H.C. CRAIG M.C.	RA APPENDIX 1
MOHIVILLE	4		Battn. marched to MOHIVILLE, arriving in billets @ 11.30 hrs. Battn. H.Q. SCOVILLE. Operation Order No.67 issued @ 17.30 hrs. Evacuations 3.O.R. To leave 2.O.R.	RA APPENDIX 2
BAILLONVILLE	5		Battn. marched to BAILLONVILLE, arriving in billets @ 13.00 hrs. Battn. H.Q. Crossroads East of Village. Operation Order No.68 issued @ 19 hrs. Evacuations 3.O.R.	RA APPENDIX 3
SOY	6		Battn. marched to SOY. arriving in billets @ 11.45 hrs. Battn. H.Q. The NUNNERY. Operation Order No.69 issued @ 18.15 hrs.	RA APPENDIX 4

Army Form C. 2118.

WAR DIARY
or
INTELLIGENCE SUMMARY.
(Erase heading not required.)

3rd BATTLN M.G.C.

Instructions regarding War Diaries and Intelligence Summaries are contained in F.S. Regs., Part II. and the Staff Manual respectively. Title pages will be prepared in manuscript.

Place	Date	Hour	Summary of Events and Information	Remarks and references to Appendices
VAUX-CHAVANNE	DEC 7		MAP MARCHE	
			Battln marched to VAUX-CHAVANNE, arriving in billets @ 14.45 hrs.	R.A.
			Battln. H.Q. VAUX-CHAVANNE, opp. CHURCH. Operation Order No. 70 issued @ 18 hrs.	APPENDIX 5
OTTRE	8		Battln. marched to OTTRE, arriving in billets @ 12.50 hrs. Battln. H.Q. OTTRE, opposite CHURCH. Operation Order No. 71 issued @ 17.00 hrs. Evacuations, 8 O.R.	R.A. APPENDIX 6
OTTRE	9		BATTLN. TRAINING. Evacuations, 2 O.R.	R.A.
"	10		Battln training. Operation order No. 72 issued @ 14.30 hrs. Evacuations 2 O.R.	R.A. APPENDIX 7
BEHO MAP.REF. I.M.	11		Battln. marched to BEHO, arriving in billets @ 13.00 hrs. Battln. H.Q. BEHO. Operation order No. 73 issued @ 19.00 hrs.	R.A. APPENDIX 8
KROMBACH	12		Battln. marched to KROMBACH, arriving in billets @ 13.30 hrs. Battln. H.Q. KROMBACH, near CHURCH. Operation order No. 74 issued @ 18 hrs. Evacuations 5 O.R.	R.A. APPENDIX 9
MANDERFELD	13		Battln. marched to MANDERFELD, arriving in billets @ 1500 hrs. B.H.Q. MANDERFELD. Operation order No. 75 issued @ 19.00 hrs. Evacuations, 6 O.R.	R.A. APPENDIX 10

Army Form C. 2118.

WAR DIARY
or
INTELLIGENCE SUMMARY.
(Erase heading not required.)

3RD BATTLN M.G.C.

Instructions regarding War Diaries and Intelligence Summaries are contained in F.S. Regs., Part II. and the Staff Manual respectively. Title pages will be prepared in manuscript.

Place	Date	Hour	Summary of Events and Information	Remarks and references to Appendices
			MAP. I.M. & I.L.	
HALLSCHLAG	DEC 14		Battn. marched to HALLSCHLAG, arriving in billets @ 12.30 hrs. B.H.Q. HALLSCHLAG. Catholic church. Operation order No. 76 issued @ 1800 hrs.	RA APPENDIX 11
DAHLEM	15		Battn. marched to DAHLEM, arriving in billets 12.25 hrs. A.H.Q. DAHLEM. Operation order No. 77 issued @ 2000 hrs. Evacuations, 4 O.R. To Leave, 1 O.R. From Leave, Lt. H.E. TIPPER.	RA APPENDIX 12
MAP. REF. I.L. RODERATH	16		Battn. marched to RODERATH, arriving in billets @ 1400 hrs. B.H.Q. RODERATH. B & C Coys, arriving @ ENGELAU @ 13 hrs. A & D Coys, arriving @ BOUDERATH @ 1500 hrs. Operation Order No. 78 issued @ 20.30 hrs.	RA APPENDIX 13
ARLOFF	17		Battn. marched to ARLOFF, arriving in billets @ 1215 hrs. B.H.Q. ARLOFF. Operation Order No. 79 issued @ 17 hrs. B & D Coys. billeted @ KIRSPENICH.	RA APPENDIX 14
EUSKIRCHEN	18		Battn. marched to EUSKIRCHEN, arriving in billets @ 11.45 hrs. B.H.Q. Corner of KIRCHSTRASSE & FRAUENBERG. ST. Operation Order No. 80 issued @ 1530 hrs. Evacuations, 4 O.R. & MAJOR J.R. BELLERBY. M.C.	RA APPENDIX 15
FUSSENICH	19		Battn. marched to FUSSENICH, arriving in billets @ 1240 hrs. B.H.Q. FUSSENICH. NEAR CONVENT. B & C Coys. billeted @ GEICH. Operation orders No. 81 issued @ 1830 hrs. Evacuations, 7 O.R. To leave, 1 O.R.	RA APPENDIX 16

Army Form C. 2118.

WAR DIARY
or
INTELLIGENCE SUMMARY.
(Erase heading not required.)

3RD Battn M.G.C.

Instructions regarding War Diaries and Intelligence Summaries are contained in F. S. Regs., Part II. and the Staff Manual respectively. Title pages will be prepared in manuscript.

Place	Date	Hour	Summary of Events and Information	Remarks and references to Appendices
			MAP I.L.	
DUREN	20		Battn marched to DUREN. arriving in Barracks @ 12.15. hrs. B.H.Q. DUREN.	R.O.
			Corner of Sud Strasse. Evacuations, 1.O.R. From Leave, 3.O.R.	
DUREN	21		Battn training. To leave, 1.O.R. From leave, 4.O.R.	R.O.
			2 tents to Lt Col Brendon D.S.O	
"	22		Battn training. To leave, 2.O.R. From leave Nil. Evacuations, 3.O.R.	R.O.
"	23		Battn training. Evacuations 12.O.R. + Officer (1) 2Lt E.G. Burke.	R.O.
			To leave, 2.O.R. From Leave, 3.O.R.	
"	24		Battn training. To leave, 2.O.R. From Leave, 1.O.R. Evacuations, 1.O.R.	R.O.
"	25		Battn training. Evacuations 2.O.R. To leave, 3.O.R.	R.O.
"	26		Battn training. To leave, 2.O.R.	R.O.
"	27		Battn training. Evacuations, 6.O.R. To leave, 2.O.R.	R.O.
"	28		Battn training. To leave, 2.O.R. Evacuations 2.O.R. Demobilization 19. O.R.	R.O.
"	29		Battn training. To leave, 2.O.R. Demobilization 19.O.R.	R.O.
"	30		Battn training. To leave, 2.O.R. & 2Lt A.O. Forster. Demobilization H.O.R.	R.O.
"	31		Battn training. To leave, 2.O.R.	R.O.

Major. Comm'dg. 3rd Batt'n M.G.C.

SECRET.

APPENDIX. 1.

3rd BATTALION MACHINE GUN CORPS

OPERATION ORDER NO. 66.

COPY NO. 13

DECEMBER 3rd. 1918.

Reference Map – ~~NAMUR~~ MARCHE – 1/100,000.
*****

1. The Battalion will march to HOHIVILLE & SCOVILLE tomorrow 9th instant.

2. The Battalion will parade on the NATOYE – EMPTINNE Road at 09.15 hours. Rear of "D" Coy. at EMBLINNE CHATEAU. Order of march – Battln. H.Q., "A" Coy., "B" Coy., "C" Coy., "D" Coy.

3. Dress and Distances as already laid down.

4. Transport will follow the Battalion.

5. One man only will march behind each vehicle.

6. Billets at present occupied will be left in a clean and sanitary condition.
One N.C.O. per Company will report at Battln. Orderly Room at 07.45 hours to hand over billets to 7th K.S.L.I.

7. Billeting party under Lieut. MORRIS will leave Q.M. Stores at 08.00 hours. The billets of the Battalion at HOHIVILLE and SCOVILLE will be taken over from 8th K.O.R.L. Billeting party should arrive at new billets by 09.00 hours.

8. Blankets and Officers' Valises will be dumped at Q.M. Stores under arrangements made by Q.M.

9. "D" Coy. will detail a rearguard consisting of one Section under an Officer to march behind the cookers. This Officer will render rearguard report to Battalion Orderly Room on arrival at destination.

ACKNOWLEDGE.

Capt. & Adt.,
3rd Battln. M.G.Corps.

Issued at 22.00 hours.
Copies to:-
1. Commanding Officer.   7. M.O.   13. War Diary ✓
2. Second in Command.   8. T.O.   14. "   "
3. O.C. "A" Coy.   9. Q.M.   15. File.
4. O.C. "B" "   10. Lt. Morris.
5. O.C. "C" Coy.   11. Lt. Duffey.
6. O.C. "D" "   12. R.S.M.

SECRET.

3rd BATTALION MACHINE GUN CORPS.

APPENDIX 2

OPERATION ORDER NO. 67.

COPY NO. 15

DECEMBER 4th 1918.

Reference Map - MARCHE - 1/100,000.

1. The Battalion will march to the NOISEUX Area tomorrow 5th inst.

2. Route - SOY - JANNEE - HETTINE - HEURE - BAILLONVILLE - NOISEUX.

3. The Battalion will parade on the MOMIVILLE - SOY Road at 08.35 hours. Head of column at Cross Roads 500 yards North of "Y" in SOY.
Order of March - Battln. H.Q., "B" Coy., "C" Coy., "D" Coy., "A" Coy.

4. Dress and Distances as already laid down.

5. Transport will follow the Battalion to the Starting Point, after which it will be Brigaded.

6. One man only will march behind each vehicle.

7. Billets at present occupied will be left in a clean and sanitary condition.

8. Billeting party under Lieut. MORRIS will leave Q.M. Stores at an hour to be notified later.

9. Blankets and Officers' Valises will be dumped at Q.M. Stores under arrangements made by Q.M.

10. "A" Coy. will detail a rearguard consisting of one Section under an Officer to march behind the cookers. This Officer will render rearguard report to Battalion Orderly Room on arrival at destination.

11. ACKNOWLEDGE.

[signature] Major
for Capt. & Adjt.,
3rd Battln. M.G.Corps.

Issued at...17.30 hours.
Copies to:-
1. Commanding Officer.   7. M.O.   13. War Diary.
2. Second in Command.   8. T.O.   14. File
3. O.C. "A" Coy.   9. Q.M.   15. R.S.M.
4. O.C. "B" "   10. Lt. Morris.
5. O.C. "C" "   11. Lt. Duffey.

Appendix 3

SECRET.

3rd BATTALION MACHINE GUN CORPS.

OPERATION ORDER NO. 68.

COPY NO. 13

DECEMBER 5th 1918.

Reference Map - MARCHE 1/100,000.

1. The Battalion will march to EREZEE - ERPIGNY Area tomorrow December 6th.

2. The Battalion will parade on the BAILLONVILLE - NOISEUX Road, head of column at Battln. H.Q. at 07.50 hours.
    Order of March - B.H.Q., "C", "D", "A", "B" Companies.

3. Dress and Distances as already laid down.

4. Transport will follow the Battalion until Brigaded.

5. One man only will march behind each vehicle.

6. Billets at present occupied will be left in a clean and sanitary condition.

7. Billeting party under Lieut. MORRIS will leave Battln. H.Q. at 07.30 hours. Lieut. MORRIS will report to the Staff Captain 9th Infantry Brigade at EREZEE at 10.00 hours.

8. Blankets and Officers' Valises will be dumped at Q.M. Stores under arrangements made by Q.M.

9. "B" Company will detail a rearguard consisting of a Section under an Officer to march behind the Transport (not behind the cookers) to collect stragglers and assist the Transport where necessary.
    The O.C. Rearguard will render Rearguard Report on arrival at destination.

10. ACKNOWLEDGE.

Capt. & Adjt.,
3rd Battln. M.G.Corps.

Issued at...19.00 hours..
Copies to:-
1. Commanding Officer.   7. M.O.   13. War Diary.
2. Second in Command.   8. T.O.   14. "   "
3. O.C. "A" Coy.   9. Q.M.   15. File.
4. O.C. "B" "   10. Lt. Morris.
5. O.C. "C" "   11. Lt. Duffey.
6. O.C. "D" "   12. R.S.M.

SECRET.

APPENDIX 4

3rd BATTALION MACHINE GUN CORPS

OPERATION ORDER NO. 69.

COPY NO. 14

DECEMBER 6th 1918.

Reference Map – MARCHE – 1/100,000.

1. The Battalion will march to VAUX CHAVANNE tomorrow December 7th.

2. The Battalion will parade on the SOY – FISENNE Road at 08.00 hours; head of column at the 6 Kilomètre Stone. Order of march – Battln H.Q., "B", "A", "D", "C" Coys.

3. Dress and Distances as already laid down.

4. Transport will follow the Battalion until Brigaded. Cookers will march with Battalion.

5. One man only will march behind each vehicle.

6. Billets at present occupied will be left in a clean and sanitary condition.
   Billets will be handed over to a Unit of the 8th Infantry Brigade. Company Seconds in Command will remain behind to hand over, with complete list of billets showing accommodation. They will receive a certificate to the effect that the billets taken over are in a clean and sanitary condition.

7. Billeting party under Lieut. MORRIS will leave Q.M. Stores at 07.30 hours. The billets at VAUX CHAVANNE will be taken over from a Unit of the 76th Infantry Brigade.

8. Blankets and Officers' Valises will be dumped at Q.M. Stores by 06.45 hours.

9. "C" Company will detail a rearguard consisting of one Section under an Officer to march behind the transport for the purpose of collecting stragglers and assisting transport if required. O.C. Rearguard will render Rearguard Report on arrival at destination.

10. A C K N O W L E D G E.

Capt. & Adjt.,
3rd Battln. M. G. Corps.

Issued at:..18.15 hours...
Copies to –
1. Commanding Officer.
2. Second in Command.
3. O.C. "A" Coy.
4. O.C. "B" "
5. O.C. "C" "
6. O.C. "D" "
7. M.O.
8. T.O.
9. Q.M.
10. Lt. Morris.
11. Lt. Duffey.
12. R.S.M.
13. War Diary.
14. "
15. File.

SECRET.

3rd BATTALION MACHINE GUN CORPS

APPENDIX 5

OPERATION ORDER NO. 70.

COPY NO. 14.

DECEMBER 7th 1918.

Reference Map - MARCHE - 1/100,000.

1. The Battalion will march to OTTRE tomorrow December 8th.

2. Route for Personnel - 3rd Class Road leading due South from the "E" in VAUX-CHAVANNE, through the "T" in DEVANT-SPILLEUW and the "H" in DERRIERE-LE-CHENE, thence by Main Road.
The Battalion will parade on the above 3rd Class Road with head on Forked Roads 100 yards North of "T" in DEVANT-SPILLEUW at 08.45 hours.
Order of march - Battln. H.Q., "A" "B" "C" "D" Coys.

3. ALL Transport will travel via HANHAY.
The Cookers will join the Battalion at Road Junction 1,000 yards South of "C" in DERRIERE-LE-CHENE. They will report to Battln. Transport Officer, at "C" Coy's H.Q. at 08.20 hours.
Remainder of Transport will be Brigaded and will move off at 08.45 hours under orders to be issued by Battln. T.O.

4. Dress and Distances as already laid down.

5. One man only will march behind each vehicle.

6. Billets at present occupied will be left in a clean and sanitary condition. Billets will be handed over to a Unit of the 8th Infantry Brigade. Company Seconds in Command will remain behind to hand over, with complete list of billets shewing accommodation. They will receive a certificate to the effect that the billets taken over are in a clean and sanitary condition.

7. Billeting party under Lieut. MORRIS will leave Q.M. Stores at 0730 ~~08.00~~ hours. The billets at OTTRE will be taken over from a Unit of the 76th Infantry Brigade.

8. Blankets and Officers' Valises will be dumped at Q.M. Stores by ~~06.30~~ 0700 hours.

9. "D" Company will detail a rearguard consisting of one Section under an Officer, to march behind the Transport for the purpose of collecting stragglers and assisting transport if required. O.C., Rearguard will render Rearguard Report on arrival at destination.

10. Arrival Reports will be rendered to Battln. Orderly Room within half an hour of arrival in billets.

11. A C K N O W L E D G E.

Issued at 18.00 hours.

Capt. & Adjt.,
3rd Battln. M.G.Corps.

Copies to-
1. Commanding Officer.
2. Second in Command.
3. O.C. "A" Coy.
4. O.C. "B" "
5. O.C. "C" "
6. O.C. "D" "
7. M.O.
8. T.O.
9. Q.M.
10. Lt. Morris.
11. Lt. Duffey.
12. R.S.M.
13. War Diary.
14. " "
15. File.

SECRET.

3rd BATTALION MACHINE GUN CORPS.

OPERATION ORDER NO. 71.

COPY NO...... 12

DECEMBER 8th 1918.

Reference Map – MARCHE – 1/100,000.

1. The Battalion will march to BOVIGNY tomorrow December 9th.

2. Route – Via JOUBIEVAL, thence by Main Road.
   The Battalion will parade on the OTTRE – JOUBIEVAL Road at 10.00 hours. head of column 1,000 yards clear of village of OTTRE.
   Order of march – Battln. H.Q., "C", "D", "A", "B" Coys.

3. Cookers will follow Battalion.
   1st Line Transport will follow Battalion as far as Main Road where it will be Brigaded.

4. Dress and Distances as already laid down.

5. One man only will march behind each vehicle.

6. Billets at present occupied will be left in a clean and sanitary condition. Billets will be handed over to a Unit of the 8th Infantry Brigade. Company Seconds in Command will remain behind to hand over, with complete list of billets showing accommodation. They will receive a certificate to the effect that the billets taken over are in a clean and sanitary condition.

7. Billeting party under Lieut. MORRIS will leave Q.M. Stores at 08.30 hours. The billets at BOVIGNY will be taken over from a Unit of the 76th Infantry Brigade.

8. Blankets and Officers' Valises will be dumped at Q.M. Stores by 08.00 hours.

9. "D" Coy. will detail a rearguard consisting of one Section under an Officer to march behind the Cookers. O.C. Rearguard will render Rearguard Report on arrival at destination.

10. Arrival Reports will be rendered to Battalion Orderly Room within half an hour of arrival in billets.

11. ACKNOWLEDGE.

Capt. & Adjt.,
3rd Battln. M.G.Corps.

Issued at...17.00 hours.
Copies to:-
1. Commanding Officer.   7. M.O.   13. War Diary.
2. Second in Command.   8. T.O.   14. "   "
3. O.C. "A" Coy.   9. Q.M.   15. File.
4. O.C. "B" "   10. Lt. Morris.
5. O.C. "C" "   11. Lt. Duffey.
6. O.C. "D" "   12. R.S.M.

SECRET.

3rd BATTALION MACHINE GUN CORPS.

OPERATION ORDER NO. 72.

COPY NO. 13

DECEMBER 10th 1918.

Reference Map - MARCHE - 1/100,000.

1. The Battalion will march to BEHO tomorrow December 11th.

2. Route - Via JOUBIEVAL, thence by Main Road.
   The Battalion will parade on the OTTRE - JOUBIEVAL Road at 09.00 hours. head of column 1,000 yards clear of village of OTTRE.
   Order of march - Battln. H.Q., "C" Coy, Divisional Band, "D", "A", "B" Coys.

3. Cookers will follow Battalion.
   1st Line Transport will follow Battalion as far as Main Road where it will be Brigaded.

4. Dress and Distances as already laid down.

5. One man only will march behind each vehicle.

6. Billets at present occupied will be left in a clean and sanitary condition.

7. Billeting party under Lieut. Morris will leave Q.M. Stores at 08.00 hours.

8. Blankets and Officers' Valises will be dumped at Q.M. Stores by 08.30 hours.

9. "B" Coy. will detail a rearguard consisting of one Section under an Officer to march behind the Cookers. O.C. Rearguard will render Rearguard Report on arrival at destination.

10. Arrival Reports will be rendered to Battalion Orderly Room within half an hour of arrival in billets.

11. A C K N O W L E D G E.

Capt. & Adjt.,
3rd Battln. M.G.Corps.

Issued at....14.30 hours.
Copies to:-
1. Commanding Officer.   7. M.O.   13. War Diary.
2. Second in Command.   8. T.P.   14.   "   "
3. O.C. "A" Coy.   9. Q.M.   15. File.
4. O.C. "B" "   10. Lt. Morris.
5. O.C. "C" "   11. Lt. Duffoy.
6. O.C. "D" "   12. R.S.M.

SECRET.

3rd BATTALION MACHINE GUN CORPS.

OPERATION ORDER NO. 75.

COPY NO. 14

DECEMBER 11th 1918.

Reference Map - I H 1/100,000.

1. The Battalion will march to KROMBACH tomorrow December 12th.

2. Route - HALDINGEN, SCHIRL, NEUBRUCK, NEUNDORF.
The Battalion will parade on the BEHO - HALDINGEN Road at 09.15 hours, head of column at Battalion Orderly Room. Order of March - Battln. H.Q., Divisional Band, "D" Coy., "A" Coy., "B" Coy., "C" Coy.

3. Cookers will follow Battalion.
1st Line Transport will be Brigaded.

4. Dress and Distances as already laid down.

5. One man only will march behind each vehicle.

6. Billets at present occupied will be left in a clean and sanitary condition. Billets will be handed over to a Unit of the 8th Infantry Brigade. Company Seconds in Command will remain behind to hand over, with complete list of billets, showing accommodation. They will receive a certificate to the effect that the billets taken over are in a clean and sanitary condition.

7. Billeting party under Lieut. HORRIS will leave Battln. Orderly Room at 08.00 hours. The billets at KROMBACH will be taken over from a Unit of the 76th Infantry Brigade.

8. Blankets and Officers' Valises will be dumped at Q.M. Stores by 07.00 hours.

9. "C" Coy. will detail a rearguard consisting of one Section under an Officer to march behind the Cookers. O.C. Rearguard will render Rearguard Report on arrival at destination.

10. Arrival Reports will be rendered to Battalion Orderly Room within half an hour of arrival in billets.

11. ACKNOWLEDGE.

Capt. & Adjt.,
3rd Battln. M. G. Corps.

Issued at ...... 19.00 hours.
Copies to -
1. Commanding Officer
2. Second in Command.
3. O.C. "A" Coy.
4. O.C. "B" "
5. O.C. "C" "
6. O.C. "D" "
7. M.O.
8. T.O.
9. Q.M.
10. Lt. Duffey.
11. Lt. Horris.
12. S.O.
13. R.S.M.
14. War Diary.
15. " "
16. File.

Appendix 9

SECRET.

3rd BATTALION MACHINE GUN CORPS

OPERATION ORDER NO. 74.

COPY NO. 15

December 12th 1918.

Reference Map I M 1/100,000.
******

1. The Battalion will march to HANDERFELD tomorrow December 13th.

2. Route – ST. VITH – ATZERATH – SCHONBERG – ANDLER.

   The Battalion will parade on the KROMBACH – NEUNDORF Road at 08.15 hours, head of column at junction of roads 700 yards North of "M" in KROMBACH.
   Order of march – B.H.Q., "D", "A", "B", "C" Coys.

3. Billets at present occupied will be left in a clean and sanitary condition. Billets will be handed over to a Unit of the 8th Infantry Brigade. Company Seconds in Command will remain behind to hand over, with complete list of billets shewing accommodation. They will receive a certificate to the effect that the billets taken over are in a clean and sanitary condition.

4. Billeting party under Lieut. MORRIS will leave Battln. Orderly Room at 07.30 hours. The billets at HANDERFELD will be taken over from a Unit of the 76th Infantry Brigade.

5. Blankets and Officers' Valises will be dumped at QM Stores by 06.30 hours.

6. "C" Coy. will detail a rearguard consisting of one Section under an Officer to march behind the Cookers. O.C. Rearguard will render Rearguard Report on arrival at destination.

7. ACKNOWLEDGE.

Issued at....18.00 hours.

Capt. & Adjt.,
3rd Battln. M.G.Corps.

Copies to –
1. Commanding Officer
2. Second in Command.
3. O.C. "A" Coy.
4. O.C. "B" "
5. O.C. "D" "
6. O.C. "C" "
7. M.O.
8. T.O.
9. Q.M.
10. S.O0
11. Lt. Morris.
13. Lt. Duffey.
14. R.S.M.
15. War Diary.
16. " "
17. File.

SECRET.

Appendix 10

3rd BATTALION MACHINE GUN CORPS.

OPERATION ORDER NO. 75.   COPY NO. 15

December 13th 1918.

Reference Map - I H 1/100,000.

1. The Battalion will march to HALLSCHLAG tomorrow December 14th.

2. Route - Cross Roads Point 572 - SCHEID.
   The Battalion will parade on the HANDERFELD - KREWINKEL Road at 10.00 hours, head of column at bend in Road 100 yards North of "H" in HANDERFELD.
   1st line transport will parade in side roads.
   Order of march - B.H.Q., "A", "B", "C", "D" Coys.

3. Billets at present occupied will be left in a clean and sanitary condition. Billets will be handed over to a Unit of the 8th Infantry Brigade. Company Seconds in Command will remain behind to hand over, with complete list of billets showing accommodation. They will receive a certificate to the effect that the billets taken over are in a clean and sanitary condition.

4. Billeting party under Lieut. MORRIS will leave Battln. Orderly Room at 08.00 hours. The billets at HALLSCHLAG will be taken over from a Unit of the 70th Infantry Brigade.

5. Blankets and Officers' Valises will be dumped at Q.M. Stores by 08.00 hours.

6. "D" Coy. will detail a rearguard consisting of one Section under an Officer to march behind the Cookers. O.C., Rearguard will render Rearguard Report on arrival at destination.

7. ACKNOWLEDGE.

Rallen
Capt. & Adjt.,
3rd Battln. M. G. Corps.

Issued at ...... 19.00 hours.
Copies to:-
1. Commanding Officer.   7. M.O.   13. R.S.M.
2. Second in Command.   8. T.O.   14. War Diary.
3. O.C. "A" Coy.   9. Q.M.   15. "   "
4. O.C. "B" "   10. S.O.   16. File.
5. O.C. "C" "   11. Lt. Morris.
6. O.C. "D" "   12. Lt. Duffey.

SECRET.

3rd BATTALION MACHINE GUN CORPS.

OPERATION ORDER NO. 76.

Appendix II

COPY NO. 14

December 14th 1918.

Reference Map – I H 1/100,000.

1. The Battalion will march to DAHLEM tomorrow December 15th.

2. The Battalion will parade on the HALLSCHLAG – KRONENBURG Road at 09.25 hours, head of column at Road Junction 700 yards North of First "A" in HALLSCHLAG.
   Order of march– B.H.Q., "B" Coy, Divisional Band, "C", "D", "A" Coys.

3. Billets at present occupied will be left in a clean and sanitary condition. Billets will be handed over to a Unit of the 8th Infantry Brigade. Company Seconds in Command will remain behind to hand over, with complete list of billets shewing accomodation. They will receive a certificate to the effect that the billets taken over are in a clean and sanitary condition.

4. Billeting party under Lieut. Morris will leave Cross Roads, HALLSCHLAG at 07.30 hours. The billets at DAHLEM will be taken over from a Unit of the 76th Infantry Brigade.

5. Blankets and Officers' Valises will be dumped at Q.M. Stores by 07.15 hours.

6. "A" Coy. will detail a rearguard consisting of one Section under an Officer to march behind the Cookers. O.C. Rearguard will render Rearguard Report on arrival at destination.

7. A C K N O W L E D G E.

Issued at ...... 18.00 hours.
Copies to:–

Capt. & Adjt.,
3rd Battln, M.G.Corps.

1. Commanding Officer. 7. M.O.   13. R.S.M.
2. Second in Command.   8. T.O.   14. War Diary.
3. O.C. "A" Coy.   9. Q.M.   15. "   "
4. O.C. "B" "   10. S.O.   16. File.
5. O.C. "C" "   11. Lt. Morris.
6. O.C. "D" "   12. Lt. Duffey.

SECRET.

Appendix 15

3rd BATTALION MACHINE GUN CORPS.

OPERATION ORDER NO. 77.   COPY NO. 15

December 15th 1918.

Reference Maps I H and I L 1/100,000.

1. The Battalion will march tomorrow December 16th —
   B.H.Q. to RODERATH,
   "A" & "D" Coys. to BOUDERATH,
   "B" & "C" Coys. to ENGELGAU.

2. The Battalion will parade on the DAHLEM – BLANKENHEIM Road at 07.55 hours; head of column at Road Junction 200 North-East of "M" in DAHLEM.
   Order of march — B.H.Q., "A" Coy., Divisional Band, "D", "B", "C" Coys.

3. Billets at present occupied will be left in a clean and sanitary condition. Billets will be handed over to a Unit of the 8th Infantry Brigade. Company Seconds in Command will remain behind to hand over, with complete list of billets shewing accommodation. They will receive a certificate to the effect that the billets taken over are in a clean and sanitary condition.

4. Billeting party under Lieut. MORRIS will leave Battalion Orderly Room at 07.30 hours. The billets at the several destinations will be taken over from a Unit of the 76th Infantry Brigade.

5. Blankets and Officers' Valises will be dumped at Q.M. Stores by 06.00 hours.

6. "C" Coy. will detail a rearguard consisting of one Section under an Officer to march behind the Cookers. O.C. Rearguard will render Rearguard Report on arrival at destination.

7. A C K N O W L E D G E.

Capt. & Adjt.,
3rd Battln. M.G. Corps.

Issued at... 20.00 hours.
Copies to—
1. Commanding Officer.   7. M.O.   13. R.S.M.
2. Second in Command.   8. T.O.   14. War Diary.
3. O.C. "A" Coy.   9. Q.M.   15. "   "
4. O.C. "B" Coy.   10. S.O.   16. File.
5. O.C. "C" "   11. Lt. Morris.
6. O.C. "D" "   12. Lt. Duffey.

3rd BATTALION MACHINE GUN CORPS,

SECRET.

Appendix 13

OPERATION ORDER NO. 78.   COPY NO........

December 16th 1918.

Reference Map - I L - 1/100,000.

1. The Battalion will march to KIRSPENICH - ARLAFF Area tomorrow December 17th.

2. B.H.Q., "B" & "C" Coys. will parade at Church RODERATH at 08.30 hours.
   Personnel of "A" & "D" Coys. will join column on the HOLZMULHEIM - EICHERSCHIED Road at Junction of Road and Path, 100 yards North-West of "W" in WEIBENSTEIN at 09.15 hours.
   Transport of "A" and "D" Coys. will join column at Cross Roads 500 yards North of 1st "M" in HOLZMULHEIM.
   Order of march - B.H.Q., "B" Coy., Divisional Band, "C", "D", "A" Coys.

3. Billets at present occupied will be left in a clean and sanitary condition.

4. Billeting party of B.H.Q., "B" & "C" Coys. will leave Church RODERATH at 07.30 hours.
   Billeting party of "A" & "D" Coys. will proceed direct to ARLAFF, meeting Lieut. MORRIS there at 09.00 hours.
   Lieut. MORRIS will report to Burgomaster, ARLAFF at 09.00 hours for billets which will be taken over from 20th K.R.R.C.

5. Blankets and Officers' Valises will be dumped at Q.M. Stores under arrangements to be made by Q.M.

6. "A" Coy. will detail a rearguard consisting of one Section under an Officer to march behind the Cookers.
   O.C. Rearguard will render Rearguard Report on arrival at destination.

7. A C K N O W L E D G E.

[signature]
Capt. & Adjt.,
3rd Battln. M.G.Corps.

Issued at....20.30 hours.
Copies to -
1. Commanding Officer.   7. M.O.   13. R.S.M.
2. Second in Command.   8. T.O.   14. War Diary.
3. O.C. "A" Coy.   9. Q.M.   15. War Diary.
4. O.C. "B" "   10. S.O.   16. File.
5. O.C. "C" "   11. Lt. Morris.
6. O.C. "D" "   12. Lt. Duffey.

Appendix 14

S E C R E T.

3rd Battalion Machine Gun Corps.

OPERATION ORDER NO. 79.   COPY NO..........

December 17th 1918.

Reference Map - I L 1/100,000.
*****

1. The Battalion will march to EUSKIRCHEN tomorrow December 18th.

2. B.H.Q., "C" and "A" Coys. will parade on the IVERSHEIM - EUSKIRCHEN Road, head of column on the Road Junction 700 yards North West of "K" in KIRSPENICH. "D" and "B" Coys. will parade on Side Road running North-West from KIRSPENICH to Main Road, with head on Road Junction above mentioned.
Time of parade - 09.45 hours.
Order of March - B.H.Q., "C" Coy., Divisional Band, "D", "A" "B" Coys.,

3. Billets at present occupied will be left in a clean and sanitary condition.

4. Billeting party under Lieut. MORRIS will leave Battalion Orderly Room at an hour to be notified later.

5. Blankets and Officers Valises will be dumped at Q.M. Stores by 0745 hours

6. "B" Coy. will detail a rearguard consisting of one Section under an Officer to march behind the Cookers.
O.C. Rearguard will render Rearguard Report on arrival at destination.

7. A C K N O W L E D G E.

Capt. & Adjt.,
3rd Battln. M.G. Corps.

Issued....17.00 hours...
Copies to -
1. Commanding Officer   7. M.O.   13. R.S.M.
2. Second in Command   8. T.O.   14. War Diary.
3. O.C. "A" Coy.   9. Q.M.   15. "   "
4. O.C. "B" "   10 S.O.   16. File.
5. O.C. "C" "   11. Lt. Morris.
6. O.C. "D" "   12. Lt. Duffoy.

APPENDIX 15
SECRET.
****

3rd BATTALION MACHINE GUN CORPS.

OPERATION ORDER NO. 80.   COPY NO........

December 18th 1918.

Reference Map I L 1/100,000.
***

1. The Battalion will march to FUSSENICH and GEICH tomorrow December 19th.

2. Route - DURSCHEVEN - ULPENICH - ZULPICH.
   The Battalion will parade on the EUSKIRCHEN - EUENHEIM Road at 09.50 hours. Head of column 1000 yards West of Railway Crossing.
   1st line Transport will parade on the same Road, head of column 500 yards East of Railway Crossing.
   Order of march - B.H.Q., "B" Coy., Divisional Band, "A", "D", "C" Coys.

3. Billets at present occupied will be left in a clean and sanitary condition.

4. Billeting party under Lieut. MORRIS will leave Battalion Orderly Room at an hour to be notified later.

5. Blankets and Officers' Valises will be dumped at Q.M. Stores by 07.45 hours.

6. "C" Coy. will detail a rearguard consisting of one Section under an Officer to march behind the Cookers.
   O.C. Rearguard will render Rearguard Report on arrival at destination.

7. A C K N O W L E D G E.

Issued at.....15.30 hours.
Capt. & Adjt.,
3rd Battln. M. G. Corps.

Copies to-
1. Commanding Officer.   7. M.O.   13. R.S.M.
2. Second in Command.   8. T.O.   14. War Diary.
3. O.C. "A" Coy.   9. Q.M.   15. "   "
4. O.C. "B" "   10. S.O.   16. File.
5. O.C. "C" "   11. Lt. Morris.
6. O.C. "D" "   12. Lt. Duffey.

Appendix 16

SECRET.

3rd Battalion Machine Gun Corps.

OPERATION ORDER NO. 81.   COPY NO. 15

December 19th 1918.

Reference Map I L 1/100,000.
*****

1. The Battalion will march to DUREN tomorrow December 20th.

2. The Battalion will parade on the FUSSENICH - FROITZHEIM Road, head of column at the point South of 2nd. "S" in FUSSENICH at 08.10 hours.
Order of March - B.H.Q., "A" Coy., Divisional Band, "B", "C", "D" Coys.

3. Billets at present occupied will be left in a clean and sanitary condition.

4. Billeting party will leave Battalion Orderly Room at 07.30 hours and will meet Lieut. MORRIS at TOWN HALL, DUREN at 09.30 hours. 2/Lt. DUFFEY will accompany the billeting party and will meet the Battalion at the junction of the STOCKHEIM - DUREN & NIEDERAU - DUREN Roads at 11.15 hours to guide the Battalion through the Town.

5. Blankets and Officers' Valises will be dumped at Q.M. Stores by 06.30 hours.

6. "D" Coy. will detail a rearguard consisting of one Section under an Officer to march behind the Cookers.
O.C. Rearguard will render Rearguard Report on arrival at destination.

7. ACKNOWLEDGE.

Capt. & Adjt.,
3rd Battln. M. G. Corps.

Issued at....18.30 hours.
Copies to:-
1. Commanding Officer.   7. M.O.   13. R.S.M.
2. Second in Command.   8. T.O.   14. War Diary.
3. O.C. "A" Coy.   9. Q.M.   15. "   "
4. O.C. "B" "   10. S.O.   16. File.
5. O.C. "C" "   11. Lt. Duffey.
6. O.C. "D" "   12. Lt. Morris.

NORTHERN DIVISION
(LATE 3RD DIVISION)

3RD BN MACHINE GUN CORPS
JAN - SEP 1919

NORTHERN DIVISION
(LATE 3RD DIVISION)

Army Form C. 2118.

WAR DIARY
or
INTELLIGENCE SUMMARY.
(Erase heading not required.)

3rd BATTLN. M. G. Corps

Place	Date	Hour	Summary of Events and Information	Remarks and references to Appendices
DUREN			1919	
JANUARY	1		Battle training. To Leave, 3. O.R. From Leave, Lt C.T. SMITH. M.C.	
"	2		Battle training, To Leave 3. O.R. Reinforcements, Lt. J.C. Williams, 2ut and 88. O.R. E.F. HOWE.	
"	3		Battle training. Evacuations 1-0-R. To Leave 3, 0-R. From Leave 1-0-R.	
"	4		Battle training. Evacuations 1-0-R. To Leave 4-0-R. DEMOBILIZATION 7.O.R	
"	5		Battle, CHURCH PARADE, To Leave 4-0-R.	
"	6		Battle training. To Leave NIL, Evacuations 5-0-R.	
"	7		Battle training Reinforcements 40-0-R. To Leave 3-0-R.	
"	8		Battle training Evacuating 2-0-R. To Leave 3-0-R.	
"	9		Battle training. To Leave 4-0-R. From Leave 1-0-R.	
"	10		Battle training, To Leave 3-0-R.	
"	11		Battle training, Evacuations 2-0-R, To Leave 3-0-R, From Leave 2-0-R.	
"			DEMOBILISATION, 15-0-R.	
"	12		Battle training, Evacuations 1-0-R. To Leave 4-0-R. From Leave 1-0-R.	
"	13		Battle training, Reinforcements 21-0-R, To Leave 2-0-R. From Leave 2-0-R.	
"	14		Battle training, Evacuations 1-0-R, To Leave 4-0-R.	

Army Form C. 2118.

WAR DIARY
or
INTELLIGENCE SUMMARY.
(Erase heading not required.)

Place	Date	Hour	Summary of Events and Information	Remarks and references to Appendices
DUREN	JAN/ 15		Battle training. Evacuation 1-O-R. Reinforcements, LT. H.V. STEPHENS AND 8.O-R. To leave MAJOR. C.F. SWAN AND 4.O-R. DEMOBILISATION 2LT. T.VOSE + 15.O-R.	O.R
	16		Battle training. Evacuation 1-O-R. Reinforcements 1-O-R. To leave LT. R.S. RYDER and 3-O-R.	O.R
	17		Battle training. To leave 2nd LT. A.H. DUFFEY. From leave 2nd LT. A.O. FORSTER.	O.R
	18		Battle training. To leave 5.O-R. From leave 1-O-R. DEMOBILISATION 18.O-R.	O.R
	19		Battle training. Evacuations 1.O-R. To leave 3.O-R. From leave 1-O-R.	O.R
	20		Battle training. To leave 4-O-R.	O.R
	21		Battle training. REINFORCEMENTS LT. F.H. CHAMPION, AND 5.O-R. To leave 3.O-R. Evacuation 2-O-R. From leave 1-O-R.	O.R
	22		Battle training. To leave, LT. C.J. DERRY, AND 4-O-R. Evacuations 1-O-R.	O.R
	23		Battle training. To leave. 3-O-R. DEMOBILISATION. J.R.BELLERBY + MAJOR. 18-O-R. M.C.	O.R

Army Form C. 2118.

WAR DIARY
or
INTELLIGENCE SUMMARY.
(Erase heading not required.)

Place	Date	Hour	Summary of Events and Information	Remarks and references to Appendices
DUREN				
DUREN	JANUARY 24		Battle training. To LEAVE, 4-O-R. From LEAVE, 1-O-R.	O.R.
"	25		STRUCK OFF STRENGTH, 2/LT. E.G. BURKE	O.R.
"			Battle training. Evacuations, 1-O-R. To LEAVE 3-O-R. From LEAVE, 1-O-R.	O.R.
"	26		(R.Q.M.S.) KELLY, W. AWARDED (The O.C.M.) (C.S.M.) SAUNDERS, E.G. (The M.S.M.)	
"			Battle training. To LEAVE, 4-O-R. From LEAVE, LT. COL. W.J. CRANSTON, D.S.O. Comdg. 3rd	
"			DEMOBILISATION, 8-O-R. (AWARDS) SGT. WILLIAMS, A. (The M.S.M.) SGT FORD, H. (M.S.M.)	
"	27		Battle training. To LEAVE, LT. A.C.C.B. SMITH. From LEAVE, 2/LT A.H. DUSSEY.	O.R.
"			(HONOURS & AWARDS) CAPTAIN & QR. MR. A.W. CRAVEN (The MILITARY CROSS.)	
"	28		Battle training. Evacuations, 1-O-R. Reinforcements 3-O-R. To LEAVE 3-O-R.	O.R.
"			From LEAVE, 1-O-R. To HOSPITAL, LT. H.T. MYNICK.	O.R.
"	29		Battle training. To LEAVE 3-O-R. From DIV. RECP. CAMP, 2/LT. H.G. TANN	O.R.
"			Reinforcements, 1-O-R. From LEAVE, 4-O-12. DEMOBILISATION 2/LT W.G. POULTON & 2-O-R.	O.R.
"	30		Battle training	O.R.
"	31		Battle training	O.R.

[signature]
LT. COL
Comdg. 3RD BATT'N M.G.C.

WAR DIARY
or
INTELLIGENCE SUMMARY
(Erase heading not required.)

Army Form C. 2118.

WO 3rd Battn. M.G. Corps

Place	Date	Hour	Summary of Events and Information	Remarks and references to Appendices
DÜREN	FEB^Y		1919	
"	1		Battle training, From Leave, 1.O.R. Demobilisation Lt. R. Summers.	OR
"	2		Battle training, Evacuation, 1-O-R.	OR
"	3		Battle training, From Leave, Lt. Ryder R.S.R.	OR
"	4		Battle training, To Leave, Capt. Allan.R. (M.C.D.C.M.) and 1-O-R.	OR
"	5		Battle training, Demobilisation, 6-O-R. From Hospital, Lt. Deaton, A.T.	OR
"	6		Battle training, Reinforcements 1-O-R. To Leave 5-O-R. To U.K. 2^{Lt} Howe. E.F.	OR
"	7		Battle training, To Leave, Capt. Craven, A.W. (M.C.) and 4-O-R.	OR
"	8		From Leave, 4-O-R. From Hospital, Lt. Myhill. H.T.	OR
"	9		Battle training, To Leave, 1-O-R. From Leave, 1-O-R. Demobilisation. Lt. J. Littler, Lt. F.H. Champion, and 1-O-R.	OR
"	10		Battle training, To Leave, 1-O-R.	OR
"	11		Battle training, To Leave, 2-O-R. From Leave. 3-O-R.	OR
"	11		Battle training, To Leave, Major St. Leger. C.D. Evacuation 1-O-R. To Leave, 2-O-R. From Leave, 4-O-R.	OR

WAR DIARY
or
INTELLIGENCE SUMMARY.
(Erase heading not required.)

Army Form C. 2118.

Place	Date	Hour	Summary of Events and Information	Remarks and references to Appendices
DUREN EEBY	12		Battle training. To Leave, Lt. A.C. Champion and 2-O-R. From Leave 8-O-R.	V&B
"	13		Battle training. To leave 3-O-R. From Leave, Lt. A. & C.G. Smith and 5-O-R.	V&B
"	14		Battle training. To Leave, 2-O-R. From Leave, 5-O-R. To U.K. Lt. Stevens, H.V.	V&B
"	15		Battle training. Evacuation, 1-O-R. Reinforcements, 1-O-R.	V&B
"	16		To Leave, Lt. H.V. Stephens, and 2-5-O-R. From Leave 8-O-R.	V&B
"	17		Battle training. To leave, 1-O-R. From Leave, 2/Lt Derry, C.J. and 2-O-R.	V&B
"	18		Battle training. Evacuations 2-O-R. From Leave, Major Swann, C.F. and 4-O-R. To Hospital, 2/Lt M. Stockdale.	V&B
"	19		Battle training. From Leave, 3-O-R. From Hospital, Lt. Burke, E.C.	V&B
"	20		Battle training. Evacuation, 1-O-R. From Leave. 2-O-R.	V&B
"	21		Battle training. From Leave Capt. Allan R. (M.C. D.C.M.) and 1-O-R.	V&B
"			Battle training. To U.K. with conducting party, Lt. Deaton, A.J. and 3-O-R.	V&B

WAR DIARY
or
INTELLIGENCE SUMMARY.
(Erase heading not required.)

Army Form C. 2118.

Place	Date	Hour	Summary of Events and Information	Remarks and references to Appendices
DÜREN				
FEBY	22		Battle training. From leave, 2-O-R.	OB
"	23		Battle training. To leave, 3-O-R. From leave, 1-O-R.	OB
"	24		Battle training. To leave 1-O-R. From leave, 3-O-R.	OB
"	25		26. O-R. and I. OFFICER, proceeded to (WEISWEILER) Guarding Electric Power Station (COAL STRIKE)	OB
"	25		Battle training. To leave, 2-O-R. From leave, Captain A.W. CRAVEN, M.G.C. and 4-O-R.	OB
"	26		Battle training. To leave, Major S. MOFFETT, M.G. and 1-O-R. From leave, 2nd HOWE. E.F. and 3-O-R.	OB
"	27		Battle training. To leave, 1-O-R. To Hospital 2Lt. A.O. FORSTER	OB
"	28		Battle training. To leave, 2-O-R.	OB

W.T. Moffett (?)
LT. COL.
COMMANDING 3RD BN. M.G.C.

Army Form C. 2118.

WAR DIARY
or
INTELLIGENCE SUMMARY.
(Erase heading not required.)

Vol 14

Place	Date	Hour	Summary of Events and Information	Remarks and references to Appendices
DUREN	MARCH 1919			
	1		Battle training Evacuations, 3-O-R. To leave 2-O-R. From leave 1-O-R.	OCL
"	2		Battle training Evacuations, 1-O-R. To leave 2-O-R. From leave, 5-O-R.	OCL
"	3		Battle training Evacuations 2-O-R, To leave, 2-O-R.	OCL
"	4		Battle training Evacuations, 3-O-R. To leave 2-O-R. From leave Forster. A.O. 2Lt.	OCL
"	5		Battle training Evacuations, 5-O-R. To leave, 2-O-R. From leave 2-O-R	OCL
"	6		Battle training Evacuations, 6-O-R. To leave 2-O-R. From leave 3-O-R. OPERATION ORDER No 88 issued @ 1700 hours	OCL
"	7		Battle training. To leave, 2-O-R	OCL
"	8		Battle training, Evacuations, 1-O-R, To leave 2-O-R, From leave 1-O-R. AND 2ND LT. A.C. CHAMPION.	OCL

Army Form C. 2118.

WAR DIARY
or
INTELLIGENCE SUMMARY.
(Erase heading not required.)

Instructions regarding War Diaries and Intelligence Summaries are contained in F. S. Regs., Part II. and the Staff Manual respectively. Title pages will be prepared in manuscript.

Place	Date	Hour	Summary of Events and Information	Remarks and references to Appendices
		1919		
DUREN	Mch 9		Battle training. To Leave, 2.O-R. Evacuations, 3-O-R.	OB
"	10		Battle training, B. Coy march to KERPEN. To Leave, 2.O-R.	OB
"	11		Battle training, B. Coy march to "EHRENFELD". C. Coy march to KERPEN. To Leave, 2.O.R.	OB
"	12		Battle training, C. Coy march to "EHRENFELD". Battⁿ Head Qrs, "A" AND "D" Coys, march to KERPEN. To Leave, 2.O-R. AND 2ⁿᵈ LT. M. GILL M From Leave, MAJOR. St LEGER, C.D.	OB
"EHRENFELD"	13		Battle training, B. H. Q. and A + D Coys, march to "EHRENFELD" From LEAVE, 2/Lt H.V. STEPHENS, AND 1-O-R. To LEAVE 2-O-R.	OB
	14		Battle training. To LEAVE, 2.O-R. From LEAVE, 2.O-R.	OB
	15		Battle training, EVACUATIONS, 4-O-R. From LEAVE, 4-O-R.	OB
	16		Battle training, Evacuations, 2.O.R. From LEAVE, ⅖ A.J. DEATON AND 1-O-R.	OB
	17		Battle training, From LEAVE, 2.O-R. EVACUATIONS, 2.O-R.	OB

Army Form C. 2118.

WAR DIARY
or
INTELLIGENCE SUMMARY.
(Erase heading not required.)

Instructions regarding War Diaries and Intelligence Summaries are contained in F. S. Regs., Part II. and the Staff Manual respectively. Title pages will be prepared in manuscript.

Place	Date	Hour	Summary of Events and Information	Remarks and references to Appendices
EHRENFELD	MARCH.			
	18		Battle training. Evacuations, 2.o.r. From Leave 2.o.r.	OW
	19		Battle training. Evacuations, 1.o.r. From leave, 2.o.r.	OW
	20		Battle training. Evacuations, 4.o.r. To leave, Capt. H.E. Blower and, 1.o.r. From Leave, 1.o.r.	OW
	21		Battle training. To Hospital Lt. H.C. Craig. To leave, 2.o.r. From Leave, 3.o.r.	OW
	22		Battle training. Re-inforcements, Lt. A.W. Lupton (M.O.C.) 2Lt. H. Mallett. 2Lt. W.D. Cattermole, Lt. F. Millner. To leave, 2.o.r. From Leave, 1.o.r.	OW
	23		Battle training. Evacuations, 1.o.r. To Leave, 2.o.r. From Leave, 3.o.r.	OW
	24		Battle training. To leave, 1.o.r. To Hospital, Lt. A.H. Duffey and 2Lt. H. Mallett. Evacuations, 3.o.r. To leave, 1.o.r.	OW
	25		Battle training. Evacuations, 3.o.r. To leave, 2Lt. S.G. Medlock. From Leave, 1.o.r.	OW

Army Form C. 2118.

WAR DIARY
or
INTELLIGENCE SUMMARY.
(Erase heading not required.)

Instructions regarding War Diaries and Intelligence Summaries are contained in F. S. Regs., Part II. and the Staff Manual respectively. Title pages will be prepared in manuscript.

Place	Date	Hour	Summary of Events and Information	Remarks and references to Appendices
	1919.			
EHRENFELD	MCH. 26		Battle training. Evacuations, 1-O-R. From Leave, 2-O-R.	OR
	27		Demobilization, 70-O-R.	OR
	28		Battle training. Evacuations, 1-O-R. To Leave, 2-O-R. From Leave 1-O-R	OR
			Battle training. From Hospital, 2/Lt. H. Mallett. To Leave, 2-O-R.	OR
			From Leave, 3-O-R. Demobilization, 22-O-R.	
	29		Battle training. To Leave, 2-O-R. From Leave, Major S. Moffett. M.C.	OR
			and 2-O-R.	
	30		Battle training. To Leave, Lt. D. Morris. and 2-O-R. Reinforcements	OR
			18 Officers. and 137. O-R.s	
	31		Battle training. To Leave, 7-O-R.s From Leave, 2-O-R.s	OR

W. Kennington Lt. Col.
Commanding 3RD BATT
M. G. C.

WAR DIARY
or
INTELLIGENCE SUMMARY.

(Erase heading not required.)

3RD BATT. M.G. CORPS

Army Form C. 2118.

WD 15

1919

Place	Date	Hour	Summary of Events and Information	Remarks and references to Appendices
EHRENFELD	APRIL 1		Battle training, Evacuations 1-O-R. To Leave, 7-O-R. From Leave, 8-O-R.	O.B.
	"		Transfer of Major S. Moffett, M.C. to 30th Batt. M.G.C. and Captain Henson, H.H.E. to U.K.	O.B.
	2		Battle training, Evacuations, 2-O-R. Reinforcements, 2/Lt. R. Rowley, and 2/Lt. W. Taylor. To Leave, 7-O-R. To Hospital and S.O.S., 2/Lt. W. Stockdale.	O.B.
	3		Battle training, To Leave, 7-O-R. From Leave, 1-O-R. Reinforcements, Major A.N. Richardson.	O.B.
	4		Battle training, To Leave, Lt. W.L. Sams, M.C. and Lt. Kirk, J.H. From Leave, 7-O-R.	O.B.
			From Leave, Capt. H.E. Blower, To Leave, 7-O-R.	
	5		Battle training. To Leave, 8-O-R.	O.B.
	6		Battle training, Evacuations, 1-O-R. To Leave, 7-O-R. Demobilization, Capt. J.C. Williams, 2/Lt. W.E. Roiser, 2/Lt. G.J. Grant, 2/Lt. A.C. Champion, Lt. S.R.S. Ryder. Departure, Revd. W. Lawson-Smith, C.F.	O.B.
RIEHL	7		Battlen marched to Riehl, Operation Order No. 83 issued @ 18-45 hrs	O.B.

Army Form C. 2118.

WAR DIARY
or
INTELLIGENCE SUMMARY.
(Erase heading not required.)

Instructions regarding War Diaries and Intelligence Summaries are contained in F. S. Regs., Part II. and the Staff Manual respectively. Title pages will be prepared in manuscript.

Place	Date	Hour	Summary of Events and Information	Remarks and references to Appendices
RIEHL	8		Battn training. To LEAVE, 7-O-R. From LEAVE, 1-O-R. REINFORCEMENT 2/LIEUT J HUNTER	
	9		Battn Ceremonial Parade - DEMOBILIZATION - Capt G.H. MATTHEWS, M.C. LIEUT H.E. TIPPER. LIEUT A.J. DEATON. 2/LT. S.R. HOLBROOK M.C. - From Leave. 2/Lt. M. McGILL. To LEAVE - 4 ORs	
	10		Battn Ceremonial Parade - To LEAVE - LIEUT J.A. ROCH M.C. + 2 ORs. Evac. 1.O.R. From LEAVE - 3 O.R's.	
	11		Battn Ceremonial Parade - To LEAVE - 4 ORs.	
	12		Battn Ceremonial Parade - INVESTITURE OF AMERICAN TROOPS - DEMOBILIZATION - MAJOR C.F. SWANN. - TO LEAVE - 4 ORs.	
	13		Battn training. To Leave - 2 ORs. From LEAVE - 2 ORs. Demobilization Evacs. 2 O.Rs. Capt H.E. BLOWER, CAPT. P. DANGERFIELD, LT. 4T.M.H.ILL	
	14		Battn training. - To LEAVE - 2/LT. T. CUNLIFFE & 1 O.R From Leave. 1.O.R. FROM HOSPITAL - LIEUT A.H. DUFFEY	
	15		Evac. 1.O.R. ATTACHMENT - Rev. T.H.E. TAPING C.F. From Leave. 1.O.R. Battn Training.	

WAR DIARY
or
INTELLIGENCE SUMMARY.

Army Form C. 2118.

Place	Date	Hour	Summary of Events and Information	Remarks and references to Appendices
	16		Demob - 2/Lt M. McGill. From Leave - 1 O.R. Evacs - 2 O.R's. Battn. Training.	
	17		Battn. Training. Demob - 1 O.R. To Leave - 2/Lt H.G.Tayn.	
	18		Battn. Training. Reinforcements - 2/Lt. C. Smith, Lt. W.E. Beaumont, 2/Lt. S.F. Pulley, 2/Lt. J.R.E. Pope, 2/Lt. T.E. Roberts, 2/Lt. J.L. Pigain, Lt. J. Storey, 2/Lt. T.H. Rees. From Hospital (Strength increase) 1 O.R.	
	19		Battn. Training. To Leave - 4 O.R's. From Leave - 5 O.R's.	
	20		Battn. Training. To Leave - 7 O.R's. From Leave - Lt. J.L. Sants M.C. + 6 O.R's. Reinf - 2/Lt. C. Shipman. Evacs - 1 O.R. To Military Prison (S of C) 1 O.R.	
	21		Battn. Training. To Leave - 2/Lt H. Mallett + 3 O.R's. From Leave - 9 O.R's	
	22		Battn. Training. Evacs - 1 O.R. To Leave - 2/Lt H. Mallett. From Leave - 1 O.R.	

Army Form C. 2118.

WAR DIARY
or
INTELLIGENCE SUMMARY.
(Erase heading not required.)

Instructions regarding War Diaries and Intelligence Summaries are contained in F. S. Regs., Part II. and the Staff Manual respectively. Title pages will be prepared in manuscript.

Place	Date	Hour	Summary of Events and Information	Remarks and references to Appendices
RUEHL	23		Battn. Training. Evacs - 2 O.R's. To Leave - 3 O.R's. From Leave - 4 O.R's. From Leave - Capt. W. Dowling M.C., 2/Lt. L. Moule, 2/Lt. F. Hope.	
	24		Battn. Training. To Leave - 5 O.R's. Demob - 2 O.R's. Reinforcement - 1 O.R.	
	25		Battn. Training. To Leave - 5 O.R's. From Leave - Lt. D. Morris & O.O.R's. Demob - 3 O.R's.	
	26		Battn. Training. To Leave - Lt. F. Winchcombe & 3 O.R's. From Leave - Lt. T.A. Rogers & 5 O.R's. Evacs - 1 O.R.	
	27		Battn. Training. To Leave - Lt. F.G.T. Labes & 5 O.R's. From Leave - 9 O.R's. Demob - Major E. Thomas, M.C. Reinforcements - 2/Lt. F.H. Filmore & 1 O.R.	
	28		Battn. Training. To Leave - 4 O.R's. Reinforcement - 1 O.R. Battn. Ceremonial Parade. From Leave - 4 O.R's.	

Army Form C. 2118.

WAR DIARY
or
INTELLIGENCE SUMMARY.
(Erase heading not required.)

Place	Date	Hour	Summary of Events and Information	Remarks and references to Appendices
RIEHL	April 29		Battn. Training. To Leave - 5 O.R's. From Leave - 4 O.R's.	O.R
	30		Battn. Training. Evacs. - 1 O.R. To Leave - 5 O.R's.	O.R

W.H. Renwick Lt. Col.
Commdg. 3rd Battn. M.G. Corps

3rd BATTALION
MACHINE-GUN
CORPS.

WAR DIARY or INTELLIGENCE SUMMARY

3RD BN. M.G. CORPS

Army Form C. 2118.

Place	Date	Hour	Summary of Events and Information	Remarks and references to Appendices
BIEHL	MAY 1		Battle training. From leave, LT. J.H. KIRK, T. CUNLIFFE AND 1-O-R.	A.
	2		Demobilization 20-O-R.	
	3		Battle training. Evacuations, 1-O-R. To leave, 4-O-R. From leave, 3-O-R.	A.
			Battle training. Evacuations, 1-O-R. To leave, 2 LT. D.J. WILLIAMS MMMMG	A.
			AND 4-O-R. From leave, 2 LT. H.G. TAVIN.	
	4		Battle training. To leave, 4-O-R.	
	5		Battle training. To Hospital, LT. A.G.C.G. SMITH. To leave LT. R.J.	A.
			HAWKINS, AND 1-O-R.	
	6		Battle training. From leave, 4-O-R.	A.
	7		Battle training. To leave, LT. A.N. MUNRO M.C. From leave, 1-O-R.	A.

WAR DIARY
or
INTELLIGENCE SUMMARY.
(Erase heading not required.)

Army Form C. 2118.

Place	Date	Hour	Summary of Events and Information	Remarks and references to Appendices
RLGWL	MAY 8		Battn. on Ceremonial Parade, Reviewed by His Royal Highness The Duke of Connaught, K.G. K.T. K.P. From Hospital, Lt. A.G.C. Smith To Leave 1.O.R. From Leave, 2 LT. H. Mallett and 7 O.R.	OK
	9		Battn training. To Leave, H.C. Graig. M.C. From Leave, 2-O-R.	R
	10		Battn training. To Leave, Lt. A. Hillman, Lt. A.H. Ward. From Leave 6 O.R.	R
	11		Battn Training. From Leave 4-O-R.	R
	12		Battn training, Evacuations 1-O-R. From Leave 5-O-R.	R
	13		Battn Training. To Leave, Lt Col. W.T. Granston D.S.O. From Leave, 3.O.R.	R
	14		Battn Training, Lt. A.H. Duffey to U.K. for M.G.C. Course From Leave 8-O-R.	Out R

Army Form C. 2118.

WAR DIARY
or
INTELLIGENCE SUMMARY

(Erase heading not required.)

Place	Date	Hour	Summary of Events and Information	Remarks and references to Appendices
RIEH L	MAY 15.		BATTLN. TRAINING. TO LEAVE, 2ᴸᵗ S.R. HOLBROOK, M.E. FROM LEAVE, 1-O-R.	2.
	16		DEMOBILIZATION. MAJOR C.D. WATTON. AND 25. O-R.	2.
			BATTLN. TRAINING, FROM LEAVE LT. F. WINCHCOMBE, AND 4-O-R.	
	17		BATTLN. TRAINING, TO LEAVE 3-O-R. DEMOBILIZATION LT. A.W. LUPTON,	2.
			LT. W.L. SAMS, LT. R.G.C.S. SMITH, LT. W.D. CATTERMOLE, 2ᴸᵗ REILLY. W.E.	
			2ᴸᵗ H. MALLETT, 2ᴸᵗ A.O. FORSTER AND 3 3. O-Rˢ.	2.
	18		BATTLN. TRAINING, EVACUATIONS 2-O-Rˢ FROM LEAVE, 4-O-Rˢ	2.
	19		BATTLN. TRAINING. TO LEAVE, 4-O-Rˢ FROM LEAVE, 1-O-R.	
	20		BATTLN. TRAINING, TO LEAVE, 4-O-Rˢ FROM LEAVE, 2-O-Rˢ	2.
	21		BATTLN. TRAINING. TO LEAVE, 2ᴸᵗ C.J. DERRY, AND 4-O-Rˢ FROM LEAVE	2.
			LT. E.J HAWKINS. AND 1-O-R	
	22		BATTLN. TRAINING. TO LEAVE. LT. C.H. ASPHAR. AND 2.O.Rˢ DEMOBILIZATION	2.
			LT. C. SHIPMAN. AND 25. O. Rˢ	

Army Form C. 2118.

WAR DIARY
or
INTELLIGENCE SUMMARY.
(Erase heading not required.)

Place	Date	Hour	Summary of Events and Information	Remarks and references to Appendices
RIEHL.	MAY.			
	23.		EVACUATIONS, 1-O-R¹. BATT'N TRAINING. FROM LEAVE, LT. A.N. MUNRO	X
			2/LT. D.J. WILLIAMS, AND 1-O-R.	
	24		BATT'N TRAINING. TO LEAVE, 2-O-R¹ FROM LEAVE, 2/LT. R. MURCH.	X
	25		BATT'N TRAINING. TO LEAVE, 2/LT. E.G. BURKE, AND 1-O-R. FROM LEAVE,	
			LT. H.C. CRAIG M.C. AND 1-O-R. DEMOBILIZATION 25-O-R³	X
	26		BATT'N TRAINING. TO LEAVE, 1-O-R. REINFORCEMENTS, LT. W.H. GREEN.	
			LT. R.W. MILLS. LT. A.E. SAWYNOR, AND 263 O-R¹ (INSPECTION OF BARRACKS BY	
			BATT'N TRAINING. TO LEAVE, MAJOR. C.G. BENNETT, AND 1-O-R. FROM LEAVE, COMMANDER VI. CORPS	
	27		LT. A. HILLMAN.	X
	28		BATT'N TRAINING. TO LEAVE, 4-O-R. FROM LEAVE, 2-O-R¹ LT. E.G.T. LAGES	X
	29		BATT'N TRAINING. TO LEAVE, H.V.W. KING, AND 4-O-R¹ TO U.K.	
			LT. F.C. MILNER, FOR OFFICER'S INSTRUCTORS AT OXFORD, GRANTED 7 days LEAVE	
			PRIOR TO COURSE. DEMOBILIZATION LT. M.S. SCHAAP AND 55 O-R¹ REINFORCEMENTS	X
			LT. J. ROSSITER, AND 3-O-R.	

Army Form C. 2118.

WAR DIARY
or
INTELLIGENCE SUMMARY.
(Erase heading not required.)

Place	Date	Hour	Summary of Events and Information	Remarks and references to Appendices
MAY.	31		BATTN TRAINING. 1ST LEAVE LT. G.G.RAY, AND 5-0-R's REINFORCEMENTS 37.0.R's.	W.

A.W. Richardson
MAJOR
COMMANDING 3RD BTN. M.G.C.

Army Form C. 2118.

WAR DIARY
or
INTELLIGENCE SUMMARY. 3RD BN M.G.C.
(Erase heading not required.)

Instructions regarding War Diaries and Intelligence Summaries are contained in F. S. Regs., Part II. and the Staff Manual respectively. Title pages will be prepared in manuscript.

Place	Date	Hour	Summary of Events and Information	Remarks and references to Appendices
RIEHL	JUNE 1		BATTLN TRAINING. TO LEAVE, 2 O.R! FROM LEAVE 7 O.R! REINFORCEMENTS 6 O.R!	MS
"	2		BATTLN TRAINING. EVACUATIONS, 6 O.R! TO LEAVE 1 O.R. REINFORCEMENTS. 5 O.R!	MS
"	3		BATTLN TRAINING. TO LEAVE 3 O.R!	MS
"	4		BATTLN TRAINING. EVACUATIONS, 1 O.R. TO LEAVE, 6 O.R! FROM LEAVE 2 O.R! REINFORCEMENTS, 60 O.R!	MS
"	5		BATTLN TRAINING, TO LEAVE, 2LT T.C. POOK AND 5 O.R! FROM LEAVE 5 O.R!	MS
"	6		BATTLN TRAINING, TO LEAVE, 3 O.R!	MS
"	7		BANK HOLIDAY. TO LEAVE, 7 O.R! FROM LEAVE, 2LT O.T. DERRY AND 1 O.R. DEMOBILIZATION. MAJOR. H.D. ST LEGER M.C. 2LT E. SIDEBOTTOM. HONOURS AWARDS. MAJOR. A.N. RICHARDSON, M.C. AWARDED THE D.S.O. MAJOR. G.G.M. GENNETT, THE M.C. MAJOR. C.E. SWAN, THE M.C.	MS

Army Form C. 2118.

WAR DIARY
or
INTELLIGENCE SUMMARY.
(Erase heading not required.)

Instructions regarding War Diaries and Intelligence Summaries are contained in F. S. Regs., Part II. and the Staff Manual respectively. Title pages will be prepared in manuscript.

Place	Date	Hour	Summary of Events and Information	Remarks and references to Appendices
RIEHL	JUNE 7.		MAJOR H.D. St. LEGER. AWARDED THE M.C. SGT. B. HARGEST. AWARDED THE D.C.M. C.Q.M.S. WALMSLEY. AWARDED THE M.S.M. SGT. WEATHERILL AWARDED THE M.S.M. CPL. W. SPICE AWARDED THE M.S.M.	
"	8		BATTLN. TRAINING. TO LEAVE. 4.O.R.s FROM LEAVE, 8.O.R.s	
"	9		BATTLN. TRAINING. EVACUATION, 3.O.R.s TO LEAVE & LT. D. MORRIS & 6.O.R.s	
"	10		BATTLN. TRAINING. REINFORCEMENTS. 4.O.R.s TO LEAVE, 2.O.R.s FROM LEAVE, 2ND LT. E. G. BURKES & 1.O.R.	
"	11		BATTLN. TRAINING. FROM LEAVE, 4.O.R.s	
"	12		BATTLN. TRAINING. TO LEAVE. 1-O-R. FROM LEAVE LT.COL.W.J. CRANSTON.D.S.O. AND 2-O-R.s	
"	13		EVACUATIONS, 2-O-R. Battln training. TO Leave. 2LT E.F.HOWE. AND. 4-O-R.s	
"	14		BATTLN TRAINING. TO LEAVE 3-O-R. FROM LEAVE 1-O-R. DEMOB. 1-O-R.	
"	15		BATTLN. TRAINING. TO LEAVE. 2-O-R. FROM LEAVE. LT. H. V. KING. DEMOB 1-O-R	
"	16		BATTLN TRAINING. TO LEAVE 6-O-R. FROM LEAVE LT. G. C. GRAY AND 6-O-R.	

WAR DIARY
or
INTELLIGENCE SUMMARY.

(Erase heading not required.)

Army Form C. 2118.

Instructions regarding War Diaries and Intelligence Summaries are contained in F. S. Regs., Part II. and the Staff Manual respectively. Title pages will be prepared in manuscript.

Place	Date	Hour	Summary of Events and Information	Remarks and references to Appendices
BIEHL	JUNE 17		Battln marched to Dabringhausen. "A" Company to Kurten. "B" Coy to Stumpff. "C" Coy to Enminghausen. D. Coy to Wermelskirchen. B.H.Q. at Dabringhausen. Demob. Lt. B. Wright. Capt. R. Allan. M.C. D.C.M. and Lt. C.T. Smith granted leave to LARME 17/6/19 to 2/6/19.	
	18		Battln Training. To leave 4-O-R. and 2Lt A. Murch proceeded to 4th Education Instructors Course 18/6/19 - 9/7/19. From Leave Maj. G.O.M. Bennett	
	19		Battln training. To leave 2nd Lt. Taylor and 2-O-R. From leave 6-O-R.	
	20		Battln training. To leave 3-O-R. From leave 12-O-R.	
	21		Battln training. To leave Lt. R. Rowley. M.C. D.C.M. Demob. Capt. R. Allan. M.C. D.C.M. and Lt. C.T. Smith M.C. D.C.M. and Lt. C.T. Smith. M.C. Demob. Capt. R. Allan. M.C. D.C.M. and Lt. C.T. Smith M.C. from leave	
	22		Battln training. To leave 2-O-R. From Leave 3-O-R.	
	23		Battln training. To leave Lt. H.V. Stephens. Maj. A.M. Richardson D.S.O.M.C. Reinforcement. Maj. C.H. Mullins. M.C.	
	24		Battln training. To leave Lt. F. Brown. and 4-O-R. From leave 1-O-R. and Lt. D. Morris.	

Army Form C. 2118.

WAR DIARY
or
INTELLIGENCE SUMMARY.
(Erase heading not required.)

Instructions regarding War Diaries and Intelligence Summaries are contained in F. S. Regs., Part II. and the Staff Manual respectively. Title pages will be prepared in manuscript.

Place	Date	Hour	Summary of Events and Information	Remarks and references to Appendices
	JUNE			
	25		Battle Training. To LEAVE 3. O-R. FROM LEAVE. 7-0-R.	
	26		Battle Training. To LEAVE 3-0-R FROM LEAVE. 8-0-R.	
	27		Battle Training. To LEAVE LT. W. H. MILLER AND 10-0-R FROM LEAVE 10-0-R.	
	28		Battle Training. TO LEAVE 10. O.R. FROM LEAVE. LT.C.T. COOK AND 9-0-R.	
	29		Battle Training. To Leave 10-0-R. From Leave 9-0-R	
	30		Battle returned by lorries. To Leave 10-0-R. From Leave 9-0-R.	

W. Brancton
Lt. Col. Commanding 363rd M.A.C.

Army Form C. 2118.

3rd BATTALION MACHINE GUN CORPS
No. BY200/10.
Date.
3RD BN. M.G.C

WAR DIARY
or
INTELLIGENCE SUMMARY.
(Erase heading not required.)

Instructions regarding War Diaries and Intelligence Summaries are contained in F. S. Regs., Part II. and the Staff Manual respectively. Title pages will be prepared in manuscript.

Place	Date	Hour	Summary of Events and Information	Remarks and references to Appendices
RIEHL	JULY 1		BATT^LN TRAINING. EVACUATION 1-O-R. TO LEAVE 10-O-R^S FROM LEAVE 3-O-R	PW7
"	2		BATT^LN TRAINING. TO LEAVE 2ND LT. T. CUNLIFFE AND 10-O-R^S FROM	PW7
	3		LEAVE 14-O-R^S. DEMOB. LT. A.N. MUNRO. M.C.	PW7
			BATT^LN TRAINING. EVACUATION 1-O-R. TO LEAVE 10-O-R^S FROM	PW7
			LEAVE 14-O-R^S.	
	4		BATT^LN TRAINING. TO LEAVE 10-O-R^S FROM LEAVE 4-O-R.	PW7
	5		REINFORCEMENTS 27-O-R^S	PW7
			BATT^LN TRAINING. EVACUATIONS 1-O-R. TO LEAVE 12-O-R^S FROM LEAVE	PW7
			2ND LT W. TAYLOR AND 7-O-R. DEMOB 1-O-R.	
	6		BATT^LN TRAINING. TO LEAVE 11-O-R^S FROM LEAVE 2-O-R.	PW7
	7		BATT^LN TRAINING. TO LEAVE 12-O-R^S. EVACUATIONS 1-O-R. FROM LEAVE 1-O-R	PW7
	8		BATT^LN TRAINING. EVACUATION 1-O-R. TO LEAVE MAJOR R.D.HODGSON M.C.	PW7
			AND 12-O-R^S FROM LEAVE LT. M.W. STEPHENS, R. ROWLEY M.C. AND 1-O-R	
	9		BATT^LN TRAINING. TO LEAVE 12-O-R. FROM LEAVE 3-O-R^S.	PW7
	10		BATT^LN TRAINING. TO LEAVE 12-O-R. FROM LEAVE 2-O-R. DEMOB. 9-O-R^S.	PW7

WAR DIARY
or
~~INTELLIGENCE SUMMARY.~~

(Erase heading not required.)

Army Form C. 2118.

3rd BATTALION MACHINE GUN CORPS.

Place	Date	Hour	Summary of Events and Information	Remarks and references to Appendices
JULY RIEHL	11		Battn training. To Leave 12-O-R's. From Leave 4-O-R. LT. F. BROWN AND MAJOR A.N. RICHARDSON D.S.O. M.C.	App 7
	12		Battn training. Evacuation 1-O-R. To Leave 18-O-R. From Leave 1-O-R. DEMOB. LT. D. MORRIS & LT. T. C. ROOK.	App 7
	13		Battn training. To Leave. LT. G.G. GRAY AND 12-O-R. From Leave LT. W.M. MILLER AND 6-O-R.	App 7
	14		Demob. 2LT. L. MOULE.	App 7
	15		Battn training. To Leave 12-O-R. From Leave 6-O-R AND LT. G. HASPAR. To Leave CAPT. A.W. CRAVEN M.C. AND 18-O-R. From LEAVE LT. HUNTER AND 5-O-R.	App 7
	16		Battn training. To Leave 10-O-R's. From Leave 7-O-R.	App 7
	17		Battn training. To Leave 10-O-R's. From Leave 7-O-R. Reinforcements 40-O-R's LT. C.S. STEVENSON, J.J. BOWLER, R. MASON (D.C.M.) W.J. JOHNSON, C.E. NICHOLS (M.C.) F.W. TRAYLE, W.M. MILNE, ROBERTSON, W. LAWSON, S. PEARSON, 2LT. P.W. BREWER LT. G.D. LOUP. 2ND LT. F.R. KOTCHIE 2ND LT. MACKIE.	App 7
	18		Battn training. To Leave 10-O-R's. Evacuations 1-O-R. From Leave 18-O-R. DEMOB. LT. J. HUNTER AND 9-O-R.	App 7

Army Form C. 2118.

WAR DIARY
or
INTELLIGENCE SUMMARY.
(Erase heading not required.)

Instructions regarding War Diaries and Intelligence Summaries are contained in F. S. Regs., Part II. and the Staff Manual respectively. Title pages will be prepared in manuscript.

Place	Date	Hour	Summary of Events and Information	Remarks and references to Appendices
RIEHL	19		Battalion training. Evacuations 1-0-R. To leave 10-0-R. From leave 10-0-R.	RWy
	20		BATTLN TRAINING. TO LEAVE 10-0-R. FROM LEAVE 6-0-R.	RWy
	21		BATTLN TRAINING. TO LEAVE 10-0-R. FROM LEAVE 6-0-R.	RWy
	22		BATTLN TRAINING. EVACUATIONS 1-0-R. TO LEAVE 10-0-R. FROM LEAVE 6-0-R.	RWy
	23		BATTLN TRAINING. EVACUATIONS 1-0-R. TO LEAVE 10-0-R. FROM LEAVE 13-0-R.	RWy
	24		BATTLN TRAINING. TO LEAVE 10-0-R. FROM LEAVE 2ND/LT CUNLIFFE 4-0-R.	RWy
	25		BATTLN TRAINING. TO HOSPITAL LT. S.G. MEDLOCK. TO LEAVE 10-0-R. FROM LEAVE 8-0-R.	RWy
	26		BATTLN TRAINING. TO LEAVE 10-0-R; FROM LEAVE 2/LT. S. PEARSON AND 15-0-R. DEMOB. 1-0-R.	RWy

Army Form C. 2118.

3rd BATTALION MACHINE GUN CORPS.
No. B.T.M.C./22

WAR DIARY
or
INTELLIGENCE SUMMARY.
(Erase heading not required.)

Instructions regarding War Diaries and Intelligence Summaries are contained in F. S. Regs., Part II. and the Staff Manual respectively. Title pages will be prepared in manuscript.

Place	Date	Hour	Summary of Events and Information	Remarks and references to Appendices
RIEHL	27		BATTLN TRAINING. TO LEAVE 10-0-R, FROM LEAVE 18-0-R, 2ⁿᵈ LT. PEARSON	R/37
	28		BATTLN TRAINING, TO LEAVE 24T R. MURCH AND 10-0-R. FROM LEAVE 12-0-R AND LT. W. LAWSON.	R/37
	29		BATTLN TRAINING, TO LEAVE 10-0-R, FROM LEAVE 14-0-R.	R/37
	30		BATTLN TRAINING, TO LEAVE 10-0-R FROM LEAVE 14-0-R AND MAJOR R.D.HODGSON + 2LT E.R.KOTCHIE. REINFORCEMENTS LT.W.F.SPREE	R/37
	31		BATTLN TRAINING, TO LEAVE 10-0-R, FROM LEAVE 2-0-R.	R/37

A.R.Richardson MAJOR.
Comdg 3ʳᵈ M.G.C.

WAR DIARY
or
INTELLIGENCE SUMMARY.
(Erase heading not required.)

Army Form C. 2118.

3rd BATTALION
MACHINE GUN
C

Summary of Events and Information 3RD BN M.G.C

Place	Date	Hour	Summary of Events and Information	Remarks and references to Appendices
REEHL	AUG. 1		BATTLN TRAINING TO LEAVE 10-O-R. FROM LEAVE 16-O-R'S	WDS
	2		BATTN TRAINING, FROM HOSPITAL 2/LT W. TAYLOR, TO LEAVE LT COL W. J. CRANSTON, D.S.O. AND 10-O-R'S FROM LEAVE 13-O-R'S 60 Reinforcements O-R'S	WDS
	3		BATTLN TRAINING, TO LEAVE 10-O-R FROM LEAVE 7-O-R DEMOB. 2nd LT J. MACKIE AND 1 O.R.	WDS
	4		BATTN TRAINING, TO LEAVE LT. W.E. BEAUMONT AND 10. O.R'S FROM LEAVE 5 O.R's.	WDS
	5		BATTN TRAINGING EVACUATION 1 O.R. TO HOSPITAL LT. H.A. HILLMAN TO LEAVE 7. O.R's FROM LEAVE LT. G.G.GRAY AND 5 O.R'S.	WDS
	6		BATTN TRAINING TO HOSPITAL LT G.G.GRAY TO LEAVE 7 O.R'S FROM LEAVE 12 O.R'S	WDS
	7		BATTN TRAINING TO LEAVE LT. W.J. JOHNSON AND 7 O.R'S FROM LEAVE 12 O.R'S	WDS
	8		BATTN TRAINING TO LEAVE 7 O.R'S FROM LEAVE 8 O.R'S	WDS

Army Form C. 2118.

WAR DIARY
or
INTELLIGENCE SUMMARY.
(Erase heading not required.)

Instructions regarding War Diaries and Intelligence Summaries are contained in F. S. Regs., Part II. and the Staff Manual respectively. Title pages will be prepared in manuscript.

Place	Date	Hour	Summary of Events and Information	Remarks and references to Appendices
RIEHL			3rd BATTN M.G.C.	
AUG	9		BATTN. TRAINING. TO LEAVE 7 O.Rs. FROM LEAVE 17 O.Rs.	
	10		DEMOB 1 OR.	
			BATTN TRAINING. TO LEAVE 7 ORS. FROM LEAVE 2 O.Rs. DEMOB 3 ORS	
	11		BATT. TRAINING TO LEAVE 7 ORS FROM LEAVE LT COL W. BRANSTON D.S.O. AND 14 ORS.	
	12		BATTN TRAINING TO LEAVE CAPT-ADJT J L PIGGIN, LT JE POPE AND 7 ORS FROM LEAVE LT W J JOHNSON AND 20 ORS DEMOB LT F C MILNER	
	13		BATTN TRAINING TO LEAVE 7 ORS FROM LEAVE 7 ORS	
	14		BATTN TRAINING TO LEAVE LT J ROSSITER M.C. AND 7 ORS FROM LEAVE 5 O.Rs	
	15		BATTN TRAINING TO LEAVE 2nd LT T E ROBERTS M.C. AND 7 ORS FROM LEAVE 20 ORs	
	16		BATTN TRAINING TO LEAVE 2nd LT S F J LEN, 2nd LT F M PILMORE AND 7 OR. DEMOB 6 ORs	
	17		BATTN TRAINING TO LEAVE LT D WILLIAMS M.C. M.M. AND 1 OR FROM LEAVE	

Army Form C. 2118.

WAR DIARY
or
INTELLIGENCE SUMMARY.
(Erase heading not required.)

Instructions regarding War Diaries and Intelligence Summaries are contained in F. S. Regs., Part II. and the Staff Manual respectively. Title pages will be prepared in manuscript.

Place	Date	Hour	Summary of Events and Information	Remarks and references to Appendices
AUG	18		BATTN TRAINING. 2ND LT A WINTER COUGHILL TO LEAVE 3RD BATTN MGC	
			2ND LT A STAMM AND 7 ORS FROM LEAVE 12 ORS	WWS
	19		BATTN TRAINING TO LEAVE 2ND LT BIG HAWKINS AND 6 ORS FROM	WWS
			LEAVE LT W E BEAUMONT, 2ND LT A LUGG AND 10 ORS	WWS
	20		BATTN TRAINING TO LEAVE LT A MASON DCM AND 6 ORS FROM	WWS
			LEAVE 6 ORS	WWS
	20		BATTN TRAINING TO LEAVE 2ND LT C SMITH AND 5 ORS FROM	WWS
			LEAVE 4 ORS	WWS
	22		BATTN TRAINING TO LEAVE LT FOX LABER AND 6 ORS FROM	WWS
			LEAVE 6 ORS. DEMOB 4 ORS	WWS
	23		BATTN TRAINING TO LEAVE 2ND LT E AWBINGUS AND 6 ORS FROM LEAVE	WWS
			7 ORS	WWS
	24		BATTN TRAINING TO LEAVE LT A E WARD AND 6 ORS FROM LEAVE	WWS
			7 ORS	WWS
	25		BATTN TRAINING TO LEAVE LT F WINCOMBE AND 6 ORS FROM LEAVE	WWS
			11 ORS TO DEMOB 4 ORS	WWS

WAR DIARY
or
INTELLIGENCE SUMMARY.

Army Form C. 2118.

(Erase heading not required.)

Place	Date	Hour	Summary of Events and Information 3RD BATTN M.G.C.	Remarks and references to Appendices
RIEHL	Aug 26.		BATTN. TRAINING TO LEAVE 2ND LT F. HOPE AND 6 O.Rs FROM LEAVE 3 O.Rs.	
	27		BATTN. TRAINING TO LEAVE LT C.S. STEVENSON AND 6 O.Rs FROM LEAVE. CAPT AND ADJT J.L PIGGIN AND 13 O.Rs	L.W.S
	28		BATTN. TRAINING TO LEAVE LT. A.W. MILLS AND 6 O.Rs FROM LEAVE LT. J.P.E. POPE AND 9 O.Rs.	L.W
	29		BATTN TRAINING TO LEAVE LT A.E. SAYNOR AND 6 O.Rs. FROM LEAVE 9 O.Rs	L.W
	30		BATTN. TRAINING TO LEAVE 2ND LT. C.J. DERRY AND 6 O.Rs FROM LEAVE LT J ROSSITER AND 9 O.Rs	L.W
	31		BATTN. TRAINING TO LEAVE LT. H.A. HILLMAN AND 6 O.Rs FROM LEAVE 2ND LT T.E. ROBERTS, 2ND LT S.F. PULLEN AND 30 O.Rs	L.W

A.Richardson
LIEUT. COLⁿ/MAJOR
C/ING 3RD BN M.G. CORPS.

Army Form C. 2118.

3rd BATTALION MACHINE GUN CORPS.
No. M32/1
Date.........

WAR DIARY
or
INTELLIGENCE SUMMARY.
(Erase heading not required.)

Instructions regarding War Diaries and Intelligence Summaries are contained in F. S. Regs., Part II. and the Staff Manual respectively. Title pages will be prepared in manuscript.

Summary of Events and Information 3RD BATTN M.G.C.

Place	Date	Hour	Summary of Events and Information	Remarks and references to Appendices
RIEHL	SEPT. 1		BATTN TRAINING. TO LEAVE. LT J.A.ROCH M.C. AND 6.O.RS FROM LEAVE 9.O.Rs	A.E.I.
"	2		BATTN TRAINING. TO LEAVE 6.O.Rs EVACUATIONS, 2.O.R FROM LEAVE. LT. D.J. WILLIAMS (O.C.M.) H.G. TAWN AND 8.O.Rs	A.E.I.
"	3		Battn training To Leave 7-O-Rs. From Leave LT E.G. HAWKINS AND 6-O-Rs.	A.E.I.
"	4		Battn training. To Leave. 2ND LT. T.A.REES AND. 6-O-Rs FROM LEAVE. LT. R. MASON (D.C.M.) AND 4-O-Rs	A.E.I.
"	5		BATTN TRAINING, EVACUATIONS, 2-O-Rs TO LEAVE 8-O-Rs FROM LEAVE 2nd C. SMITH, AND 7-O-Rs	A.E.I.
"	6		BATTN TRAINING, EVACUATIONS 3-O-Rs TO LEAVE 7-O-Rs SPECIAL LEAVE TO FRANCE LT. IN H. GREEN. FROM LEAVE 7-O-Rs DEMOB. 16-O-Rs.	A.E.I.
"	7		BATTN TRAINING TO LEAVE 7-O-Rs FROM LEAVE. LT. W. PHILLIPS AND 7-O-Rs	A.E.I.

Army Form C. 2118.

WAR DIARY
or
INTELLIGENCE SUMMARY.
(Erase heading not required.)

Instructions regarding War Diaries and Intelligence Summaries are contained in F. S. Regs., Part II. and the Staff Manual respectively. Title pages will be prepared in manuscript.

Place	Date	Hour	Summary of Events and Information	Remarks and references to Appendices
SEPT	8		BATTLN. TRAINING. TO LEAVE 7-0-R⁵. FROM LEAVE. LT. LEES F.Q.T. AND 3-0-R¹. DEMOB. LT.W.F. SPREE. LT.F.M. ELDRIDGE AND 7-0-R⁵.	A.S.I.
	9		BATTLN. TRAINING. EVACUATIONS 2-0-R⁵ TO LEAVE 7-0-R⁵ PROM LEAVE 5-0-R¹.	A.S.I.
	10		BATTLN. TRAINING. TO LEAVE 3-0-R⁵ FROM LEAVE. LT. MILLS R.W. LT. HILLMAN A.A. 2 LT. F. HOPE DEMOB. 6 OFFICERS.	W.S.I.
	11		BATTLN. TRAINING. TO LEAVE 3-0-R¹ AND 2 LT E.G. BURKE FROM LEAVE 8-0-R¹. DEMOB. 8 OFFICERS AND 10-0-R¹.	A.S.I.
	12		BATTLN. TRAINING. TO LEAVE. LT.H.G. CRAIG AND 3-0-R¹ FROM LEAVE. LT. A.G. WARD. LT. E. WINCHCOMBE. C.S. STEVENSON AND 4-0-R⁵.	A.S.I.
	13		BATTLN. TRAINING. EVACUATIONS 3-0-R⁵. TO LEAVE 3-0-R¹ FROM LEAVE 4-0-R³	W.S.I.
	14		BATTLN. TRAINING. EVACUATIONS 1-0-R¹ TO LEAVE 3-0-R⁵. FROM LEAVE. LT. A.E. SAYNOR AND 3-0-R¹	A.S.I.
	15		BATTLN. TRAINING. TO LEAVE 4-0-R¹. FROM LEAVE. LT. W.H. GREEN AND 4-0-R¹	W.S.I.

WAR DIARY
or
INTELLIGENCE SUMMARY

(Erase heading not required.)

Army Form C. 2118.

Instructions regarding War Diaries and Intelligence Summaries are contained in F. S. Regs., Part II. and the Staff Manual respectively. Title pages will be prepared in manuscript.

Place	Date	Hour	Summary of Events and Information	Remarks and references to Appendices
SEPT	16		BATTLN. TRAINING. TO LEAVE. 3-0-R³ FROM LEAVE. 3.0-R¹ DEMOB.	A.S.I.
			4. OFFICERS AND 7-O-R³.	
	17		BATTLN. TRAINING. TO LEAVE. 2-0-R³ FROM LEAVE. LT. J.A. ROCH	A.S.I.
			LT. D. STOREY. AND 12.0-R¹. DEMOB. 69.0-R¹.	
	18		BATTLN. TRAINING. TO LEAVE. 2-0-R¹.	A.S.I.
	19		BATTLN. TRAINING. TO LEAVE. CAPT. H. WILKINS AND 2-0-R¹.	A.S.I.
			FROM LEAVE. 3-0-R¹ DEMOB. 20-0-R¹.	
	20		BATTLN. TRAINING. TO LEAVE. 2-0-R¹. FROM LEAVE. 11-0-R³.	A.S.I.
	21		BATTLN. TRAINING. TO LEAVE. 2-0-R. FROM LEAVE. LT. H. C. CRAIG.	N.S.I.
			2 LT. C.J. DERRY	
	22		BATTLN. TRAINING. TO LEAVE. 2-0-R¹ FROM LEAVE. 8-0-R¹	A.S.I.
	23		BATTLN. TRAINING. TO LEAVE. 2-0-R¹ FROM LEAVE. 12-0-R¹ DEMOB. 5-0-R³	A.S.I.
	24		BATTLN. TRAINING. TO LEAVE. 1-0-R. FROM LEAVE. 5-0-R³	A.S.I.
	25		BATTLN. TRAINING. TO LEAVE. LT. E.E. HOWE. AND 1-0-R³. EVACUATION. 10.R	A.S.I.
			FROM LEAVE. 5.O.R.	
	26		BATTLN. TRAINING. TO LEAVE. MAJOR. R.D. HODGSON. LT. W. TAYLOR. FROM LEAVE	A.S.I.
			4.O.R.	

WAR DIARY
or
INTELLIGENCE SUMMARY.
(Erase heading not required.)

Army Form C. 2118.

Instructions regarding War Diaries and Intelligence Summaries are contained in F.S. Regs., Part II. and the Staff Manual respectively. Title pages will be prepared in manuscript.

Place	Date	Hour	Summary of Events and Information	Remarks and references to Appendices
RIEHL	SEPT 27		BATTLN TRAINING. TO LEAVE LT. G.J. BOWLER. FROM LEAVE 3-O-R'. DEMOB. 35-O-R'.	A.S.I. A.S.I.
	28		BATTLN TRAINING. FROM LEAVE. 3-O-R'.	
	29		BATTLN TRAINING. FROM LEAVE 2-O-R'.	A.S.I.
	30		BATTLN TRAINING.	A.S.I.

W. Fermor. Lt. Col.
3rd Bn M.G. Corps.

www.ingramcontent.com/pod-product-compliance
Lightning Source LLC
Chambersburg PA
CBHW080830010526
44112CB00015B/2486